T0215182

Communications in Computer and Information Science   **890**

Commenced Publication in 2007
Founding and Former Series Editors:
Phoebe Chen, Alfredo Cuzzocrea, Xiaoyong Du, Orhun Kara, Ting Liu,
Krishna M. Sivalingam, Dominik Ślęzak, Takashi Washio, and Xiaokang Yang

Editorial Board Members

More information about this series at http://www.springer.com/series/7899

Jude Hemanth · Thushari Silva ·
Asoka Karunananda (Eds.)

Artificial Intelligence

Second International Conference, SLAAI-ICAI 2018
Moratuwa, Sri Lanka, December 20, 2018
Revised Selected Papers

 Springer

Editors
Jude Hemanth
Karunya University
Coimbatore, India

Thushari Silva
University of Moratuwa
Moratuwa, Sri Lanka

Asoka Karunananda
University of Moratuwa
Moratuwa, Sri Lanka

ISSN 1865-0929   ISSN 1865-0937 (electronic)
Communications in Computer and Information Science
ISBN 978-981-13-9128-6   ISBN 978-981-13-9129-3 (eBook)
https://doi.org/10.1007/978-981-13-9129-3

This Springer imprint is published by the registered company Springer Nature Singapore Pte Ltd.
The registered company address is: 152 Beach Road, #21-01/04 Gateway East, Singapore 189721, Singapore

Preface

Artificial intelligence (AI) has now won unprecedented recognition as the fuel for the Fourth Industrial Revolution. Undisputedly, AI has become the main ingredient of the smart computational solutions for real-world problems in all areas including business, health, engineering, science, defense, and social sciences. Developments in AI have increasingly reduced the gap between man and machines. Numerous works have shown not only brain empowerment with AI but also building machines with biological brains is becoming a reality.

The Second SLAAI-International Conference on Artificial Intelligence (SLAAI-ICAI 2018), which was held on December 20, 2018, at University of Moratuwa, Sri Lanka, offered a platform for researchers around the world to share their smart innovations in the field of AI. SLAAI-ICAI received submissions from several countries including Russia, China, India, and Sri Lanka and maintained a 52% acceptance rate. Every submitted paper went through a rigorous double-blind review process. Each paper received at least three reviews. Where issues remained, additional reviews were commissioned. The SLAAI-ICAI covered ten major areas including mainly machine learning, deep learning and robotics, and natural language processing.

Three distinguished speakers, who gave plenary talks illustrating prospective directions for the field were Prof. Vilas Wuwongse, (University Advisor for Research and Information Technology, Sakon Nakhon Rajabhat University, Thailand), Prof. George Rzevski, (Emeritus Professor, Complexity and Design Research Group, The Open University, UK) and Prof. Jude Hemanth (Karunya University, India).

We gratefully acknowledge the support of the Organizing Committee, conference Program Committee session chairs, and reviewers, panel of judges, authors of the papers and council members of the SLAAI for their untiring effort to make the conference a success.

June 2019

Asoka Karunananda
Jude Hemanth
Thushari Silva

Organization

Conference Chair

Asoka S. Karunananda   University of Moratuwa, Sri Lanka

General Chair

Valentina Emilia Balas	Aurel Vlaicu University of Arad, Romania
Victor Hugo Costa de Albuquerque	University of Fortaleza, Brazil
Aboul Ella Hassanien	Cairo University, Egypt

Technical Program Chairs

Jude Hemanth D.	Karunya University, India
A. T. P. Silva	University of Moratuwa, Sri Lanka

Conference Executive Secretary

D. D. M. Ranasinghe   The Open University of Sri Lanka, Sri Lanka

Conference Treasurer

N. M. Wagarachchi   University of Ruhuna, Sri Lanka

Advisory Board Members

Nalin Wickramaarachchi	University of Moratuwa, Sri Lanka
A. R. Weerasinghe	University of Colombo, Sri Lanka
Rangaraj M. Rangayyan	University of Calgary, Canada
Ramona Lile	Aurel Vlaicu University of Arad, Romania
Daniela Elena Popescu	University of Oradea, Romania
Valentina Emilia Balas	Aurel Vlaicu University of Arad, Romania
Aboul Ella Hassanien	Cairo University, Egypt
Daniela Lopez De Luise	Computational Intelligence and Information Systems Lab, Argentina
Mohammed Majid Al-Riafe	Goldsmiths University of London, UK
A. P. Madurapperuma	The Open University of Sri Lanka
K. G. H. U. W. Ratnayake	The Open University of Sri Lanka
Bernadetta Kwintiana Ane	University of Stuttgart, Germany
Ali Ismail Aawad	Lulea University of Technology, Sweden
Janos Botzheim	Tokyo Metropolitan University, Japan

Fuqian Shi	Wenzhou Medical University, China
Vania Vieira Estrela	Universidade Federal Fluminense (UFF), Brazil
Yunhong Kelly Xu	Kunming University of Science and Technology, China

Organizing Co-chairs

Sagara Sumathipala	University of Moratuwa, Sri Lanka
Budditha Hettige	General Sir John Kotelawala Defence University, Sri Lanka
Ruwan D. Nawarathna	University of Peradeniya, Sri Lanka
Sidath Liyanage	University of Kelaniya, Sri Lanka

Publicity and Logistics Co-chairs

| H. W. H. Premachandra | Wayamba University of Sri Lanka, Sri Lanka |
| W. A. C. Weerakoon | University of Kelaniya, Sri Lanka |

Sponsorship Co-chair

| K. S. D. Fernando | University of Moratuwa, Sri Lanka |

Contents

Intelligence Systems

A Preliminary Study on Kinematic Analysis of Human Hand   3
  C. N. Savithri, R. Kevin, and E. Priya

Fuzzy Logic Based Backtesting System   15
  Erandi Praboda and Thushari Silva

Six-State Continuous Processing Model for a New Theory of Computing. . . .   32
  Chinthanie Weerakoon, Asoka Karunananda, and Naomal Dias

Locating the Position of a Cell Phone User Using GSM Signals   49
  Shazir Shafeeque, G. S. N. Meedin, and H. U. W. Ratnayake

Neural Networks

Modeling of Hidden Layer Architecture in Multilayer Artificial
Neural Networks.   67
  Mihirini Wagarachchi and Asoka Karunananda

A Novel Hybrid Back Propagation Neural Network Approach
for Time Series Forecasting Under the Volatility   79
  R. M. Kapila Tharanga Rathnayaka and D. M. K. N. Seneviratna

Flood Forecasting Using Artificial Neural Network for Kalu Ganga   92
  Dhananjali Gamage and Kalani Ilmini

Role of Deep Neural Network in Speech Enhancement: A Review   103
  D. Hepsiba and Judith Justin

Intelligent Time of Use Deciding System for a Melody to Provide
a Better Listening Experience   113
  M. W. Sohan Janaka, H. U. W. Ratnayake, and I. A. Premaratne

Game Theory

Invoke Artificial Intelligence and Machine Learning for Strategic-Level
Games and Interactive Simulations   129
  Nishan Chathuranga Wickramarathna and Gamage Upeksha Ganegoda

Ontology Engineering

An Ontological Approach for Knowledge Representation of Dental
Extraction Forceps 147
    Shanmuganathan Vasanthapriyan

Ontology Based Online Tourist Assistant...................... 161
    Pramodya Mendis, Sachini Siriwardene, Ruwini Wijesiri,
    Upali Kohomban, and Subha Fernando

Natural Language Processing

Digital Assistant for Supporting Bank Customer Service 177
    Dinithi Weerabahu, Agra Gamage, Chathurya Dulakshi,
    Gamage Upeksha Ganegoda, and Thanuja Sandanayake

A Novel Dialogue Manager Model for Spoken Dialogue Systems Based
on User Input Learning 187
    M. F. Ahmed Shariff and Ruwan D. Nawarathna

Text Mining-Based Human Computer Interaction Approach
for On-line Purchasing....................................... 200
    Nadeeka Malkanthi and Thashika D. Rupasinghe

Feature Based Opinion Mining for Hotel Profiling 219
    Dilum Gunathilaka, Shamila Pathirana, Sasanka Senarathne,
    Jithmi Weerasekara, and Thushari Silva

Agent Based System

A Hybrid Agent System to Detect Stress Using Emotions and Social Media
Data to Provide Coping Methodologies 235
    Ridmal Liyanagamage, Shakina Kitchilan, Roshan Maddumage,
    Shazeeka Kitchilan, Nishantha Kumarasinghe, and Subha Fernando

Thinking Like Humans: A New Approach to Machine Translation 256
    Budditha Hettige, Asoka Karunananda, and Gorge Rzevski

Rice Express: A Communication Platform for Rice Production Industry..... 269
    M. A. S. T. Goonatilleke, M. W. G. Jayampath, and B. Hettige

Signal and Image Processing

Diagnosis of Coronary Artery Diseases and Carotid Atherosclerosis
Using Intravascular Ultrasound Images 281
    K. V. Archana and R. Vanithamani

Performance Analysis: Preprocessing of Respiratory Lung Sounds   289
  G. Shanthakumari and E. Priya

A Classification Based Approach to Predict the Gender
Using Craniofacial Measurements   301
  Maneesha M. M. Arachchi, Lakshika S. Nawarathna, Roshan Peiris,
  and Deepthi Nanayakkara

An Optimized Predictive Coding Algorithm for Medical
Image Compression.   315
  J. Anitha, P. Eben Sophia, and D. Jude Hemanth

Palm Vein Recognition Based on Competitive Code, LBP and DCA
Fusion Strategy.   325
  Xiyu Wang and Hengjian Li

Author Index   335

Intelligence Systems

A Preliminary Study on Kinematic Analysis of Human Hand

C. N. Savithri[1(✉)], R. Kevin[2], and E. Priya[1]

[1] Department of Electronics and Communication Engineering,
Sri Sairam Engineering College,
Sai Leo Nagar, West Tambaram, Chennai 600044, India
{savithri.ece,priya.ece}@sairam.edu.in
[2] Department of Mechanical Engineering, Sri Sairam Engineering College,
Sai Leo Nagar, West Tambaram, Chennai 600044, India
kevin9821@gmail.com

Abstract. The human hands represent an intricate engineering, exquisitely to carry out a variety of tasks. Mimicking human hand is the most challenging task due to the complex structure while, considering the tasks performed by hand. Developing hand prosthesis requires modeling of human hand and the study of its motion capabilities. A human hand model presented in this paper resembles anatomical hand, considering its restrictions and similar motions of the human hand. A 3D model of prosthetic hand that is similar to structure of an adult hand is created using CATIA software. The trajectories and motion of hand model are derived by Simscape toolbox in MATLAB environment. The deformation and strain distribution is obtained using ANSYS software to ensure that hand model will be able to withstand the load it is intended to. Thus the model ratifies for the maximum load and the deformation it would experience on the application of load.

Keywords: Human hand model · Simscape · Kinematic analysis · CATIA · ANSYS

1 Introduction

The human hand is the terminal part of arm that performs functions like grasping and manipulating objects with great dexterity. Limb may be lost due to accidents, medical conditions, or due to congenital defects. Amputees are increasing in number day by day. The prosthetic hand can substitute for a missing limb and mimic its function to a great extent [1]. The foremost problem with commercially available prosthetic hand is the lack of the Degrees of Freedom (DoFs) for grasping [2]. Modeling of prosthetic hand to hold the objects dexterously requires understanding the structure and control of human hand [3, 4]. Biomechanics of finger is difficult to understand owing to the complexity involved in actuation of joints. Recent research focuses on design, modeling and control of prosthetic hands by kinematic analysis [5–7]. The motion of fingers can be studied with a simplified model neglecting the elements that has minor impact on motion. Several methods to study the kinematics of human hand include bond graph

© Springer Nature Singapore Pte Ltd. 2019
J. Hemanth et al. (Eds.): SLAAI-ICAI 2018, CCIS 890, pp. 3–14, 2019.
https://doi.org/10.1007/978-981-13-9129-3_1

method, obtaining equations for joints and solving those equations. These equations in turn obtain the torque that drive fingers and joints. Kinematic analysis of human hand by bond graph method is arduous. Simmechanics is a powerful and sophisticated tool for the study of mechanical system in an easy way. Simscape facilitates to model and modify the structure of human hand or simulate the motion to obtain the trajectory by optimizing the parameters. Simscape environment helps in simulating physical model of the complex system despite the complexity and DoF involved. Simscape helps to obtain the dynamic model of the system without solving cumbersome mathematical equations, thus saving time and effort [8]. Recent work identifies the importance of kinematic analysis of human hand. The motion of middle finger is studied based on Denavit–Hartenberg (DH) convention and the respective kinematic model of the middle finger is presented [2, 9]. Kinematic model of hand with 16 DoF is developed and the joint torques for various hand movements are calculated [10]. The kinematic behavior of human hand can be described by a set of mathematical equations. The hand can be modeled as a mechanical system consisting of disjoint parts interconnected by joints. The response of each finger joint in the presence of a proportional integral derivative controller is studied. Literature reveals that mechatronic based structure of four fingers is created and a unity feedback proportional integral (lag) controller together with saturation limiter is utilized to control the rotation of actuation module in these fingers [11, 12]. A robotic hand capable of producing ten grip patterns is developed in their work, authors discussed about the compromise between grip pattern, number of motors required to actuate and placement of motor [13]. Finite element method is used to perform a structural analysis of a prosthetic hand prototype during the cylindrical and tip grasp. Through geometric relations, a set of equations are developed in order to define the position of the prosthesis elements from the position of the actuator. The loads in the numerical analysis are calculated by modeling a static analysis, in which the forces that the fingers of the prosthesis can exert at the tip are obtained [14]. A prosthetic hand prototype is analyzed using finite element method and implemented the prosthetic hand prototype by hydraulic actuators. Authors have analyzed two positions of their prototype such as wide hand open and the other for an intermediate position [15].

The motivation for this paper is to study the motion curves of fingers and trajectories of fingers through simulation of human hand model. The paper is structured as follows: Sect. 2 explains structure of human hand and kinematics of hand model. The experimental results and analysis with above mentioned methods is detailed in Sect. 3. Conclusions are summarized in Sect. 4.

2   Methodology

2.1   Skeletal Structure of Human Hand

Human hand has a palm and four fingers (index, middle, ring and little finger) and a thumb. The anatomical structure of a palm-finger system is shown in Fig. 1. There are 27 bones in the hand together with muscles, tendons and associated structure. There are three phalanges namely, distal, middle and proximal phalanx from each fingertip to base of the finger except the thumb. The joints between phalanges are the Distal Inter Phalangeal (DIP) joint, the Proximal Inter Phalangeal (PIP) joint, Metacarpo Phalangeal (MP) joint, and the Carpo Metacarpal (CM) joint. The MP joint has two DoF (adduction/abduction and flexion/extension), while the DIP and PIP joints have only one DoF (flexion and extension). The CM joint is neglected due to small operating range. The thumb unlike other fingers, is a complex structure with only distal and proximal phalange preceding the metacarpal bone. The joints present in the thumb are Inter Phalangeal (IP) joint, MP joint, and CM joint. The CM joint has two DoF (flexion/extension and adduction/abduction) which enables thumb opposition.

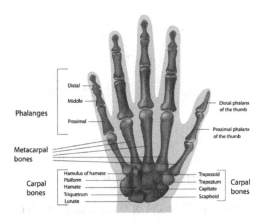

Fig. 1. Anatomy of human hand. Adopted from human anatomy library [16]

2.2 Block Diagram

Figure 2 shows block diagram of the complete system. The foremost step is to develop a CAD model of hand. The motion curve for each finger is obtained using MATLAB by plotting finger tip's position at each time instant. The CAD model of hand is imported to simscape environment for performing the kinematic analysis. Finally, hand model is tested against deformation and strain by importing the hand model to ANSYS environment.

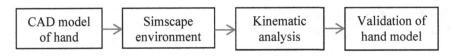

Fig. 2. Block diagram of the complete system

2.3 Kinematic Model of Human Hand Structure

The hand has a unique shape and habituates to the environment [17]. The structure and functionality of the natural hand has to be studied before attempting to design a prosthetic hand. The trajectories and motion of fingers can be obtained from simplified kinematic model of human hand.

Figure 3 shows the human hand model joints and phalanges. There are few considerations before the kinematics of human hand is studied. They are:

1. Wrist is modeled as three simple independent, orthogonal revolute joints having one DoF.
2. MCP, PIP and DIP joints are considered as revolute joints having one DoF.

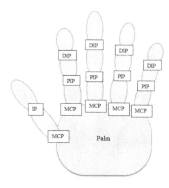

Fig. 3. Human hand model

The next step is to create a 3D model of human hand which requires the structural characteristics such as length of each phalange, width of each finger, joints in a finger. The hand model developed in this work has 15 DoF. Table 1 provides the dimensions of each element that aid in modeling of the prosthetic hand.

Table 1. Dimensions of human hand

Finger name	First link		Second link		Third link	
	Length (cm)	Width (cm)	Length (cm)	Width (cm)	Length (cm)	Width (cm)
Little	2.5	2.5	2.5	2.5	2.5	2.5
Ring	3	3	3	2.5	2.5	2.5
Middle	3.5	3	3	3	2.5	2.5
Index	3	3	3	3	2.5	2.5
Thumb	4	3	3	3		
Palm	7	10				

Finger consists of set of links coupled together by joints. The joints are modeled as revolute joints which allow relative rotation about an axis of about one DoF. The values of the joint variables are known from which the position and orientation of the finger, are determined from the forward kinematics namely the DH convention [18]. In case of revolute or rotational joint, the angles between the links are described by the joint variables. The constraints of human hand can be categorized into three types:

Type I are called static constraints owing to anatomy of hand which defines the limits to the finger. q_1, q_2, q_3, q_{4x}, q_{5x}, q_{6x} represents joint variables. The motion of fingers are described by inequalities presented in Eq. (1)

$$
\begin{aligned}
-90° &\leq q_1 \leq +90° \\
-15° &\leq q_2, q_3, q_{4x} \leq +15° \\
0° &\leq q_{5x}, q_{7x} \leq 90° \\
0° &\leq q_{6x} \leq 90°
\end{aligned}
\tag{1}
$$

Type II constraint are called dynamic constraints that describes the limits when the joint are in movements. It provides the relationship between DIP and PIP joint and are approximated as in Eq. (2)

$$
q_{DIP} \cong \frac{2}{3} q_{PIP}
\tag{2}
$$

Type III constraints are difficult to analyze and are not included in this study.

2.4   3D Hand Model Using CATIA

The prosthetic hand is modeled and assembled by CATIA V5R20 version. Initially, each part of the finger is modeled in part design which comes under the mechanical design. The 2D design of each part is created by using basic 2D tools in the workbench. Later the index finger, thumb finger, middle finger, ring and little finger are modeled. Next the profiles of the fingers are drawn and once it is completed, the model is exported from workbench option. The 2D model thus developed can be converted into a 3D model by selecting the revolution operation on choosing the revolve tool. After modeling all these parts, the model is saved in a file for easy retrieval. Finally for assembling the modeled parts, the assembly design option is selected which opens the assembly window. The modeled parts can be imported by clicking on product option and existing component. Once all the parts are imported, they need to be organised. The transition tools about X, Y and Z axis is used to move the parts and arrange in the order. The parts are fixed firmly by opting several constraints about its origin and axes. The final product is saved and stored in the 'igs' file extension. Figure 4(a) shows the hand model created using CATIA software.

Figure 4(b) shows the simscape model of human hand while Fig. 4(c) shows the internal equivalent blocks of thumb finger. Joints are modeled using revolute joint allowing one DoF. Table 2 shows the blocks used and their functionality for easy interpretation.

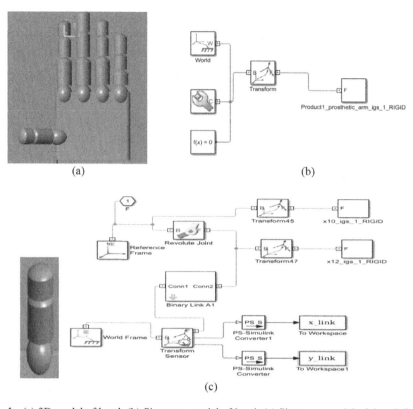

Fig. 4. (a) 3D model of hand, (b) Simscape model of hand, (c) Simscape model of thumb finger

Table 2. Functions of blocks used in 3D model

Group	Block	Name	Explanation
Bodies		Transform	Applies a time-invariant transformation between two frames
		World	The assembly origin of a CAD translated into a model becomes the World (Co-ordinate System (CS)) origin
	$f(x) = 0$	Solver configuration	The solver configuration block specifies the solver parameters that the model needs before the simulation could begin Each topologically distinct Simscape block diagram requires exactly one solver configuration block to be connected to it

(*continued*)

Table 2. (*continued*)

Group	Block	Name	Explanation
Joints		Revolute	This block represents a joint with one rotational degree of freedom. One revolute primitive provides the rotational degree of freedom. The base and follower frame origins remain coincident during simulation
Frames and transform		Transform sensor	Transform sensor measures the spatial relationship between two frames
Utility	PS S	Ps-Simulink converter	Convert physical signal into Simulink output signal
Sinks	simout	To workspace	Write data to workspace

3 Results and Discussion

The motions of hand especially the flexion and extension of the hand are studied by considering the constraints of natural hand. Simplified model is obtained with the following considerations:

1. Abduction or adduction movement is not allowed for central fingers
2. Wrist is a solid body with zero deformation
3. Only the last phalange of the thumb moves

The kinematic chains for each finger are described to realize the model. The kinematic constraints are translated into a MATLAB code. The values of the joint variables are used to compute the fingertip's current position. The movable joint takes the lowest value and rises to maximum value and vice-versa as soon as motion ceases for full extension to full flexion. Figure 5(a) shows the fingertip orientation for central fingers and Fig. 5(b) shows the fingertip orientation for thumb.

Figure 6 shows the fingertip trajectories in flexion motion. The range given by Eq. (1) can be reversed and the fingertip trajectories in extension motion can be obtained. It can be observed from the motion curves and trajectories of finger model that it resembles the trajectories of human finger and hence can be used to develop prosthetic prototype.

The next step is to create a 3D model of hand using CATIA software with the dimensions of an adult as given in Table 1. This hand model is imported to simscape environment by converting the hand model to 'xml' file extension and smimport instruction. The structural properties of the model are also imported while the hand model is converted. Figure 4(a) shows corresponding simscape blocks after importing the hand model. Figure 4(b) shows the simscape blocks of a thumb finger.

Figure 7 shows the converted model in simscape environment. Figure 7(a) shows initial position of thumb and Fig. 7(b) shows the final position of thumb. It is observed that the hand model obeys the constraints of human hand.

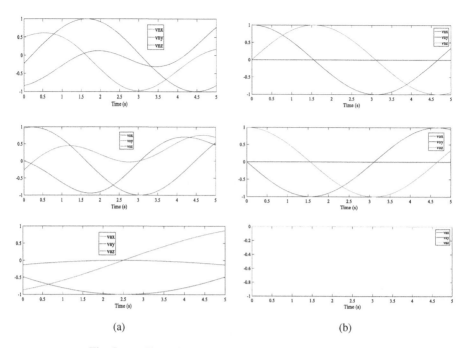

(a)   (b)

Fig. 5. (a) Fingertip orientation of central fingers, (b) thumb

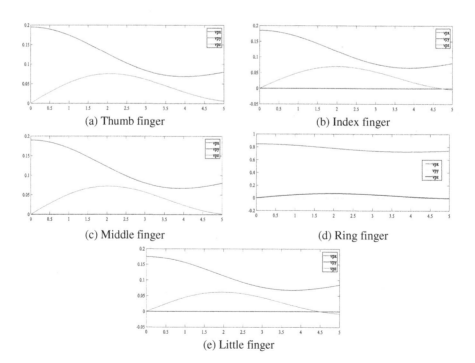

(a) Thumb finger   (b) Index finger

(c) Middle finger   (d) Ring finger

(e) Little finger

Fig. 6. Fingertip trajectories in flexion motion

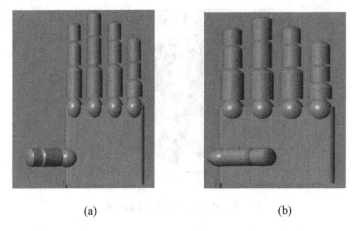

(a)   (b)

Fig. 7. (a) Thumb in initial position, (b) final position

The final step is the ratification of the 3D hand model using ANSYS software to ensure the withstanding capacity while suitable load is applied. A static structural analysis is performed in this environment. The steps involved in accomplishing Finite Element Method (FEM) simulation are:

1. Construction of geometric model
2. Creation of finite element mesh for the prototype
3. Definition of loading conditions
4. Solving the analysis
5. Generation of the results for the analysis

Properties such as material, density are defined for the hand model in ANSYS environment. Finite element mesh is created by discretization of the hand model using tetrahedral elements considering the surface complexity of hand as shown in Fig. 8. Loading conditions are defined such that, the force with different magnitude is applied on upper side of palm making all other parts as fixed and validated against deformation and strain.

The distribution of deformation and strain when a load of 10 N applied to anterior palm is shown in Fig. 9(a) and (b) while this analysis is done the posterior side of palm and other parts are kept fixed. Results demonstrate that maximum deformation and strain of 6.67×10^{-8} mm and 4.31×10^{-9} respectively near wrist as presented by red color in color bar. The blue color indicates the parts are fixed and hence experiences no deformation on these fixed parts.

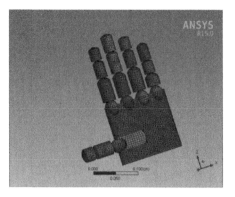

Fig. 8. Mesh of the hand model

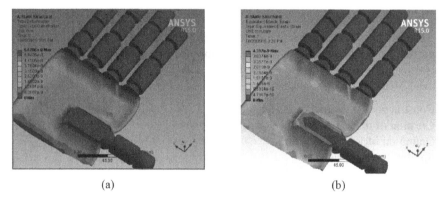

(a)   (b)

Fig. 9. (a) Total deformation distribution with force of 10 N, (b) Strain distribution force of 10 N

4 Conclusion

Human hand is an astonishing example for a highly complex system capable of performing variety of grasps [19]. The knowledge and understanding of the elements and functions of natural hand is essential for developing a prosthetic hand. It can also find applications in gesture recognition, animation industry etc. Kinematic study of human hand helps to measure the quantities that describe motion. In this work, geometry of an adult hand is described. A model of human hand is developed taking into consideration the constraints of natural hand. MATLAB simscape is an efficient tool to study the kinematics of human hand as it provides visualization of the solution graphically while inherently solving complex mathematical equations. The motion curves for each finger are obtained using DH convention. It is inferred from the results that the flexion and extension curves are similar to the anatomical human hand. Static structural analysis of hand model is carried out to ensure proper actuation during loading conditions. Further to validate the developed human hand model the deformation and strain distribution are carried out in the ANSYS environment, while a load of 10 N is applied. Results demonstrate that the deformation and strain are found to be negligible for the considered load. Thus it can be concluded that the model developed in this is work can be implemented in creating a prosthetic hand. The novel contribution in this work involves the creation of hand model mimicking the exact dimension of human hand. The future work is to analyze the model for various hand actions such as open, close, spherical grasp and point. The challenge is to decide on actuators and suitable material to achieve a light weight and robust affordable prosthesis.

References

1. Schwarz, R.J., Taylor, C.L.: The anatomy and mechanics of the human hand. Artif. Limbs **2** (2), 22–35 (1955)
2. Ungureanu, L., Dragulescu, D.: Modeling a human finger as an automatic system. In: 11th International Conference on Vibration Engineering, Timisoara, Romania, 27–30 September 2005
3. Yang, J., Pitarch, E.P., Abdel-Malek, K., Patrik, A., Lindkvist, L.: A multi-fingered hand prosthesis. Mech. Mach. Theory **39**, 555–581 (2004)
4. Rakibul, H., Vepar, S.H., Hujijbert, H.: Modeling and control of the Barrett hand for grasping. In: 15th International Conference on Computer Modelling and Simulation. Cambridge University, Cambridge, 10–12 April 2013
5. Vavrinčíková V., Hroncová D.: Modeling of robot dynamics in the SimMechanics environment. ATP J. Plus Intell. Motion Syst. 60–64 (2009). ISSN 1336-5010 (in Slovak)
6. Dung, L.T., Kang, H.-J., Ro, Y.-S.: Robot manipulator modeling in matlab-SimMechanics with PD control and online gravity compensation. In: Proceedings of the 5th IEEE International Forum on Strategic Technology, IFOST 2010, 13–15 October 2010
7. Boros, T., Lamár, K.: Six-axis educational robot workcell with integrated vision system. In: Proceedings of 4th IEEE International Symposium on Logistics and Industrial Informatics LINDI 2012, Smolenice, Slovakia, pp. 239–244 (2012). ISBN 978-1-4673-4518-7
8. Fedák, V., Ďurovský, F., Üveges, R.: Analysis of robotic system motion in SimMechanics and MATLAB GUI environment. In: MATLAB Applications for the Practical Engineer. InTech (2014). https://doi.org/10.5772/58371
9. Ungureanu, L., Drăgulescu, D.: Modeling a human finger as an automatic system. In: Proceedings of SACI, pp. 69–75 (2005)
10. Serbest, K., Cilli, M., Yildiz, M.Z., Eldogan, O.: Development of a human hand model for estimating joint torque using MATLAB tools. In: 2016 6th IEEE International Conference on Biomedical Robotics and Biomechatronics (BioRob), June, pp. 793–797. IEEE, New York (2016)
11. Tasar, B., Gulten, A., Yakut, O.: Modeling, simulation and control of prosthetic hand using SimMechanics. Int. J. Curr. Eng. Technol. **8**(2), 206–212 (2018)
12. Bahadur, R., Mahmood, A.: Prosthetic hand module using electromechanical actuators: a simulation. In: 2016 19th International on Multi-topic Conference (INMIC), December, pp. 1–5. IEEE, New York (2016)
13. Hota, R.K., Korrapati, M., Kumar, C.S.: Kinematic design of a linkage driven robotic hand for prosthetics capable of achieving ten grips. In: 2016 International Conference on Robotics and Automation for Humanitarian Applications (RAHA), December, pp. 1–6. IEEE, New York (2016)

14. Lealndash, J.A., Torres-San Miguel, C.R., Carbajalndash, M.F., Martinez-Saez, L.: Structural numerical analysis of a three fingers prosthetic hand prototype. Int. J. Phys. Sci. **8**(13), 526–536 (2013)
15. Stanciu L., Stanciu, A.: Designing and implementing a human hand prosthesis. In: Vlad S., Ciupa R.V., Nicu A.I. (eds) International Conference on Advancements of Medicine and Health Care through Technology. IFMBE Proceedings, vol 26. Springer, Berlin, Heidelberg (2009). http://doi.org/10.1007/978-3-642-04292-8_88
16. Human Anatomy Library: Anatomy of the left hand (2016). http://humananatomylibrary.com/anatomy-of-the-left-hand/anatomy-of-the-left-hand-3d-human-anatomy-model-human-anatomy-library/
17. Dragulescu, D., Ungureanu, L.: Human hand modeling. Al II-lea Simpozion Internaţional de Mecanică Teoretică şi Aplicată "Dimitrie Mageron", Iasi, pp. 365–372 (2005)
18. Ungureanu, L., Stanciu, A.: Modeling the motion of the human hand. In: The 11th International Conference on Vibration Engineering, Timişoara, pp. 111–116 (2005)
19. Ungureanu, L., Stanciu, A., Menyhardt, K.: Actuating a human hand prosthesis: model study. In: 2nd WSEAS International Conference on Dynamical Systems and Control, Bucharest Romania (October 2006)

Fuzzy Logic Based Backtesting System

Erandi Praboda[⊠] and Thushari Silva

Faculty of Information Technology, University of Moratuwa,
Moratuwa, Sri Lanka
erandipraboda@gmail.com, thusharip@uom.lk

Abstract. Identification of favorable trading opportunities is crucial in financial markets as it could bring additional increment in profits. Backtesting is one of the process which consists of analyzing the past price movements and predict the best possible trading strategy. Current approaches focus only on exact matching of market values. In order to overcome deficiencies in current approaches, this research proposes a fuzzy logic based approximate matching approach by using the technical indicators and trading rules. The evaluation results demonstrate that finding approximate matching places for a particular trading strategy has a positive contribution to successful trading and an average trader can be successful in trading buy following those fuzzy logic based trading strategies.

Keywords: Backtesting · Fuzzy logic · Approximate matching · Exact matching

1 Introduction

In the financial market like the stock market, forex market and crypto currency market variety of technical indicators are used to make trading decisions [1]. A set of trading rules developed on top of the technical indicators is called as the trading strategies in the field of financial market. The process of checking the viability of these sets of rules by applying the on the historical data without risking any actual capital is called as backtesting. Backtesing is a practice that followed by the traders before they go to the real time trading. Traders will adjust their trading strategies based on the backtesting results to the direction where it will return more profit. Early days the backtesting was followed by series of manual calculations, but today with the enhancement in the field of software industry, different types of software have come to alive with the aim of automating this backtesting process. Even though various numbers of backtesting tools are commercially available since they are having some serious limitations, it is critically important to build a high-performance, high-fidelity backtester.

This research integrates the concept of analyzing the past price movement in the financial market with the elements of fuzzy logic in order to build a successful methodology to do the backtesting. Past price movements of the financial market can be analyzed by using technical indicators [1]. Technical indicator is a mathematical formula that computes a series of price based data points which represent a pattern over some period of time and assists traders to make selling and buying decisions [2]. Other

© Springer Nature Singapore Pte Ltd. 2019
J. Hemanth et al. (Eds.): SLAAI-ICAI 2018, CCIS 890, pp. 15–31, 2019.
https://doi.org/10.1007/978-981-13-9129-3_2

than the basic functionality of the available back testing systems this tool will provide two main features including hybrid matching of trading strategy against the historical data and Maximum execution efficiency. Therefore, these two features which differentiate this Backtesting via hybrid matching module from existing back testing tools.

The rest of the paper is organized as follows: Sect. 2 outlines the review and research of relevant literature, followed by the proposed solution. The implementation is presented in the Sect. 4 and experimental results and analysis presented in Sect. 5. We conclude the paper with a conclusion.

2   Related Works

The process of testing trading strategy based on the historical data to ensure its feasibility before the trader risks any actual capital is known as backtesting [4]. This process is mainly based on the underlying theory that the trading strategy that was successful in the past is likely to be succeed in the future. Early studies of backtesting were mainly focused on testing one indicator at a time. At this edge the researchers use backtesting to determine the accuracy of an indicator when generating the buy and sell signals based on that indicator. After such studies were carried out over a hundred years in 1992 Brock et al. [5] conducted an experiment using 26 variations of moving average and trading range breaks. These two indicators were backtested on the Dow Jones Industrial Average over 100 years from 1887 to 1986 [5]. In 1998, a follow up study carried out by Bessembinder and Chain [6] and determined that when compensating for trading costs, the strategies analyzed by Brock were not significantly more profitable than a buy and hold approach. This implies that although the technical indicators are enriched of some kind predictive ability, they were unable to disprove the weak form of the efficient market hypothesis. Another follow up study conducted by Lo et al. in 2000 was able to implement a computer based model to detect analyzed the chart patterns from 1962 to 1996 on NYSE [7]. Since most of these studies are based on backtesting one indicator at once the researchers paid more attention to investigate whether the combine indicators can be used to evaluate the viability of the trading strategy. As a result of that in 2007 Elaine Loh used a combine model which is consisting of two indicators: moving average and a stochastic oscillator [8]. When this model was backtested on Asia Pacific stock exchanges, the authors could prove that when moving averages were accurate only 50% of the time, the method which used two indicators was accurate 75% of the time [8]. This study shows that combining indicators can eliminate the noise and increase the accuracy and efficiency of trading strategy. Therefore, it is necessary to develop a backtesting tool which provides the facility to backtest combining strategies. Thus, we followed the hybrid approach in the proposed method. Traders always required to backtest their algorithm with different set of parameters and based on different time frames and different time period and different currency pairs. An enhanced back testing tool which has the capability of backtesting a trading strategy with approximate and exact matching is presented below.

3 Proposed Solution

The proposed method uses the fuzzy logic to design new tools to backtest trading strategies. In this proposed solution high performance is achieved by using multi-threads. In order to achieve high accuracy both exact and approximate matching are followed. As illustrated in Fig. 1 Hybrid matching module consists of a Data feeder, Chart Generator and Indicator Calculator which calculate the relevant indicators based on the trading strategy. Both exact matching algorithm and approximate matching algorithm generate the buy and sell signals and as the final step these buy and sell signals are used to calculate the final back testing results. The major components of this proposed system can be further detailed as follows.

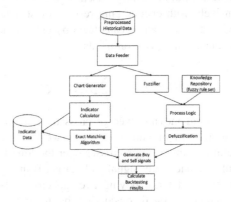

Fig. 1. Overall design of Hybrid Matching Module

3.1 Data Management Module

Data feeder manages access to historical price data from the API through the internet. There is a separate API that has been developed for this research work and it provides necessary preprocessed historical data within a specific time period accommodating clients' request. The developed REST API is capable of sending the relevant price data within a specific date range. Forex historical data consists of Date, Time, Open, High, Low, Close and Volume. This system has an internal cache of historical data which enhances the performance by minimizing the access to the external API. When the data feeder is triggered, it searches in the internal cache first and if the requested data is not available.

3.2 Chart Generating Module

The main objective of the Chart Generating module is plot the historical price data against the date, plot the indicators against the date and time and indicate the sell and buy signals on price data chart.

3.3   Indicator Calculator

This sub module is dedicating for calculating the necessary indicators for a particular trading strategy. It consists of the necessary logic to calculate the technical indicators.

3.4   Exact Matching Module

Under the exact matching module five standard buy and sell trading models are developed based on their relevant technical indicators. The technical indicators used under this module can be listed as follows.

3.4.1   Moving Average Cross Over

This is a simple but powerful trading strategy used by the most of the forex traders. It has been studied extensively with encouraging results, most notably study by Brock et al. in 1992 [5]. Moving average can be calculated by using following formula here, where Price (n) denote the closing price on n^{th} day.

$$\text{Moving Average} = \sum_{n-5}^{n} \frac{price(n)}{5} \tag{1}$$

The most commonly used moving average cross over trading strategy has been built from using the short term moving average as well as the long term moving average. If the short term moving average crosses over the long term moving average the trading strategy will generate a buy signal and market is thought to be trending up on the other hand, if the short term moving average crosses below the long term moving average sell signal is generated considering that the uptrend has been replaced by the down trend [11].

3.4.2   Moving Average Convergence/Divergence (MACD)

MACD is a very popular indicator used in technical analysis to measure the momentum in security. In late 1970 this indicator was introduced by Gerald Apple. The MACD denotes the difference between two given moving averages. Upward momentum indicates when the short term moving average is above the long term moving average or when the MACD is positive. On the other hand, when the MACD is negative, the short term moving average is below the long term moving average and suggest a downward momentum [12]. MACD can be constructed by using followings.

$$\text{MACD} = \text{SEMA - LEMA} \tag{2}$$

Where SEMA is the Short term EMA of closing prices and LEMA is the Long term EMA of closing prices (LEMA).

9 day EMA of the MACD line (Signal Line)

$$\text{EMA} = \text{Price (T)} * m + \text{EMA (T}-1) * (1-m) \tag{3}$$

When T represent day and k is the no of days that the exponential moving average should be calculated. m is computed as m = 2/(k + 1). According to the rules when the

MACD crosses above the signal line buy signal is generated. The sell signal is generated when the MACD crosses below the signal line.

3.4.3 Bollinger Bands

This method is used to compare the relative price level and the volatility over a particular period of time. The volatility of the price level is computed by taking the standard deviation of the security prices. The middle line of the Bollinger Bands is computed by taking the k-period moving average of the price series. Then by calculating $x\sigma$ distance from the middle line it is possible to obtain the upper line, while obtaining the lower line by taking $-x\sigma$ distance, where x is a positive constant and σ is the standard deviation computed over a moving window of K periods [3]. When the close price of the currency pair crosses above the signal line it system will indicate a sell signal and while close price crosses below the signal line it will generate a buy signal.

3.4.4 Relative Strength Index (RSI)

RSI is a most popular and useful momentum oscillator developed and introduced by J. Welles Wilder in 1978 [3]. Basically, this indicator compares the magnitudes of the recent gain and recent losses and it converts to a number between 0 to 100. If the RSI is greater than 70 it is considered as a good place to sell a particular currency fair and according to the RSI trading strategy if the RSI value is above 70 it indicate a best place to sell and if it is below 30 then it indicate a buy signal. Following equation are used to calculate RSI value.

$$RSI = 100 - \frac{100}{1 + RS} \tag{4}$$

$$Average\ Gain = Total\ Gain/n \tag{5}$$

$$Average\ Loss = Total\ Losses/n \tag{6}$$

$$RS = \frac{Average\ Gain}{Average\ Loss} \tag{7}$$

3.4.5 Stochastic Oscillator

It is a momentum indicator comparing the closing price of a security to the range of its prices over a certain period of time. It can be calculated by using the following formula. Buy and Sell signals are created when the %Y crosses through a three-period moving average, which is called the %C.

$$\%Y = 100\,(D - L14)/(H14 - L14) \tag{8}$$

where D - the most recent closing price, L14 – Low value of the 14 previous trading sessions, H14 – The highest price traded during the 14 period, %Y - Current market rate for a particular currency pair and %C – 3 period moving average of %Y.

3.5   Approximate Matching

The main purpose of this module is to find out the places within historical data where a particular trading strategy has been applied with some slight differences and evaluate the viability of a trading strategy based on those approximate matching places. In order to find out those approximate matching place fuzzy logic has been used. Here the Mamdani fuzzy inference system is followed as the fuzzy inference system [13]. Therefore, this module consists of several sub components: Fuzzification, Knowledge Repository, and Logic Processing Unit. Under this module five fuzzy trading strategies which correspond to the trading strategies mention under Exact Matching Module were developed. Table 1 lists these five fuzzy trading strategies with the relevant parameters.

Table 1. Fuzzy trading strategies

Trading strategy name	Parameters
Fuzzy simple moving average crossover	• Short-term window size
	• Long-term window size
	• Fuzzy Threshold value
Fuzzy MACD	• Short-term window size
	• Long-term window size
	• Signal line window size
	• Fuzzy Threshold value
Fuzzy Bollinger bands strategy	• Lookback period
	• Band standard deviations
	• Fuzzy Threshold value
Fuzzy RSI	• Lookback period
	• Fuzzy Threshold value
Fuzzy stochastic oscillator	• %Y – first (?) Lookback period
	• %C- second (?) Lookback period
	• Fuzzy Threshold value

3.5.1   Fuzzification

The process of transforming real scalar (crisp) values into fuzzy linguistic variable using fuzzy membership function stored in the fuzzy knowledge base is known as fuzzification [14]. In this research following input variables and parameters were used for the fuzzification process under different trading strategy and the input variables of under different trading strategy can be defined as follows. Several input variables has been normalized and scaled to − 100 to 100 [15].

Fuzzy Moving Average Crossover Strategy

$$NMA = 100 * ((FMA - SMA)/LMA) \qquad (9)$$

Where NMA- Normalized moving average, FMA- Fast Moving Average or short term moving average,
SMA- Slow Moving Average or long term moving average
Fuzzy MACD strategy

$$fuzzyMACDInput = 100 * (MACD - SignalLine/MACD) \qquad (10)$$

Fuzzy Bollinger Bands Strategy

$$fuzzyInputUpperBand = 100 * (close - upperBand/close) \qquad (11)$$

$$fuzzyInputlowerBand = 100 * (close - lowerBand/close) \qquad (12)$$

Fuzzy RSI Strategy

$$fuzzyRSIOne = 100 * (RSI - 70)/RSI \qquad (13)$$

$$fuzzyRSITwo = 100 * (RSI - 30)/RSI \qquad (14)$$

Fuzzy Stochastic Oscillator

$$fuzzyStochasticInput = \%Y - \%C \qquad (15)$$

Figure 2 represents the fuzzy membership function which is used in the fuzzification process of Fuzzy Simple Moving Average cross over strategy and Fuzzy MACD strategy. As illustrated in the Fig. 2 triangular membership function has been used, it will be defined based on the fuzzy Threshold values.

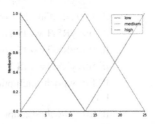

Fig. 2. Fuzzy Membership Function for input variables

3.5.2 Fuzzy Rules

Normally there are three types of decisions that can be used in the process, they are riskless choice, decision making under uncertainty and risky choice. The system is trying to implement decision making under uncertainty. These Decisions are made based on fuzzy rules. Fuzzy rules allow approximate reasoning by including the facts about rules and linguistic variables according to the fuzzy set theory [16]. Usually fuzzy rules are expressed in terms of an IF-THEN statement [17]. The knowledge base used by different trading strategy can be defined as Table 2.

Table 2 Fuzzy rule base

Trading strategy	Fuzzy rules
Fuzzy moving average crossover strategy	IF SMA IS High THEN Signal IS Buy
	IF SMA IS Normal THEN Signal IS Hold
	IF SMA IS Low THEN Signal IS Sell
Fuzzy MACD strategy	IF fuzzyMACDInput IS High THEN Signal IS Buy
	IF fuzzyMACDInput IS Normal THEN Signal IS Hold
	IF fuzzyMACDInput IS Low THEN Signal IS Sell
Fuzzy Bollinger bands strategy	IF fuzzyInputUpperBand IS High THEN Signal IS Buy
	IF fuzzyInputUpperBand Normal THEN Signal IS Hold
	IF fuzzyInputUpperBand IS Low THEN Signal Hold
	IF fuzzyInputlowerBand IS High THEN Signal IS Sell
	IF fuzzyInputlowerBand Normal THEN Signal IS Hold
	IF fuzzyInputlowerBand IS Low THEN Signal Hold
Fuzzy RSI strategy	IF fuzzyRSIOne IS High THEN Signal IS Buy
	IF fuzzyRSIOne Normal THEN Signal IS Hold
	IF fuzzyRSIOne IS Low THEN Signal Hold
	IF fuzzyRSITwo IS High THEN Signal IS Sell
	IF fuzzyRSITwo IS Normal THEN Signal IS Hold
	IF fuzzyRSITwo IS Low THEN Signal Hold
Fuzzy stochastic oscillator	IF fuzzyStochasticInput IS High THEN Signal IS Buy
	IF fuzzyStochasticInput IS Normal THEN Signal IS Hold
	IF fuzzyStochasticInput IS Low THEN Signal IS Sell

3.5.3   Logic Processing Unit

This takes the output of the fuzzification process and the knowledge repository as the inputs. Fuzzified inputs are applied to the antecedents of the fuzzy rules. If a given fuzzy rule has multiple antecedents the fuzzy operator (AND or OR) is used to obtain a single number that represents the results of the antecedent evaluation [18]. The output of the Logic Processing Unit is a signal on a normalized domain on which two different fuzzy sets, BUY, HOLD, and SELL are defined. Figure 3 defines the output membership function used in this system.

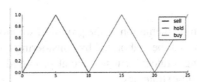

Fig. 3. Fuzzy membership function for output variables.

3.5.4   Defuzzification

The process of mapping the fuzzy space defined over an output universe of discourse into non-fuzzy action. The method used in this work is the centroid of area (COA) [19]. This method provides crisp values based on the center of the gravity of the fuzzy set. Equation 16, defines the formula that is used for the defuzzification when the membership function is discrete [20].

$$F = \frac{\sum_i^K \mu(Zi)(Zi)}{\sum_i^K \mu(Zi)} \tag{16}$$

Here the defuzzified value has been denoted as F, Zi indicates the sample element, K represents the number of elements in the sample and $\mu(Zi)$ is the membership function.

3.6   Calculating Backtesting Results

After identifying the Buy, Sell and Hold signals by using the approximate matching and exact matching modules the next step is a calculation of the backtesting results. The main aim of this module is presenting the viability of the trading strategy with some statistical figures like equity curve which can be understood by the user easily. This receive a set of signals and create a series of positions by allocating against the cash component. In order to construct the Mark to market (MTM) portfolio followings are calculated [21].

Positions for every day;

$$Holdings = Position * Closing\ Price \tag{17}$$

$$Cash = Initial\ Capital - Total\ Holdings \tag{18}$$

$$MTM = Cash + Positions * Closing\ Price \tag{19}$$

4   Implementation

This section presents the implementation of the proposed solution mentioned in Sect. 4. The rest of the explanation will be elaborated by considering the moving average cross over strategy as the trading strategy, but the actual proposed solution is extended to backtest five standard trading strategies.

4.1   Preliminaries

The following methods are assumed to be declared in advance when deriving the algorithms.

get(url, params): Allow to send an api request to get the data from the server, which is located at the web address provide by the property *url* and allow to pass the relevant parameters by setting the values to the *params* property. A json object containing the relevant price data is returned by the API as a response to this get request. If values has not been set for the property *params* then default values will be set.

rolling_mean(value, window_size): Calculate moving average of value based on the window size. *generate_signals()*: This method is responsible for generating BUY and SELL signals (1and 0) based on the rules of trading strategy as explained under Exact Matching Module. As an example, if the trading strategy is Moving Average Cross Over, Then the implementation of this method will be as follows.

```
if (signals['short_mavg'] > signals['long_mavg']){
signals['signal'] = 1.0 }
else{
signals['signal'] = 0.0 }
```

cumsum(): Calculate the cumulative sum.

pct_change(): Return the percent change over given number of period. By default the period that used to shift for making percent change is 1.

Antecedent(universeVariable, label): This function will input the variables to the fuzzy control system. There are two parameters one is a one dimensional array and the other one is the name of the universe variable or array.

Consequent(universeVariable, label): This function will output the variables to the fuzzy control system. There are two parameters one is a one dimensional array and the other one is the name of the universe variable or array.

$$f(y,d,e,f) = \begin{cases} 0, & y \leq d \\ \frac{y-d}{e-d}, & d \leq y \leq e \\ \frac{f-y}{f-e}, & e \leq y \leq f \\ 0, & f \leq y \end{cases} \tag{20}$$

The parameter d and f are located the feet of the rectangle and the parameter e is located the peak.

Rule(antecedent, consequent): Defining the rules in a fuzzy control system by connecting the antecedent to consequent

ControlSystem(rules): provide the base class to fuzzy control system. If the rules are provided as a parameter the system is initialized with the given set of fuzzy rules.

ControlSystemSimulation(controlSystem):Calculates the results from fuzzy control system. A fuzzy control system object will be passed as a parameter.

compute(): Simulate fuzzy control system by calculating the value of fuzzy output.

4.2 Algorithm for Exact Matching of Moving Average Using Cross Over Strategy

```
url ← "http://api_url"
json_data ←get(url)
file_path ← "E:/Data.csv"
signals ← DataObject.create()
portfolio ← DataObject.create()
signals['signal'] ← 0.0
short_window ←50
long_window ←150
initial_capital ← 100000
price_data_csv ← convert_to_csv(json_data)
price_data ← read_csv(file_path)
signals['short_mavg'] ← rolling_mean(price_data['Close'], short_window)
signals['long_mavg'] ← rolling_mean(price_data['Close'], long_window)
signals['signal'] ←generate_signals()
signals['possitions'] ←generate_diff()
portfolio['holdings']←multiply(signals['possitions'],price_data['Close'])
portfolio['cash']←
          initial_capital – cumsum (portfolio['holdings'])
portfolio['total']←portfolio['cash']+cumsum(portfolio['holdings'])* price_data['Close']
portfolio['return']← pct_change(portfolio['total'])
```

4.3   Algorithm for Approximate Matching of Moving Average Using Cross Over Strategy

```
url ← "http://api_url"
json_data ←get(url)
file_path ← "E:/Data.csv"
signals ← DataObject.create()
portfolio ← DataObject.create()
signals['signal'] ← 0.0
short_window ←50
long_window ←150
initial_capital ← 100000
price_data_csv ← convert_to_csv(json_data)
price_data ← read_csv(file_path)
signals['short_mavg'] ← rolling_mean(price_data['Close'], short_window)
signals['long_mavg'] ← rolling_mean(price_data['Close'], long_window)
signals['fuzzyInput'] ← 100*((signals ['short_mavg'] - signals['long_mavg']) / signals['short_mavg'])
normalizedInput ← Antecedent(arange(-1, 1, 0.00001)
fuzzyOutput ← Consequent(arange(0,3,0.001), 'fuzzyOutput')
normalizedInput['low'] ← trimf(normalizedInput.universe, [-1, -1, 0])
normalizedInput['medium'] ←trimf(normalizedInput.universe, [-1, 0, 1])
normalizedInput['high'] ← trimf(normalizedInput.universe, [0, 1, 1])
fuzzyOutput['low'] ← trimf(fuzzyOutput.universe, [0, 0.5, 0])
fuzzyOutput['medium'] ← trimf(fuzzyOutput.universe, [0, 0.5, 1])
fuzzyOutput['high'] ← trimf(fuzzyOutput.universe, [2.0, 2.5, 3.0])
rule1 ← Rule(normalizedInput['low'] , fuzzyOutput['low'])
rule2 ← Rule(normalizedInput['medium'], fuzzyOutput['medium'])
rule3 ← Rule(normalizedInput['high'] , fuzzyOutput['high'])
movingAverage_ctrl ← ControlSystem([rule1, rule2, rule3])
movingAverageCrossOver ← ControlSystemSimulation(movingAverage_ctrl)
 for x in signals['fuzzyInput']:
 movingAverageCrossOver.input['normalizedInput'] ←      round(x,5)
 movingAverageCrossOver.compute()
 signals['signal'][short_window:][i] ← movingAverageCrossOver.output['fuzzyOutput']
 if movingAverageCrossOver.output['fuzzyOutput']< 1.0:
  signals['signal'][short_window:][i] ← -1
 else:
  if movingAverageCrossOver.output['fuzzyOutput']> 1.0 and
movingAverageCrossOver.output['fuzzyOutput']< 2.0:
   signals['signal'][i] ← 0
  else:
   signals['signal'][i] ← 1
 signals['possitions'] ←generate_diff()
 portfolio['holdings']←multiply(signals['possitions'],        price_data['Close'])
 portfolio['cash']←
               initial_capital – cumsum (portfolio['holdings'])
 portfolio['total']←
 portfolio['cash']+cumsum(portfolio['holdings'])* price_data['Close']
portfolio['return']← pct_change(portfolio['total'])
```

5 Evaluation

Over a 5 year period starting from 31/1/2013 to 31/1/2018 data was collected with out of sample evaluation over a recent years with sliding window of one year period. The portfolio performance of 5 best strategies was evaluated and compared to benchmark strategies. Sample sizes should be mentioned.

OPTIMIZED-VERIFY-EVALUATE methodology was used to evaluate the proposed solution as in [22]. The first strategy was adjusted or optimized over the in the sample data, then verified over more recent out of sample data and finally evaluated over another set of more recent sample data. Data set were divided into three data sets as shown in Table 3. Each data set is consists of an OPTIMIZE, VERIFY and EVALUATE date ranges. EVALUATE date range remain constant for each data set.

Table 3 Data set used for evaluation

Data set name	Optimize years	Verify years	Evaluate years
401	4	0	1
311	3	1	1
302	3	0	2

For the evaluation of the trading strategies following matrixes were calculated for each and every strategy.

5.1 Sharpe Ratio

This ratio defines how much excess return traders are receiving for the extra volatility that bear for holding a riskier asset. In 1966, William Sharp derived a formula to calculate the Sharpe ratio [23]. Nowadays it has become a most referenced risk/return measure used in finance. The formula used for calculating shape ratio can be defined as follows [24].

$$SR(m) = (r - R)/Std(m) \qquad (21)$$

Where m is the investment, r is the average rate of return of m, R is the best available rate of return of a risk-free security and Std(m) is the standard deviation of r.

The greater the Sharpe ratio means the better ratio between the return and additional risk. Usually the a strategy which is having a Sharpe ratio greater than 1 is acceptable by the investors and when the Shape ratio getting increase the acceptance of the trading strategy gets increased.

5.2   Maximum Drawdown

This is an indicator of the risk of a portfolio chosen based on a specific strategy. It gives a measurement of the largest drop from peak to bottom in the value of a portfolio before a new peak is achieved [25]. Here for calculating the maximum drawdown and Eq. 22 is used [26].

$$MDD = \frac{(PV - LV)}{PV} \tag{22}$$

MDD is Maximum Drawdown of a given strategy, PV is peak value before largest drop and LV is the lowest value before new high established [27].

5.3   Compound Annual Growth Rate (CAGR)

This provides the annual growth rate of an investment over a specified period of time longer than one year. This rate tells what the traders have at the end of the investment period [28]. The calculation of CAGR can be done by using the formula mentioned as Eq. 23 [29].

$$CAGR = (E/B)^{1/n} - 1 \tag{23}$$

Here E is the value at the investment beginning and B is the value at the investment end and n is the number of periods.

As shown in the Fig. 4, the system generates the graphical view of the closing price with the corresponding trading signals (buy = up arrow, sell = down arrow), and a graphical view of the account equity curve.

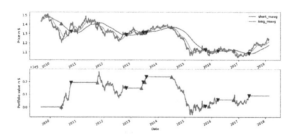

Fig. 4. Graphical view is provided by Exact Matching Module

Evaluation results of the system for the standard and fuzzy trading strategies with respect to the above mentioned matrixes are shown in Tables 4 and 5.

Table 4 Evaluation results

Data set: 2016-01-01/2017-01-01
Currency Pair: EUR/USD

Strategy	Sharp ratio	CARG	MDD
Moving average cross over	− 0.36365	−0.02992	−16.9011
Fuzzy moving average cross over	1.154825	0.02992	−16.9011
MACD	0.019602	0.02881	15.9910
Fuzzy MACD	0.132493	0.07891	17.8984
Stochastic	0.123907	−0.03239	−8.78734
Fuzzy stochastic	0.234295	0.05673	−8.78713
RSI	0.342323	−0.06831	12.3454
Fuzzy RSI	0.345381	−0.10075	9.09849
Bollinger band	0.435668	0.12467	−4.99878
Fuzzy bollinger band	0.689839	0.124600	5.67648

Table 5 Evaluation results

Data set: 2017-01-01/2018-01-01
Currency Pair: EUR/USD

Strategy	Sharp ratio	CARG	MDD
Moving average cross over	0.213237	0.25641	12.34447
Fuzzy moving average cross over	−0.484823	0.25778	12.55436
MACD	0.154310	−0.36414	10.45812
Fuzzy MACD	0.167682	−0.12894	12.43695
Stochastic	−0.564892	0.78262	−8.546433
Fuzzy stochastic	−0.349485	0.78231	−7.215457
RSI	0.213468	0.12596	14.5766
Fuzzy RSI	0.487940	−0.22535	23.9878
Bollinger band	0.697578	0.12425	−23.190
Fuzzy Bollinger band	0.697937	0.23155	24.2452

6 Conclusion

The results of the system show that the fuzzy logic based trading strategy developed under the approximate matching module perform better than the standard trading strategies and thus significantly improve the overall performance of the system and this confirms that the fuzzy logic based approximate matching module have a positive contribution to a successful trading system. Once the successful trading strategy has been developed and verified, traders can be successfully applied it real time to make the trading decisions. Selecting the right currency pair is important as selecting the trading strategy because the different currency pair has different price pattern and a specific strategy doesn't work same for all currency pairs. As well as the trading strategies backtested over historical data are no guarantee that it will perform well in another time period, therefore the traders should always remember this when they applied the backetested trading strategies in real time. For the Evaluation of the system only five years price data has taken into the account, but in order to increase the confidence in the trading system, it can be tested over more than five years and verify whether it maintain the consistent performance. On the other hand the evaluation and analyzing processes are manual processes in this system, but it is possible to significantly reduce the time and effort by automating more of the evaluation process. In the future this research work will further extend to backtest additional trading strategies and their combinations.

References

1. Ren, C.: The Investor's Guide to Technical Analysis. McGraw-Hill, New York (2004)
2. Schwager, J.: Getting Started in Technical Analysis. Wiley, New York (1999)
3. Colby, R., Meyers, T.: The Encyclopedia of Technical Market Indicators. Irwin Professional Publishing, New York (1998)
4. Achelis, S.: Technical Analysis from A to Z. McGraw Hill, New York (2001)
5. Brock, W., Lakonishok, J., Lebaron, B.: Simple technical trading rules and the stochastic properties of stock returns. J. Finance **47**(5), 1731–1764 (1992)
6. Sullivan, R., Timmermann, A., White, H.: Data-snooping, technical trading rule performance, and the bootstrap. J. Finance **54**(5), 1647–1691 (1999)
7. Lo, A., Harry, M., Wang, J.: Foundations of technical analysis: computational algorithms, statistical inference, and empirical implementation. J. Finance **55**, 1705–1765 (2000)
8. Park, C.-H., Irwin, S.H.: What do we know about the profitability of technical analysis? J. Econ. Surv. **21**(4), 786–826 (2007)
9. Metatrader4: MetaTrader 4 Official Release. https://www.metatrader4.com/en/company/140. Accessed 20 July 2017
10. VonAltrock, C.: Fuzzy Logic and Neurofuzzy Applications in Business and Finance. Prentice-Hall, Inc., Upper Saddle River (1997)
11. Weissman, R.: Mechanical Trading Systems: Pairing Trader Psychology with Technical Analysis. Wiley, Hoboken (2005)
12. Achelis, B.S.: Technical Analysis from A to Z, pp. 199–200. McGraw Hill, New York (2001)
13. Naranjo, R., Meco, A., Arroyo, J., Santos, M.: An intelligent trading system with fuzzy rules and fuzzy capital management. Int. J. Intell. Syst. **30**(8), 963–983 (2015)
14. Russell, S., Norvig, P.: Artificial Intelligence: A Modern Approach, 2nd edn. Pearson Educational Inc., Upper Saddle River (2003)
15. Gamil, A., El-fouly, R., Darwish, N.: Stock technical analysis using multi agent and fuzzy logic. In: Proceedings of the World Congress on Engineering, vol. 1, pp. 142–147 (2007)
16. Yager, R.R., Lotfi, A.Z. (eds.): An Introduction to Fuzzy Logic Applications in Intelligent Systems, vol. 165. Springer, Berlin (2012)
17. Castillo, O., Melin, P., Kacprzyk, J., Pedrycz, W.: Type-2 fuzzy logic: theory and applications. In: IEEE International Conference on Granular Computing, 2007. GRC 2007, pp. 145–145 (2007)
18. Iancu, I.: A Mamdani type fuzzy logic controller. In: Fuzzy Logic-Controls, Concepts, Theories and Applications. InTech (2012)

19. Zimmermann, H.-J.: Fuzzy control. In: Fuzzy Set Theory—And Its Applications, pp. 203–240. Springer, Dordrecht, (1996). http://doi.org/10.1007/978-94-010-0646-0
20. Patyra, M.J., Grantner, J.L., Koster, K.: Digital fuzzy logic controller: design and implementation. IEEE Trans. Fuzzy Syst. 4(4), 439–459 (1996)
21. Christoffersen, P., Pelletier, D.: Backtesting value-at-risk: a duration-based approach. J. Financ. Econom. 2(1), 84–108 (2004)
22. Zeigenbein, S.: A Fuzzy Logic Stock Trading System Based on Technical Analysis (2011)
23. Lo, A.W.: The statistics of sharpe ratios. Financ. Anal. J. 58(4), 36–52 (2002)
24. Zakamouline, V., Koekebakker, S.: Portfolio performance evaluation with generalized sharpe ratios: beyond the mean and variance. J. Bank. Finance 33(7), 1242–1254 (2009)
25. Pospisil, L., Vecer, J.: Portfolio sensitivity to changes in the maximum and the maximum drawdown. Quant. Finance 10(6), 617–627 (2010)
26. DataCamp Community: Python For Finance: Algorithmic Trading. https://www.datacamp.com/community/tutorials/finance-python-trading. Accessed 8 Apr 2018
27. Perlin, M.S.: Evaluation of pairs-trading strategy at the Brazilian financial market. J. Deriv. Hedge Funds 15(2), 122–136 (2009)
28. Barth, M.E., Elliott, J.A., Finn, M.W.: Market rewards associated with patterns of increasing earnings. J. Account. Res. 37, 387–413 (1999)
29. Soliman, M.T.: The use of DuPont analysis by market participants. Account. Rev. 83(3), 823–853 (2008)

Six-State Continuous Processing Model for a New Theory of Computing

Chinthanie Weerakoon[1(✉)], Asoka Karunananda[2], and Naomal Dias[3]

[1] Department of Statistics & Computer Science, University of Kelaniya,
Kelaniya, Dalugama, Sri Lanka
chinthanie@kln.ac.lk
[2] Department of Computational Mathematics, University of Moratuwa,
Moratuwa, Katubedda, Sri Lanka
asokakaru@uom.lk
[3] Department of Computer Systems Engineering, University of Kelaniya,
Kelaniya, Dalugama, Sri Lanka
ngjdias@kln.ac.lk

Abstract. In contrast to the computation in Von-Neumann Architecture, the human mind executes processing in the brain by improving speed and accuracy over execution cycles. Further, it has been postulated that the memory is a result of continuous processing and is not separated from processing in the human mind. Similar to that mind model, a six-state continuous processing model with the states New, Ready, Running, Blocked, Sleep and Terminate, has been proposed to implement a special compiler which consists of conditionally evolving memory that aids in improving performance in conventional computation by exploiting 24-Casual Relations explained in Buddhist Theory of Mind. The experiments have been conducted to demonstrate how the proposed computing model increases the performance of execution of source codes and compilers. The result shows a clear increase of performance in computation by avoiding overloading the memory, and ensuring the execution of high quality code segments at the right time.

Keywords: Continuous processing · Six-state processing model · Evolving smaller memory · Special compiler · 24-causal relations

1 Introduction

Improving performance of computation has been a constant research challenge. The current approaches to computation have been primarily based on Von-Neumann Architecture (VNA) [1] which considers memory and processor as separated but connected distinct units [2]. It is a well-known fact that efficiency in execution on Von-Neumann architectures has been suffering from access time between CPU and memory (Von-Neumann Bottleneck) [3]. In this context, numerous researches have been conducted to offer both hardware and software solutions for improving computational

© Springer Nature Singapore Pte Ltd. 2019
J. Hemanth et al. (Eds.): SLAAI-ICAI 2018, CCIS 890, pp. 32–48, 2019.
https://doi.org/10.1007/978-981-13-9129-3_3

efficiency. For instance, hardware solutions such as caches, registers, and buffers have been introduced to improve the performance of memory [4]. Processor technologies are also rapidly growing with hardware architectural design, and multiple cores [3]. In contrast to hardware solutions, some software solutions have also been introduced to realize enhanced computations in various manner. Among others, parallel computing [6], evolutionary computing [7], incremental computing [8], neural computing [9], and Agent technology [10] can be cited as examples. Further software solutions to improve computational efficiency have been introduced in research in Operating System [11]. However, in comparison with software technologies, hardware technologies in computing has grown rapidly over the last 4 decades [5]. This has hindered in not being able to exploit the power of modern hardware for computations. As such developing software solutions for improving performance turn out to be a research problem.

We have been researching into developing a new software solution for improving computational efficiency. Our approach is inspired by the fact that computation in human mind does not separate memory from processor, and the processing speed and accuracy in processing improves over the cycles in the mind. The execution in the mind also evolves by starting from a small memory which updates over the time. Modelling of the evolving smaller memory comes to a research challenge. It should be noted that Von-Neumann architecture does not talk of evolution in computation over the cycles. The above inspiration has led us to research into Buddhist Theory of mind and found that memory can be modelled as a result of processing. We have developed a six-state processing model that comprises the states, namely New, Ready, Running, Blocked, Sleep and Terminate to implement evolvable memory that leads to improving performance in computation. The experimental results show a significant improvement in the performance of execution of the program in consecutive cycles.

The rest of the paper is organized as follows. Section 2 critically reviews the related work and we define the research problem. Section 3 is on Methodology showing the Buddhist theoretical foundation of the new theory of computation mimicking how execution takes place in the mind. Section 4 presents the testing scenarios and how we have evaluated the new model. Then, the last two sections discuss the experimental results, the significance of the work, and the possible applications of the new model concluding the work.

2   Related Work

This section describes various attempts to come up with different computational solutions that have contributed to improving efficiency in computations. We cover hardware solutions and software solutions in this regard. The software solutions are discussed at the system software level and application level.

2.1   Hardware Solutions

Moore's law [5], in every year processing speed of computers are supposed to be improved. In fact, development in processing speed now can go beyond Moore's prediction with the introduction of nanotechnology to the industry. In addition to the smaller memories such as different cache memories (L1, L2, and L3) [4] and registers [3], different kinds of memories, such as RAM, DRAM and EEPROM [3] were introduced with increasing capacities [2]. Further, the size of the computer has been decreased by increasing the density [3] of the electronic chips and other such components. However, still, the memory arrangements are much slower than the processor [6].

2.2   Operating Systems Solutions

Processing Models in OSs have been evolved from Two-State model to Seven-State Model. Two-State model, which has the states running and not-running is improved by adding ready and blocked queues instead of no-running state to hold ready and blocked processes separately [16], hence introducing Three-State model [17]. Further, including the information on 'after the completion of the execution' and 'before loading the newly defined processes into the memory', two other states such as exit, and new were joined, presenting the Five-State model.

However, a process to be promptly executed must be completely loaded into the main memory. In this case, if the main memory is fully filled with blocked processes and a virtual memory is absent, the processor will be idling until a waiting event occurs. The delays exist in Input/Output (I/O) activities and the memory access are highly affecting on this idling. As a result, the researchers introduced two Suspend states namely Ready/Suspend and Blocked/Suspend designing the seven-state model. This model allocates the space in main memory for the Ready or Blocked processes with higher priorities by sending the Ready or Blocked processes with lower priorities into the secondary storage. Since, disk I/O is faster than the other I/O such as printer I/O or tape I/O, swapping generally improve the performance of the system. However, the delays exist in memory access and I/O activities are not still fully solved.

2.3   Software Solutions

Multi Agent Systems (MAS) implements the process of problem solving by message passing in a team [10]. This technology is inspired by the behavior of massive structures such as bee colonies and ant colonies. MAS can offer a new paradigm for parallel distributed and concurrent computing on Von-Neumann architecture. This technology is ideal for generating emergent solutions, but rather weak in improving efficiency in computation, because some applications requires thousands of agents running at the same time. Genetic Algorithms (GA) provides the basis for evolutionary computing as inspired by the Darwinian theory of evolution [18]. GA has been applied for CPU scheduling. For example, they have used GA approaches in optimizing the waiting time [19] or maximizing CPU utilization or throughput [20]. GA can generate better quality solutions over generations, but GA is very much resource hungry during computation on both memory and CPU. Incremental computation is an approach to model systems where the data changes incrementally [21]. Simply, this concept allows in updating the outcome [8] or efficiently executing the program [22] when the input is altered [8, 22].

The above software solutions have predominantly concerned with modelling of real world systems with many entities which are interconnected, operated in parallel and distributed manner in dynamically changing environments. They have not been interested in generating better quality solution more efficiently over cycles. As such these software solutions are interested in solving certain real-world problems, but not necessarily improving computational efficiency and accuracy. More importantly, there has not been any attempt to come up with a model that executes programs in a manner similar to how minds execute. We notice this as negligence within the computing community, because mind is most cited best computer in the nature.

3 Methodology

This section discusses our approach and the effort on introducing a novel computing model. First, this describes the theoretical base and natural inspirations we had for this research. Then, our approach is presented and the description of the new model comes next. The last subsection of this section explains how the proposed computing model has been implemented in a fraction calculator.

3.1 Towards the New Processing Model

Better explanations for the human mind can be found from the Buddhist theory of mind. Therefore, in forming the continuous processing model, we exploit [12–14, 23] 24-causal relations explained in Patthana Prakarana [24] in Buddhist theory of mind.

The Buddhist theory explains everything as conditional phenomena. Similarly, the mind is also explained as a continuous thought process that emerges and continues as per the conditions [15]. Furthermore, how this arousal happened making the contin-uation of the process [19, 20], could be explained by a set extracted from 24-Causal Relations [15, 24] in Buddhist theory.

From 24-Causal Relations, this research uses a set of 15 out of 24 causal relations [14] as in Table 1 to explain the continuous processing in the human mind.

The conditions accomplish three major functions such as producing, supporting and maintaining. Then, 24-causal relations also assist the model by the way of doing above one or more functions to move from a conditioned state to a conditioning state [15]. These causal relations have been used in forming the actions in the transitions of the processing model as seen in the Table 1. According to the Table 1, the three concepts

Table 1. Causal relations in forming the actions of the processing model

Causal relation	Major function/Action formed in the model
Object (*Ārammana*)	Recognize the external or internal input
Root (*Hētu*)	Creation of a process for a given operation, can support the continuation of the system by being established
Co-Nascence (*Sahajāta*)	Produce the related things together
Association (*Sampayuktha*)	Related things exist and get deleted together
Mutuality (*Aññamañña*)	Related things help each other for the execution and to exist
Pre-Dominance (*Adhipati*)	The process with the highest priority dominates the system
Presence (*Atthi*)	Make the space or time available
Support (*Nissaya*)	Make the ground for execution
Pre-Nascence (*Purējāta*)	Activating new processes by loading them to the memory to execute them later
Proximity (*Anantara*)	Make no interval between two processes and maintain the continuity
Karma (*Karma*)	Execution of ready processes
Repetition (*Āsēvana*)	Execution over generations
Disappearance (*Vigata*)	Delete the unnecessary or inefficient processes/modules/instructions
Post-Nascence (*Pacchajāta*)	Make the continuation of a blocked process by a newly occurred event
Karma-Result (*Karma – Vipaka*)	Producing the results of execution

Co-Nascence (*Sahajāta*), Association (*Sampayuktha*), and Mutuality (*Aññamañña*), together do the classification [15] of related things such as relevant libraries/instructions/operations or data.

Finally, in the absence of causal relations, requirements such as an input, an event, an action or all the necessities for re-organizations (No further improvements or executions), the process can be terminated. Rest of the actions are clear in Table 1.

3.2   Continuous Processing of Human Mind: Real-World Scenarios

This research had a great insight from the real-world scenarios such as how a student take short notes, how they prepare for their exams doing tutorials and accessing larger knowledge bases [12], and how all the skilled workers do their tasks [13]. Some of these examples were already discussed in [12] and [13]. As another example, it is possible to highlight how the medical student becomes a veteran doctor with the time. This example can be used to emphasize the smaller memory or the small compiler in the human mind evolves with the time. It improves with experience, knowledge and organization through continuous processing, which depends on the input and the practice.

3.3 Our Approach

The proposed processing model consists of two process categories, namely 'Internal Processes' and 'External Processes'. The 'Internal Process' is similar to the internal process of human mind, which occur due to mind input (internal input), which is most probably related to the currently executing process in the mind. Further, the 'External Process' is similar to the internal process of the human mind, which occur due to an external input that comes through one of the other sense-doors [15].

In the context of the computer, an external input is a user input or such other input, which comes from external environment. Initially, the system starts with the internal process and the operation is randomly selected from the list of operations currently stored in the initial smaller memory through which the instructions stored in the knowledge base are accessed. Once an external input comes in, the system switch to the external process. Only if the current internal process is in 'Sleep' state, the system can accept an external input. After switching to the external process, the system can switch back to the internal process if there is no external input present. However, if no external input present, then the internal process can be continued with the operations, which are related to the most recent external input. In such a way, the system performs continuous processing.

While, executing through continuous processing over generations, the model does a set of actions which includes, identifying the input and operations, adding libraries for new operations, classifying the relevant operations with relevant data and instructions, prioritizing them accordingly, creating frequently occurring operating modules, and deleting unnecessary data, or unnecessary or inefficient modules and instructions. Such a way, smaller memory is evolved with the relevant entries. Moreover, these actions can happen in both the process categories encountering them in a single flow. Further, the actions such as additions, classification, prioritization and deletion can be aggregated into the single task 'Organizing'. Therefore, by repeating this organizing task, the system gains improvements. Additionally, the output of each process can be produced internally or externally depending on the process category.

3.4 New Processing Model

This subsection explains the new processing model that imitates the continuous processing model of the human mind. The newly introduced processing model consists of six states, namely, 'New', 'Ready', 'Running', 'Blocked', 'Sleep', and 'Terminate'.

Initially, a newly created process is in the 'New' state. Next, if a process is activated and organized, such a process is in 'Ready' state. Subsequently, if a process has been executing on a processor that particular process is in 'Running' state. After completing the execution, the process is transferred to the 'Sleep' state, which allows another process to initiate, execute or continue. In addition to that, a process can be in 'Blocked' state, if the process is waiting until a certain requirement to be fulfilled. Finally, the processes that are no longer required any modification or need any execution, can be terminated from the system, and such processes can be in 'Terminate' state. Figure 1 clearly shows the states and the transitions of the new processing model. The major purpose of this model is to maintain the continuity and update the system, especially the memory, round by round.

Fig. 1. State transition diagram of the new processing model

3.5   Implementing the Proposed Model in a Fraction Calculator

A Fraction Calculator (FC) has been implemented by incorporating the proposed continuous processing model. This can calculate the results of the expressions of fractions, fractions with whole parts, more than two fractions (no restriction on the length of the expression), and sub-expressions of fractions with brackets, with the operations addition, subtraction, multiplication, and division.

Similar to the human mind, this FC has two types of processes, namely internal processes and external processes. First, the FC starts with an internal process, which occurs due to an internal expression that was formed by the system itself by selecting an arbitrary operation from an existing list of operations in the smaller memory and arbitrary set of fractions. Then, it produces internal results. The system switches to the external process due to an expression of fractions given by the user as an external input. Here, the results are visible to the user. If no external input is available, the system switches back to the internal process. At this time, the internal expression is formed with the operations that were most recently used in the external expression.

FC starts with an initial smaller memory. It consists of records related to the operators in use. For example, for the plus operator, the relevant record with four items is (+, 1, 1, SumCalcModule), the first item shows the symbol of the operator, and the second item denotes the priority level of the operator. The third item shows the number of alternative algorithms, which can be used in calculating the addition of given two fractions. The last item of the record gives the name of the library file required for the addition of fractions.

With the help of both internal and external processes, FC continuously does its executions through the smaller memory. Meanwhile, as mentioned in the last paragraph of the above Sect. 3.3 a set of actions has been taken place. Through these actions, the smaller memory has been changing over execution cycles improving the performance of the FC.

The major actions in the FC can be briefly described as follows:

- Identify the input and operations: The expressions can be classified depending on the operators and the fractions in the expression:

    1. An expression with a new operator: The expression consists of an operator, which is not currently stored in the memory.

2. An expression with a different operator: The incoming operator is different from the operator, which is most recently operated. (the set of fractions can be similar)
3. An expression with a same operator: The incoming operator is similar to the operator, which is most recently applied, but with a different set of fractions.
4. Same Expression: Incoming expression can be exactly similar to the most recently executed expression. (Both the list of operators and the fractions are similar in the order.)
5. Frequent Expression: An expression that is recently inserted in many times is categorized as a frequent expression.

- Adding libraries for new operations: If the expression consists of a new operator, then the relevant instruction set to accomplish the particular operation should be added to the system as a library file, through the given interface. Then, a relevant record is automatically added to the smaller memory.

  For example, if there is no record related to the division in the smaller memory, when an expression with division operator is entered, FC identifies the incoming expression as an expression with a new operator. Then, FC allows to add the library file with the relevant set of instructions, and to set the priority for the operator, while adding the record (d, 2, 1, DivCalcModule) to the smaller memory. (Note: Here, instead of '/', 'd' is used as the division operator, since, '/' is used as the fraction operator)

- Classifying the relevant operations with relevant data and instructions, and prioritizing them accordingly for the execution: Once, an expression is entered, FC dynamically creates a module calling relevant instructions in relevant library files with related to the given operator/s. Then, compiles it and executes with the given data according to the assigned priorities.

- Creating frequently occurring operating modules: Initially, the FC starts with a common java file called "SubMain.java", in which the source code is dynamically changed by loading relevant libraries and algorithms as necessary, depending on the operation to be accomplished. Further, distinct modules for each and every operation will not be saved until the system identifies execution nature of the operations as frequent or infrequent. Over the execution cycles, the system identifies how frequent the operations come into action and then the system creates modules for the operations, which execute more frequently.

  That means, the module that creates dynamically, will not be specifically saved unless the frequent use of respective operator is evident. After, executing the same module for a certain number of times in nearby execution cycles, the module is labelled as a frequently using module and is permanently stored in the memory as seen in Fig. 2(b). Further, the record in the smaller memory related to the particular operator is updated with a fifth item indicating the name of the module as seen in the Fig. 2(a). Then, the module can be directly accessed through the smaller memory.

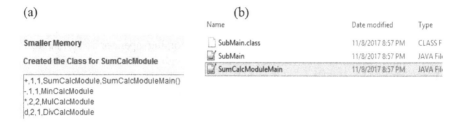

(a)

Smaller Memory

Created the Class for SumCalcModule

+,1,1,SumCalcModule,SumCalcModuleMain()
-,1,1,MinCalcModule
*,2,2,MulCalcModule
d,2,1,DivCalcModule

(b)

Name	Date modified	Type
SubMain.class	11/8/2017 8:57 PM	CLASS F
SubMain	11/8/2017 8:57 PM	JAVA Fil
SumCalcModuleMain	11/8/2017 8:57 PM	JAVA Fil

Fig. 2. Create the module for frequently occurring plus operator. (a) Updated record in the smaller memory, (b) File is created and stored

- Deleting unnecessary data, or unnecessary or inefficient modules and instructions: Since, there are many algorithms to compute a single task, the prototype of the proposed system will find the most efficient algorithm over the execution cycles and keep it by removing inefficient algorithms from the pool of algorithms bound to the particular task.

Here, it is possible to give an example from the multiplication. Initially, there are two alternative algorithms as MulCalc1() and MulCalc2() to accomplish multiplication. Through, cycles of executions, FC determines the most efficient algorithm using time values recorded in each execution cycle. Then, the FC removes the inefficient algorithm. At the same time, the number of algorithms for the multiplication is changed from two to one in the smaller memory.

Further, if a particular module or an instruction is no longer necessary for the system, then that can be removed from the system. Currently, the decision for such a removal is taken if the particular module has not been used within a certain time duration. Further, the respective record is automatically removed from the smaller memory.

4 Testing and Evaluation

This section presents the testing and evaluation process conducted over the FC, which has been incorporated with the proposed continuous processing model.

During this testing process, we keep the focus on two major modifications gained through execution cycles, which improve the processing power of the FC. The first modification is "Create and Save the computing modules for frequently executing operations", while "Remove inefficient algorithms and Select the most efficient algorithm" is being the second modification.

Testing Scenario 1: Create and Save the computing modules for frequently executing operations over execution cycles.

Since the process variation can produce non-normal data [25], this analysis was conducted for the operations separately. (This paper discusses Plus Operator only)

The hypothesis, which was tested in this scenario, is;

H_0: There is no difference between the means of the two samples (before and after applying modifications through continuous processing) of time values.
(No Performance Improvement over program execution cycles) (H_0: $\mu_D = d_0$, $d_0 = 0$)
H_1: The mean value of the sample time values recorded before organizing memory is greater than the mean value of the sample time values recorded after organizing memory.
(Performance has improved over program execution cycles) (H_1: $\mu_D > d_0$, $d_0 = 0$)

Method: First, a set of 100 expressions of fractions with plus operator were selected. Then, those were executed before the modification and recorded the time taken by each expression for the execution in Nanoseconds. In the same way, after the modification, the time values were recorded for the same set of expressions. This recording process was conducted in subsequent execution cycles.

As seen in Fig. 3, it was able to see a clear difference between the time values of two samples.

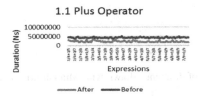

Fig. 3. Graph of time values recorded before and after applying the modifications to the FC with plus operator.

The same set of expressions of fractions has been used to measure the two outcomes, hence producing paired samples. Further, the study over these kinds of paired samples is called as a crossover study [26]. Furthermore, the relevant statistical test recommended [27] to perform a crossover study is paired t-test or Wilcoxon Signed Rank test or Sign test. The latter two are non-parametric tests. However, the paired t-test is more powerful [27, 28] than Wilcoxon Signed Rank test and Sign test. The two non-parametric tests are considered as alternatives [27] for the paired t-test.

However, the paired-t test can be applied only if the paired samples satisfy three conditions. The first condition is samples should be in continuous scale [29], the second condition is the set of differences of paired samples should have a normal distribution [29]. The last condition is the set of differences of paired samples should have no outliers [28]. Then, only if the set of differences seriously violates the above second and third conditions [27], and has a symmetric continuous distribution [30], Wilcoxon Signed Rank test must be applied. Finally, if the set of differences violates all the above conditions, Sign test must be applied [29, 30].

Then, as the second step in Testing Scenario 1, the samples were analysed to determine which test could be applied in these paired samples. For that, it was necessary to determine whether the samples satisfy the said conditions.

The first condition to check was whether the samples were in continuous scale. Since the time data recorded at time intervals [28] in nanoseconds these paired samples and their differences are belonged to continuous scale [30].

The second condition to check was whether the set of differences of the paired samples has a Normal distribution.

In this case, the Anderson Darlin (AD) test [31] was used to check the normality and the probability plot of difference was drawn.

Referring the graph of Fig. 4, which was drawn with Minitab;

(a)   (b)

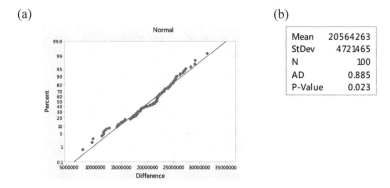

Fig. 4. Probability plot of difference drawn with Minitab (a) Probability plot (b) Values

P–Value$_{calculated}$(0.023) > P–Value$_{tabulated}$(0.01) and AD$_{calculated}$(0.885) < AD$_{calculated}$ (1.035) [31].

Hence, Normality is proved.

The last condition to check was whether the differences of the paired samples have significant outliers. For this, the Grubbs' test [32] was applied as follows using Minitab. Figure 5 shows the outlier plot and respective values.

(a)   (b)

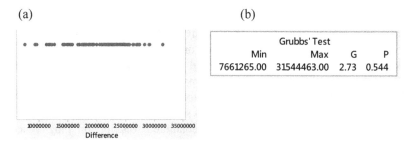

Fig. 5. Outlier plot of difference (a) Outlier plot (b) Values

Outlier Test with Difference: Significance level $\alpha = 0.01$.
Null hypothesis : All data values come from the same normal population.
Alternative hypothesis : Smallest or largest data value is an outlier.

Grubbs' Test:
Consider the values in the Table 2.;

Table 2. Values from Grubbs' test

Variable	N	Mean	StDev	Min	Max	G	P
Difference	100	20564263	4721465	7661265	31544463	2.73	0.544

Since, P−Value$_{calculated}$ = 0.544 > P−Value$_{tabulated}$ (= 0.01, Significance Level), the null hypothesis cannot be rejected and No outlier at the 1% level of significance.

Thus, the differences between the paired samples satisfy all the conditions.

After checking the conditions, it was determined that the most relevant test to do this analysis was paired t-test and it was not necessary to go for the alternatives.

Finally, the paired t-test was applied for the paired samples with a 99% significance level.

Test Statistics:

$$T = \frac{\bar{D} - \mu_D}{S_d/\sqrt{n}} \qquad , T_{calculated} = t = \frac{\bar{d} - d_0}{s_d/\sqrt{n}}$$

$\bar{D}$ = Random variable of mean of differences of samples
μ_D = Mean of Differences of population   n = Sample Size
$\bar{d}$ = Mean of Differences of samples (Estimate of $\bar{D}$)
S_d = Random variable of standard deviation of differences of samples

Paired t-test for the difference between Before Create and After Create the particular module:

Table 3. Values for the paired-t test (addition)

	N	Mean	StDev	SE Mean
Before select	100	43311188	2706548	270655
After select	100	22746925	4253045	425304
Difference	100	20564263	4721465	472147

From Table 3;

$s_d/\sqrt{n}$ = SE Mean = 472147 s_d = StDev = 4721465

$\bar{d}$ = 20564263   n = N = 100

99% lower bound for mean difference: 19447822

T–Test of mean difference = 0 (vs > 0): T–Value = 43.55 P–Value = 0.000

Hence, $T_{calculated} = \bar{d}/(s_d/\sqrt{n}) = 43.55$

$T_{table}(99, 0.01)$ = 2.365 (degree of freedom = N − 1 = 99) = > $T_{calculated}$ > T_{table}

Further, the calculated P-value is less than the table P-value (significance level-0.01)

Therefore, the null hypothesis can be rejected and it is possible to conclude that there is a significant improvement in the system after the modification as the mean value of the sample recorded before the modifications (Create and Save the computing modules for frequently executing addition operation) is greater than the mean value of the sample recorded after the modification.

Testing Scenario 2: Remove inefficient algorithms and Select the most efficient algorithm in Multiplication.

The hypothesis, which was tested in this scenario, is;

H_0: There is no difference between the means of the two samples of time values.

(No Performance Improvement over program execution cycles) (H_0: $\mu_D = d_0$, $d_0 = 0$)

H_1: The mean value of the sample time values recorded when using the inefficient algorithm is greater than the mean value of the sample time values recorded with the selection process and thereafter.

(Performance has improved over program execution cycles) (H_1: $\mu_D > d_0$, $d_0 = 0$)

Method: Our goal was to determine whether the system had gained an improvement in its execution after removing inefficient algorithms and selecting the most efficient algorithm.

During the testing process it was able to decide that the most efficient algorithms in multiplication is MulCalc1() from MulCalc1() and MulCalc2(), since MulCalc2() takes a longer time than MulCalc1(). (This cannot be decided even if the time complexity has been considered earlier).

If a programmer has used MulCalc2() without knowing its inefficient nature, it would be definitely time consuming and need more processing. Therefore, in early execution cycles, allocating some pre-processing time for the selection and then continue with the most efficient algorithm improves the performance of the computing system, than using the inefficient algorithm.

The sample time values recorded during the selection process and the time values recorded when using the inefficient algorithm can be seen in Table 4 for a given set of twenty expressions. Then, for both cases, total time durations were calculated as seen in the last row of Table 5. (Selection Process = 2323140714 Ns, Inefficient Algorithms (MulCalc2()) = 2786388917 Ns).

Table 4. Selection process vs inefficient algorithm

| Expression | Selection | | Time taken by the inefficient algorithm (M2) in nanoseconds |
	Duration (Ns)	Method	
1/2*2/3	116316738	M1	
1/2*2/3	128066758	M2	272323879
:	:	:	:
1/5*4/6	53335011	M1	
1/5*4/6	166784509	M2	127790389
1/5*5/6	41904696	M1	160376426
2/3*1/4	55239494	M1	124228894
:	:	:	:
3/4*1/5	43070573	M1	127886944
3/4*2/5	55433363	M1	143891059
Total Time	**2323140714**		**2786388917**

Such twenty total values were recorded from twenty samples of different sets of twenty expressions as seen in Table 5.

Table 5. Sample total values for selection process and inefficient algorithm (M2)

Sample	Selection (Ns)	MulCalc2() (Ns)
1	**2323140714**	**2786388917**
2	2134226128	2471722339
:	:	:
19	2785844294	3185859802
20	2138863042	2473804734

As in the above Testing Scenario 1, after checking for the conditions, the paired t-test was applied to the data in Table 5.

From Table 6;

Table 6. Values for the paired-t test (selection process)

	N	Mean	StDev	SE mean
M2	20	2769338332	322477375	72108133
With selection	20	2456718655	361500451	80833958
Difference	20	312619678	125888527	28149530

$$s_d/\sqrt{n} = \text{SE Mean} = 28149530 \qquad\qquad s_d = \text{StDev} = 125888527$$

$$\bar{d} = 312619678 \qquad\qquad\qquad n = N = 20$$

99% lower bound for mean difference: 312619678

T−Test of mean difference = 0 (vs > 0): T−Value = 11.11 P−Value = 0.000

Hence, $T_{\text{calculated}} = \bar{d}/(s_d/\sqrt{n}) = 11.11$

$T_{\text{table}}(99, 0.01) \qquad = 2.539(\text{degree of freedom} = N - 1 = 19) = > T_{\text{calculated}} > T_{\text{table}}$

Therefore, the null hypothesis can be rejected and it is possible to conclude that there is a significant improvement in the system after the selection as the mean value of the sample recorded when using the inefficient algorithm is greater than the mean value of the sample recorded during the selection process and thereafter.

5 Discussion

Since the proposed model has continuous processing and an internal process, the system with the new processing model can gain self-improvements over generations with the help of the actions mentioned in the above Sects. 3, eventhough the external inputs or external processes are absent. Further, in the FC, if the incoming expression is longer, then at the end of the evaluation of the expression (for example, $\frac{7}{10} + 8\frac{1}{7} + \frac{12}{15} * \left(\frac{1}{2} + \frac{5}{9} - \frac{1}{12}\right) * \frac{11}{20} - \frac{2}{3} + 5\frac{6}{8} + \frac{4}{5} - \frac{7}{13} + \frac{3}{19} + \frac{6}{17} + \frac{3}{4}$), the system could gain improvements. In addition to that, since the model identifies and classifies the incoming inputs, the time taken by the expression evaluation can be improved, especially if the input is classified under the "Same Expression" category.

By applying paired t-test with 99% confidence level, it was able to prove that the proposed continuous processing model helps to improve the performance of a system, when executes over the generations.

On the contrary, when the current computer processes the same input for several times, it gains improvements neither in the process nor in the result.

In fact, all the terms used for the new model are currently existing terms. However, the transitions are more functional than the existing transitions as explained in Sect. 3. Especially, New-Ready, Running-Ready, Blocked-Ready, Running-Sleep, Ready-Ready, and Ready-Terminate are differently defined exploiting causal relations explained in Buddhist Theory of Mind.

Furthermore, the new model is advanced than the incremental computing, since the new model refines the entire system through a continuous process, not only the parts related to the modified input. On the other hand, 'Repetition' and 'Classification' can be shown as the major concepts. Ultimately, the new processing model totally depends on the fundamental core concepts, which was explained in Sect. 3. However, in improving the existing computing models such as GA or Agent technology, the model proposed here can be used.

6 Conclusion

The proposed model can be adopted in different ways. Some of such adoption suggestions are mentioned below. First, one can think of integrating this model into the kernel of the operating system. For example, this concept can be used in applying suitable scheduling algorithms in the operating system by identifying the patterns of repetitive processes. Further, this can be used within the inference engine of an expert system. Within this particular environment, this model can be used in handling knowledge entities/facts/rules and resolving the facts and rules. Moreover, in a development environment, this model can be applied in a compiler or an interpreter. Then, this model can help the developer to improve the software in subsequent execution cycles as seen in the fraction calculator (maybe during the testing cycles). Finally, the company can hand over more efficient software to the client. Even within a program, using this proposed model, it is possible to enhance the computing power of the program over the time. (Fraction calculator consists of both a compiler, which compiles the incoming expressions, and an executor, which evaluates expressions and gives results).

It can be concluded that the proposed processing model, which has six states, was proved as a performance improver for the continuously processing computing systems. Further, this model can be integrated to the other soft computing mechanisms to enhance their computing power. At last, this model can be adapted in to different systems where they have continuous processing. Aviation or military based monitoring Systems can be shown as an example for the systems, which have continuous processing. Overall, it is possible to say that this new processing model produce a new approach for computing.

References

1. Godfrey, M.D., Hendry, D.F.: The computer as von Neumann planned it. IEEE Ann. Hist. Comput. **15**(1), 11–21 (1993)
2. Abd-El-Barr, M., El-Rewini, H.: Fundamentals of Computer Organization and Architecture. Wiley, Hoboken (2005)
3. Stallings, W.: Computer Organization and Architecture: Designing for Performance. Pearson Prentice Hall, Upper Saddle Rive (2010)
4. Smith, A.J.: Cache memories. ACM Comput. Surv. **14**(3), 473–530 (1982)
5. Moore, G.E.: Moore's Law at 40. Chapter 7, in Understanding Moore's Law: Four decades of innovation edited by D. C. Brock, Philadelphia, PA.: Chemical Heritage Foundation, pp. 67–84 (2006)
6. Gebali, F.: Algorithms and Parallel Computing. Wiley, Hoboken (2011)
7. Eiben, E.A., Smith, A.J.: Introduction to Evolutionary Computing. Springer, Heidelberg (2015)
8. Hammer, M.A., et al.: Incremental computation with names. ACM SIGPLAN Not. **50**(10), 748–766 (2015)
9. Russell S.J., Norvig P.: Artificial Intelligence: A Modern Approach. Prentice Hall, Upper Saddle River (2015)

10. Wooldridge, M.J.: An Introduction to Multiagent Systems, 2nd edn. Wiley, Chichester (2009)
11. Silberschatz, A., Galvin, P.B., Gagne, G.: Operating System Concepts, 9th edn. Wiley, Hoboken (2016)
12. Weerakoon, W.A.C., Karunananda, A.S., Dias, N.G.J.: A tactics memory for a new theory of computing, pp. 153–158 (2013)
13. Weerakoon, W.A.C., Karunananda, A.S., Dias, N.G.J.: Conditionally evolving memory for computers, pp. 271–271 (2015)
14. Weerakoon, W.A.C., Karunananda, A.S., Dias, N.G.J.: New processing model for operating systems. University of Kelaniya, pp. 29 (2016)
15. Bodhi, B.: Comprehensive Manual of Abhidhamma: The Psychology of Buddhism (Abhidhammattha Sangaha). Buddhist Publication Society (2006)
16. Stallings, W.: Operating Systems: Internals and Design Principles, 7th edn. Prentice Hall, Boston (2012)
17. Tanenbaum, A.S., Boss, H.: Modern operating systems, 4th edn. Pearson/Prentice Hall, Upper Saddle River (2015)
18. De Jong, K.A.: Evolutionary Computaion: A Unified Approach. The MIT Press, Cambridge (2006)
19. Siregar, M.U.: A new approach to CPU scheduling: genetic Round Robin. Int. J. Comput. Appl. $47(19)$, 18–25 (2012)
20. Sharma, M., Sindhwani, P., Maheshwari, V.: Genetic algorithm optimal approach for scheduling processes in operating system. Int. J. Comput. Sci. Netw. Secur. $14(5)$, 91–94 (2014)
21. Carlsson, M.: Monads for incremental computing. In: The Seventh ACM SIGPLAN International Conference on Functional Programming, pp. 26–35 (2002)
22. Hammer, M.A., Phang, K.Y., Hicks, M., Foster, J.S.: Adapton: composable, demand-driven incremental computation (2014)
23. Weerakoon, W.A.C., Karunananda, A.S., Dias, N.G.J.: Enhancing the functionality of rule-based expert systems. In: 4th International Conference on Advances in Engineering Sciences and Applied Mathematics, Kuala Lumpur, Malaysia, p. 93 (2015)
24. Suwisi Pratya: Pattana Prakarana, Abhidhamma Pritaka, Buddha Jayanthi Tipitaka Series 52 (3) (2006)
25. Colton, J.: Detecting and analyzing non-normal data. In: Tampa American Society for Quality (ASQ) Meeting, Minitab Inc., Florida (2014)
26. Cleophas, T.J., Zwinderman, A.H.: SPSS for Starters and 2nd Levelers, 2nd edn. Springer, Heidelberg (2015)
27. Meek, G.E., Ozgur, C., Dunning, K.: Comparison of the t vs. Wilcoxon signed-rank test for likert scale data and small samples. JMASM $6(1)$, 91–106 (2007)
28. Imam, A., Mohammed, U., Abanyam, C.M.: On consistency and limitation of paired t-test, Sign and wilcoxon sign rank test. IOSR-JM $10(1)$, 01–06 (2014)
29. Gupta, S.C., Kapoor, V.K.: Fundamentals of Mathematical Statistics. Sultan Chand & Sons (2007)
30. Walpole, R.E.: Probability and Statistics for Engineers and Scientists. Pearson Education, Boston (2012)
31. Stephen, M.A.: The Anderson-Darlin Statistics. Department of Statistics, Stanford University, Stanford, California (1979)
32. Grubbs, F.E.: Procedures for detecting outlying observations in samples. Am. Stat. Assoc. Am. Soc. Qual. $11(1)$, 1–21 (1969)

Locating the Position of a Cell Phone User Using GSM Signals

Shazir Shafeeque$^{(\boxtimes)}$, G. S. N. Meedin, and H. U. W. Ratnayake

Department of Electrical and Computer Engineering,
The Open University of Sri Lanka, Nawala, Nugegoda, Sri Lanka
soozu082@gmail.com, {gsnad,udithaw}@ou.ac.lk

Abstract. Mobile devices are increasingly popular today and mobile location-based services are considered as a profitable opportunity for service providers. Position tracking is essential in implementing many of the new location based services in cellular networks. Mobile positioning technology has become an important area of research as well for emergency and commercial services. There are different ways to track a precise location of a mobile phone or a user. The most widely spread method is the use of built-in GPS module, or the cell tower triangulation. However, most people do not use GPS location service all the time and as a result cellular mobile network based mobile positioning has been an alternative method for tracking. Moreover, these methods have many problems such as low accuracy, high equipment cost, rapid cell-site modifications, and the need of advanced infrastructure. Therefore, a requirement is there to develop a cost effective, accurate, mobile positioning method to replace the current low accuracy and costly methods which use cellular mobile network. In this research project, an Android application was developed to fetch location parameters of connected nearest base stations of a cell phone to locate the coordinates of each and every base station using Google geo-location API. There, combinations of three base station coordinates were used to calculate the approximate location using Pearson Correlation Coefficient approach. Approximated locations were optimized using a Genetic Algorithm to locate final estimated location. This paper discusses the proposed system and the implementation of the proof of concept.

Keywords: Mobile location-based services · Google geo-location API ·
Genetic algorithm · Pearson correlation coefficient

1 Introduction

In our daily life, cell phone has become an essential necessity. Knowing where someone is probably the most comforting thought that the technology has provided nowadays. Mobile positioning technology has become an important area of research for emergency as well as for commercial services. Mobile positioning in cellular networks will provide several services [1] such as, proximity based marketing, travel information using location based service, mobile workforce management, fraud preventions and location based alerting systems.

© Springer Nature Singapore Pte Ltd. 2019
J. Hemanth et al. (Eds.): SLAAI-ICAI 2018, CCIS 890, pp. 49–63, 2019.
https://doi.org/10.1007/978-981-13-9129-3_4

There are different ways to track a precise location of a mobile phone and a user. The most widely spread method is use of built-in GPS (Global Positioning System) module, or cell tower triangulation. GPS is a network of orbiting satellites that send precise details of their position in space back to earth. The signals are obtained by GPS receivers such as navigation devices and are used to calculate the exact position, speed and time at the location. The accuracy of GPS data depends on many factors such as the quality of the GPS receiver, the position of the GPS satellites at the time the data was recorded, the characteristics of the surroundings (buildings, tree cover, valleys, etc.) and even the weather. Specifications for many GPS receivers indicate their accuracy to be within about 3 to 15 m, 95% of the time [2]. This assumes the receiver has a clear view of the sky and has finished acquiring satellites.

However, many people do not use GPS location service all the time in their smartphones [3]. So the other way of tracking is using cell tower triangulation. Cell tower triangulation is similar to GPS tracking in many ways. Multiple towers are used to track the phone's location by measuring the time delay that a signal takes to return to the towers from the phone. However, the accuracy of such a tracking technique is not high. This paper describes a method to improve the accuracy of such a tracking technique using Genetic Algorithm.

The rest of this paper is organized as follows. Section 2 is the literature survey related to this research. Section 3 gives the methodology of the research including the system design and implementation. Section 4 provides results and discussion, and finally the conclusion and future work.

2 Literature Survey

Various techniques for identifying the location of a device can be divided into network centric, handset centric methods or a combination of both [4]. Network centric techniques locate a device based on information supplied by the network or with help of a number of mobile phone base stations, and no handset enhancements are necessary. Handset centric methods require an upgrade to the mobile device as the location is calculated by the mobile phone itself from signals received from base stations. Satellite based technologies, such as GPS are examples for handset-centric positioning. Cell of Origin (COO), Time of Arrival (TOA), Angle of Arrival (AOA), Time Difference of Arrival (TDOA), and Enhanced Observed Time Difference (E-OTD) are the relevant location technologies for network based mobile phone tracking.

Cell of origin (COO) [5, 6] is the least accurate but the cheapest because it does not require individual phones or network infrastructure to be altered.

Time of Arrival (TOA) [7] is based on the precise measurement of the arrival time of a signal transmitted from a mobile device to several receiving sensors. The TOA technique requires very precise knowledge of the transmission start time(s), and must ensure that all receiving sensors as well as the mobile device are accurately synchronized with a precise time source. A drawback of the TOA approach is the requirement for precise time synchronization of all stations, especially the mobile device.

The technique known as Angle of Arrival (AOA) [8] determines the location of a user by measuring the angles from which a mobile phone's signals are received by two or more base stations. Because the mobile device is moving, this is not a very accurate method. Base stations need AOA equipment to identify the direction of the telephone signal.

The Time Difference of Arrival (TDOA) [9] technique measures the time it takes for a mobile phone signal to reach the receiving tower and two additional towers. The signal travel time allows determining the user's distance from each tower, which in turn allows to calculate the position of the user.

Enhanced Observed Time Difference (E-OTD) [6] uses triangulation between at least three different base stations to provide more accurate location identification than Cell-ID. The distance between the handset and the base station is calculated according to the different times it takes a signal to reach the base stations once it leaves the handset. E-OTD only works on GSM and GPRS networks, requires an upgrade of mobile network infrastructure and software loading to base stations to ensure compatibility. Base stations must be equipped with location measurement units (LMUs) and, when measuring the signal from the mobile phone, LMUs can triangulate the user's position.

3 Methodology

This section of the paper describes the system design and implementation of the system. Figure 1 below illustrates the system architecture of the system.

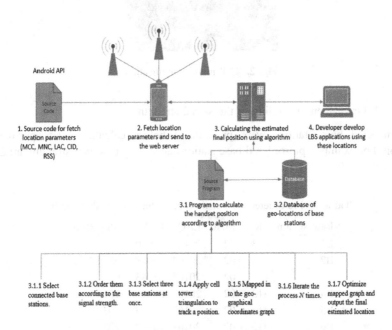

Fig. 1. Overall system architecture

Methodology followed is explained under seven steps in this section. The flow of the system is as follows.

Step 1: Select connected base stations

A typical mobile phone receives radio signals from neighboring cells in the time it is connected to a macro cell. When it is connected, all neighboring cells send their own unique parameters to the handset (MCC, MNC, LAC, CID and RSS). Using those parameters we can geographically locate the position of a base station using Google geo-location API. To fetch those parameters, an Android application was developed with runtime permissions as illustrated in Fig. 2.

Fig. 2. Cell monitor application

Step 2: Order them according to the signal strength

Connected base stations were pre-ordered before calculating an approximate location. For example, pre-ordered base stations according to signal strength are given in Table 1.

Table 1. Pre-ordered base stations according to signal strength

Base station	MCC	MNC	LAC	CID	RSS (dBm)
B1	413	02	20167	35060	−79
B2	413	02	20167	35068	−95
B3	413	02	20167	35083	−99
B4	413	02	20167	35058	−101
B5	413	02	20167	35069	−103
B6	413	02	20167	19769	−103
B7	413	02	20167	35076	−107

Step 3: Select three base stations at once

The program selects three base stations at a time to calculate an approximate location of a user. For example, if a cell phone connected to 6 base stations, it can have 20 different combinations. The group selection is given in Fig. 3.

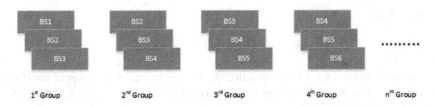

Fig. 3. Group selection

Step 4: Apply Pearson Correlation Coefficient (PCC) technique to calculate an approximate position

The Pearson correlation coefficient is a measure of the strength of the linear relationship between two variables. Here, it was obtained using the linear relationship between signal attenuation (L) and received signal strength (R) applying the equation of Okumura-Hata model. The derivation of this linear equation is shown below.

This method minimize the influence of disturbance, barriers, or NLOS (Non-Line of sight) errors on performance.

GSM signal propagation and attenuation can be described by Okumura-Hata model as follows.

$$L = 69.55 + 26.16 \log_{10}(f_c) - 13.82 \log_{10}(h_b) - a(h_m)$$
$$+ [44.9 - 6.55 \log_{10}(h_b)] \log_{10}(d)$$

Where,

f_c – Carrier frequency
h_b – Height of the base station
h_m – Height of the mobile station (cell phone)
d – Distance of propagation
L – Attenuation
$a(h_m)$ – Correction function which is decided by the environment

$$a(h_m) = \begin{cases} (1.1 \log_{10} f_c - 0.7)h_m - 1.56 \log_{10}(f_c) + 0.8 smallcity \\ 8.29(\log_{10}(1.54h_m))^2 - 1.1(f_c \leq 300MHz)bigcity \\ 3.2(\log_{10}(11.75h_m))^2 - 4.97(f_c > 300MHz)bigcity \end{cases}$$

Then, we get

$$L = a_1 \log(d) + b_0$$

Where $a_1 = [44.9 - 6.55 \log_{10}(h_b)]$ *and*

$$b_0 = 69.55 + 26.16 \log_{10}(f_c) - 13.82 \log_{10}(h_b) - a(h_m)$$

Such that

$$R_0 = T_0 - a_1 \log(d) - b_0 + C_0$$

Where R_0 denotes the RSSI in practice, T_0 denotes transmitting power of the BS in practice, which is generally a time invariant constant, and C_0 denotes a constant for different antenna gain. Let?

$$b_1 = T_0 - b_0 + C_0$$

Then

$$R_0 = -a_1 \log(d) + b_1 \tag{1}$$

The RSSI in theory is,

$$R = T - (44.9 - 6.55 \log(h_0)) \log(d) - b + C$$

Where R denotes the RSSI in theory, T denotes the transmit power of the BS in theory, C denotes constant for different antennas, and h_0 is a predicted value of h_b. Let? $a_2 = (44.9 - 6.55 \log(h_0))$ and $b_2 = T - b + C$, Then

$$R = -a_2 \log(d) + b_2 \tag{2}$$

According to (1) and (2), we can get

$$R_0 = \frac{a_1}{a_2} R - \frac{a_1 b_2}{a_2} + b_1,$$

$$T_0 - L + C_0 = \frac{a_1}{a_2} R - \frac{a_1 b_2}{a_2} + b_1,$$

$$L = -\frac{a_1}{a_2} R + \frac{a_1 b_2}{a_2} - b_1 + C_0 + T_0,$$

$$L = A.R + B$$

Where $A = -\frac{a_1}{a_2}$ and $B = \frac{a_1 b_2}{a_2} - b_1 + C_0 + T_0$.

As we can see, there is a liner relationship between L and R. Pearson's Correlation Coefficient (PCC) quantifies the liner relationship between vectors:

$$r = \frac{\sum_{i=1}^{n}(x_i - \bar{X})(y_i - \bar{Y})}{\sqrt{\sum_{i=1}^{n}(x_i - \bar{X})^2 \sum_{i=1}^{n}(y_i - \bar{Y})^2}}$$

if absolute value of PCC is smaller than 1.

When it is close to 1, the liner relationship between the two vectors will be stronger. The algorithm is as follows:

(1) Put a mesh grid in the coverage area of the home base station (usually the nearest base station), to which GSM device belongs.
(2) Traverse every node on mesh grid and calculate the PCC of $\vec{L}$ and $\vec{R}$.
(3) Find the node with absolute PCC value closest to 1 as the position (Fig. 4).

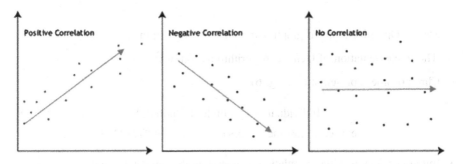

Fig. 4. Pearson correlation coefficient variations

Step 5: Mapped in to the geo-graphical coordinates graph

The approximated point was mapped into a graph for optimization purpose as shown below (Fig. 5).

Step 6: (3-5) Iterate the process N times

Iterations = N,

$$N = \frac{n!}{r!(n-r)!}$$

n – Number of connected base stations
r = 3 (Always take 3 base stations at once)

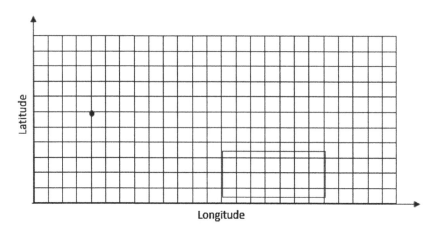

Fig. 5. Coordinates graph

Step 7: Optimize mapped graph using Genetic Algorithm

The implementation of Genetic Algorithm as follows,

- Chromosome representation (Fig. 6)

$$Individual = \{Latitude, Longitude\}$$
$$e.g.\ chromosome = \{6.914229143, 79.87732343\}$$

- Initial population Initial population is created with completely random solutions of 10.

```
//Create a random individual
public void generateIndividual(double minLat, double maxLat, double minLong, double maxLong){
        Random random = new Random();
        genes[0] = minLat + (maxLat - minLat) * random.nextDouble();
        genes[1] = minLong + (maxLong - minLong) * random.nextDouble();
}

                    (maxLat - minLat)    //Latitude varience
                    (maxLong - minLong)  //Longitude varience
```

Fig. 6. Code snippet for generate random chromosome

- Fitness evaluation
  Fitness evaluation is done using the formula of distance between two points(Fig. 7).

  The objective function is,

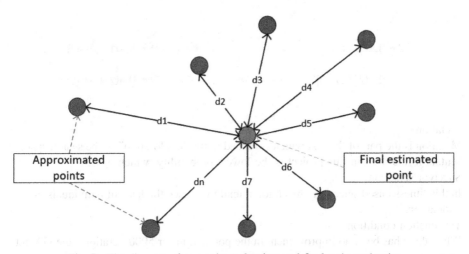

Fig. 7. The diagram of approximated points and final estimated point

$$f = d1 + d2 + d3 + \ldots + dn$$

Where $n =$ number of points

$$f(x,y) = \sqrt{(x-x1)^2 + (y-y1)^2} + \sqrt{(x-x2)^2 + (y-y2)^2}$$
$$+ \sqrt{(x-x3)^2 + (y-y3)^2} + \ldots$$
$$+ \sqrt{(x-x_n)^2 + (y-y_n)^2}$$

Then the fitness function is,

$$F = \frac{1}{f(x,y)}$$

if sum of distance is low, get higher fitness,
if sum of distance is high, get lower fitness

Parent selection
Selection of parent is done using the tournament method. Select K individuals from the population at random and select the best out of these to become a parent. The same process is repeated for selecting the next parent.
Crossover
One-point crossover method was used to generalize the next generation. The crossover rate 50%.

P1 = {Lat1, Long1} ⟶ C1 = {Lat1, Long2}

P2 = {Lat2, Long2} ⟶ C2 = {Lat2, Long1}

Mutation

Mutation is the part of the GA which is related to the "exploration" of the search space. Mutation rate used in this project is the lowest probability, which is 1.5%

Survivor selection

In this fitness based selection, the children tend to replace the least fit individuals in the population.

Termination condition

When there has been no improvement in the population for 5000 iterations, the GA get terminated.

4   Results and Discussion

This section presents the results of implemented prototype which was tested at real time locations. Then final estimated location is compared with the actual location. The final estimated location in Dematagoda is given in Fig. 8.

The algorithm was tested with same inputs at different times to analyze the outputs.

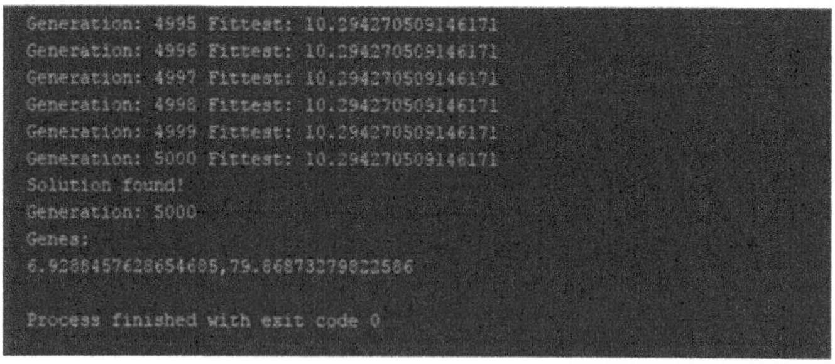

Fig. 8. Final estimated location in Dematagoda

It was observed that there are no changes in outputs after a number of significant iterations (Figs. 9 and 10).

The final estimated location in Borella Junction is given in Fig. 11.

Error of final estimated location (Dematagoda) – 17.38 m (Figs. 12 and 13)
Error of final estimated location (Borella Junction) – 32.39 m (Figs. 14 and 15)

One of the difficulties faced during the implementation phase was the lack of precise open source databases regarding service provider's cell tower locations due to security reasons. Online open source databases from Google and Yandex were used as

Fig. 9. Difference between estimated location and actual location [Dematagoda]

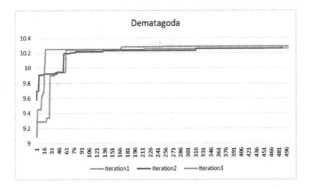

Fig. 10. Fitness evaluation over generations for three iterations [Dematagoda]

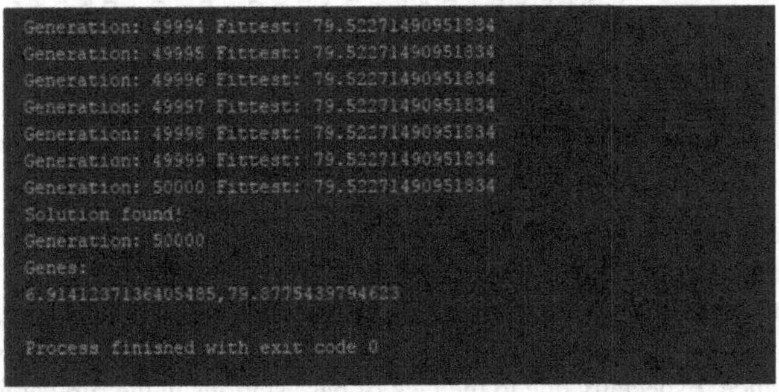

Fig. 11. Final estimated location in Borella Junction

an alternative solution to this problem. In this project, Google API was used to fetch coordinates of base stations. However, the data sets given in the database are not precise. Since the actual location of base stations cannot be given to the algorithm as

Fig. 12. Difference between estimated location and actual location [Borella Junction]

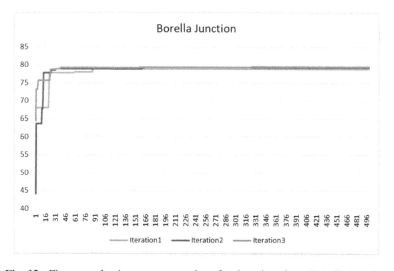

Fig. 13. Fitness evaluation over generations for three iterations [Borella Junction

inputs it directly affects the estimated outputs. Error can be reduced by feeding actual locations of base stations to the algorithm.

The major drawback of the implemented project is that the user at least need to connect with three or more base stations at once. Otherwise the algorithm will provide poor performance. Especially due to the lack of base stations in the rural areas accuracy of the results could be low.

The cell coverage area is determined by the base station output power and the environment. Things such as trees, hills, buildings and land formations will affect the coverage of the area. In city areas there is generally a larger number of users and also more obstructions.

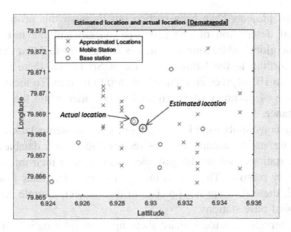

Fig. 14. illustrated the estimated location and the actual location in Demategoda

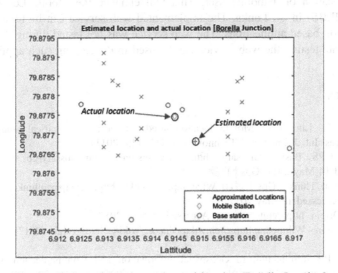

Fig. 15. Estimated location and actual location [Borella Junction]

5   Conclusion

Wireless network positioning systems have become very important in recent years. Various location-based services in wireless communication networks depend on mobile positioning. Commercial examples range from low-accuracy methods based on cell identification to high-accuracy methods combining wireless network information and satellite positioning. However, most people do not use GPS location services at all, except when they need. So the wireless networks positioning systems need to be improved. Locating the position of a mobile user with a high degree of accuracy is a research interest that holds the key to a breakthrough in many service challenges faced by operators in the wireless communication world.

Many research projects have been carried out to solve this problem. This paper described a detail description of one proposed system and the test results. While studying about the global addressing system it is being identified that the longitude per distance vary according to the latitude. In case of Sri Lanka, there is a variation of approximately 6° to 10° degrees in latitude from top to bottom. To locate a mobile user with higher degree of accuracy, it is required to consider while the calculations are dealing with distance.

The following constraints were identified during the implementation of this project. To locate a mobile station accurately, it is required to have a database with precise locations of base stations. But service providers do not share their information of base stations for security reasons. Though online open source databases from Google and Yandex are used, these data are not precise. In this project, Google API was used to fetch coordinates of base stations.

In future, if service providers share their updated information of base stations through an API, it will create a good opportunity to increase the accuracy of final estimated location of a mobile user. That will enhance the Mobile Location Base Services (MLBS) in Sri Lanka. The implemented web service can be used in developing location based applications. The web service was not tested during this project. With adequate testing the web service can be used in developing such applications.

References

1. Chen, P.T., Lin, Y.S.: Mobile location-based services: an empirical study of user preferences. Int. J. Inf. Educ. Technol. **1**(5), 416–425 (2011)
2. GPS - GPS Basics Glossary. http://www.gps-basics.com/glossary/gps.shtml (2017). Accessed 14 May 2017. Gps | 世論
3. What Japan Thinks: Gps | 世論 What Japan Thinks. http://whatjapanthinks.com/tag/gps/ (2017). Accessed 17 May 2017
4. Cell of Origin. http://etutorials.org. Accessed 15 May 2017
5. Cell of origin - Wikipedia. https://en.wikipedia.org/wiki/Cell_of_origin (2017). Accessed 15 May 2017
6. Abdalla, R.: Introduction to Geospatial Information and Communication Technology (GeoICT). Springer, Cham (2016). https://doi.org/10.1007/978-3-319-33603-9
7. Jais, M.I., Ehkan, P., Ahmad, R.B., Ismail, I., Sabapathy, T., Jusoh, M.: Review of angle of arrival (AOA) estimations through received signal strength indication (RSSI) for wireless sensors network (WSN). In: 2015 IEEE 2015 International Conference on Computer, Communication, and Control Technology (I4CT 2015), April 21–23 in Imperial Kuching Hotel, Kuching, Sarawak, Malaysia
8. Al-Sahli, S., Amro, A., Kassir, M.M., Noamani, D.: Direction Finding Application for GSM Networks. Beirut: Department of Electrical and Computer Engineering, American University of Beirut
9. Bai, Y. B., et al.: A new algorithm for improving the tracking and positioning of cell of origin. In: IEEE 2015 International Association of Institutes of Navigation World Congress, Prague, Czech Republic (2015)
10. Gorra, A.: An analysis of the relationship between individuals' perceptions of privacy and mobile phone location data—a grounded theory study. Chapter 2, Leeds Metropolitan University, UK

11. Lumbini, C., Balasuriya, N.: An improved pedestrian tracking algorithm for NLOS cellular environments. In: 2015 IEICE 2015 10th Asia-Pacific Symposium on Information and Telecommunication Technologies (APSITT), pp. 127–129. (2015)
12. Zhang, Y., Member, IEEE, Liu, H., Fu, W., Zhou, A., Mi, L.: Localization algorithm for GSM mobiles based on RSSI and pearson's correlation coefficient. In: 2014 IEEE International Conference on Consumer Electronics (ICCE), pp. 284–285 (2014)

Neural Networks

Modeling of Hidden Layer Architecture in Multilayer Artificial Neural Networks

Mihirini Wagarachchi[1(✉)] and Asoka Karunananda[2]

[1] Department of Interdisciplinary Studies, University of Ruhuna,
Galle, Sri Lanka
mihirini@is.ruh.ac.lk
[2] Department of Computational Mathematics, University of Moratuwa,
Katubedda, Moratuwa, Sri Lanka
asoka@mrt.ac.lk

Abstract. A generated solution for an artificial neural network (ANN) may result in complex computations of neural networks, deployment, and usage of trained networks due to its inappropriate architecture. Therefore, modeling the hidden layer architecture of artificial neural networks remains as a research challenge. This paper presents a solution to achieve the hidden layer architecture of artificial neural networks which is inspired by some facts of neuroplasticity. The proposed method has two phases. First, it determines the number of hidden layers for the best architecture and then removes unnecessary hidden neurons from the network to enhance the performance. Experimental results in several benchmark problems show that the modified network shows better generalization than the original network.

Keywords: Artificial neural networks · Delta values · Hidden layer architecture · Peak search algorithm

1 Introduction

Artificial neural networks are mathematical and computational models for predicting and decision making, inspired by the functions of the biological nervous system. Also, they are very advanced modelling systems, capable to solve many highly complex tasks with good generalization. The generalization power of an Artificial Neural Network strongly depends on its hidden layer architecture. In general, as there are enough data to capture the complexity of the given task, multi-layered architectures show better performance than shallow ones for many real-valued applications [1, 2]. However, this solution of architecture may not be computationally optimized. In addition, using both too large and too small number of hidden neurons show advantages as well as disadvantages. When the network is too large it learns fast [3] and can form complex decision regions as the problem requires and show better fault tolerance in damage conditions [4]. However, when there are too many parameters generalization ability declines as it fails to distinguish similar neurons. On the other hand, networks with too few parameters show better generalization nevertheless, neurons in these networks not learn data properly [5]. Apart from the many approaches on hidden layer architecture in

© Springer Nature Singapore Pte Ltd. 2019
J. Hemanth et al. (Eds.): SLAAI-ICAI 2018, CCIS 890, pp. 67–78, 2019.
https://doi.org/10.1007/978-981-13-9129-3_5

ANN, we find that most of them do not have a good theoretical background. Hence, the determining the hidden layer architecture remains as an unsolved problem.

The method presents in this paper is inspired by the finding from the neuroscience, that the human brain has a neural network with more than 100 billion neurons, yet our activities are performed by a simpler neural network with a much lesser number of neurons [6]. Furthermore, in biological neural networks, the neurons that do not significantly contribute to the network performance will naturally be disregarded [7]. According to neuroplasticity, biological neural networks can also solicit the activations of neurons in the proximity of the active neural network to improve the performance of the network. On the same line, it hypotheses that for a given complex-trained artificial neural network, we can discover a network, which is much more simplified than the originally given architecture, but still performs in similar or better. Thus, the procedure described in this paper starts with a trained, complex network and first reduces the number of hidden layers by using a peak search algorithm and next eliminates the disregard neurons by computing the correlation coefficient of summation of delta values [8] and the cycle error.

The next section discusses the theoretical fundamentals for modeling hidden layer architecture. In Sect. 3 problem with the method of solving is formulated. The empirical results are presented in Sect. 4. Finally, Sect. 5 gives the conclusion.

2 Towards Theoretical Fundamentals for Hidden Layers

Artificial neural networks are created by mimicking the functional behavior of the human brain. One of the most important and fascinating properties of the human brain is its ability to adapt to the surrounding environment by changing its neural structure. Until recently scientists and the philosophers in the field of neuroscience worked with the notion that the human brain is immutable and hard wired. It was postulated that no new neurons are born and functions of brain structures are fixed [9]. The recent studies show that these assumptions are no longer correct and brain functions change throughout one's life [10]. It is one of the important capabilities of the human brain to organize its structure and function itself in order to provide an output for various inputs to get from its surrounding environment. This change of brain neurons and its pathways to adapt to the surrounding environment is called the neuroplasticity and also referred to as the brain plasticity [11, 12].

2.1 Neuronal Structure of the Human Brain

Neurons are the most important specialized cells in the nervous system that transmits the signals throughout the body. They are known as information-processing units in the brain responsible for receiving and transmitting information. Neurons act in different ways in sensing external and internal stimuli, in transmitting the information and controlling the muscle actions.

At the birth, infant brain consists of more than 80 billion of neurons and 1000 trillions of synaptic connections. These neurons and synaptic connections grow rapidly until 2 years of age. While he grows the weak neurons and synapses are removed from the human brain by strengthening the remaining. The synaptic connections of an adult brain have only about half of that an infant brain.

The biological nervous system composed with central nervous system (CNS) and peripheral nervous system (PNS). The CNS consists of the brain and the spinal code. The PNS is composed of the cranial nerves that emerge from the brain and spinal code. The main parts of the brain are cerebrum, cerebellum, and brainstem. The Largest part among them is the cerebrum, which is split longitudinally into two large hemispheres; the left hemisphere and the right hemisphere. The cerebrum has both gray and white matter. The gray matter, which is the outermost layer of the cerebrum, is called the cerebral cortex. The cerebral consists of four lobes; frontal, parental, temporal and occipital. Neocortex is the largest part of the cerebral cortex and many functions such as intelligence, memory, creativity, emotions, touch, vision, hearing and speech etc. are controlled by the neocortex.

2.2   Layered Structure of the Neocortex

The neocortex is the outermost part of the cerebral hemisphere with a thickness of 2-4 mm. The neocortex consists of 'grey matter' of the brain or neuronal cell bodies and unmyelinated fibers surrounding the 'deeper white matter' in the cerebrum [13]. It believes that all the higher level cognitive functions, such as sensory perception, planning and decision making happen in the neocortex. It is interesting to observe that layered structure of the neocortex. Generally, neocortex of the mammal's brain consists 6 layers and each layer has its own function different from others. The first layer, the outermost layer of neocortex contains only few inhibitory cells. i.e. only dendrites and axons which go to deeper layers can be found from this layer. Gradually, the complexity of neuronal structure increases to layer by layer and the 6th layer contains many different cells in white matter. The structure of this function is not homogeneous [14, 15]. However, the six-layered neocortex is unique to the mammalian brain structure. Other than mammalians only fish and reptiles have neocortex and they have only 3 layered structure.

2.3   Positive and Negative Effects of Neuroplasticity

Majority of the remodeling of human brain takes place from infant level to adolescence. But this process continues its changes throughout one's lifespan. These changes can happen in both positive and negative directions to respond to intrinsic and extrinsic influences [16]. So that the remodeling of brain shows both positive and negative outcomes, that depend on the above features.

Positive neuroplasticity improves brain and body health. Also, it enhances the capacity for creativity and memory. It has been shown that by expanding the synaptic plasticity, new skills can be developed. Physical exercises and meditation cause for better cognition and improve the functions of the aging brain. In the occasion, when a child has a disorder in some function such as hearing, then the brain removes those neurons and axons which does not serve himself and replaced the new neurons which are able to develop new skills. This gives a child a second chance to develop his skills. In addition, more efficient communication between sensory and motor pathways, slowing down pathological processes, promoting recovery of sensory losses and improved motor control are some positive outcomes of the neuroplasticity.

Synaptic pruning always does not yield only positive outcomes. The loss of extra neurons and pathways may cause difficulties in recovering from a brain injury. Eliminating excess neurons limit the ability to develop new pathways to bypass the damaged neurons. Moreover, under-pruning of synapses slows down the functions of the human brain. For instance, it believes that children and adolescents get mental disorder such as autism due to having excess synapses in the brain. Because synapses are the endpoint of neurons and neurons connect and communicate with each other through synapses and excessive synapses may maximize the effects of these brain functions. That is having synapses more than necessary can cause some symptoms such as oversensitivity to noise and social experiences in addition to the epileptic seizures due to the more electrical signals being transmitted through neurons [17].

2.4   Artificial Neural Networks and Human Brain

The human brain, which is having the phenomenal power is the most complex organ in the human body. The extraordinary power of the human brain is far beyond that of any supercomputer today. The mechanism of the human brain is absolutely different from the conventional 'Von Neumann' architectural computer. A Von Neumann computer works step by step sequentially through an algorithm [23]. But brain is a massively parallel and highly complex information-processing structure. Among a big crowd in a town we can recognize a friend or identified a voice in a noisy station. Is there any machine to model such complex behavior? The artificial neural networks are developed to mimicking some of these fascinating features of human brain.

In the human brain, dendrites receive signals, which project from other neural cells and pass them to the cell body. When accumulated signals in cell body reach to a certain threshold limit, the neuron fires and electrical impulses are passed through axon. At the end each axon is branched into number of synaptic knobs, also known as axon terminals. With synaptic connects, it connects to other neighboring neurons and signal passes to those adjacent neurons through the synapses. Some synapses get positive outcomes from dendrites and they influence neurons to fire while some get negative outcomes and weaken the signals. Approximately, a single neuron connects to 10^5 synapses and it believes that the human brain contains about 10^{16} synaptic connections.

ANNs are created to model this functional behavior of the human brain by directly transferring the concept of neurons. The neurons or basic elements are represented by nodes or artificially designed neurons. The axons are corresponding to the connections between neurons. Dendrites and cell body are represented by combining and activation functions respectively. The synaptic weights of artificial neural networks represent the synapses of central nervous system. The concept of training of artificial neural networks came from the psychologist Donald O. Hebbs famous theory "When an axon of cell A is near enough to excite cell B or repeatedly or persistently takes part in firing it, some growth process or metabolic change takes place in one or both cells such that A's efficiency, as one of the cells firing B, is increased" [22]. However, it is still a challenge to model human brain artificially. The Biological neurons and neuronal activity are far more complex than artificially created neurons. Generally, neurons in human brain do not simply sum the weighted inputs and the dendritic mechanisms in biological systems are much more elaborate. Also, real neurons do not stay on until the inputs change and the outputs may encode information using complex pulse arrangements.

This project is based on the fact that a large number of neurons and synapses of the infant brain eliminates while he learns. In the same line, we hypothesized that a large-sized network can be pruned and obtain a simpler network by removing disregard neurons while training. On the other hand, we employ the concept of the layered architecture of the neocortex. As layered structure cause to the intelligence of mammal's brain, we assume that an ANN with many layers provide better generalization than a single-layered structure.

3   Our Approach to the Modeling of Hidden Layer Architecture

Determining the hidden layer architecture is a great challenge in artificial neural networks. Although there are many approaches to determine the hidden layer architecture in ANN, we find that these methods have various shortcomings and hence, the problem of hidden layers remains as an unsolved problem. As a solution to that, this paper presents a pruning method to determine the hidden layer architecture of artificial neural networks. The proposed approach is inspired by the fact that nature is always overestimated. It has been observed in human behavior, most probably losing one organ, still, people can perform up to some level. That is when one part of the brain damage, some other neurons maximize their functions to compensate the damaged ones. In the same line, we hypothesized that any given large ANN can be reduced to a smaller sized network by trimming the hidden layer architecture and resultant network show same or better performance as the original. The approach of hidden layer architecture of this project has two phases. Firstly, it determines the number of hidden layers and then prunes unnecessary neurons from hidden layers to attain an optimal architecture.

3.1   Determining the Number of Hidden Layers

It is known that large networks with several hidden layers show better generalization than shallow ones [18, 19], however, if it continues the increasing of hidden layers generalization reaches to a peak level and then either remain in that level or starts to decline [20]. So that, first we introduce the following peak-search algorithm to determine the number of hidden layers in the network which gives the best generalization. The algorithm is designed by two assumptions. (1) While increasing the layers, generalization increases and reached to peak-value and then either decreases or continues with the same value.

(2) Any large network can be pruned to a smaller sized one without degrading its performance.

The process starts with a trained network which contains a large number of hidden layers (H) and hidden neurons (N). The backpropagation algorithm was used to train the network.

The Algorithm

Let the generalization of k hidden layers be G_k. Suppose that the number of hidden neurons in layer i is n_i. Then

$$n_1 + n_2 + \ldots + n_H = N$$

Assume that the peak value lies between two values L and R, where L and R are left and right ends of the intervals respectively.

Step 1:   Insert G_H

                      Compute G_1

If $G_1 = 100$, the network with best generalization contains 1 hidden layer
Else, let $L = 1$ and $R = H$

Step 2: Compute M and G_M

(where $M = \left[\dfrac{L+R}{2} \right]$ and [ ] denotes the integer part of the number)

Step 3: if $G_L \leq G_M < G_R$, replace L by M

      Else if $G_L \geq G_M > G_R$, replace R by M.

Eles if $u_L \leq u_M \geq u_R$, compute

$$m_1 = \left[\frac{L+M}{2} \right] \quad \text{and} \quad m_2 = \left[\frac{M+R}{2} \right].$$

If $G_L < G_{m_1} > G_M \geq G_{m_2} \geq G_R$, replace R by m_1

Else if, $G_L \leq G_{m_1} \leq G_M < G_{m_2} > G_R$ replace L by m_2

Else if $G_L \leq G_{m_1} \leq G_M \geq G_{m_2} > G_R$, replace L by m_1 and R by m_2

Step 4: Repeat Step 2 and Step 3 until $R - L = 1$.
Step 5: The number of hidden layers of the network with best generalization ability is
          $\max\{L,R\}$.

If the algorithm ends with a j number of hidden layers, then the total number of hidden neurons remain in the network is

$$n_1 + n_2 + \ldots + n_j$$

The worst case arises when if $G_L \leq G_M \geq G_R$.

By applying the above algorithm to a large-sized complex network, a simpler network with better generalization can be obtained. However, yet there may some neurons whose contribution to the error decay process is negligible. Consequently, the following procedure will remove such neurons from the current network.

3.2 Eliminating Unimportant Neurons

The network obtained by the above algorithm has a fewer number of hidden layers and hidden neurons but performs better than the originally fed one. Nevertheless, still, this architecture may contain neurons whose contribution in the error decay process is negligible. The second phase of this project removes all such neurons from the net-work, obtained by the above peak-search algorithm by considering the delta values [21, 22] of the backpropagation algorithm. The delta values of the output layer and hidden layer neurons are given as follows.

For the output layer, delta value of the neuron k is given by

$$\delta_k = f_o'(net_k)(d_k - y_k)$$

Where, f_o' is the activation function defined for output layer and d_k and y_k are the desired and actual outputs respectively.

The delta value of neuron i of any hidden layer is

$$\delta_i = f_h'(net_i) \sum_k \delta_k w_{ki}.$$

Where f_h' is the pre-defined activation function of the hidden layer, w_{ki} is the connection weight of the neurons i of hth layer to the neuron k of $(h + 1)^{th}$ layer. These delta values are used in updating the connection weights as follows.

$$w_{ki}^h(n + 1) = w_{ki}^h(n) + \eta \delta_i^h(n) f_h(n)$$

Where, h is the number of hidden layers in the network and η is the learning rate.

According to the above equation, zero delta values imply that there is no update of the particular weights. Therefore, hidden neurons with zero delta values do not con-tribute to decrease the cycle error. So those hidden neurons whose delta value is zero, are identified as fewer salience neurons and eliminate them from the network.

Empirical results show that very often, there is a correlation between the summation of delta values of hidden layers and the output error which can be positive or negative. Thus, we use this correlation to identify the removable neurons. In this paper, this correlation is denoted by $\gamma_{\delta_h, E}$

$$\gamma_{\delta_k, E} = corr\left(\sum_{k=1}^{n_h} \delta_k, E\right)$$

Therefore, to obtain more precise network, the correlation defined in the above is used. If the correlation is positive, minimal architecture obtains by removing neurons with positive delta values. In contrast, when the correlation is negative, neurons with negative delta values remove to obtain the desired architecture. However, in both cases, neurons which have infinitesimal delta values are removing. The pruning has the same meaning of synaptic pruning in neuroscience. It facilitates changes in neural configu-ration by removing weak neurons and synapses while strengthening the remaining.

As in synaptic pruning, while pruning the weak neurons and the synaptic connections from the ANN architecture, it merges the similar neurons to strengthen their functions.

3.3 Merge the Similar Neurons

The whole process of pruning neurons is inspired by the concepts of neuroplasticity and synaptic pruning. While pruning unnecessary neurons from the human brain it increases the functions of the remaining. In similar, this process maximizes the weights of synaptic connection while removing the unimportant neurons. However, the effect of the weights of those neurons for the error decay process is not negligible. Hence, while removing, the neurons connections weights merge with similar neurons to obtain more efficient network. Similar weights vectors refer weights vectors with the same orientation.

Let the jth neuron of hidden layer h be identified as a removable neuron. Suppose $V = (v_{ij})_{p \times q}$ and $W = (w_{ij})_{q \times r}$ are the input and the output vectors of layer h respectively.

When removing j^{th} neuron, the row vector $V^{R_j} = [v_{j1}, v_{j2}, \ldots, v_{jq}]$ and the column vector $W^{C_j} = [w_{1j}, w_{2j}, \ldots, v_{qj}]^T$ will be removed and while removing they merge with similar vectors. So that, when two vectors V^{R_j} and V^{R_k} are similar, if

$$\left\langle \frac{V^{R_j}}{V^{R_j}}, \frac{V^{R_k}}{V^{R_k}} \right\rangle = 1$$

Thus, if neuron j in layer h is identified as the removable neuron. V^{R_k} and W^{C_j} are the similar vectors to V^{R_j} and W^{C_i} respectively. Then V^{R_k} merges with V^{R_j} and W^{C_j} merges with W^{C_i}.

4 Experiments and Results

All the experiments carried on this project is presented here. To assess the effectiveness of the proposed method in determining the hidden layer architecture, the number of simulations carried out in different fields. All the experiments were done for fully connected feedforward networks with supervised learning.

The performance of the artificial neural network depends on several parameters such as hidden layer architecture, learning rate, the activation function, etc. This project concerns the hidden layer architecture of the network. So that all the other parameters made constants throughout the training and testing process. The log sigmoid and linear functions were used as activation functions of hidden and output layers respectively. For each case learning rate of the backpropagation algorithm was fixed at 0.1 initially, all the weights were chosen randomly and normalized. Each network trained by using the backpropagation algorithm and stopping criteria was decided as the difference between the error of two successive iterations became less than 10^{-4} or pre-decided maximum number of iterations. The brief description of each data set is discussed in the next section and Table 1 depicts each network with its initial conditions. All the data sets are chosen from UCI machine learning repository [23].

Next, we come to our main task of this research, determine the hidden layer architecture. As the first step of this task, we use the peak search algorithm discussed in the Sect. 3 to determine the number of hidden layers in the most appropriate network. As shown in the following Table 1, Initial networks contained 10–20 hidden layers were taken as the inputs and the structure of hidden neurons in each layer with k hidden layers is given as

$$n_1 - n_2 - \ldots - n_k$$

If the network obtained by the peak search algorithm has $j(\leq k)$ hidden layers, new structure of hidden neurons is

$$n_1 - n_2 - \ldots - n_j$$

So that, at the first stage $n_{j+1} + n_{j+2} + \ldots + n_k$ number of neurons prune from the network, while improving the generalization and reducing the training time.

Table 2 gives a comparison of the size and performance of the new neural network and the originally considered large-sized network. Where H and N denote the number of hidden layers and the total number of hidden neurons in the network respectively. Accuracy is the percentage of correct responses to the total number of outputs on the testing set.

As it has shown in Table 2 below, all the data sets except Banknote, Flare and Glass are given better generalization than the original ones. Cancer set reduces its size by 60% while improving performance by 36.7%. Climate and Diabetes sets are able to remove about 80% of hidden neurons from the original network. This is a significant factor as small networks reduce the computer cost and training time.

The 3 sets Banknote, Flare, and Glass continue their highest generalization once it reaches to the maximum value. Therefore, they do not show any performance in accuracy in the peak search algorithm but the sizes have been reduced by a substantial number of neurons.

Table 1. Details of initial network architectures

Data set	Number of inputs	Number of outputs	Number of instances	Training patterns	Testing patterns
Banknote	4	2	1372	1029	343
Cancer	9	2	699	525	174
Card	51	2	690	518	172
Climate	14	2	540	405	135
Diabetes	8	2	768	576	192
Flare	25	3	1066	800	266
Glass	9	7	214	160	54

Table 2. Results of peak search algorithm

Data set	Initial network			Network obtained by the peak search algorithm		
	H	N	Accuracy %	H	N	Accuracy %
Banknote	12	1032	100	2	172	100
Blood	15	360	87.2	6	168	87.7
Cancer	10	260	62.7	4	104	99.4
Card	12	546	53.5	4	70	89.5
Climate	10	400	92.6	2	80	97.8
Diabetes	15	570	63.5	3	114	82.8
Flare	12	780	89.8	8	540	89.8
Glass	10	160	100	4	48	100

The main objective is training the network is to reduce the error between the desired and actual outputs. Thus, the networks acquired by the above algorithm still may have some neurons, which do not contribute to the error decay process. So that, as described in the previous section, we compute the correlation ($\gamma_{\delta_k, E}$) between the cycle error and the summation of delta values to identify such neurons. The results are shown in Table 3.

It is clear that most of the networks have a good correlation between the cycle error and the summation of the delta values. Surprisingly, this correlation changes its sign alternatively from layer to layer and most probably the last layer shows negative such correlation with the error.

Next, determine the removable nodes according to Sect. 3 above. If a particular neuron shows the poor contribution in the error decaying process in all the training cycle that could be recognized as a removable neuron. While removing, the neurons with the same orientation are merged to reduce more possible nodes and weight connections. Table 4 gives the final network architectures in each problem. These results show that this method reduces the number of hidden neurons by a huge amount. For example, in the 'Blood' problem, more than 90% of neurons remove from the original network. In the other sets also, this amount exceeds 40%.

Table 3. Correlation coefficients

Data Set	$\gamma_{\delta_1, E}$	$\gamma_{\delta_2, E}$	$\gamma_{\delta_3, E}$	$\gamma_{\delta_4, E}$	$\gamma_{\delta_5, E}$	$\gamma_{\delta_6, E}$	$\gamma_{\delta_7, E}$	$\gamma_{\delta_8, E}$
Banknote	−0.18	0.11						
Blood	0.99	−0.91	0.91	−0.91	0.90	−0.91		
Cancer	0.89	−0.89	0.83	−0.89				
Card	0.96	−0.96	0.95	−0.97				
Climate	0.88	−0.90						
Diabetes	−0.83	0.83	−0.83					
Flare	−0.14	−0.15	−0.15	0.15	−0.14	0.14	−0.13	0.17
Glass	0.83	−0.83	0.82	−0.86				

Table 4. Performance of the new model

Data Set	N	Accuracy	Neuron reduction on pruning (%)	Neuron reduction on whole process (%)
Banknote	172	100	0.0	83.3
Blood	16	88.2	90.5	95.6
Cancer	94	99.4	9.6	63.8
Card	62	89.5	11.4	88.6
Climate	64	97.8	20.0	84.0
Diabetes	109	82.8	4.4	80.9
Flare	428	89.8	20.7	45.1
Glass	48	100	0.0	70.0

5 Conclusion

This paper presents a technique to find a smaller sized simple network from a given complex architecture of an artificial neural network. The method was inspired by some facts on neuroplasticity and synaptic pruning. As human brain eliminates its neurons while learning from the environment, this model removes a large amount of neurons from the original large sized network and attain a smaller sized network, which is much simpler than the original, yields better performance and reduces the computational time.

References

1. Liu, Y., Starzyk, J.A., Zhu, Z.: Optimizing number of hidden neurons in neural networks. EeC **1**(1), 6 (2007)
2. Amini, J.: Optimum learning rate in back-propagation neural network for classification of satellite images (IRS-1D). Sci. Iran. **15**(6), 558–567 (2008)
3. Castellano, G., Fanelli, A.M., Pelillo, M.: An iterative pruning algorithm for feedforward neural networks. IEEE Trans. Neural Netw. **8**(3), 519–531 (1997)
4. Lippmann, R.: An introduction to computing with neural nets. IEEE ASSP Mag. **4**(2), 4–22 (1987)
5. LeCun, Y.: Generalization and network design strategies. In: Connectionism in Perspective, vol. 19, pp. 143–155. Elsevier, Amsterdam (1989)
6. Herculano-Houzel, S.: The remarkable, yet not extraordinary, human brain as a scaled-up primate brain and its associated cost. Proc. Natl. Acad. Sci. **109**(Suppl. 1), 10661–10668 (2012)
7. Sousa, A.M., Meyer, K.A., Santpere, G., Gulden, F.O., Sestan, N.: Evolution of the human nervous system function, structure, and development. Cell **170**(2), 226–247 (2017)
8. Wagarachchi, N.M., Karunananda, A.S.: Optimization of multi-layer artificial neural networks using delta values of hidden layers. In: IEEE Symposium on Computational Intelligence, Cognitive Algorithms, Mind, and Brain, pp. 80–86 (2013)
9. Vollmer, L.: Change Your Mind: Neuroplasticity & Buddhist Transformation. All Theses and Dissertations (ETDs), 928 (2010). http://openscholarship.wustl.edu/etd/928
10. Pascual-Leone, A., Amedi, A., Fregni, F., Merabet, L.B.: The plastic human brain cortex. Annu. Rev. Neurosci. **28**, 377–401 (2005)

11. Eggermont, J.J.: The Correlative Brain: Theory and Experiment in Neural Interaction. Springer, New York (1990)
12. Chrol-Cannon, J., Jin, Y.: Computational modeling of neural plasticity for self-organization of neural networks. BioSystems **125**, 43–54 (2014)
13. Wells, R.B.: Cortical neurons and circuits: a tutorial introduction. Unpublished Paper (2005) www Mrc Uidaho Edu
14. Mountcastle, V.B.: The columnar organization of the neocortex. Brain **120**(4), 701–722 (1997)
15. Thomson, A.M.: Neocortical layer 6, a review. Front. Neuroanat. **4**, 13 (2010)
16. Shaffer, J.: Neuroplasticity and positive psychology in clinical practice: a review for combined benefits. Psychology **3**(12), 1110 (2012)
17. Children with Autism Have Extra Synapses in Brain. Columbia University Medical Center. http://newsroom.cumc.columbia.edu/blog/2014/08/21/children-autism-extra-synapses-brain/. Accessed: 10 Aug 2017
18. LeCun, Y., Bengio, Y., Hinton, G.: Deep learning. Nature **521**(7553), 436–444 (2015)
19. Hinton, G.E., Osindero, S., Teh, Y.-W.: A fast learning algorithm for deep belief nets. Neural Comput. **18**(7), 1527–1554 (2006)
20. Wagarachchi, M., Karunananda, A.: Optimization of artificial neural network architecture using neuroplasticity. Int. J. Artif. Intell. **15**(1), 112–125 (2017)
21. Wagarachchi, N.M., Karunananda, A.S.: Novel technique for optimizing the hidden layer architecture in artificial neural networks. Am. Int. J. Res. Sci. Technol. Eng. Math. **4**(1), 1–6 (2013)
22. Wagarachchi, N.M., Karunananda, A.S.: Towards a theoretical basis for modelling of hidden layer architecture in artificial neural networks. In: 2nd International Conference on Advances in Computing, Electronics and Communication, pp. 47–52 (2014)
23. Prechelt, L.: PROBEN 1: a set of benchmarks and benchmarking rules for neural network training algorithms. Univ., Fak. für Informatik (1994)

A Novel Hybrid Back Propagation Neural Network Approach for Time Series Forecasting Under the Volatility

R. M. Kapila Tharanga Rathnayaka[1]([⊠]) and D. M. K. N. Seneviratna[2]

[1] Department of Physical Sciences and Technology,
Faculty of Applied Sciences, Sabaragamuwa University of Sri Lanka,
Belihuloya, Sri Lanka
kapiar@appsc.sab.ac.lk
[2] Department of Interdisciplinary Studies, Faculty of Engineering,
University of Ruhuna, Galle, Sri Lanka
seneviratna@is.ruh.ac.lk

Abstract. An Artificial Neural Network (ANN) algorithms have been widely used in machine learning for pattern recognition, classifications and time series forecasting today; especially in financial applications with nonlinear and non-parametric modeling's. The objective of this study is an attempt to develop a new hybrid forecasting approach based on back propagation neural network (BPN) and Geometric Brownian Motion (GBM) to handle random walk data patterns under the high volatility. The proposed methodology is successfully implemented in the Colombo Stock Exchange (CSE) Sri Lanka, the daily demands of the All Share Price Index (ASPI) price index from April 2009 to March 2017. The performances of the model are evaluated based on the best two forecast horizons of 75% and 85% training samples. According to the empirical results, 85% training samples have given highly accurate in their testing process. Furthermore, the results confirmed that the proposed hybrid methodology always gives the best performances under the high volatility forecasting compared to the separate traditional time series models.

Keywords: Back propagation neural network · Geometric Brownian motion · Autoregressive integrated moving average · Colombo stock exchange · Hybrid forecasting approach

1 Introduction

Capital Investment in the stock market is the easiest and fastest way of building a healthy financial foundation for future life. In the past few decades, stock markets have become more institutionalized to invest large investment funds to the general public [1]. As a result, financial managers around the world have been spent their time to simulate the stock prices purposively in order to make them in profitable investments. However, making decisions in equity markets still have been regarding as one of the biggest challenge in the modern economy, because of the numerous type of economic booms, policies and reforms.

© Springer Nature Singapore Pte Ltd. 2019
J. Hemanth et al. (Eds.): SLAAI-ICAI 2018, CCIS 890, pp. 79–91, 2019.
https://doi.org/10.1007/978-981-13-9129-3_6

As a real world practice, two common approaches have been widely using in financial theories and practices to predict stock prices. They are as technical analysis tools and fundamental analysis methods [2]. The technical theories believe that the past patterns of the price behaviors repeat itself tends to recur in the future again. Furthermore, the fundamental analysis is a method of evaluating a security and assesses, by examining related economic, financial, and other qualitative and quantitative factors. However, the modern financial indices have been exhibiting unpredictable random walk path and estimate the near predictions are hard and impossible to outperform without taking any additional risk with the traditional time series approaches which are developed based on the normality, linearity and stationary conditions [3].

During the last few decades, miscellaneous types of new methodologies have been developed under different scenarios. Some of which are only applicable in theoretical aspects. However, most of these new approaches are combined both traditional as well as modern network approaches such as Artificial Neural Network (ANN), fuzzy logic and exhibited both continuous and discrete dynamic behaviors [4].

The Combining of both traditional linear (Autoregressive integrated moving average (ARIMA), Support Vector Machine algorithm (SVM), exponential smoothing model) and modified nonlinear approaches, building combined forecasting mechanisms have emerged new way in the finance since 2000. Various types of methodologies have been proposed in the literature. For instance, Zhang et al. (2003) introduced a novel hybrid methodology based on ARIMA and ANN models [4]. Theoretically, Zhang et al. methodology can be explained under the linear and nonlinear domains. They assumed that the ARIMA model fitting contains only the linear component and their residuals contain just only the nonlinear behavioral patterns [5].

As a result of these complications regards to the traditional time series approaches, the main purpose of this study is to take an attempt to develop Artificial Neural Network (ANN) and Geometric Brownian Motion (GBM) based new hybrid forecasting approach to handle incomplete, noise and uncertain data estimating in multidisciplinary systems. Because of the less sensitivity for error term assumptions, high tolerate noises, robustness and heavy tails, multilayer perceptron with Back propagation ANN algorithms are more suitable for mapping non-linear data patterns than traditional time series mechanisms. The new proposed network architecture mainly consists of input, hidden and one output layers. Furthermore, as the hidden and output layers by using the hyperbolic tangent sigmoid nonlinear transfer function and linear transfer functions, the proposed methodology designed for one-step-ahead forecast. Indeed, the ARIMA model is used as a comparison mode. The proposed methodology is successfully implemented for forecasting price indices in the Colombo Stock Exchange (CSE), Sri Lanka.

The rest of the paper is set out as follows. The estimated new ANN methodology is described in Sect. 2. The Sect. 3 presents the experimental findings and ends up with concluding remarks with Sect. 4.

2 Methodology

Time series forecasting is a dynamic research area that has been drawing considerable attention for solving the miscellaneous type of applications in the real world today. The proposed methodology of this study mainly consists of three major parts to forecasting stock market indices under the different scenarios. They are; Geometric Brownian motion (GBM) approach, artificial neural network and GBM based new hybrid approach and model comparison study based on traditional time series methods.

2.1 The Geometric Brownian Motion

The Geometric Brownian motion approach is one of the significant methodology which has been widely using in finance for making proper decisions under the random walk behavioural patterns.

The daily stock market price index S_t is said to be a stochastic process represents the most closed up-to-date valuation of index until trading commences again on the next trading day [4]. Let we assume that, the stock market price index S_t has a Geometric Brownian Motional behavior's and represents as a stochastic differential equation as Eq. (1) [5].

$$dS_t = \mu S_t \delta t + \sigma S_t dW_t \tag{1}$$

Where, the W_t is a Winner process with μ and σ constants. Where; the mean of the distribution of percentage drift μ and the volatility or sample standard deviation are given by Eqs. (2) and (3) respectively [6];

$$\mu = \bar{S} = \frac{1}{M}\sum\nolimits_{t=1}^{M} S_t \tag{2}$$

$$\sigma = r = \sqrt{\frac{1}{(M-1)\delta t}\sum\nolimits_{t=1}^{M}(R_t - \bar{R})^2} \tag{3}$$

The S_t and S_{t-1} denotes the asset values of the ith and it's previous day market values respectively. Moreover, if the price on two consecutive days was not available, it would be assumed that the price remained unchanged and hence return is zero. Let's apply the techniques of separation of variable and integrating Eq. (1) with respect to t;

$$\int_0^t \frac{dS_t}{S_t} = \int_0^t (\mu\, dt + \sigma dW_t)\, dt \tag{4}$$

Let's we assume that the initial condition of W_0 is 0. Furthermore, the $\frac{dS_t}{S_t}$ relates to the $d(\ln S_t)$ and term S_t is under the Ito process [7].

$$d(\ln S_t) = \frac{dS_t}{S_t} - \frac{1}{2}\sigma^2 dt \qquad (5)$$

$$d(\ln S_t) = \mu t + \sigma w_t - \frac{1}{2}\sigma^2 dt \qquad (6)$$

The analytical solutions of the Eq. (6) is given by [8];

$$S_t = S_0 \exp\left(\left(\mu - \frac{1}{2}\sigma^2\right)t + \sigma w_t\right) \qquad (7)$$

The Eq. (7) shows continuous stochastic process of Geometric Brownian motion that can be used for simulated the forecast of stock market indices.

The following algorithm can be used for forecasting data with lage number of sample observations.

```
%Assuming the following parameters
s=0; % Daily asset prices
R= ((s(t)-s(t-1)*100))/s(t-1); % asset returns
M= (0:1: N); % total number of observations
MU=sum (R)/ (M); % drift rate
TS=1% constant time difference between two samples
SIGMA= sqrt([sum(r-MU)^2]/((M-1)*(TS))) ;% volatility rate
T = (0:1: N) *TS; time interval
%Geometric Brownian Morton Approach
WT = sqrt(TS) *[0; cumsum(randn(N,1))]; % approximation to the
Normal distribution
W = (MU - 0.5*SIGMA^2) *T + SIGMA * WT
GBM =  s(0)* exp( W ); assets forecasting
```

2.2   The Novel GBM-ANN Hybrid Method for Forecasting

As a result of high volatility and unstable patterns, the traditional time series fore-casting approaches can't achieve successes in both linear and non-linear domains. According to the literature, none of the methodologies still haven't been making suf-ficient for these circumstances. So, combined methodologies under the linear auto-correlation structure and non-linear weighted average component have created high accuracy forecasting than single model approaches.

The proposed new hybrid methodology composed with two main phases based on their linear and non-linear domains as follows [9].

$$Y_t = L_t + N_t \qquad (8)$$

Where; L_t and N_t denote the linear autocorrelation and non-linear component of the time series pattern Y_t respectively. In the initial step, the GBM with Ito' lemma approach approaches is used to forecast the stock market indices under the stationary and non-stationary conditions.

As a next step, the residual of the linear component is evaluate using the Eq. (9).

$$e_t = Y_t - \hat{L}_t \tag{9}$$

Where e_t denotes the residual of the GBM and $\hat{L}_t$ presents the forecasted value of the estimated time series at time t. However, if we can see any non-linear behavioral patterns in residuals, as a next step, the ANN modeling approach is used to discover the non-linear behavioural patterns.

$$e_t = f(e_{t-1}, e_{t-2}, e_{t-3} \ldots, e_{t-n}) + \varepsilon_t \tag{10}$$

$$\hat{y}_t = \hat{L}_t + \hat{N}_t \tag{11}$$

Where n represents the input nodes and f is the non-linear function which determined based on ANN approach. The newly proposed BPNN Algorithm for forecasting non-linear behaviours as follows.

2.3 BPNN Algorithm for Forecasting Non-linear Behaviours

The back propagation neural network (BPNN) algorithm was introduced first time in the 1970s, but it was successfully applied for real world applications in 1986 by David et al. The BPNN algorithm is summarized under five-steps as follows [10].
Step 1:   Define Inputs

Consider the forms of error data series. $\varepsilon_t = \{e\}_t$; where $t = 1, 2, \ldots, n$.
Step 2:   Define Neural Network paradigms (Hidden layers, Input and Output neurons)

The back propagation algorithm is a method for training the weights in a multilayer feed-forward neural network [11]. As such, it requires a network structure to be defined of one or more layers where one layer is fully connected to the next layer. The general structure of the back propagation neural network can be expressed as Eqs. (12), (13) and (14) [12, 13].

$$net_j = \sum_{i=1}^{m} w_{ij} X_i; \quad j = 1, 2, \ldots, n \tag{12}$$

$$R_j = f_{hidden}(net_j) = f\left(\sum_{i=1}^{m} w_{ij} x X_i\right) \tag{13}$$

$$Y_k = f_{output}\left(\sum_{j=1}^{n} w_{jk} R_i\right); \quad k = 1, 2, \ldots z \tag{14}$$

Where, X_i, R_j, Y_k and w_{jk} represent the inputs and outputs of the hidden layer, outputs of the network and the connection weights respectively [14, 15].

Step 3:   BPNN forecasting

The identified BPNN network is used here to forecast $(n+1)^{th}$ error point. The network is run 1000 iterations [16, 17]. The proposed network architectural model consists of single hidden layer connected feed forward network include single input layer, hidden layer and output layer as follows in Fig. 1.

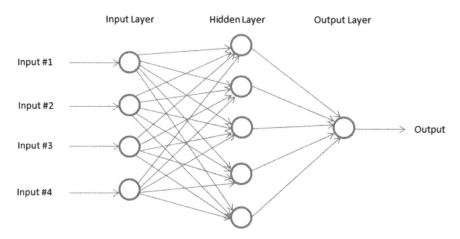

Fig. 1. Typical three layered feed-forward neural network [18, 19]

Step 4:   Implementation

The current study, MAE and MAPE are utilized to evaluate the accuracy one-step ahead forecast. The error measures are as follows [20–23].

$$MAE = \left| S_i - \widehat{S}_i \right| \tag{15}$$

$$MAE = \left| \frac{S_i - \widehat{S}_i}{S_i} \right| \tag{16}$$

Where S_i and $\widehat{S}_i$ are the actual value of the original series and predicted value from the proposed hybrid model respectively. The smaller values of these error measures are considered to find the more accurate forecast result among the focused models.

The proposed hybrid model exploits the unique feature of GBM and ANN in determining different patterns. Tues, it creates an additional advantage to model linear and nonlinear patterns separately by using by separate models and then combine the forecasts to improve the overall modeling performances [20].

3 Results and Discussion

3.1 Data Preprocessing

The proposed methodology is evaluated using All Share Price Index (ASPI), Colombo stock exchange, Sri Lanka from April 2009 to March 2017 were extracted and tabulated for our calculations. The data source consisted 1926 observations, first 85% of 1637 daily observations were used during the training (in-sample or training sample) and the remaining 288 (about 15% of the sample) were considered as the out of sample to test the generalization capabilities of proposed models. The visual inspection of the daily ASPI pattern in Fig. 2 indicates that the data observations contain considerable noise with significant non-linear trend with considerable volatility during the sample period of time.

Fig. 2. Time series plot of ASPI

As a next step, unit root test used to test whether the ASPI time series variable existence of stationary of unit root or not. In the current study three different methods namely Augmented Dickey–Fuller test (ADF), Phillips–Perron test (PP) and KPSS test were used (Table 1).

Table 1. Unit root test result_level data

		t-statistic	Prob*.
Augmented Dickey-Fuller test statistic		−29.916	0.0000
Test critical values:	1% level	−3.9646	
	5% level	−3.4130	
	10% level	−3.1285	
Phillips-Perron test statistic		−30.2394	0.0000
Test critical values:	1% level	−3.9646	
	5% level	−3.4130	
	10% level	−3.1285	

(continued)

Table 1. (*continued*)

		t-statistic	Prob*.
KPSS test statistic (LM test)		0.13079	0.0000
Asymptotic critical values*	1% level	0.2160	
	5% level	0.1460	
	10% level	0.1190	

According to the ADF and PP results in Table 2, only the first difference data stationary under the 0.05 level of significance. Furthermore, KPSS test results confirmed that, data series is stationary after making the series in their first differences.

3.2   Data Modeling and Forecasting

The current study was carried out based on four different volatility measurements in order to find best volatility model of GBM for forecasting stock price indices in CSE. They are as Simple volatility (SV), Log volatility (LV), High and low volatility (HLV) and High-Low Close volatility (HLCV).

Table 2. GBM forecasting for different volatility methods

Error	SV	LV	HLV	HLCV
MAPE (%)	0.2425	0.1997	0.0889	0.0328*
MAD	17.1055	14.086	6.276	2.332*

The error accuracies of MAPE and MAD results in Table 2 suggested that High-Low Close volatility (HLCV) method has achieved minimum error accuracy comparing other three methods. So, in the next step, HLCV based Geometric Brownian motion with Ito's Lemma approach was used to assess the out-of-sample forecasting performance for the horizon of one month ahead. As a next step, the residual were measured. The behaviours of the residuals presented a non-randomly dispersed around the horizontal axis. So in the next step, suitable BPNN learning algorithm is employed to forecast error demands estimated based on one-step-ahead forecasting's.

In the initial stage, the network settings were fixed with 0.01 learning rate and single hidden layer neuron. Furthermore, to generate the accuracy results, the network was trained 1000 times. The same procedure was repeated step by step up to the number of hidden layer neuron equal 8 with respect to the constant learning rate. The estimated results can be summarized as Table 3.

Table 3. ANNs with different no. of hidden neurons

No. of neurons	ASPI testing (15%)		
	MAE	RMSE	MAPE (%)
1	38.124	56.376	0.54
2	38.973	58.456	0.52
3	37.657	57.879	0.51
4	35.456*	55.354*	0.49*
5	38.146	57.983	0.52
6	38.986	58.892	0.54
7	39.875	58.994	0.56
8	38.765	58.013	0.61

*Denotes the model with the minimum error values

In practice, the minimum error accuracies can be used to identify the best model. According to the results in Table 3, the minimum value of MAE (35.456), RMSE (55.354) and MAPE (0.49) indicated that, the number of four hidden neurons is given best performances than others. Furthermore, to find the best learning rate, the selected numbers of hidden neurons were fixed and the learning rate was increased step by step from 0.01 to 0.08 with 0.01 increments. The results suggested that BPNN (1-4-1) with 0.06 learning rates is employed 1000 times to forecast best one-step-ahead forecasting ASPI price index.

To find more accurate results, best two forecast horizons of 75% and 85% training sample sizes are used and their error measures MAE and MAPE are summarized in Table 4.

Table 4. Forecasting performances

Sample	Model	One-step-ahead forecast	Actual value	Error accuracy testing		
				MAD	MSE	MAPE (%)
75% Training sample	ARIMA	7203.72	7235.25	31.53	994.1	0.435
	GBM	7215.67		19.58	383.3	0.270
	ANN-ARIMA	7218.69		16.56	274.2	0.227
	ANN-GBM	7232.54		2.71	7.344	0.037
85% Training sample	ARIMA	7017.05	7020.8	3.75	14.06	0.053
	GBM	7021.67		0.87	0.75	0.012
	ANN-ARIMA	7018.506		2.29	5.26	0.038
	ANN-GBM	7020.572		0.22*	0.05*	0.003*

*Denotes the model with the minimum error values

The Table 5 results suggested that, 85% testing sample gives the best performance with minimum MAD, MSE and MAPE (%) with 0.228, 0.051984 and 0.324 respectively. Furthermore, results show that while applying neural networks alone can improve the forecasting accuracy over than single ARIMA. The same scenario can be seen in their separate forecasting's as displayed result in Fig. 3.

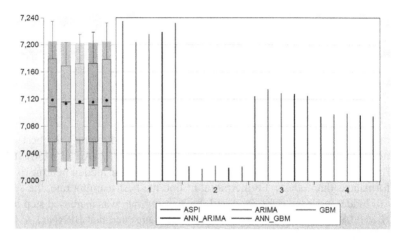

Fig. 3. One-step-ahead forecast forecasting for ASPI

The results concluded that, combining linear and nonlinear models together, the overall forecasting errors can be significantly reduced than separate single models. In ASPI scenario, the proposed ANN-GBM hybrid model always gives the best performances with compared to the single models (Fig. 4).

Table 5. The model accuracy for coming week

Model accuracy	Forecasting accuracy (%)			
	ARIMA	GBM	ARIMA-ANN	ARIMA-GBM
MAD (%)	13.08	9.94	5.39	2.31*
MAE	267.76	161.49	45.71	6.75*
RMSE	16.36	12.70	6.76	2.59*

*Denotes the model with the minimum error values

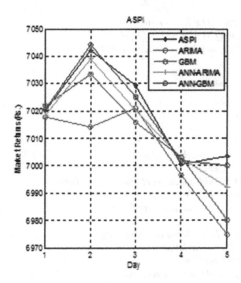

Fig. 4. ASPI forecasting for coming week

4   Conclusion

According to the literature, most of the studies have been using time series forecasting methods as their benchmark. So this is a first time in literature used GBM and ANN based hybrid approach to test the effectiveness of stock market forecasting. The empirical study results suggested that the proposed methodology have given high accurate predictions regarding the one – day head forecasting under the volatility.

As a next step as a comparison mode, the selected ARIMA models, GBM, and proposed ARIMA-ANN/GBM-ANN hybrid method were used to assess the out-of-sample forecasting performance for the horizon of one week ahead (testing sample) and the corresponding results are summarized in Table 4 and Fig. 2. According to the error analysis results, new proposed ARIMA-GBM is highly accurate (less than 10%) with lowest RMSE error residuals.

Acknowledgments. This work was supported by the Research Grant (SUSL/RE/2017/04), Sabaragamuwa University of Sri Lanka, Belihuoya, Sri Lanka.

Codes and Mat Lab Program for Proposed Hybrid Methodology

The new hybrid methodology is more appropriate to handle incomplete, noise and non-linear random time sequences with limited data samples. The proposed algorithm is as follows.

```
x=input variable; t=target variable; k=new; f=0;
Q = size(x,2);  Q1 = floor(Q*0.95);  Q2 = Q-Q1;
ind = randperm(Q); ind1 = ind(1:Q1); ind2 = ind(Q1+(1:Q2));
x1 = x(:,ind1);
t1 = t(:,ind1);
x2 = x(:,ind2);
t2 = t(:,ind2);
net = feedforwardnet(2);
net=configure(net,x,t);
net=init(net);
net.trainFcn = 'trainlm';  % Levenberg-Marquardt
net.trainParam.epochs = 1000;
net.trainParam.mu = 0.05; %Minimum performance gradient
net.trainParam.mu_dec = 0.1; %Initial mu
net.trainParam.mu_inc = 10; %mu decrease factor

net.trainParam.mu_max = 1e25; %mu increase factor
net.trainParam.show = 25; %Maximum mu
% Choose a Performance Function
net.performFcn = 'mse';  % Mean squared error
net.layers{1}.transferFcn = 'tansig';
net.layers{2}.transferFcn = 'purelin';
% Choose Plot Functions
net.plotFcns = {'plotperform','plottrainstate','ploterrhist', ...
'plotregression', 'plotfit'};
net.trainparam.showWindow=false;
numNN = 1000;
nets = cell(1,numNN);
for i=1:numNN
%disp(['Training ' num2str(i) '/' num2str(numNN)])
nets{i} = train(net,x1,t1);
end
%Eroor Comparison
n=numNN;w1;k1=cell(1,n);
for i=1:n
if w1(i)==min(w1)
    k1{i}=i;
else
    k1{i}=0;
end
```

References

1. Mishra, T., Kapoor, V.: Financial trends prediction using the back propagation neural network and YQL. Int. J. Comput. Appl. **144**(10), 20–26 (2016)
2. Willmot, P.: Introduces Quabtitative Finance 2. Wiley, New York (2007)
3. Dmouj, A.: Stock Price Modelling: Theory and Practice. Vrije Universiteit, Amsterdam (2006)

4. Omar, A., Jaffar, M.M.: Forecasting share price of small size companies in Bursa Malaysia using geometric brownian motion. J. Int. Appl. Math. Inf. Sci. **8**, 107–112 (2014)
5. Brewer, K.D., Feng, Y., Kwan, C.C.Y.: Geometric Brownian motion, option pricing, and simulation: some spread sheet-based exercises in financial modelling. Spread Sheets Educ. **7** (2), 1–28 (2012)
6. Kim, K.-j.: Artificial neural networks with evolutionary instance selection for financial forecasting. Expert Syst. Appl. **12**(1), 202–220 (2006)
7. Kryzanowski, L., Galler, M., Wright, D.W.: Using artificial neural networks to pick stocks. Financ. Anal. J. **3**(2), 40–333 (1993)
8. Huang, M., Chen, M., Lee, S.: Integrating data mining with case-based reasoning for chronic diseases prognosis and diagnosis. Expert Syst. Appl. **32**(3), 856–867 (2007)
9. Morgan, D.P., Scofield, C.L.: Neural Networks and Speech Processing. Kluwer Academic Publishers, Dordrecht (1991)
10. Postali, F.A.S., Picchetti, P.: Geometric brownian motion and structural breaks in oil prices: a quantitative analysis. Energy Econ. **28**, 506–522 (2006)
11. Qi, M.: Handbook of Statistics. Elsevier B.V., Amsterdam (1996)
12. Rathnayaka, R.M.K.T., Seneviratna, D.M.K.N, Jianguo, W.: A hybrid statistical approach for stock market forecasting based on artificial neural network and ARIMA time series models. In: International Conference on Behavioral, Economic and Socio-cultural Computing (BESC), Nanjing, China, pp. 33–38 (2015)
13. Rathnayaka, R.M.K.T., Jianguo, W., Seneviratna, D.M.K.N.: Geometric brownian motion with Ito's lemma approach to evaluate market fluctuations: a case study on Colombo stock exchange. In: International Conference on Behavioral, Economic, and Socio-Cultural Computing (BESC2014), Shanghai, China, pp. 25–29 (2014)
14. Rathnayaka, R.M.K.T., Seneviratna, D.M.K.N., Jianguo, W.: An unbiased GM(1,1)-based new hybrid approach for time series forecasting. Grey Syst. Theory Appl. **6**(3), 322–340 (2016)
15. Reddy, K., Clinton, V.: Simulating stock prices using geometric Brownian motion: evidence from Australian companies. Aust. Account. Bus. Finance J. **10**(3), 23–47 (2016)
16. Roman, J., Jameel, A.: Back propagation and recurrent neural networks in financial analysis of multiple stock market returns. In: 29th Annual Hawaii International Conference on System Sciences (1996)
17. Seneviratna, D.M.K.N., Rathnayaka, R.M.K.T.: Rainfall data forecasting by SARIMA and BPNN model. IOSR J. Math. **6**(3), 57–63 (2017)
18. Seneviratna, D., Chen, D.: Using feed forward BPNN for forecasting all share price index. J. Data Anal. Inf. Process. **2**, 87–94 (2014)
19. Seneviratna, D., Shuhua, M.: Forecasting the twelve month treasury bill rates in Sri Lanka. IOSR J. Econ. Finance **1**(1), 42–47 (2013)
20. Zhang, G., Patuwo, B.E., Hu, M.Y.: Forecasting with artificial neural networks. Int. J. Forecast. **14**, 35–62 (1998)
21. Yuan, Y.: Study on Financial Market Investment Portfolio Selection Based on Genuine Correlation Matrix. In: Qu, X., Yang, Y. (eds.) IBI 2011. CCIS, vol. 268, pp. 329–334. Springer, Heidelberg (2012). https://doi.org/10.1007/978-3-642-29087-9_51
22. Wang, J., Deng, S.: Fluctuations of interface statistical physics models applied to a stock market model. Nonlinear Anal. Real World Appl. **9**, 718–723 (2008)
23. Nasseri, M., Asgahari, K., Abedini, M.: Optimized scenariofor rainfall forecasting using genetic algorithm coupled with artificial neural network. Expert Syst. Appl. **35**(3), 1415–1421 (2008)

Flood Forecasting Using Artificial Neural Network for Kalu Ganga

Dhananjali Gamage[✉] and Kalani Ilmini[✉]

Faculty of Computing, General Sir John Kotelawala Defence University,
Colombo, Sri Lanka
dgdhananjali@gmail.com, kalaniilmini@kdu.ac.lk

Abstract. Floods are among the natural disasters that cause human hardship and economic loss. Establishing a viable flood forecasting and warning system for communities at risk can mitigate these adverse effects. However, establishing an accurate flood forecasting system is still challenging due to the lack of knowledge about the effective variables in forecasting. The present study has indicated that the use of artificial intelligence, especially artificial neural networks is suitable for flood forecasting systems and identify the input variables, feed them to the ANN and train the model. Then test the model using test data and predict flood level in Kaluthara and Ratnapura area using that ANN model.

Keywords: Natural disasters · Artificial intelligence ·
Artificial neural network (ANN)

1 Introduction

Natural disasters like floods, drought, Tsunamis, create numerous hazards including risk to human life, disturbance of transport and communication networks, damage to buildings and infrastructure, and the loss of agricultural crops. Floods in Sri Lanka occur mainly during the monsoon season in which major floods in Kalutara and Rathnapura districts usually occur during the Southwest Monsoon Season (May–September). While preventing a natural disaster like flood is not a practical task, but prevention and protection policies are required that aim to reduce the vulnerability of people and public and private property.

Flood forecasting and prediction capabilities evolved slowly during the 1970s and 1980s. However, recent technologies like ANN have had a major impact on forecasting methodologies. ANNs, is a method that is inspired by the structure and functional characteristics of biological neural networks and it is a subset of machine learning. ANNs are mainly used in areas such as prediction and classification. ANN includes input layer which is responsible for getting input data to the network, hidden layer or more than one hidden layers responsible for extracting hidden patterns from the input

© Springer Nature Singapore Pte Ltd. 2019
J. Hemanth et al. (Eds.): SLAAI-ICAI 2018, CCIS 890, pp. 92–102, 2019.
https://doi.org/10.1007/978-981-13-9129-3_7

data and output layer for return the response of the network. The main feature of artificial neural networks is the iterative learning process in which training data cases are presented to the network one at a time while adjusting the weights associated with the input values. After all cases are presented, the process often starts over again. During the learning stage, the network learns to predict the correct output label of training samples by adjusting the weights. A training dataset in machine learning is a set of data used to identify potential relationships between data. A test set is the set of data used to assess the effectiveness of a predictive relationship. In this paper, a computational model using ANNs is developed to identify the likelihood of floods happen in Kalutara and Rathnapura districts of Sri Lanka by exploring the underlying mechanisms of the flood occurrences. In this study, The ANNs have been trained with back propagation algorithm, which is uniquely intended to solve non-linear least square complications.

2 Literature Review

2.1 Related Works

Utilizations of ANNs in hydrology are gauging every day water requests [15] and flow forecasting [16]. Zhu and Fujita utilized NNs to forecast stream 1 to 3 h in the future. They used three circumstances in applying ANNs: (a) off-line, (b) online, and (c) interval runoff prediction. The off-line model represents a linear relationship between runoff and incremental total precipitation. The on-line model assumes that the predicted hydrograph is a function of previous flows and precipitation. The interval runoff prediction model represents a modification of the learning algorithm that gives the upper and lower bounds of forecast. They have been found that the on-line model worked well but that the off-line model failed to accurately predict runoff [16].

An ANN, utilizing contribution from the Eta model and upper air environment, has been created for anticipating the likelihood of precipitation and quantitative precipitation forecast for the Dallas-Fort Worth, Texas, area. This study gave forecasts that were remarkably accurate, especially for the quantity of precipitation, which is paramount importance in forecasting flooding events [6].

The application related to flood forecasting is a study done to model rainfall-runoff processes [9]. They have been developed an ANN model to study the rainfall runoff process in the Leaf River basin, Mississippi. The system was contrasted with conceptual rainfall runoff models, such as Hydrologic Engineering Center (HEC)-I the Stanford Watershed Model, and linear time series models. In the examination, the ANN was found to be the best model for one stage ahead predictions.

Recently, functional networks were added to the ANN tools. Bruen and Yang investigated their use in real time flood forecasting. They have been applied two types of functional networks, separate and associatively functional networks to forecast flows for different lead times and compared them with the regular ANN in three catchments.

They have been demonstrated that functional networks are comparable in performance to NNs, as well as easier and faster to train [1].

The feasibility of using a hybrid rainfall-runoff model that used ANNs and conceptual models was studied by Chen and Adams. Using this approach, they have been investigated the spatial variation of rainfall and heterogeneity of watershed characteristics and their impact on runoff. They have been demonstrated that ANNs were effective tools in nonlinear mapping. It was also determined that ANNs were useful in exploring nonlinear transformations of the runoff generated by the individual sub catchments into the total runoff of the entire watershed outlet. They have been concluded that integrating ANNs with conceptual models shows promise in rainfall runoff modeling [3].

2.2 Technology Adopted

2.2.1 ANN

The idea of ANNs goes back to the third and fourth Century B.C. with Plato and Aristotle, who figured hypothetical clarifications of the brain and thinking processes. S. McCulloch and W. A. Pitts were the first modern theorists to publish the fundamentals of neural computing. This exploration started significant interest and work on ANNs [12]. During the mid to late twentieth century, examination into the advancement and utilizations of ANNs quickened significantly with a few thousand papers on neural modeling being published [10].

A good meaning of ANN, is given by Haykin [7] telling ANN as a hugely parallel combination of basic processing unit which can obtain knowledge from environment through a learning process and store the knowledge in its associations. ANN definitions [4, 5, 13, 14] highlight Processing Elements and the learning algorithm. Rojas [14] noticed that we still don't completely comprehend the figuring system of a natural neuron and that is the reason we favor processing units rather than artificial neuron Learning is well-defined as modifying synaptic weight to capture information in [4, 5, 7, 14]. In [7] and [5] it is also noted that ANN can modify its own topology.

As of late, a lot of work has been done in applying ANNs to water assets. Capodaglio et al. (1991) utilized ANNs to forecast sludge bulking. The authors discovered that ANNs performed similarly well transfer function models and better than linear regression and ARMA models. The disadvantage of the ANNs is that one can't find the inner workings of the procedure. An examination of the coefficients of stochastic model conditions can uncover valuable data about the arrangement under investigation; there is no real way to acquire comparable information about the weighing matrix [2].

2.2.2   Back-Propagation Algorithm

The improvement of the back-propagation algorithm was basic to future advancements of ANN methods. The technique, which was created by several researchers independently, works by altering the weights interfacing the units in progressive layers. Muller and Reinhardt wrote one of the earliest books on ANNs. The archive gave essential clarifications and spotlight on ANN modeling [13]. Hertz, Krogh, and Palmer exhibited an examination of the hypothetical parts of ANNs [8].

2.2.3   K Fold Cross Validation

Cross-validation is a process that can be used to estimate the quality of artificial neural network. In k-fold cross validation during the training phase use different values for the training technique's parameters and also try different number of hidden nodes and find the best values for number of hidden nodes and training parameters. With these, finally train the network using all data and best number of hidden nodes and training parameters [11].

3   Methodology

See Fig. 1.

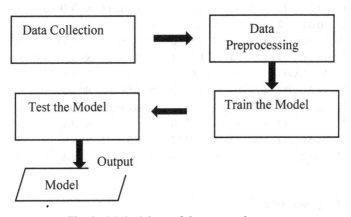

Fig. 1.   Methodology of the proposed system

3.1   Data Collection

Weather related historical data (May 2007 to May 2017) of Kalu Ganga of Sri Lanka including daily rainfall, water level of four sub basins, flood related historical data have been collected from the Department of Irrigation of Sri Lanka (Table 1).

Table 1. Data that extract from the Department of Irrigation according to the four sub basins in Kalu Ganga. W column shows the water level and R column shows the rainfall according to the date. S column shows the status of each basin like Normal, Alert, Minor Alert, Major Alert

1	Date	Ellagawa			Putupaula			Rathnapura			Millakanda		
2		W	R	S	W	R	S	Q	R	S	W	R	S
3	30-Apr-17	6.98	0	N	1.37	0	N	2.4	16	N	5.02	0	A
4	1-May-17	3.74	0	N	0.3	0	N	0.17	0	N	0.47	0	N
5	2-May-17	3.71	0	N	0.45	0	N	0.14	0	N	0.49	29	N
6	3-May-17	3.75	0	N	0.44	0	N	0.13	0	N	0.43	0	N
7	4-May-17	3.88	0	N	0.44	0	N	0.16	1	N	0.52	0	N
8	5-May-17	3.81	0	N	0.47	0	N	0.3	0	N	0.7	43	N
9	6-May-17	3.94	3	N	0.41	5	N	0.18	17	N	0.54	9	N
10	7-May 17	3.88	5	N	0.33	0	N	0.17	14	N	0.6	3	N
11	8-May-17	4.38	10	N	0.42	30	N	0.78	0	N	2.47	0	N
12	9-May-17	4.96	1	N	0.54	0	N	0.8	91	N	2.66	3	N
13	10-May-17	5.14	0	N	0.4	0	N	1.45	5	N	1.08	1	N
14	11-May-17	4.95	0	N	0.32	0	N	1	13	N	0.8	3	N
15	12-May-17	4.72	0	N	0.39	0	N	0.9	51	N	1.16	0	N
16	13-May-17	4.81	0	N	0.36	0	N	1.15	5	N	0.96	0	N
17	14-May-17	5.15	0	N	0.43	0	N	1.6	2	N	0.72	0	N
18	15-May-17	6.45	3	N	1.35	4	N	1.98	14	N	3.29	5	N
19	16-May-17	4.86	0	N	0.68	0	N	0.98	0	N	1.4	0	N
20	17-May-17	4.42	0	N	0.56	0	N	0.75	0	N	1.19	0	N
21	18-May-17	4.78	34	N	1.2	11	N	0.76	7	N	3.52	160	N
22	19-May-17	4.35	0	N	0.57	0	N	0.55	0	N	1.54	0	N
23	21-May-17	4.28	6	N	0.46	2	N	0.58	7	N	1.25	16	N
24	22-May-17	4.18	0	N	0.33	2	N	0.43	5	N	0.98	2	N
25	23-May-17	4.28	3	N	0.21	0	N	2	2	N	0.91	6	N
26	24-May-17	5.09	13	N	0.42	2	N	2.3	37	N	0.99	8	N
27	25-May-17	8.14	22	N	1.9	79	N	6.33	81	A	4.44	162	N

3.2   Data Preprocessing

There are four sub basins situated along the Kalu Ganga. Namely from top to bottom they are Ratnapura, Ellagawa, Millakanda, Putupaula. First, status column is decoded to number type in order to feed to the network. The coding representation is 0 represents 0, alert represents 1, minor alert is represented using 2 and for major alert it is 3.

Table 2. Preprocessed data set

Date	Ellagawa			Putupaula			Rathnapura			Millakanda		
	W	R	S	W	R	S	Q	R	S	W	R	S
30-Apr-17	6.98	0	0	1.37	0	0	2.4	16	0	5.02	0	1
1-May-17	3.74	0	0	0.3	0	0	0.17	0	0	0.47	0	0
2-May-17	3.71	0	0	0.45	0	0	0.14	0	0	0.49	29	0
3-May-17	3.75	0	0	0.44	0	0	0.13	0	0	0.43	0	0
4-May-17	3.88	0	0	0.44	0	0	0.16	1	0	0.52	0	0
5-May-17	3.81	0	0	0.47	0	0	0.3	0	0	0.7	43	0
6-May-17	3.94	3	0	0.41	5	0.18	0.18	17	0	0.54	9	0
7-May 17	3.88	5	0	0.33	0	0	0.17	14	0	0.6	3	0
8-May-17	4.38	10	0	0.42	30	0	0.78	0	0	2.47	0	0
9-May-17	4.96	1	0	0.54	0	0	0.8	91	0	2.66	3	0
10-May-17	5.14	0	0	0.4	0	0	1.45	5	0	1.08	1	0
11-May-17	4.95	0	0	0.32	0	0	1	13	0	0.8	3	0
12-May-17	4.72	0	0	0.39	0	0	0.9	51	0	1.16	0	0
13-May 17	4.81	0	0	0.36	0	0	1.15	5	0	0.96	0	0
14-May-17	5.15	0	0	0.43	0	0	1.6	2	0	0.72	0	0
16-May-17	6.45	3	0	1.35	4	0	1.98	14	0	3.29	5	0
17-May-17	4.86	0	0	0.68	0	0	0.98	0	0	1.4	0	0
18-May-17	4.42	0	0	0.56	0	0	0.75	0	0	1.19	0	0
19-May-17	4.78	34	0	1.2	11	0	0.76	7	0	3.52	160	0
20-May-17	4.35	0	0	0.57	0	0	0.55	0	0	1.54	0	0
21-May-17	4.28	6	0	0.46	2	0	0.58	7	0	1.25	16	0
22-May-17	4.18	0	0	0.33	2	0	0.43	5	0	0.98	2	0
23-May-17	4.28	3	0	0.21	0	0	2	2	0	0.91	6	0
24-May-17	5.09	13	0	0.42	2	0	2.3	37	0	0.99	8	0
25-May-17	8.14	22	0	1.9	79	0	6.33	81	1	4.44	162	0
29-May-17	13.29	2	3	6.65	18	3	7.02	4	1	9.66	19	3
30-May-17	12.33	47	3	6.02	21	3	6.92	25	1	8.46	53	3
31-May-17	11.06	5	2	5.3	0	3	6.78	40	1	7.62	38	2

Although, the domain knowledge obtain by the data analysis and at the latter part of the river, the previous sub basin data is used to increase the accuracy of the system. For instance, when training the for Millakanda sub basin Rathnapura and Ellagawa data is used as inputs.

Table 2 shows the preprocessed dataset obtained after applying preprocessing techniques described. W column shows the water level and R column shows the rainfall according to the date as previously. S column shows the status of each basin like 0, 1, 2, and 3. These data is used to train the neural network model for each sub basin. Next section discusses the how data have been used to predict the flood level of each sub basin.

3.3   Train the Model

In order to build the flood prediction model, a predictive model is developed in the study.

Ratnapura sub basin:
Inputs for the Ratnapura sub basin are rainfall, water level of the Rathnapura sub basin and previous day status. Output is the level of flood in the Ratnapura sub basin.
Ellagawa sub basin:
There can be an impact of upper sub basins to the lower sub basins. So, inputs for the Ellagawa sub basin are the current rainfall, current water level and previous day status of the Ratnapura sub basin and the current rainfall, current water level of Ellagawa sub basin and previous day status. Output of this basin is the level of flood in the Ellagawa sub basin.

Millakanda sub basin:
Millakanda sub basin is the third sub basin along the river from Adam's peak to sea. So, it has inputs of Ratnapura and Ellagawa sub basins. Inputs for the Millakanda are current rainfall, current water level and previous day status of the Ratnapura sub basin, current rainfall, current water level and previous day status of the Ellagawa sub basin and the current rainfall, current water level of Millakanda sub basin and previous day status.
Output is the level of flood in the Millakanda sub basin.
Putupaula sub basin:
As Putupaula is the last sub basin along the river from top to bottom it gets all other three sub basins status as the inputs. So, inputs for the Putupaula are current rainfall, current water level and previous day status of the Ratnapura sub basin, current rainfall, current water level and previous day status of the Ellagawa sub basin, current rainfall, current water level and previous day status of the Millakanda sub basin and the current rainfall, current water level of Putupaula sub basin and previous day status. By using these as inputs model output the level of flood in the Putupaula sub basin.

Code 1 includes to Keras implementation of the ANN Model for the sub basin, Ellagawa.

Code 1. Keras implementation of the ANN Model.

```
from keras.models import Sequential
from keras.layers import Dense

import numpy

import matplotlib.pyplot as plt

dataset=numpy.loadtxt("sample
ellagawa.csv",delimiter=",")

X=dataset[0:2830,0:7]
Y=dataset[0:2830,7]

X_test=dataset[2830:3530,0:7]
Y_test=dataset[2830:3530,7]

model = Sequential()
model.add(Dense(15,input_dim=2,
activation='relu'))
model.add(Dense(15, activation='relu'))
model.add(Dense(1, activation='sigmoid'))

model.compile(loss='binary_crossentropy',optim
izer='adam', metrics=['accuracy'])

history=model.fit(X,Y,epochs=150,
validation_split=0.3,batch_size=10)

plt.plot(history.history['acc'])
plt.plot(history.history['val_acc'])
plt.title('model accuracy')
plt.ylabel('accuracy')
plt.xlabel('epoch')
plt.legend(['train','validate'],loc='upper
left')
plt.show()

scores = model.evaluate(X_test, Y_test)
print("\n%s:          %.2f%%"          %
(model.metrics_names[1], scores[1]*100))
model.save("ellagawa1.h5")
```

3.4   Test the Model

The values of flood level have been forecasted for the period of one year from May 2017 to May 2018. These predicted values are then compared to the actual weather data from May 2017 to May 2018 to evaluate the accuracy and the reliability of the developed time series model.

Ratnapura Sub basin:
The model is trained using the inputs as mentioned in the Sect. 3.3 and accuracy of the model is 100%. Figure 2 shows the train and test accuracy obtained in Ratnapura sub basin. Table 3 shows the training, validation and testing accuracy for Ratnapura sub basin.

Ellagawa Sub basin:
As mentioned in the Sect. 3.3, the model is trained with using upper sub basin data and the Ellagawa sub basin. Accuracy of the model is 99.14%. Figure 3 shows the train and test accuracy obtained in Ellagawa sub basin. Table 3 shows the training, validation and testing accuracy for Ellagawa sub basin.

Millakanda Sub basin:
The model is trained using the data as mentioned in the Sect. 3.3 and accuracy of the model is 96.43%. Figure 4 shows the train and test accuracy obtained in Millakanda sub basin. Table 3 shows the training, validation and testing accuracy for Millakanda sub basin.

Putupaula sub basin:
The model is trained using all sub basin's data. Accuracy of the model is 98.57%. Figure 5 shows the train and test accuracy obtained in Putupaula sub basin. Table 3 shows the training, validation and testing accuracy for Putupaula sub basin.

Table 3. Summary of training, validation and testing accuracy for each sub station

Sub basin	Training accuracy	Validation accuracy	Testing accuracy
Ratnapura	99.2%	96.6%	100%
Ellagawa	98.9%	99.2%	99.14%
Millakanda	96.4%	96.5%	96.86%
Putupaula	98.2%	98.7%	98.57%

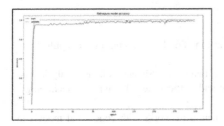

Fig. 2. Train and test accuracy obtained in Ratnapura sub basin.

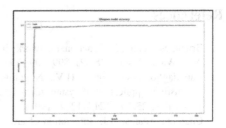

Fig. 3. Train and test accuracy obtained in Ellagawa sub basin.

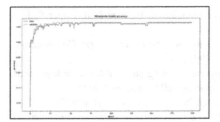

Fig. 4. Train and test accuracy obtained in Millakanda sub basin.

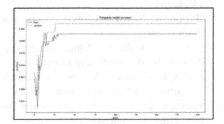

Fig. 5. Train and test accuracy obtained in Putupaula sub basin.

4 Discussion

The literature shows that ANN technology has been accounted for to give sensibly great answers for conditions where there are unpredictable systems that are (a) Poorly defined and understood using mathematical equations, (b) problems that deal with noisy data or involve pattern recognition, (c) situations where input data is incomplete and ambiguous by nature. It is a result of these qualities, that it is trusted an ANN could be connected to show model the daily rainfall-runoff relationship and predict flood.

The current research work focuses on food forecasting using ANN for Kalu Ganga. In this study we have created the model to four sub basins Ratnapura, Ellagawa, Millakanda, Putupaula.

5 Future Works

In the current data set most of the data are recorded as the "Normal" and there are few "Alerts", "Minor Alerts" and "Major Alerts", because of that test accuracy of the system is varying. As a solution for that have to increase the dataset. Furthermore, to handle class unbalanced problem k-fold cross validation technique can be used. Next stage of the current research work is to improve the accuracy of the system using k-fold cross validation technique.

References

1. Bruen, M., Yang, J.: Functional networks in real time flood forecasting-a novel application. Adv. Water Resour. **28**(92), 899–909 (2005)
2. Capodaglio, A.G., Jones, H.V., Novotny, V., Feng, X.: Sludge bulking analysis and forecasting: application of system identification and artificial neural computing technology. Water Res. **25**(10), 1217–1224 (1991)
3. Chen, J., Adams, B.J.: Integration of artificial neural networks with conceptual models in rainfall-runoff modeling. J. Hydrol. **318**(14), 232–249 (2006)
4. Eberhart, R., Shi, Y.: Computational Intelligence. Morgan Kaufmann, Burlington (2007)
5. Gurney, K.: An Introduction to Neural Networks. CRC Press, Boca Raton (2003)
6. Hall, T., Brooks, H.E.: Precipitation forecasting using a neural network. Weather Forecast. **14**(3), 338–345 (1999)
7. Haykin, S.: Neural Networks: A Comprehensive Foundation. Prentice Hall, Upper Saddle River (1999)
8. Hertz, J., Krogh, A., Palmer, R.: Introduction to the Theory of Neural Computation. Addison-Wesley Publishing Company, Boston (1991)
9. Hsu, K.L., Grupta, H.V., Sorooshian, S.: A superior training strategy for three-layer feed forward artificial neural networks. Technique report no. HWR no. 96–030 (1996)
10. Kohonen, T.: An introduction to neural computing. Neural Netw. **1**, 3–16 (1988)
11. McCaffrey, J.: Understanding and using k-fold cross validation for neural networks (2013)
12. McCulloch, W.S., Pitts, W.: A logical calculus of the ideas immanent in nervous activity. Bull. Math. Biol. **5**, 115133 (1943)
13. Muller, B., Reinhardt, J., Strickland, M.T.: Neural Networks an Introduction. Springer, Berlin (1995)
14. Rojas, R.: Neural Networks: A Systematic Introduction. Springer, Berlin (1996)
15. Zhang, S.P., Watanabe, H., Yamada, R.: Prediction of daily water demands by neural networks. Paper presented at the stochastic and statistical methods in hydrology and environmental engineering, University of Waterloo, Waterloo, Ontario, Canada (1993)
16. Zhu, M., Fujita, M.: Application of neural networks to runoff forecast. Paper presented at the stochastic and statistical methods in hydrology and environmental engineering, University of Waterloo, Waterloo, Ontario, Canada (1993)

Role of Deep Neural Network in Speech Enhancement: A Review

D. Hepsiba[1]([⊠]) and Judith Justin[2]

[1] Department of Instrumentation Engineering,
Karunya Institute of Technology and Sciences, Coimbatore, Tamil Nadu, India
hepsiba@karunya.edu
[2] Department of Biomedical Instrumentation Engineering,
Avinashilingam Institute for Home Science and Higher Education for Women,
Coimbatore, Tamil Nadu, India
hodbmieaul@gmail.com

Abstract. This paper presents a review on different methodologies adopted in speech enhancement and the role of Deep Neural Networks (DNN) in enhancement of speech. Mostly, a speech signal is distorted by background noise, environmental noise and reverberations. To enhance speech, certain processing techniques like Short-Time Fourier Transform, Short-time Auto-correlation and Short-time energy can be adopted. Features such as Logarithmic Power Spectrum (LPS), Mel-Frequency Cepstral Coefficients (MFCC) and Gammatone Frequency Cepstral Coefficient (GFCC) can be extracted and given to DNN for noise classification, so that the noise in the speech can be eliminated. DNN plays a major role in speech enhancement by creating a model with a large amount of training data and the performance of the enhanced speech is evaluated using certain performance metrics.

Keywords: Speech enhancement · Deep Neural Network · Feature extraction · Background noise · Speech signal

1 Introduction

Speech enhancement plays an important role in processing of any speech signal because it tends to be easily affected by different problems such as interference due to environmental noise, background noise and reverberations. Speech enhancement techniques are implemented to eliminate the environmental noise that disturbs the target speech signal and to retrieve the clean speech for applications such as Automatic Speech Recognition (ASR) [21, 22], mobile speech communication, speaker recognition, hearing aids [25, 26] and speech coding [23, 24]. Speech enhancement [1, 2] helps in improving the intelligibility and perceptual quality and also helps in the reduction of noise distortion of a speech signal degraded by adverse conditions. The different types of speech enhancement techniques developed in the past years are spectral subtraction [4], iterative wiener filtering [5], minimum mean square error [6], Kalman Filtering [15] and optimally modified log spectral amplitude [19, 20]. The presence of musical noise in the enhanced speech is the major drawback of these traditional techniques.

© Springer Nature Singapore Pte Ltd. 2019
J. Hemanth et al. (Eds.): SLAAI-ICAI 2018, CCIS 890, pp. 103–112, 2019.
https://doi.org/10.1007/978-981-13-9129-3_8

Compared to the other traditional techniques Minimum Mean Square Error (MMSE) gives better quality of enhanced speech with lower musical noise [38, 39].

Non-linear DNN based regression models [3] are developed with training data, depending on different conditions and considering factors such as types of noise, noisy speech, noise from speakers and Signal-to-Noise Ratios (SNRs). The performance of the DNN is limited in adverse conditions and in real time noisy situations. To overcome this limitation, and to improve the generalization capability for detecting varying inputs, the training set is formed with hundreds of different noise types. This attempt proved to be efficient in managing the non-stationary behavior of noise and the different categories of unseen noise. This is done by equalizing the global variance of enhanced speech features [6] and the reference clean speech features for reducing the over-smoothing problem. The drop out training [7] is applied on the datasets of neural network when overfitting problem arises. Noise Aware Training (NAT) is done [8] by adding noise information in the DNN inputs to improve the noise robustness and performance in DNN-based speech enhancement systems.

When the need is to separate the noise from the speech signal or to separate a target source from a mixture data, the Non-negative Matrix Factorization (NMF) plays a major role. NMF has a wide scope in acoustic signal detection, speech enhancement, speech recognition in adverse environment, acoustic source separation and many more [9–12]. To increase the performance of NMF target data extraction algorithm with source subspace overlap, the estimation of encoding vectors is done by DNN to reconstruct the desired source data vectors [13]. The mixture data given to the DNN for training includes the clean speech and the noise generated from the interfering sources. DNN modeling is done by mapping the data vectors to its corresponding encoding vectors. Instead of using NMF for separation of clean speech from the mixture data, DNN can be used in two stages: first for separation of clean speech from noisy speech and second for enhancing the clean speech [17]. Another approach for enhancing speech using NMF is the exemplar-based speech enhancement technique [14], where the training clean speech and noisy data are taken in time-frequency representations. Speech and noise have varied modulation frequency content, hence, the Modulation Spectrogram feature holds good in separating the speech and noise in an efficient manner.

Time-Frequency masking is another methodology implemented when background noise causes the major problem [27]. This method improves the magnitude and phase response of the noisy speech through estimating the complex ideal ratio mask in real and imaginary domains. Here the DNN is made to learn the mapping between the reverberant speech and the complex ideal ratio mask [28].

Improved Least Mean Square Adaptive Filtering (ILMSAF) [16] helps in overcoming the drawbacks such as reduced performance in low SNR environments and poor adaptability in different noisy environments. Adaptive filter coefficients estimated by Deep Belief Network (DBN) helps in efficient noise removal. DNN acts as a noise classifier and based on the noise classification the filter parameters are chosen for removing noise.

The most commonly occurring problem in the DNN based algorithm is the reduced performance in mismatched noise condition [3, 6]. To get rid of this problem it is mandatory to have more noise types in the training set. DNN based feature extraction can also be done to achieve speech enhancement, by learning the mapping in linear-frequency spectral domain [18]. Applying pre-enhancement in the spectral features of the DNN input could help in recovering clean speech features.

The rest of the paper is organized as follows. Section 2 discusses on the different types of databases of clean speech and noise signals. Section 3 elaborates on the processing methodologies adopted for the speech signal. Role of DNN in speech enhancement is explained in Sect. 4.

2 Databases

Database refers to both the clean speech data and noisy speech data that can be utilized for the research findings. The clean speech data is taken from the TIMIT corpus [31]. NTT database [34] has clean speech utterances in eight different languages (English, American English, Japanese, German, Chinese, Spanish, French and Italian). The DARPA-RM [29] database is suitable for training the supervised learning system. Noisy data is taken from Noisex-92 [32], Aurora-2 [30] and Speechdat-Car US (SDC) database [33]. Common noise types taken for training and testing the DNN are Babble, Restaurant, Street, Cafeteria, Machine gun, White, Volvo, Factory1, Buccaneer, etc.

3 Processing

The properties of the speech signal vary with time, and hence, the short-time processing methods that periodically repeat for the waveform duration are utilized. The following are the different processing techniques adopted in the processing of speech signal.

3.1 Short-Time Energy

Short-time energy helps in differentiating the voiced and unvoiced sounds in a speech signal. Thus, the speech and the background noise can be easily detected. The variation in short-time energy [37] determines the difference between the voiced and unvoiced speech segments. The short-time energy is high for voiced segments and low for unvoiced segments and very low for silent speech.

The short-time energy is represented as given in Eq. (1)

$$E_{\hat{n}} = \sum_{m=-\infty}^{\infty} (x[m]w[\hat{n}-m])^2 \qquad (1)$$

where

$E_{\hat{n}}$-Energy of the sample n in the signal x
w-Window
m-Number of frames in the signal

3.2   Short-Time Fourier Transform

The Short-Time Fourier Transform (STFT) is the most powerful tool in any audio signal processing, especially in speech signal processing [35]. When a signal with changing frequency such as music, audio signal and speech signal is taken for noise removal, instead of analyzing the whole signal, STFT helps in analyzing the smaller divisions of the signal. The STFT is a function of both time and frequency, therefore, it is represented as time-frequency distribution [36].

The Short-Time Fourier Transform is computed using Eq. (2)

$$X[n, \lambda] = \sum_{m=-\infty}^{\infty} x[n + m]w[m]e^{-j\lambda m} \tag{2}$$

where

$n \in Z$ is a time index and $\lambda \in R$ is a normalized frequency index

3.3   Short-Time Autocorrelation

Autocorrelation is a technique that compares the original signal with the time-delayed version of itself. The Short-Time Autocorrelation is the autocorrelation function of the windowed segment of the speech signal. The voiced and unvoiced speech can be decided based on the peaks of the autocorrelation function [16].

The Short-Time Autocorrelation is denoted as given in Eq. (3)

$$R_{\hat{n}}[k] = \sum_{m=-\infty}^{\infty} (x[m]w[\hat{n} - m])(x[m + k]w[\hat{n} - k - m]) \tag{3}$$

where

$R_{\hat{n}}$ – Short-time autocorrelation at sample n in the signal x
w – Window

4   Deep Neural Networks for Speech Enhancement

DNN has wide scope in audio recognition, speech recognition, speech enhancement and other domains. DNN is a feedforward network and has the capability to model non-linear relationships. The DNN is trained with a collection of data comprising the clean and noisy speech. Different features such as Log-Power Spectra (LPS), Mel Cepstral Coefficients (MFCC) and Gammatone Frequency Cepstral Coefficients (GFCC) are extracted from the speech signal to model the DNN. During training stage, the DNN is made to learn the mapping function and the relationship between the noisy and clean speech, where the noisy data with different levels of Signal-to-Noise Ratio (SNR) are considered. In some cases, DNN is used for noise classification, where adaptive filter coefficients are selected according to the determination of noise. DNN plays a major role in separation of the source signal from the mixed signal by decreasing the interference and distortion.

4.1   Pre-training DNN with Noisy Data

A collection of clean speech and noisy speech data represented by the log spectra features are given to the regression based DNN model in the training phase. After training, the enhanced log power spectra features are given as input to the DNN model. The DNN concatenates the time axis information in the form of multiple frames and frequency axis information in the form of log spectral features as the input feature vector for DNN learning [3].

It is observed that the performance of DNN based method gives better results compared to the logarithmic minimum mean square error (L-MMSE) method [19, 20, 40] for estimating the noise corrupted target speech. The DNN enhanced spectrogram shows no musical noise and lies closer to the original clean speech spectrogram than the L-MMSE enhanced speech. From the study made on the subjective preference evaluation, it is observed that, on an average, 76.35% of subjects have preferred DNN-based enhanced speech instead of L-MMSE enhanced speech under one or two mismatched noisy environments [3].

4.2   Drop Out Training and Noise Aware Training in DNN

The main drawback in the estimated clean speech is over-smoothing. Equalizing the global variance of estimated clean speech and reference clean speech reduces this problem to an extent. In order to remove the mismatch between the training and testing conditions caused by the different types of noise and various SNR conditions, the drop out training methodology could be adopted. Drop out Training [6] is implemented in DNN by randomly removing certain percentage of neurons from the input, intermediate or hidden layer and treated as a model. Sometimes drop out training causes decrease in performance for matched conditions but gives robustness for mismatched conditions. To give a clean picture on the noise information, Noise Aware Training [6] is done by feeding the DNN with noisy speech samples and subsequent estimation of noise. Thus, the DNN gets trained to determine the clean speech signal.

The DNN enhanced speech suppresses the non-stationary noise and results in less residual noise compared to L-MMSE enhanced speech [41]. From the study made from the subjective preference evaluation, it is observed that, on an average, 78% of the subjects have preferred DNN enhanced speech over the L-MMSE enhanced speech. It is inferred that, the DNN-based speech enhancement system is more efficient in dealing with real world noisy speech in different languages and various recording conditions that is not included in the training [6].

4.3   DNN Based Encoding Vector Estimation

Non-negative Matrix Factorization (NMF) technique is a conventional method which is used to extract encoding data vectors [9, 12]. The performance of conventional NMF based method degrades as the strength of the noise sources increase. The concept of regression is used for estimating the encoding vectors from a mixture of data given. The mixture data and encoding vectors are mapped and learned by DNN [13].

From performance metrics such as Signal to Distortion Ratio (SDR), Signal to Interference Ratio (SIR), Signal to Artifacts Ratio (SAR) [42] and Perceptual Evaluation of Speech Quality (PESQ) [43], it is observed that the performance of DNN based NMF is good compared to the conventional NMF based techniques and DNN based separation in both matched and mismatched conditions [13].

4.4   DNN Based Noise Classification

Filter parameters play a major role in removal of noise. The filter parameters vary depending on the type of noise. DNN helps in classification of noise and selection of the filter coefficients according to the noise type. In the training phase, the Improved Least Mean Square Adaptive Filtering (ILMSAF) model is trained for different noise types. The enhancement of speech is done by selecting the ILMSAF model according to noise type. The adaptive filter coefficients play a major role in improving the perceptual quality of enhanced speech [16].

The ILMSAF based speech enhancement algorithm with DNN gives better results in terms of speech objective quality measures than the Wiener filtering method used for speech enhancement [44]. The ILMSAF based speech enhancement algorithm with DNN gives a good response in high SNR conditions and extraordinary response in low SNR conditions [16].

4.5   Source Separation and Enhancement Using DNN

The Single Channel Source Separation (SCASS) helps to separate audio source from the mixed signal [45, 47]. The most popular method is the Non-negative Matrix Factorization (NMF) and nowadays DNN is implemented for source separation also [48, 50]. Source separation is adopted by two methods using DNN. The first method maps the features of the mixed signal onto features of the source signal [49, 50]. In the second method, the spectral mask of the mixed signal is mapped, and therefore it contributes to each source in the mixed signal [51]. These methods are used for separating the sources that is distorted due to interference by other sources and distortions. Distortion is eliminated in two stages: In the first stage, the signals are denoised from the background noise, and is termed as the separation stage. Quality of the signal is enhanced in the second stage, which is the enhancement stage [17].

The separation is either done by NMF or DNN and the enhancement is done by DNN using two methods. In the first method, the separated signal is enhanced individually for each source using its own trained DNN. In the second method, a single DNN is used to enhance all the separated sources together. In both the methods, discriminative training is adopted to train the DNN in the enhancement stage. The observations made from the SIR and SDR values show that the quality of the separated sources is improved by decreasing the interference and distortions [17].

4.6 DNN Based Speech Enhancement Systems

Generally, DNN is trained in different conditions such as noise type, gender of the speaker and Signal to Noise Ratio (SNR), to ensure the generalizing capability of the DNN based speech enhancement system [53, 56] in terms of Speech Quality (SQ) and Speech Intelligibility (SI) [2]. A comparison is made in terms of noise specific, speaker specific, and signal-to-noise (SNR) specific system performance with respect to noise general, speaker general and SNR general systems. A single DNN based Speech Enhancement (SE) system has been designed for a specific noise type, speaker & SNR, is compared with the general DNN based SE system designed for various noise types, speakers & SNR and the short-time spectral amplitude minimum mean square error (STSA-MMSE) based Speech Enhancement algorithm [58].

From the performance metrics speech quality and speech intelligibility, it is observed that the DNN based SE system has good generalizing capability when exposed to unseen noise types and speakers. The DNN trained with only one type of noise, one type of speaker and one type of SNR performs excellent when compared with the general DNN based SE system trained with a variety of noise types, speakers and SNR [52].

5 Conclusion

Deep Neural Network is an emerging technique in speech enhancement and has a wide scope for research. Various processing techniques applicable for the enhancement of speech are discussed. The DNN in speech enhancement can be trained in multiple conditions and tested in mismatched conditions to test the efficiency of the network. The performance of the enhanced speech signal is evaluated with different performance metrics such as Short-Time Objective Intelligibility (STOI) score, Perceptual Evaluation of Speech Quality (PESQ), Signal to Distortion Ratio (SDR), Signal to Interference Ratio (SIR) and Signal to Artifact Ratio (SAR).

Thus, it can be concluded that the Deep Neural Network plays a major role in speech recognition, speech enhancement, audio separation and noise classification.

References

1. Benesty, J., Makino, S., Chen, J.D.: Speech Enhancement. Springer, New York, NY (2005)
2. Loizou, P.C.: Speech Enhancement: Theory and Practice. CRC Press, Boca Raton, FL (2013)
3. Xu, Y., Du, J., Dai, L.-R., Lee, C.-H.: An experimental study on speech enhancement based on deep neural networks. IEEE Signal Process. Lett. **21**(1), 65–68 (2014)
4. Boll, S.: Suppression of acoustic noise in speech using spectral subtraction. IEEE Trans. Acoust. Speech Signal Process. **ASSP-27**(2), 113–120 (1979)
5. Lim, J.S., Oppenheim, A.V.: Enhancement and bandwidth compression of noisy speech. Proc. IEEE **67**(12), 1586–1604 (1979)

6. Xu, Y., Du, J., Dai, L.-R., Lee, C.-H.: A regression approach to speech enhancement based on deep neural networks. IEEE/ACM Trans. Audio Speech Lang. Process. **23**(1), 7–19 (2015)

7. Hinton, G.E., Srivastava, N., Krizheysky, A., Sutskever, I., Salakhutdinoy, R.R.: Improving neural networks by preventing co-adaptation of feature detectors (2012)

8. Seltzer, M., Yu, D., Wang, Y.: An investigation of deep neural networks for noise robust speech recognition. In: Proceedings of ICASSP, pp. 7398–7402 (2013)

9. Jin, Y.G., Kim, N.S.: On detecting target acoustic signal based on negative matrix factorization. IEICE Trans. Inf. Syst. **E93-D**(4), 922–925 (2010)

10. Wilson, K.W., Raj, B., Smaragdis, P., Divakaran, A.: Speech denoising using nonnegative matrix factorization with priors. In: Proceedings of IEEE International Conference on Acoustics, Speech, and Signal Processing, pp. 4029–4032 (2008)

11. Weninger, F., Geiger, J., Wllmer, M., Schuller, B., Rigoll, G.: The Munich 2011CHiME challenge contribution: NMF-BLSTM speech enhancement and recognition for reverberated multisource environments. In: Proceedings of 1st International Workshop on Machine Listening in Multisource Environments (CHiME), pp. 24–29 (2011)

12. Grais, E.M., Erdogan, H.: Single channel speech music separation using non-negative matrix factorization and spectral masks. In: Proceedings of International Conference on Digital Signal Process, pp. 1–6 (2011)

13. Kang, T.G., Kwon, K., Shin, J.W., Kim, N.S.: NMF-based target source separation using deep neural network. IEEE Signal Process. Lett. **22**(2), 229–233 (2015)

14. Baby, D., Virtanen, T., Gemmeke, J.F., Van Hamme, H.: Coupled dictionaries for exemplar-based speech enhancement and automatic speech recognition. IEEE/ACM Trans. Audio Speech Lang. Process. **23**(11), 1788–1799 (2015)

15. Grancharov, V., Samuelsson, J., Kleijin, B.: On causal algorithms for speech enhancement. IEEE Trans. Audio Speech Lang. Process. **14**(3), 764–773 (2006)

16. Li, R., et al.: ILMSAF based speech enhancement with DNN and noise classification. Speech Commun. **85**, 53–70 (2016)

17. Grais, E.M., Roma, G., Simpson, A.J.R., Plumbley, M.D.: Two-stage single-channel audio source separation using deep neural networks. IEEE/ACM Trans. Audio Speech Lang. Process. **25**(9), 1773–1783 (2017)

18. Lee, H.-Y., Cho, J.-W., Kim, M., Park, H.-M.: DNN-based feature enhancement using DOA-constrained ICA for robust speech recognition. IEEE Signal Process. Lett. **23**(8), 1091–1095 (2016)

Cohen, I., Berdugo, B.: Speech enhancement for non-stationary noise environments. Signal Process. **81**(11), 2403–2418 (2001)

20. Cohen, I.: Noise spectrum estimation in adverse environments: improved minima controlled recursive averaging. IEEE Trans. Speech Audio Process. **11**(5), 466–475 (2003)

21. Li, J., Deng, L., Haeb-Umbach, R., Gong, Y.: Robust Automatic Speech Recognition: A Bridge to Practical Applications, 1st edn. Academic, Orlando (2015)

22. Li, B., Tsao, Y., Sim, K.C.: An investigation of spectral restoration algorithms for deep neural networks-based noise robust speech recognition. In: Proceedings of Interspeech, pp. 3002–3006 (2013)

23. Li, J., et al.: Comparative intelligibility investigation of single-channel noise reduction algorithms for Chinese, Japanese and English. J. Acoust. Soc. Am. **129**(5), 3291–3301 (2011)

24. Li, J., Sakamoto, S., Hongo, S., Akagi, M., Suzuki, Y.: Two-stage binaural speech enhancement with Wiener filter for high-quality speech communication. Speech Commun. **53**(5), 677–689 (2011)

25. Levitt, H.: Noise reduction in hearing aids: an overview. J. Rehabil. Res. Dev. **38**(1), 111–121 (2001)
26. Chern, A., Lai, Y.H., Chang, Y.-P., Tsao, Y., Chang, R.Y., Chang, H.-W.: A smartphone-based multi-functional hearing assistive system to facilitate speech recognition in the classroom. IEEE Access **5**, 10339–10351 (2017)
27. Williamson, D.S., Wang, Y., Wang, D.: Complex ratio masking for monaural speech separation. IEEE/ACM Trans. Audio Speech Lang. Process. **24**(3), 483–492 (2016)
28. Williamson, D.S., Wang, D.L.: Time-frequency masking in the complex domain for speech dereverberation and denoising. IEEE/ACM Trans. Audio Speech Lang. Process. **25**(7), 1492–1501 (2017)
29. Price, P., Fisher, W.M., Bernstein, J., Pallet, D.: The DARPA 1000-word resource management database for continuous speech recognition. In: Proceedings of IEEE International Conference on Acoustics, Speech, and Signal Processing, New York, NY, USA, pp. 651–654 (1988)
30. Hirschand, H.G., Pearce, D.: The AURORA experimental framework for the performance evaluations of speech recognition systems under noisy conditions. In: Proceedings of ISCA ITRWASR, pp. 181–188 (2000)
31. Garofolo, J.S.: Getting started with the DARPA TIMIT CD-ROM: an acoustic phonetic continuous speech database. NIST Technical Report (1988)
32. Varga, A., Steeneken, H.J.M.: Assessment for automatic speech recognition: II. NOISEX-92: a database and an experiment to study the effect of additive noise on speech recognition systems. Speech Commun. **12**(3), 247–251 (1993)
33. Moreno et al.: Speech dat-car: a large database for automotive environments. In: Proceedings of International Conference on Language Resources and Evaluation, Athens, Greece, pp. 1–6 (2000)
34. Multi-Lingual Speech Database for Telephonometry, NTT Advanced Technology Corporation, San Jose, CA, USA (1994)
35. Allen, J.B.: Application of the short-time Fourier transform to speech processing and spectral analysis. In: Proceedings of IEEE ICASSP-82, pp. 1012–1015 (1982)
36. Cohen, L.: Time-Frequency Analysis. Englewood Cliffs, Prentice-Hall, Upper Saddle River (1995)
37. de-la-Calle-Silos, F., Stern, R.M.: Synchrony based feature extraction for robust automatic speech recognition. IEEE Signal Process. Lett. **24**(8), 1158–1162 (2017)
38. Cappe, O.: Elimination of the musical noise phenomenon with the Ephraim and Malah noise suppressor. IEEE Trans. Speech Audio Process. **2**(2), 345–349 (1994)
39. Hussain, A., Chetouani, M., Squartini, S., Bastari, A., Piazza, F.: Nonlinear Speech Enhancement: An Overview. In: Stylianou, Y., Faundez-Zanuy, M., Esposito, A. (eds.) Progress in Nonlinear Speech Processing. LNCS, vol. 4391, pp. 217–248. Springer, Heidelberg (2007). https://doi.org/10.1007/978-3-540-71505-4_12
40. Cohen, I., Gannot, S.: Spectral Enhancement Methods. In: Benesty, J., Sondhi, M.Mohan, Huang, Y.A. (eds.) Springer Handbook of Speech Processing. SH, pp. 873–902. Springer, Heidelberg (2008). https://doi.org/10.1007/978-3-540-49127-9_44
41. Ephraim, Y., Malah, D.: Speech enhancement using minimum mean square log spectral amplitude estimator. IEEE Trans. Acoust. Speech Signal Process. **ASSP-33**(2), 443–445 (1985)
42. Vincent, E., Gribonval, R., Fevotte, C.: Performance measurement in blind audio source separation. IEEE Trans. Audio Speech Lang. Process. **14**(4), 1462–1469 (2006)
43. ITU, Perceptual Evaluation of Speech Quality (PESQ): an objective method for end-to-end speech quality assessment of narrowband telephone networks and speech codecs ITU-T Rec. p. 862 (2000)

44. Li, R., Bao, C., Xia, B., Jia, M.: Speech enhancement using the combination of adaptive wavelet threshold and spectral sub-traction based on wavelet packet decomposition. In: 2012 IEEE 11th International Conference on Signal Processing (ICSP), vol. 1, pp. 481–484 (2012)

45. Virtanen, T.: Monaural sound source separation by non-negative matrix factorization with temporal continuity and sparseness criteria. IEEE Trans. Audio Speech Lang. Process. **15**(3), 1066–1074 (2007)

46. Smaragdis, P.: Convolutive speech bases and their application to supervised speech separation. IEEE Trans. Audio Speech Lang. Process. **15**(1), 1–12 (2007)

47. Smaragdis, P., Shashanka, M., Raj, B.: A sparse non-parametric approach for single channel separation of known sounds. In: Neural Information Processing Systems, Vancouver, BC, Canada, Dec 2009, pp. 1705–1713

48. Grais, E.M., Roma, G., Simpson, A.J.R., Plumbley, M.D.: Single channel audio source separation using deep neural network ensembles. In: Proceedings of 140th Audio Engineering Society Convention, Paper no. 9494 (2016)

49. Huang, P.-S., Kim, M., Hasegawa-Johnson, M., Smaragdis, P.: Singing-voice separation from monaural recordings using deep recurrent neural networks. In: Proceedings of International Society for Music Information Retrieval Conference, pp. 477–482 (2014)

50. Huang, P.-S., Kim, M., Hasegawa-Johnson, M., Smaragdis, P.: Deep learning for monaural speech separation. In: Proceedings of IEEE International Conference on Acoustics, Speech, and Signal Processing, pp. 1562–1566 (2014)

51. Weninger, F., Hershey, J.R., Roux, J.L., Schuller, B.: Discriminatively trained recurrent neural networks for single-channel speech separation. In: Proceedings of IEEE Global Conference on Signal and Information Processing, pp. 577–581 (2014)

52. Kolbæk, M., Tan, Z.-H.: Speech intelligibility potential of general and specialized deep neural network based speech enhancement systems. IEEE/ACM Trans. Audio Speech Lang. Process. **25**(1), 153–167 (2017)

53. Lee, T., Theunissen, F.: A single microphone noise reduction algorithm based on the detection and reconstruction of spectro-temporal features. Proc. R. Soc. Lond. A Math. Phys. Sci. **471**, 2184 (2015)

54. Huang, P.-S., Kim, M., Hasegawa-Johnson, M., Smaragdis, P.: Joint optimization of masks and deep recurrent neural networks for monaural source separation. IEEE/ACM Trans. Audio Speech Lang. Process. **23**(12), 2136–2147 (2015)

55. Liu, D., Smaragdis, P., Kim, M.: Experiments on deep learning for speech denoising. In: Proceedings of INTERSPEECH, pp. 2685–2689 (2014)

56. Wang, Y., Chen, J., Wang, D.: Deep neural network based supervised speech segregation generalizes to novel noises through large-scale training. Dept. Comput. Sci. Eng. Ohio State Univ., Columbus, OH, USA, Technical Report OSU-CISRC-3/15-TR02 (2015)

57. Hendriks, R.C., Gerkmann, T., Jensen, J.: DFT-Domain Based Single-Microphone Noise Reduction for Speech Enhancement: A Survey of the State of the Art. Synthesis Lectures on Speech and Audio Processing, vol. 9, pp. 1–80. Morgan & Claypool, SanRafael, CA (2013)

58. Erkelens, J., Hendriks, R., Heusdens, R., Jensen, J.: Minimum mean square error estimation of discrete Fourier coefficients with generalized Gamma priors. IEEE/ACM Trans. Audio Speech Lang. Process. **15**(6), 1741–1752 (2007)

Intelligent Time of Use Deciding System for a Melody to Provide a Better Listening Experience

M. W. Sohan Janaka[✉], H. U. W. Ratnayake, and I. A. Premaratne

Department of Electrical and Computer Engineering,
The Open University of Sri Lanka, Nawala, Nugegoda, Sri Lanka
sohanjanaka101@gmail.com, {udithaw,iapre}@ou.ac.lk

Abstract. Understanding a melody or a song is quite a difficult task for any machine. This research proposes to analyze notations of the music melodies and to decide the best time to play, sing or listen for any given melody by using the knowledge of Hindustani music trained in an Artificial Neural Network. In the proposed system, pre-process module identifies the Aroha, Awaroha, Vadi and Sanwadi Swara of the melody. Those characteristics that are identified from the pre-process module are input to the Artificial Neural Network (ANN). The system uses the expert knowledge of the Hindustani Raagadari music to train the ANN designed and developed using Tensorflow deep learning platform. Training data set for the learning process has been of size 450 whereas testing data set has been 44 from the total of 494 Raaga details. Trained ANN could achieve a testing accuracy of 84%.

Keywords: Artificial Neural Network (ANN) · Music · Expert knowledge · Raaga · Gaana Samaya · Tensorflow

1 Introduction

People have thousands of songs in their personal computers (PCs), laptops or smartphones. However, most of the times they do not prefer to choose the songs manually and listen to those songs, because they already know what song will be played in the sequence. This may not be the best sequence to arrange the songs to be played at any given time.

This problem will be minimized if the listener decided to listen to a radio station instead of him/her choosing songs. In a radio station, the songs will be played by a professional artist. He/she will carefully choose the music which will match to the current time of the day and will also control the rhythm flow between songs.

The first solution is very good although listener will have to listen to a radio station with commercials and sponsors' advertisements eventually. The second solution is to use a shuffler, which is very popular among music listeners. However, a shuffler cannot understand the melody or rhythm of songs and it randomly plays a song from the playlist. Therefore, this is also not a good experience for the music listener. There is no clear-cut rule to determine the time of use of a melody. This research examines the time

© Springer Nature Singapore Pte Ltd. 2019
J. Hemanth et al. (Eds.): SLAAI-ICAI 2018, CCIS 890, pp. 113–126, 2019.
https://doi.org/10.1007/978-981-13-9129-3_9

Table 1. Learning and Testing results of the ANN.

	Test details	Learning accuracy	Max testing accuracy
1	No hidden layers	49.16%	56%
2	1 layer sigmoid (20 nodes)	75.00%	66%
3	1 layer relu (20 nodes)	77.50%	70%
4	2 layers relu (20 nodes, 15 nodes)	92.08%	76%
5	2 layers sigmoid (20 nodes, 15 nodes)	86.67%	74%
6	3 layers sigmoid (20 nodes, 15 nodes, 10 nodes)	90.20%	80%
7	3 layers relu (20 nodes, 15 nodes, 10 nodes)	92.29%	78%
8	4 layers sigmoid (20 nodes, 15 nodes, 10 nodes, 10 nodes)	68.75%	52%
9	4 layers relu (20 nodes, 15 nodes, 10 nodes, 10 nodes)	95.21%	82%
10	4 layers relu (20 nodes, 15 nodes, 10 nodes, 10 nodes) with dropout layers	77.71%	64%
11	5 layers relu (25 nodes, 20 nodes, 15 nodes, 10 nodes, 10 nodes) with dropout layers	93.75%	82%
12	4 layers relu (25 nodes, 20 nodes, 15 nodes, 10 nodes) with dropout layers	96.45%	84%

of use identifying method practiced in Hindustani Raagdari Music which is referred to as "Gaana Samaya" in Music terminology.

There is no procedure or a set of rules to decide the "Gaana Samaya" for a melody based on a particular Raaga. Experienced musicians are able to define it based on their experience and expert knowledge. This research is focused on how well an ANN could be utilized to achieve this target. For this purpose a suitable pre-processing algorithm, training method, and the infrastructure of an ANN are investigated.

In the proposed system using notation of the melody, pre-process module identify the Aroha, Awaroha, Vadi and Sanwadi Swara of the melody. The training data set is created based on the characteristics of Hindustani Raaga to train an ANN model. A web application is developed to deploy the prototype. The rest of this paper is organized as follows. Section 2 is the literature survey related to this research. Section 3 describes the Design of the System while Sect. 4 discusses the Implementation. Section 5 provides Evaluation and Test Results and finally, Sect. 6 describes Conclusion and Future Work.

2 Literature Survey

Since this research involves study of two domains, background analysis of Hindustani Music and an overview of Artificial Neural Networks will be discussed in this section.

2.1   Hindustani Music

Music is considered as the art of combining vocal or Swara from music instruments (or both) to produce beauty of form, harmony, and expression of emotion. There are many genres of music styles. Hindustani music, Western music, Pop, Rock and Ghazal are some of them. Music is considered a universal language which can express emotions.

Swara. Swara is a Sanskrit word, meaning sound or note. In Hindustani music, there are 7 main Swara called Shuddha Swara. Each Shuddha Swara is traditionally originated to imitate the sound of a different animal, and some have additional meanings of their own [1]. Also, each Swara is associated with one of the seven chakras of the body [1].

There are two main variations in some of these Swara, these are called "Komala" and "Thiwra" There are four Komala Swara Ri, Ga, Da and Ni and Ma is the only Thiwra swara. Komala and Thiwra Swara are denoted as follows,

$$ ඵ ග ධ නි ම' $$

A dot above a letter indicates that the note is sung one octave higher (Uchcha), and a dot below indicates one octave lower (Mandra). Or, if a note with the same name as follows,

Octave higher - ස, ර, ග, ම, ප, ධ, නි

Octave lower - ස ,ර ,ග, ම, ප, ධ, නි

Raaga. According to Indian classical music, Raaga is comparable to a melodic mode in Western music. It is a central feature of classical Indian music. However, it has no direct translation to concepts in the classical Western music. Each Raaga consists of an array of melodic structures with musical motifs and considered to have the ability to affect the emotions of the audience. Raaga provides a musical framework for a musician to build his/her melody [2].

- Every Raaga should have characteristics as follows,
- Raaga should be born from a Thaat
- Raaga consists of at least five Swara
- Raaga should have at least one or more Rasa
- Raaga should have an Aroha and Awaroha
- "Sa" Swara cannot be neglected
- Raaga should have a Vadi and Samvadi Swara
- A Raaga cannot neglect the Swara "Ma" and "Pa" at the same time.

Aroha. Aroha is the ascending pattern of Swara in a Raaga. The pitch increases as this goes up from Shadja (Sa) to the Ucha Shadja (Sa) [3].

e.g. Aroha of kafi Raaga:- ස ,ර ,ග ,ම ,ප ,ධ ,නි ,ස

Awaroha. Awaroha is the descending pattern of Swara in a Raaga. The pitch decreases as this goes from Ucha Shadja (Sa) to the Shadja (Sa) [3].

Eg Awaroha of kafi Raaga:- ස ,නි , ධ ,ප ,ම ,ග , ර ,ස

Vadi. Vadi is the most important Swara of a Raaga. It is not the most played note but refers to a note of special significance. It is usually the Swara which is repeated the greatest number of times, and often it is the Swara on which the singer can pause for a significant time [3].

Samvadi. The Samvadi is the second-most prominent (though not necessarily second-most played) Swara of a Raaga [3].

Gaana Samaya. Nature of the day changes in every minute. Relative to the nature of the day, human nature and feelings are also changing. According to the Hindustani music, every Raaga has a Gaana Samaya, which recommends what time of the day that particular Raaga should be sung. It ensures that the beauty of the Raaga is not be marred by the time of the day it is sung. The Rasa which means sentiments that are evoked by a particular Raaga that the artist is responsible for evoking may be enhanced by following the time-cycle recommendation for Raagas [2].

In summary, playing a melody differ in Gaana Samaya from morning to evening. Each raaga has very particular symbolic associations particularly with the time of day or with the seasons and is also believed to convey a particular aesthetic mood to listeners. As in all the Indian arts, the musician who plays a raga endeavours to convey a certain mood to an audience and to awaken corresponding feelings within them [2].

In Hindustani music, the day time is divided in to 4 parts and night time is divided into 4 parts considering that day time is the duration between sunrise to sunset and night time is the duration between sunset to sunrise.

Day time	Night time
6:00 am- 9:00 am Diva Prathama Praharaya	6:00 pm - 9:00 pm Rathi Prathama Praharaya
9:00 pm - 12:00 am Rathi Dewana Praharaya	9:00 pm - 12:00 am Rathi Dewana Praharaya
12:00 pm – 3:00 pm Diva thewana Praharaya	12:00 am – 3:00 am Rathi thewana Praharaya
3:00pm – 6:00 pm Diva sivwana Praharaya	3:00 am – 6:00 am Rathi sivwana Praharaya

Assuming sunrise at 6:00 am and sunset at 6:00 pm

There have been several research projects to identify the basic characteristics of a song according to the Hindustani Classical Raaga music [4–6].

2.2 Artificial Neural Networks

According to [7], an Artificial Neural Network can be considered as a "computing system made up of a number of simple, highly interconnected processing elements, which process information by their dynamic state response to external inputs". A neural network has many numbers of nodes, and generally, there are 3 kinds of nodes. Input Nodes, Output Nodes, Hidden Nodes. The input nodes take in information, which should be pre-processed to a form which can be numerically expressed. This information is presented as activation values and then passed throughout the network. Based on the connection strengths (weights), inhibition or excitation, and transfer functions, the activation value is passed from node to node. Each of the nodes sums the activation values it receives and modifies the value based on its transfer function.

A deep net is a neural network with a large number of nodes and hidden layers. Owing to deep learning, computation models consisting of several processing layers can easily learn data representations with different levels of abstraction [8].

Deep neural nets widely use backpropagation algorithm as the learning mechanism. In many instances, Backpropagation is used due to shortcomings in other algorithms [7]. Though there are many advantages there are disadvantages like *vanishing gradient* that occurs often in deep learning systems. Due to this problem, there could be issues with the accuracy and the length of training duration.

The cost value is constantly calculated while the training of a neural net is carried out. The cost refers to the difference between the predicted output of the net and the actual output from a set of labelled training data. In order to lower the cost, small adjustments are made to the biases and weights again and again until the potentially lowest value is reached. The neural network tends to train slowly when the gradient is small, and it trains quickly when the gradient is high [9].

2.3 Similar Systems

Every raaga has this "Gaana samaya" which is the best time period to perform that raaga. However, still there is no programme or software system which could able to analyze or understand the particular melody and decide the best time ("Gaana samaya") for that melody. There are similar kinds of research that has been done, as follows.

- Basic Pattern Generation for Kalpana Swara Synthesis Using Graphical Approach [11]

  Many patterns of swaras will be weaved within the boundary of raaga, thaala and laya (or tempo) of music to give a pleasing and soothing effect. This paper presents various algorithms used for generating basic patterns for the "kalpana swara". These basic patterns are widely used while constructing "kalpana swara" [11].

  (* kalpan aswara is raga improvisation within a specific tala in which the musician improvises in the Indian music solfege (sa, ri, ga, ma, pa, da, ni) after completing a composition)

- Method for parametrically sorting music files [12]

  It is a method for sorting music files. A parameter to be used in sorting is selected either by the player or by the user. A random number is generated and Weights are assigned to the parameter and the random number. These values are then used to calculate the sorting criteria for each file. The files are then sorted by their sorting criteria, generating a playlist [12].

- Automatic Raaga Identification System For Carnatic Music Using Hidden Markov Model [6]

  As for as the Human Computer Interactions (HCI) is concerned, there is a broad range of applications in the area of research in respective of Automatic Melakarta Raaga Identification in music. The pattern of identification is the main object for which, the basic mathematical tool is utilized. This paper therefore introduces a procedure for Raaga. Identification with the help of Hidden Markov Models (HMM) which is rather an appropriate approach in identifying Melakarta Raagas.

This proposed approach is based on the standard speech recognition technology by using Hidden continuous Markov Model [6].

- Raaga identification using clustering algorithm [5]

  The frequencies of different Swaras are calculated using the Pitch Detection Algorithm. A study of comparison between the inbuilt Pitch Detection Algorithm and the standard music analysis tool is used to obtain pitch frequency of Swaras. Here, a Clustering Algorithm is proposed to identify the nearest matching Swaras and thereby identifying the Raaga. The Clustering Algorithm is used to test several Raagas and those Raagas identified are found to be accurate [5].

- Object oriented classification and pattern recognition of Indian Classical Ragas [4]

  In this paper, a new method is being proposed for making a catalogue of different melodious audio stream into some specific featured classes based on object oriented modeling. The classes have some unique features to be specified and characterized; depending upon those properties of a particular piece of music it can be classified into different classes and subclasses. The concept is developed considering the non-trivial categorization problem due to the vastness of Indian Classical Music (ICM). It is expected that the novel concept can reduce the complication to the objective analysis of the classification problem of ICM [4].

- An Expert System to Generate Chords for Melodies Composed in Eastern Music Format [10]

  This research has been carried out to find an intelligent system to generate chords for melodies which has been composed without considering chords initially. In western music, melodies are composed alongside with chords which specify the rules for composing. Even though, the concept of a chord is not practiced in Hindustan music, modern musicians are now adapting the chords and use western instruments for great listening experience. The chord generation is considered as the expert knowledge, which is usually carried out by a musician with a trained ear. Therefore, beginners with less experience face difficulties when deciding a chord. In this research, an expert system has been proposed, to generate chords based on music knowledge [10].

3   Design of the System

The first major task in the design of the system is the design of the pre-processing algorithms which can identify the basic characteristics of a song according to the Hindustani Classical Raaga music. These characteristics once numerically expressed will be the outputs of this pre-processing algorithm as well as the inputs for the ANN.

The front end of the system is a web interface which use bootstrap and JavaScript to convert songs in Musical Instrument Digital Interface (MIDI) to music notation. Music notation thus generated is input to the pre-processing algorithm to identify Aroha, Awaroha, Vadi, Sanvadi and the result is given as a string array. A simplified block diagram of the modules which are directly connected to the user interface is shown in Fig. 1.

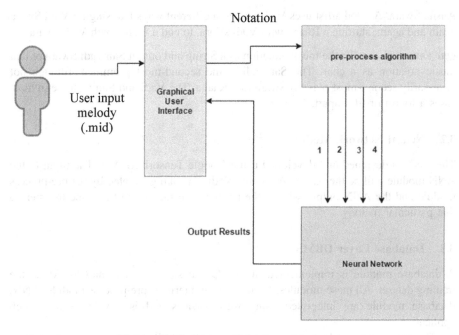

Fig. 1. Block diagram of the proposed system

3.1 Pre-process Module

This module extracts the notes from MIDI file and generate Aroha, Awaroha, Vadi and Sanvadi as outputs. This algorithm consists of four functions.

1. Aroha
2. Awaroha
3. Vadi
4. Sanwadi

gen_Aroha - will take music notation as a String and output Aroha of the music notation as a char array. Aroha is the ascending scale of Swara in a Raaga. The pitch increases as this goes up from Shadja (Sa) to the Ucha Shadja (Sa).

gen_Awaroha - will take music notation as a String and output Awaroha of that music notation as a char array. Awaroha is the descending scale of Swara in a Raaga. The pitch decreases as this goes to from Ucha Shadja (Sa) to the Shadja (Sa).

gen_Vadi - will take music notation as a String and output Vadi Swara of that music notation as a char. Vadi is the most sonant or most important Swara of a Raaga. It is usually the Swara which is repeated the greatest number of times, and often it is the Swara on which the singer can pause for a significant time. The specialty of any Raaga depends on Vadi Swara and because of this, the Vadi Swara is also called the Jeeva Swara or the

Ansha Swara. A good artist uses Vadi Swara in different ways like singing Vadi Swara again and again, starting a Raaga with Vadi swara, to end a Raaga with Vadi swara.

gen_samwadi   - will take music notation as a String and output Samvadi Swara of that music notation as a char. The Samvadi is the second-most prominent (though not necessarily second-most played) Swara of a Raaga. The Vadi and Samvadi are in most cases a fourth or fifth apart.

3.2   Neural Network Module

The ANN is designed and developed using Google Tensorflow API. The input to the ANN module will be the Aroha, Awaroha, Vadi, Sanvadi generated by the pre-process module and the ANN output will be the prediction result of the best time to listen to that particular melody.

3.3   Database Layer DBMS

A database module is implemented in MySQL to store the data and to extract the training dataset. All these modules: front end web interface, pre-process module, ANN, database module are integrated using web services and is developed as a web application.

Though there is evidence of existence of nearly 600 Raaga in classical Hindustani music only 494 could be collected for this research. Currently, there are around 500 Raaga to be found in Sri Lanka. Hibernate ORM Framework has been used for the implementation of the database layer and pre-process. First, it was required to convert all values into numerical values and then those numerical values were input to train the neural network. Then the data normalization process was done and finally, two Comma Separated Values (CSV) files were generated and both having 494 rows.

- Data_In.csv

Fig. 2. Format of the Data_In.csv

- Data_Label.csv

  Format of the Data_In.cvs is shown in Fig. 2,

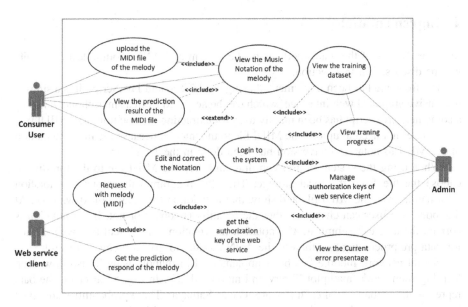

Fig. 3. Use case diagram of the system

There are 3 different kinds of users associate with the system for different use cases. Use case diagram of the system is shown in Fig. 3.

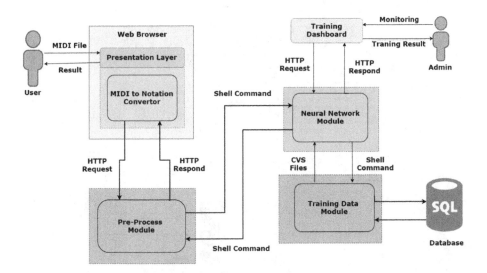

Fig. 4. Overall system design

There are 6 main modules in the proposed system. Interfacing and communication between those main modules are illustrated in Fig. 4 shown below.

4   Implementation

Implementations of the main modules of the system and ANN module testing results will be discussed in this section.

The front end has been implemented using html, CSS, and JavaScript. It is a simple, responsive graphical web interface, which can be accessed from a smartphone, tablet or a computer. Java script has been mainly used for extracting the notation from MIDI file. A user does not need to upload the MIDI file to the internet because the implementation of the MIDI to notation conversion has been done in the JavaScript.

When using the system, a user can drag and drop the MIDI file to the top div, or choose the file from the local storage. Then the program will extract the notation information from the MIDI file and show that notation in the notation text window. At this point, the user can check whether the notation is correct or not. If the notation is correct, the user can submit it. The notation information will be sent to a web service for data pre-processing and then to the ANN module to give a prediction result.

Neural network module has been implemented in python using Tensorflow deep learning framework, mathplot library and numpy library. In Fig. 5 bar chart, the bars represent the probability of each Prahara (Gaana Samaya). These probabilities are given by the neural network module corresponding to the input MIDI file.

Fig. 5. Example of a test MIDI file

Structure of the neural network is shown is Fig. 6.

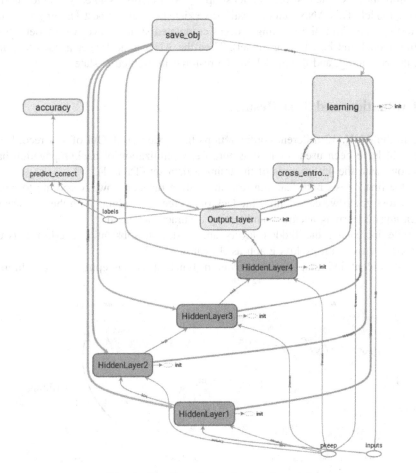

Fig. 6. Structure of neural network module

Hidden Layers. Hidden Layers mainly consist of Input, Weights Tensor, Bias, multiplication function, addition, function Activation function (Relu) and dropout layer.

Output Layer. Output layer is pretty similar to the hidden layers, but output layer does not contain a dropout layer and uses the softmax activation function.

Softmax function is selected as the activation function of output layer because of the binary behaviour of the label dataset (Data_Label.csv). Output tensor of the output layer is a 2nd order Tensor (z x 8)

Learning. For learning this ANN uses the Adam Optimizer. Adam is an optimization algorithm that can be used instead of the classical stochastic gradient descent procedure to update network weights iterative based in training data. Adam was presented by Diederik Kingma and Jimmy Ba.

Saving and restoring ANN model. The tf.train.Saver class provides methods to save and restore models. The tf.saved_model.simple_save function is an easy way to build a tf.saved_model. This ANN automatically saves its status at the best learning rate and best testing rate. After the learning process completed system have two models (best learning model and best testing model). Then the ANN is no longer needed to learn from the beginning, and the model can be restored in prediction state.

5   Evaluation and Test Results

To train the ANN, 12 different configurations have been used. Out of 494 records of Raaga, 44 have been used for testing purpose. Optimization of backpropagation has been done with the 450 records of the training data set (Table 1).

In the first 3 tests both learning rate and testing rates are low. According to cross entropy loss graph we can identify the lack of degree of freedom. With the increase in hidden layers, learning accuracy and testing accuracy increased.

While increasing the hidden layers and nodes, a substantial overfitting issue appeared in cross entropy loss graph as shown in Fig. 7.

It was identified that ReLU activation function is susceptible to overfitting.

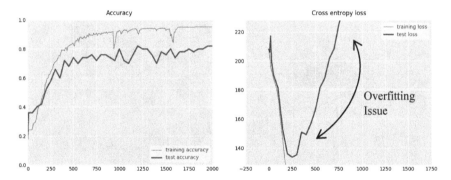

Fig. 7. Overfitting Issue in test 5

Therefore, a dropout mechanism has been added to the hidden layers after test 9. Then overfitting issue was controlled, although accuracy was decreased. In the fully connected 4 hidden layer architecture with sigmoid function showed poor performance. Therefore, testing continued with ReLU activation function with the dropout mechanism. A fully connected 5 hidden layer architecture did not show any improvement relative to the 4 hidden layers. Therefore (test 12) fully connected 4 hidden layers with 4 dropout layers and softmax output layer became the most optimized neural network configuration for this solution. With the variations of nodes finally (test 12) neural network archived 96.45% learning accuracy and 84% test accuracy with stable accuracy curve and cross entropy loss curve after 3000 iterations to 5000 iterations.

5.1   ANN Training Dashboard

Training dashboard has been implemented using TensorBoard feature of the Tensorflow API. It is capable of displaying training accuracy, learning accuracy, data flow path, distribution of the weights and biases of an ANN. A screenshot of the scalars tab of the training dashboard can be seen in Fig. 8. TensorBoard's Scalar Dashboard visualizes scalar statistics that vary over time. Using these two graphs admin can monitor the learning accuracy and cross entropy loss of the ANN real-time.

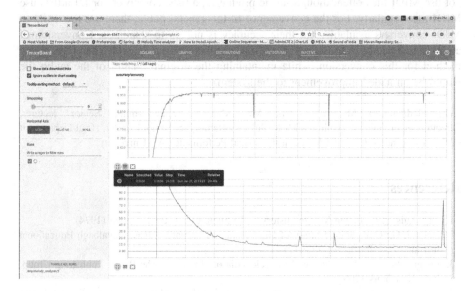

Fig. 8. Accuracy and cross entropy loss graph

6   Conclusion and Future Work

Every melody has an emotional significance and a symbolic association combined with season and time called "Gaana Samaya". This research was carried out to identify the best time to play, sing or listen for any given melody. The melody could have been created using one or more raaga. For this purpose a web application has been created integrating the user interface and an ANN capable of predicting the "Gaana Samaya". The optimum neural network has archived 96.45% learning accuracy and 84% test accuracy.

However, it must be noted that there exist some aspects of the domain of music which is difficult to explain logically. There are many popular controversial theories such as;

- Bilawal Raaga which is very popular among musicians associates Gaana Samaya as day – 1. However, there is another theory that the Bilawal do not have a one specific Gaana Samaya, it can be used in any Prahara both day and night.
- Jathi of Bageshwari Raaga is said to be Odhav - Sampoorna(5-7), though there is another idea that Jathi of Bageshwari is sampurna – sampurna (7-7).

Therefore, in the domain of music one problem can have both successful and controversial answers at the same time. A total number of 494 Raaga data has been used for the learning and testing process:,for training (450) and testing (44). However, there is a large number of Raagas composed from ancient times which have been destroyed or difficult to find. This work can be carried out further by finding more details of Raagas. Increase in the number of Raagas may leads to better testing accuracy.

In the proposed system, users can only upload MIDI files. The general public does not use MIDI files often, though music producers, artists, composers or DJ artists use MIDI files regularly. For the convenience of the general public there are few MP3 to MIDI converters available, but their accuracy is not up to standards. Conversion of audio files (melody/instruments) into MIDI is still at a research level. Therefore, a new method for this conversion, while maintaining the original quality of the audio file would be an added improvement to the system.

Acknowledgements. Music advisers Mr. Mahinda Senevirathne; Senior lecturer, Director/Career Guidance Unit and Mr K. Sujeewa Ranasighe; Senior lecturer, Head/Department of the North Indian Classical Music at the Visual Performance Art University.

References

1. Nijenhuis, E.T.: Indian Music: History and Structure. E.J. Brill, Leiden (1974)
2. Binathi, G.: Comparative Study of Hindustani and Carnatic Ragas. Dayalbagh Educational Institute, Dayalbagh, Agra (2012)
3. Lochtefeld, J.G.: The Illustrated Encyclopedia of Hinduism. The Rosen Publishing Group, Inc., New York (2002)
4. Chakraborty, S., De, D.: Object oriented classification and pattern recognition of Indian classical ragas. In: 1st International Conference on Recent Advances in Information Technology (RAIT) (2012)
5. Kumar, K.P., Rao, M.S.: Raaga identification using clustering algorithm. In: International Conference on Electrical, Electronics, and Optimization Techniques (2016)
6. Prasad Reddy, P.V.G.D., Rao, B.T., Sudha, K.R.: Automatic Raaga identification system for Carnatic music using hidden Markov model. Glob. J. Comput. Sci. Technol. **11** (2012)
7. Dongare, A.D., Kharde, R.R., Kachare, A.D.: Introduction to artificial neural network. Int. J. Eng. Innov. Technol. (2012)
8. LeCun, Y., Bengio, Y., Hinton, G.: Deep learning. Nature **521**, 436–444 (2015)
9. Crunch'n Numbers: Deep learning-convolutional neural networks for image classification (2017) http://john-cd.com/blog/2017/03/08/Deep-Learning. Accessed 20 September 2017
10. Yasith Chathuranga, E.A.D., Ratnayake, H.U.W., Premaratne, I.A.: An expert system to generate chords for melodies composed in eastern music format. In: IEEE International Conference on Computer, Communications and Electronics, pp. 501–504 (2017)
11. Padyana, M., Thomas, B.A.: Basic pattern generation for Kalpana Swara synthesis using graphical approach. Int. J. Comput. Sci. Trends Technol. **4**(3), 384–388 (2016)
12. Hartley, P.: Method for parametrically sorting music files. Google Patents (2001)

Game Theory

Invoke Artificial Intelligence and Machine Learning for Strategic-Level Games and Interactive Simulations

Nishan Chathuranga Wickramarathna
and Gamage Upeksha Ganegoda[✉]

Faculty of Information Technology,
University of Moratuwa, Katubedda, Sri Lanka
nishan.chathuranga@outlook.com, upekshag@uom.lk

Abstract. Computer games are an important sector of the digital economy, computer and entertainment industry are very sophisticated in many ways in the current context of technology. They've gone beyond entertainment needs, and the computer game paradigm and technology together are now increasingly used in education, training, storytelling, and wherever it's necessary to create an appealing and engaging environment. More realism in virtual and artificial environments and more real interfaces to the users can be considered as two main advantages that we get using these techniques. Instead of pre-defined hard coded scripts driving these environments, we will be able to create just the environment and its relative mechanics, so the artificial intelligence could introduce tailored challenges and scenarios to the environment. This paper proposes a Behavioral Driven Procedural Content Generation methodology together with Ternary Neural Networks to be used in interactive strategy-based simulations for effective decision making. This is vital because current approaches like Experience Driven Procedural Content Generation algorithms can be very flexible and one small change could trigger complex changes in the system. Using another model created by using player behavior will be specifying the clamping conditions so the AI is capable of stabilizing itself.

Keywords: Artificial intelligence · Computer games · Machine learning · Simulations · Procedural content generation

1 Introduction

Computer algorithms that can make games work are almost as old as the computer games itself, but their usability is limited because they cannot generate terrain, levels and other artwork or game content. The next big problem that increasing need to solve how to use sophisticated artificial intelligence techniques like machine learning and neural networks to design new games and simulations that will go pass human imagination. But in some areas like health care, ethics and law, inability to comprehend traditional and precedent approaches in a clear weakness when it comes to use AI, but in computer games, that very thing is strength that can push the boundaries and introduce new levels of creativity. Not to mention the high reduction in cost of

© Springer Nature Singapore Pte Ltd. 2019
J. Hemanth et al. (Eds.): SLAAI-ICAI 2018, CCIS 890, pp. 129–143, 2019.
https://doi.org/10.1007/978-981-13-9129-3_10

development life cycle. Key areas that are identified as current and most promising areas are as follows [1].

1. Search and planning
2. Automated narratives
3. Modeling players
4. Non-player characters' behavior manipulations
5. Game designing with the aid of AI
6. Games as benchmarks for AI

Main reasons and motivations for this review is to give proper and structured knowledge about existing AI related techniques and how they can be used for commercial games and simulations to enhance the user experience and for better problem modeling. AI in common commercial computer games is mainly are focusing on the interactions between the game and the player, that being said they are also cannot be considered as high-level AI programs because what they do is simulating intelligence that the player will eventually consider as real AI. Main research areas as per the end user has been given in Fig. 1.

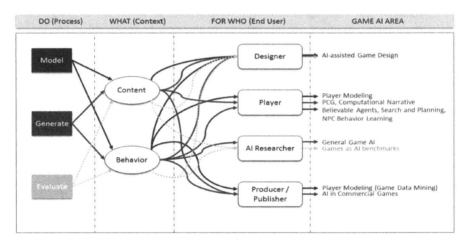

Fig. 1. End user perspective of the identified game AI areas. Each AI area follows a process (model, generate or evaluate) under a context (content or behavior) [1].

Approaches to learn NPC behavior mainly focuses on the use of techniques like reinforcement learning, and to learn behaviors that games can be played evolutionary algorithms like temporal difference learning can be used [2].

Another effective aspect of AI for games is techniques to analyze and interpret data generated by users; this is also demanded by the industry. A linear unchangeable static way is used to design traditional computer games. But game industry realized only recently that computer games can be created in such a way that it can target to meet user expectations like any other custom software and then it can be marketable highlighting those qualities. Problem faced is that in spite of all these researches and theories that are being put forth, games that are able to adapt and deliver personalized content to the user expectations and deliver tailored content is still a developing idea. No major commercial games use AI to study player behavior and use it to dynamically change the game narrative [3].

If there is an ability to create virtual environments or game worlds that are and more reactive more relatable to individual users (game players), what's needed is the ability to collect data on those players for understanding their way of play. This means that enemies will be able to learn your pattern of combat and challenge you, Non-player characters will feel the naturality in conversing with the player, narratives will adapt and push users for more interactive goals.

Game theory; a powerful tool to analyze and design distributed algorithms that where you have little knowledge over the environment. Although it is considered as a non-evolving timeline, because the players pursue their own goals [4].

1.1 AI as a General-Purpose Technology (GPT)

There are some early concrete indications of these innovations guarantee, the current jumps in AI. Execution being the most conspicuous illustration. Be that as it may, in the meantime, estimated efficiency development in previous decade is being decreased fundamentally. This deceleration of efficiency is extensive, reducing efficiency development considerably or a greater amount of its level in the decade going before the stoppage. It is far reaching, having happened all through, numerous substantial developing economies too.

With the development of deep neural networks and other new approaches that are discussed later in this text it is observable that it is possible to overcome the problems in hand. These will be surely helpful to automating manufacturing processes, will provide better decision-making concepts and will be final invention of mankind [5].

In the near future it is predicted that it will connect human reasoning and clever systems to achieve a more profitable society. Altogether, as ascertained that computerized reasoning and AI could contribute up to $15.7 trillion to the worldwide economy by 2030. This is by considering the total of development crosswise over medicinal services, vehicles, monetary administrations, transportation, coordination, retail, utilities, military and assembling [6]. Development of artificial intelligence enabled players for complex real time strategy (RTS) games is currently in many ways an evolving trend. In computer games, game elements that can interrelate and converse with uses is a must because in that way the players will feel immersive and engaging environment [7, 8].

1.2 Adaptive Educational Games

The problem of integrating learning content into learning games has been approached by researches in many perspectives and angles, a common approach for this is still not available. A system has been proposed as an integration of Instructional Management System - Learning Design (IMSLD) during the learning process design, on one hand as a consistent subject specific language between the educators and the game developer or development team, because of the similarity between computer game design and

IMSLD elements, and because of, to adapt and evolve the game to the preferences and expectations of the user [9].

Learners who prefer to be taught are differentiated using these methodologies "inductively" by deducing rules and principles, and foundations, or "deductive," presenting them with these principles, their outcomes, and utilities. By defining the style of learning (of the learner), the corresponding learning activities can be easily adjusted [10].

AI is used to improve gameplay of a player and to support player's entertainment; this is a well-known fact and always been there in the field of computer games. Starting with player modeling, player motion, lighting for adaptive environments, camera control for intelligent behavior to non-player characters and their abilities [12].

AI in computer games should adjust the game world to player's expectations and settings by manipulating proper variables for challenge and entertainment. If the player is not challenged by the game, game engine should understand this and increase the difficulty of the game, and if the player is challenged game should lover the difficulty in the game. In current games this is done by predefined values that are set by the player. The game engine should use information provided by the player previously to model the behavior using age, gender or preferences using monitoring mechanisms while the game is running; i.e. dynamically [13].

The assessor will inform the adaptive mechanism of his/her current knowledge, for example, when mastering the addition operations. The next level indicates the operation of subtraction and so on. For a player who performed well in earlier stage, the adaptive mechanism chooses the most difficult learning activity for the next stage [11].

Here the discussion is about how to use Artificial Intelligence and Machine Learning to model player behavior and use it in decision generating systems as simulations. Forthcoming sections of this review paper is organized and categorized into following key aspects. Sections two introduces Artificial Neural Networks to be used in commercial games and how to advance their efficiency and how Markov Decision Processes improve decision making and understanding the situation in hand properly. third section emphasize how Procedural Content Generation can be used to model user experience. Self-play reinforcement learning and importance is described in section four. How to use artificial intelligence for virtual agents has been analyzed in section five and emphasizes the collaborative discourse theory as assistive mechanism to users while introducing mind attribution to model human-like characters. Section six describes an efficient bio monitoring system to gather data about the user. Section seven discusses all the aspects and sums up the subject and concludes the paper with major findings in section eight.

2 Neural Networks and Decision Processes

Use of deep convolutional neural networks has recently been having huge advances. Handling various input sizes in also a challenge with Deep Neural Networks (DNN) and to handle the game dynamics. As solutions, two main ideas are being discussed. The first idea was a set of designed features. One with the highest score is chosen after considering all possible action or outcomes. The second concept is to implement a DNN that takes input as a session of frames. It will be able to extend the architecture for analyzing images and visual content. For the convolutions to be applied, the game is coded in from of a stack matrix.

2.1 Ternary Neural Networks

The storage requirements and computational requirement for DNNs are much higher. Because of this issue their usability in situation where you have limited resources is limited. Ternary Neural Networks (TNN) could be the answer to make DNNs more resource efficient. It uses teacher student approach where the teacher network is trained with stochastically activating ternary neurons. Both networks in terms of design are having the same architecture. Student network weights are the terrorized that of the teacher networks weights. Ternarization Performance – Student networks ability to imitate teacher network. Classification Performance – Benchmarking has been done with several datasets, error rate on MNIST, which is the most studied dataset in deep learning is 1.67% [14].

New hardware that can be tailored to this TNNs can be built. In this study, proposes TNN for deep resource learning applications. To design special hardware and ensure their availability for integrated applications that lacks resources, a student-teacher training approach for TNNs is used. TNNs has been demonstrated the high performance in terms of use of resources efficiently and accuracy in recent experiments [14].

2.2 Markov Decision Processes

Using MDPs and decision models that are able to learn from large data sets and generate alternative decision paths via simulations and predicting multiple scenarios can help decision making processes much more efficient and the ability to understanding the situation in hand properly.

By designing problem formulations, it is theorized that the ability to approximate optimal decisions even in complex environments and finally reaching or pass human understanding and decision-making abilities is possible. By combining humans and AI programs, it is believed to maximize the potential of such systems. It has the ability to functions as advanced telemedicine services and decision support systems everywhere.

Sequence of iterated decisions are made overtime, Markov decision processes (MDPs) are one of most realistic and accurate ways to be implemented in an uncertain dynamic environment to get optimal policies or decisions [2, 15].

The Markov approach provides a structured and deterministic method to evaluate probabilistic actions over non-principled and uncertain scenarios. Because of limited resources and unpredictable human behavior, and variable response times this is considered to be the most ideal [15].

MDP has shown that it is possible to model a problem efficiently in a virtual environment and can be used to make decisions to handle complex problems.

3 Procedural Content Generation

Procedural Content Generation (PCG) is semiautomatic or sometimes automatically generating levels, characters, maps, textures and narratives or quests, terrain, stories, dialogue, rule sets and weapons through algorithms [1]. PCG is used in computer games to improve the storyline that can be re-playable, providing a new scenario or narrative every time the player tries to play the game and effectively helpful to reduce cost, effort, to save memory or storage space.

Argument expands beyond entertainment. These game-based concepts are used for simulations, training and education/decision support systems. Militaries need dynamic and previously undefined scenarios to train and simulate the outcomes of tactical decision that they make on the battlefield or any other means.

3.1 Experience-Driven PCG

Important area for human computer interaction. According to demand and need of the user, user experience is more personalized via real time adjustments and cognitive modeling.

The Experience Driven Procedural Content Generation (EDPCG) (described in detail in Fig. 2) is generic method that can be applied in many areas of human computer interaction. Stages of emotional behaviors and detecting affective behaviors for representing affect-driven systems are very important for closed loop human computer interaction. A game should be adaptive to the player which has not been achieved previously where only the illusion has been given of AI via NPCs in number of games studied such as pong, Tetris, FPS and games for education [16].

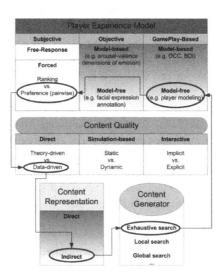

Fig. 2. The EDPCG framework in detail. The gradient grayscale-colored boxes represent a continuum of possibilities between the two ends of the box while white boxes represent discrete, exclusive, options within the box [16].

First, what's needed is to redefine the content, by dividing game into blocks, so that at any given point based on the player need, the model can search through the locks and present the player with content that will optimize the experience of the player. Main components of the model can be segmented into four main steps. Modeling Player Experience, often modeled as a function of game content and player's characteristics. Content Quality, the content that are being generated by model is analyzed and related to the modeled experience. Representation, to maximize performance and efficiency, robustness and reliability of the content is represented accordingly. Content Generator, the content space is searched for blocks that enhances the experience with respect to the model generated.

The most straightforward way to come up with an experimental model is to get direct input from players about experience they had a model that experience in evaluation functions. Subjective Player Experience Model (PEM) only take into account these self-reports and reports that are coming indirectly from the expert systems or external observers of the algorithms. Subjective PEMs are (most of them) are based closely on free reaction of players while playing the game or data retrieved by force via questionnaires etc.

In Objective PEM, real-time player tracking with recorded player behavior will be investigated for modeling. There are many ways to do this. Most of them are physiological signals, such as respiration, skin responses, electromyography, motion tracking and in some cases speech [17].

Main concept behind Gameplay-based PEM actions of the player is linked to experience that he might gather since game affect the cognitive processes of the player and his focus.

3.2 Search-Based PCG

Search-based procedural content generation can be considered as interesting field with two main components. First being a test function that does not reject or accept the proposed content, but it assigns a value using an evaluation function to the content. Second being the ability to generate new content by evaluation the value given to the previous content thus producing new content with higher grades.

The search-based PCG may always do not have to be coupled together with evolutionary computation. Here also it is possible to apply heuristic search strategies as well. If the search space of a game is being traversed it must be represented regardless of the algorithms that has been chosen to grade the content, key decision that is made here is the design of the evaluation function. To represent the content in the search space the answer to the question, how to map the genotypes (data that are being handle by evolutionary algorithm) to phenotypes (data that are evaluated by the evolutionary algorithm). In a game context, a genotype is the instructions to create a level of a game, where a phenotype can be considered as an actual game level.

Evaluation function assigns a grade or a scalar to the content items that are being generated. The grade accurately reflects the suitability of the content to use in the game and can be considered as the negative of a "cost" function.

4 Self-play Reinforcement Learning

Now let's look into the problem of mastering a concept, or given set of goals, ultimately a computer game without using human knowledge on the subject. So far, all these techniques that is presented requires human supervision or human interaction with the system/algorithm to perform its function efficiently. The long-term target of AI is a computer algorithm that can self-learn, AlphaGo AI of DeepMind became the world's first computer program to win the GO game by defeating the world champion.

But how? Search tree of this AI evaluated the optimum positions and picked moves using DNNs, both supervised learning and reinforcement learning has been used to construct this. Human expert moves (in Go game) has been used to train the algorithm using supervised learning and from self-play; using reinforcement learning. This is a breakthrough in computer AIs, which is a reinforcement learning algorithm which can learn without the guidance of humans, human data or knowledge about the rules of the domain. It had given access to only the rules of the game. Algorithms learned the game by playing the game against itself becoming its own teacher [18].

This new approach is using two DNNs: one to return move possibilities namely the policy network and another to return position evaluations, the value network. Supervised learning was used to train the policy network initially, to predict expert human selections and moves with high accuracy, then the value network is predicted to winner of the game by playing the game with itself and trained itself by using that outcomes [18]. It took three days to complete the training shown in Fig. 3. The same reinforcement self-learning approach also can be used for the games Chess and Shogi by generalizing [19].

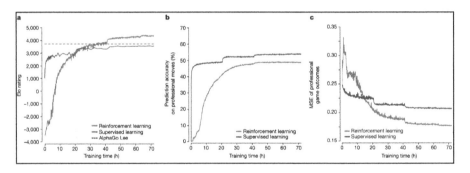

Fig. 3. Evaluations of AlphaGo Zero. a. Self-play reinforcement learning performance. b. Accuracy of the predictions over human expert moves. c. Mean Squared Error of human expert gameplay outcomes [18].

This utilize this new approach for simulations, better forecasting models, better predictions algorithms for utilizations in many areas, as an example space exploration and military need can be taken as high priority problems that human race face in the present day can be addressed. Disaster management and humanitarian relief missions can be well formed if this type of technology is at for our disposal.

5   Artificial Intelligence for Virtual Agents

Virtual agent in a computer game is commonly referred to is a human represented in graphical entity, mostly in three-dimensional form. These agents expected to be realistic including expressions and communicative abilities. Autonomous behavior control systems and algorithms has to integrated with these agents to mimic human behavior. There are algorithms even to control eye movements (eye gaze) of these agents. In the future, it is expected to develop tools and systems that allows these agents to be freely reactive within a virtual environment [20].

One important research area in this domain is distributed cooperative control of multi-agent systems, which is used in very large number of applications including hazardous environment exploring, disaster management by search and rescue, surveillance for military and reconnaissance etc. [21].

The virtual agents that are in games or virtual environments should have all these functionalities. In addition, they should overcome the problems that they are faced today. Mainly these agents could be NPCs, or any other object that will be independently operational but could be manipulated via player's actions.

Planning the motion of these agents is as important as their behavior. As an example, simulating the behavior of group of people have large number of applications such as emergency evacuation, personal training, urban planning etc. [21]. To ensure the realistic or intelligent behavior of these agents, collision free path planning is a must. The Multi-Agent Navigation Graph data structure is used to generate these paths and if integrated with simulations and strategy games, the accuracy of the results generated could be drastically increased as shown in Fig. 4.

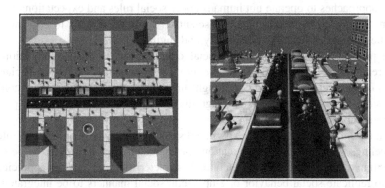

Fig. 4. Crowd simulation with moving agents in an environment with buildings and sidewalks, cars are dynamic obstacles, Multi-agent Navigation Graph system performing navigation with 200 agents [23].

This algorithm calculates the maximal distance or space for a group of agents that are moving with different goals and does not in need of separate path planning mechanism. Local and global collision avoiding mechanisms are present in this algorithm to adaptive and dynamic agent behavior. Using continuum dynamics-based crowd behavior simulations is a new approach in this domain [22]. Even though this system addresses the problem of local collision, it does not guarantee the global collision avoidance because the path of each agent needs to be computed separately.

Proximity of the agent to nearest site from the 2nd nearest agent is used to plan the local planning. A second order Voronoi diagram is used to calculate the closest agent [23]. Voronoi diagrams are the main proximity data structure in geometry in motion planning [24, 25]. One interesting emerging concept is using the fundamental driving forces of human-human collaboration theories to human computer interaction. Collaborative discourse theory is one of the major research areas that will help the intelligent systems to have better interactions with humans. Imagine two humans working on one task that involves a shared context of some sort like a spreadsheet, then replace one of the human users with a system.

In a computer-generated simulation may be in a virtual environment for a complex problem or scenario may have many outcomes and many options. If there are no guidance and since these types of complex systems cannot be simplified any further, another system to guide the user is proposed. The agent has to have some model about the problem domain and the tasks and should carry out a conversation about them to eliminate conflicts, this is known as the discourse state. Collaborator should have an accurate discourse state and an algorithm to update it [26].

When it comes to modeling human-like agents in a virtual setting, the uncanny valley theory is of great assistance. Main idea is to illustrate how complex human-like agents can introduce or mimic strong feelings once they have reached a high level of realistic behavior while maintaining imperfections as well.

Attribution of some human mental capabilities is very important when it comes to modeling human-like characters. Most modern computers and robots follow a goal directed approaches to operate but humans apply social rules and expectations for their decision making. Some researchers and scientists apply these rules to AIs and introduced the concept of machine personality and digital mind.

The primary cause for modeling social cognition and emotion perception in a human replica can be recognized via *uncanny valley* model [27]. Digital social cognition is one aspect of this study, although, the agents in a computer game could be considered as a vessel for computer programs or scripted content and if not properly tuned could appear as a nonhuman behavior.

Even though the results of this experiment showed that many people like to interact, share feelings with human-like replications or characters, but want them to be operational within a given limited set of behavioral characteristics and may not appreciate the ability to replicate social behavior or empathetic social manners to be integrated with them [27].

Digital systems with the power to calculate and demonstrate feelings, or at least reproduce some form of emotional cognitive ability has been given new ethical standards [28]. Process has already begun; some people have shown that expectations and social rules can be integrated with robots and other goal driven systems [29].

6   Relationship with Biometric Data

As described earlier in Sect. 3, recording human vital signs via sensors has to be done to gather data about the player experience and player behavior. Data gathered from these sensory platforms are not as much of a representation of the player because no sensor is smart enough to capture human feelings or no evolutionary algorithm has the complexity of human brain. So, we need to identify what features to be mapped to an evolutionary algorithm so it will be able to create a player experience model to be used in behavior driven procedural content generation. Elevation of heart rate, increased respiration rate, certain brain activities can be identified as and mapped to emotional states of the player. Movement of body and intensive heart rate data combination could reveal energy consumption of the body [30].

But all these sensor platforms have to connected to the body from multiple connections, leaving no room for portability. Portable system to monitor heart rate, oxygen saturation of blood, breathing patterns of infants has been developed but even that has sensors connected with physical connections to the processing platform [31].

A multisensory platform with wireless capabilities has been introduced that implements multiple sensors to acquire data, digital and analog signal processing abilities, calculate secondary parameters from primary data (use ECG to get heart rate.) and transmit data.

Major system components of the sensor platform are shown in Fig. 5. Of course, this level of complex system is not required to a game platform but the portability and efficiency introduced in this system can be utilized to any sensor network.

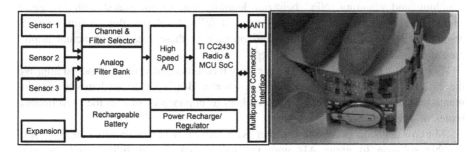

Fig. 5. Top level diagram of sensor platform (left) and assembled device (folded) (right) [32].

Current similar devices are consisting of rigid components, but this device is flexible. Multiple layers in the device ensured reduction in size and comfort as a wearable as shown in Fig. 5 (right). For this to work properly, firmware with buffers, signal processing, signal conditioning capabilities with efficient power supply systems has to be integrated. This system uses an accelerometer, a thermistor and to measure the user's ECG [32].

This system is just a data acquisition device. When it comes to computer games, the processing of this data has to be analyzed and used to reflect user behavior and the AI must be capable of properly mapping the outcomes to the gameplay timeline.

7 Discussion

Connecting virtual and physical worlds is not an easy task. With aid of machine learning and neural networks human race can push the boundaries of decision-making systems. Strategy games are important in this aspect because they demand high level of thinking and planning to play them. The game itself has to generate challenging environment for the players (if it is a simulation: to the users) otherwise overtime the players will be able to learn and defeat the underlying algorithms are fake AIs that are just sticking into pre-defined routines.

Militaries, space exploration, drug testing etc. are largely depending on computer simulations but use of human factor to these algorithms is still an underdeveloped area. Since both strategy level games and simulations in this context can be put into a one container so problems faced by both areas can addressed via common set of solutions.

This paper proposes a methodology to apply machine learning to track and analyze the behavior of the users or players and make the computer game adapt to them. It also proposes to user ternary neural networks to implement this in applications because efficient management of resources in a portable environment is highly recommended. Findings of this review can be applied successfully to the interactive simulations where the decisions are made based on predictions and strategic analysis. A new concept called *Behavior Driven Procedural Content Generation* is introduced as a new research area and/or as a branch to Experience Driven PCG.

Game AI can be integrated to control the context or the behavior of the game. Designer and use AI assistance to design the game. For the player experience enhancement, player modeling, PCG, computational narrative, believable agents, searching and planning, NPC behavior learning can be integrated with the game engines. AI in commercial games is not yet fully developed due to limitation of resources. Research has been done and popular in these areas while actual implementation issues still needs to addressed.

Use of Ternary Neural Networks is highly recommended when it comes to improve the efficiency while still using existing hardware. But layer driven hardware implementations are also introduced by researchers to enhance or sustain the performance issues of TNNs.

Markov decision processes together with ternary neural networks can provide a feasible solution to game AIs with predictive analysis capabilities and dynamic decision-making processes. The basic idea behind this concept is to analyze a problem from the user's perspective and provide the solutions (can be one or many solutions) that is most relevant to the current context. The problem that one person faces, can be different from someone else. As a solution, the system is forced to maintain a track of not only user experience but also user behavior, hence the Behavior Driven PCG.

AlphaGo Zero computer demonstrated high accuracy of self-learning, without any human involvement to the learning process. Another interesting input could be if the AI can map the feelings of the user which are responses to the AI's actions. This data then can be used to model human-like characters and these characters will be able to mimic human emotions. To maintain mutual understanding between AI and the user, a guidance agent can be implemented as a low-level AI, which will assist the high-level

AI and the user simultaneously to maintain communication and to keep the required amount of interactivity as described in Sect. 5.

All the characters and object in this virtual environment can be treated as virtual agents and can be manipulated via computer algorithms [33]. Goal is to use artificial intelligence equipped with all these described functions together with sensor network to monitor important vital signs of the subject to generate a model of the player and customize starting from application interfaces up to entire game or simulation itself. Most of the next generation games and interactive graphical simulations will be based on Virtual Reality and Augmented Reality [34]. So, finding better ways to interface and integrate these systems will be the key to address complex problems which will be faced by human race in the future.

8 Conclusion

As the popularity of computer games are increasing, novel ways to analyze and deliver user tailored content becomes the next level upgrade to game mechanics. Artificial Neural Networks and Procedural Content Generation can be used to achieve the required level of advancements to computer games; strategic level games must use this because they can be converted into interactive simulations that can be used as decision support systems for various causes like strategy planning for military and space exploration.

All the necessary research areas and technologies has been identified and elaborated as per the current state of them. Wide range of numerous aspects have been evaluated with familiar concepts like reinforcement leaning up to mind attribution. Still many more improvements await but the main idea of the approach is to show that systems which can record behavioral data and demonstrate human-like behavior by using that data are possible.

By using all or some these approaches, a new research area has been identified as *Behavior Driven PCG*, where the game engine AI will collect and analyze user behavior and customizes the environment according to the user. The fundamental human desire to control their environment is the key force here, even the content is generated and tailored to user preference, still the notion of control is powerful that actual control. Also, this personalization helps to stop information overload in the system. Game designers will not have design everything like game environment and characters, the integrated AI will take care of many things saving money and time.

Acknowledgement. This review paper is built and extends on currently underway and previously published research papers and surveys that were put forth by referenced authors. The author of this review would like to thank the supervisor for her useful comments and immense guidance given in need.

References

1. Yannakakis, G.N., Togelius, J.: A panorama of artificial and computational intelligence in games. IEEE Trans. Comput. Intell. AI Games **7**(4), 317–335 (2015)
2. Beck, R., Pauker, S.G.: The Markov process in medical prognosis. Med. Decis. Mak. **3**(4), 419–458 (1983)
3. Lucas, S.M., Mateas, M., Preuss, M., Spronck, P., Togelius, J.: Artificial and computational intelligence in games (Dagstuhl Seminar 12191). In: Dagstuhl Reports, vol. 2, pp. 43–70, no. 5 (2012)
4. Lucas, S.M., Mateas, M., Preuss, M., Spronck, P., Togelius, J.: Artificial and computational intelligence in games: integration. In: Seminar: 1998 ACM Subject Classification I.2.1 Artificial Intelligence – Games, 25–30 January 2015
5. Agrawal, A., Gans, J., Goldfarb, A.: What to expect from artificial intelligence. Sloan Management Review (2017)
6. Brynjolfsson, E., Rock, D., Syverson, C.: Artificial intelligence and the modern productivity paradox: a clash of expectations and statistics. NBER Working Paper No. 24001, November (2017)
7. Kim, M., Kim, K., Kim, S., Anind, K.D.: Performance evaluation gaps in a real-time strategy game between human and artificial intelligence players. IEEE Access **6**, 13575–13586 (2018)
8. Perez-Liebana, D., Samothrakis, S., Togelius, J., Lucas, S., Schaul, T.: General video game AI: competition, challenges and opportunities. In: Proceedings of AAAI Conference on Artificial Intelligence, pp. 4335–4337 (2016)
9. Baldiris, S., Graf, S., Fabregat, R.: Dynamic user modeling and adaptation based on learning styles for supporting semi-automatic generation of IMS learning design. In: ICALT, 11th IEEE International Conference on Advanced Learning Technologies, 6–8 July 2011, Athens, Georgia, USA
10. Gardner, H.: Multiple Intelligences: The Theory in Practice. Basic Books, New York (1993)
11. Hamdaoui, N., Idrissi, M.K., Bennani, S.: AMEG: adaptive mechanism for educational games based on IMSLD and artificial intelligence (2015)
12. Herik, H.J., Donkers, H.H.L.M., Spronck, P.H.M.: Opponent modelling and commercial games. In: Proceedings of the IEEE Symposium on Computational Intelligence and Games (CIG'05) (2005)
13. Hamdaoui, N., Idrissi, M.K., Bennani, S.: Serious games in education, towards the standardization of the teaching-learning process. In: EMET, 18–20 July 2014
14. Alemdar, H., Leroy, V., Prost-Boucle, A., Pétrot, F.: Ternary neural networks for resource-efficient AI applications
15. Bennett, C.C., Hauser, K.: Artificial intelligence framework for simulating clinical decision-making: a markov decision process approach. Artif. Intell. Med. **57**, 9–19 (2013)
16. Yannakakis, G.N., Togelius, J.: Experience-driven procedural content generation. IEEE Trans. Affect. Comput. **2**(3), 147–161 (2011)
17. Picard, R.W., Vyzas, E., Healey, J.: Toward machine emotional intelligence: analysis of affective physiological state. IEEE Trans. Pattern Anal. Mach. Intell. **23**(10), 1175–1191 (2001)
18. Silver, D., et al.: Mastering the game of Go without human knowledge. Nature **550**, 354–358 (2007)
19. Silver, D., et al.: Mastering chess and shogi by self-play with a general reinforcement learning algorithm (2017)

20. Das, A., Hasan, M.M.: Eye gaze behavior of virtual agent in gaming environment by using artificial intelligence. In: 2013 International Conference on Electrical Information and Communication Technology (EICT) (2013)
21. Ge, X., Han, Q., Ding, D., Zhang, X., Ning, B.: A survey on recent advances in distributed sampled-data cooperative control of multi-agent systems. Neurocomputing **275**, 1684–1701 (2018)
22. Tu, X., Terzopoulos, D.: Artificial fishes: physics, locomotion, perception, behavior. In: Glassner, A. (ed.) SIGGRAPH 1994: Proceedings of the 21st Annual Conference Series on Computer Graphics and interactive techniques, 24–29 July 1994, Orlando, Florida, pp. 43–50. ACM SIGGRAPH. ACM Press. ISBN 0-89791-667-0
23. Sud, A., Andersen, E., Curtis, S., Lin, M., Manocha, D.: Real-time path planning for virtual agents in dynamic environments (2013)
24. Okabe, A., Boots, B., Sugihara, K.: Spatial Tessellations: Concepts and Applications of Voronoi diagrams. Wiley, New York (1992)
25. Choset, H., Burdick, J.: Sensor based motion planning: the hierarchical generalized Voronoi graph. In: Algorithms for Robot Motion and Manipulation, pp. 47–61. AK Peters (1996)
26. Rich, C., Sidner, C.L., Lesh, N.: Applying collaborative discourse theory to human–computer interaction. AI Mag. **22**(4), 15–26 (2001)
27. Stein, J.-P., Ohler, P.: Venturing into the uncanny valley of mind—the influence of mind attribution on the acceptance of human-like characters in a virtual reality setting. Cognition **160**, 43–50 (2017). https://doi.org/10.1016/j.cognition.2016.12.010
28. Waytz, A., Gray, K., Epley, N., Wegner, D.M.: Causes and consequences of mind perception. Trends Cogn. Sci. **14**, 383–388 (2010)
29. Nass, C., Moon, Y.: Machines and mindlessness: social responses to computers. J. Soc. Issues **56**(1), 81–103 (2000)
30. Halsey, L.G., et al.: Acceleration versus heart rate for estimating energy expenditure and speed during locomotion in animals: tests with an easy model species, homo sapiens. Zoology (Jena) **111**(3), 231–241 (2008)
31. Neuman, M.R.H., et al.: Cardiopulmonary monitoring at home: the CHIME monitor. Physiol. Meas. **22**(2), 267–286 (2001)
32. Chuo, Y., et al.: Mechanically flexible wireless multisensor platform for human physical activity and vitals monitoring. IEEE Trans. Biomed. Circuits Syst. **4**, 281–294 (2010)
33. Niazi, M.A., Hussain, A., Kolberg, M.: Verification & validation of agent based simulations using the VOMAS (virtual overlay multi-agent system) approach
34. Lugmayr, A., Zhu, K., Ma, X.: Artificial intelligence meets virtual and augmented realities

.

Ontology Engineering

An Ontological Approach for Knowledge Representation of Dental Extraction Forceps

Shanmuganathan Vasanthapriyan[(✉)]

Department of Computing and Information Systems,
Sabaragamuwa University of Sri Lanka, Belihuloya, Sri Lanka
priyan@appsc.sab.ac.lk

Abstract. Tooth extraction is a common surgical procedure in the dental field. If the procedure is carried out without proper knowledge about the tooth and the extracting instruments, it may lead to complexity on extraction procedure or even cause damages to the patients' jaws. Therefore, the information and knowledge must be provided in a structured and complete way and in a context specific manner. Initially, information regarding the dental extraction forceps were gathered from the experts in the field, considering the importance of sharing the knowledge on dental extraction. Subsequently, an ontology on dental extraction forceps was developed. Next, the developed ontology was evaluated by ontology experts in an iterative approach. Finally, a knowledge sharing portal was developed and validated. We strongly believe that our dental extraction knowledge sharing portal can support the dental students, dentists as well as their assistants to improve the sharing of knowledge and learning practices.

Keywords: Dental · Knowledge sharing · Ontology · Extraction

1 Introduction

A tooth is one of the hardest parts in most of the vertebrates which is calcified structure and situated inside jaws [1]. Tooth performs a very important function of the body which is breaking down of foods. It also gives aesthetic value to the appearance of a person. Dentistry is a branch of medicine which deals with the dentition, and related structures and tissues in the face. A dental extraction is the removal of teeth from its socket in the jaws [1, 2]. There are many reasons for dental extractions but mainly done if a tooth has been damaged by decay or broken [3]. Other reasons are such as a crowded mouth, infection, supernumerary or malformed tooth, and even because of cosmetic purposes (to remove tooth of poor appearance). Oral surgery is the branch of dentistry that deals mainly with extractions [1]. There are two types of extractions: (i) A simple extraction, which is performed on a tooth which can be seen inside the mouth. In a simple extraction procedure, the dentist will hold the tooth with specialized pliers called "extraction forceps" and move them back and forth in order to loosen the tooth from the jaw before getting rid off the tooth [4]. (ii) A surgical extraction, which is a more complex procedure done by the surgeon.

© Springer Nature Singapore Pte Ltd. 2019
J. Hemanth et al. (Eds.): SLAAI-ICAI 2018, CCIS 890, pp. 147–160, 2019.
https://doi.org/10.1007/978-981-13-9129-3_11

The forceps is an exaggerated version pair of pliers. It is made up of three parts; the blades, the joint and the handles. In general, forceps which are designed for the extraction of anterior (front) teeth in the maxilla (upper), the blades and handles are in the same line while for the maxilla posterior (back) teeth the handles form a curve with the blades. In forceps used for the extraction of mandibular (lower) teeth, the blades and handles are at an angle of approximately ninety degrees between them [4].

Sometimes different types of terms are used to express the same idea. Due to various forms, general nature and incomplete information, the knowledge will not reach everyone [5]. In addition, the computer must clearly understand the meaning or semantics of the information. Semantic web enables this understanding of computers [6]. The ontologies will be a powerful mechanism for the knowledge provided in semantic web [7]. Ontologies have various usages such as natural language processing, knowledge management, intelligent integration of information, e-commerce, and semantic web [8]. Structured view of domain knowledge is provided by ontology. It also acts as a repository of concepts in the domain [9]. This structured view is necessary to help knowledge sharing, knowledge aggregation, information retrieval, and question answering. According to Thomas Gruber [11], *"an ontology is an explicit specification of a conceptualization"*.

Furthermore, the environment has been decided to examine a particular Sri Lankan hospital. The key reasons are based on the geographical location of the researcher, practicality, and ease of access to those hospitals and comparative nature of the study data due to the same economic and regulatory regimes surrounding their operation by the same authority of the hospital.

The aim of this work is to contribute to an improvement in the management and usage of dental extraction forceps in hospitals by developing an ontology-driven solution that organizes and describes clearly related knowledge. The remainder of the paper is organized as follows. Section 2 describes the literature review and the related work. Section 3 discusses the designing approach for modelling dental extraction forceps. The discussions regarding the research are described in Sect. 4. Section 5 concludes this paper and presents directions for future work.

2   Literature Review and Related Works

One of the commonest surgical procedure in the dental surgery is tooth extraction [3]. Dentists need to be very careful when performing tooth extraction. Even though enough efforts are applied to perform tooth extractions some accidents may happen when proper instruments are not used [12]. Sometimes it may lead to slipping of the forceps from the tooth to affect the other tooth or jaw or even partial removal of the tooth [13].

All the tooth in human is not in the same shape and size. So, each tooth needs to be extracted using different types of dental extraction forceps. Choosing the appropriate extraction forceps is the important part for the protection of jaws and another neighboring tooth which will be affected if the forceps slips away while extracting. If the specific extraction forceps are not used for a tooth, then there will be more complications [14] such as incomplete extraction in which a tooth root remains in the jaw, prolonged bleeding, swelling, bruising, nerve injury or even extraction of the wrong tooth [1].

Further, if proper extraction forceps are used by the dentist, his or her extraction will be easy as each extraction forceps are made by using the knowledge of physics. For example, extraction forceps are made smaller in size for children in order to apply less force and larger in size for adults in order to apply more force. If we take another example, the tooth on deep end in the jaw (wisdom tooth) needs a different mechanism to extract than the tooth in the front part of the jaw (incisors) [4]. So extraction forceps are made "L" shape for the deeper end and straight for central area. Therefore, usage of specific extraction forceps for the specific tooth is very important for patients' health as well as for the easiness of the dentist. Since, different terminologies are used it is very important to have a sound knowledge in each and every equipment and their relation to tooth.

Modelling knowledge by using ontologies in the medical domain is an active research field [15]. Even though health sector is being supported by number of biomedical ontologies such as GALEN, the Unified Medical Language Source, the Systemic Nomenclature of Medicine which focus on general scope of the biomedical domain [16], and the Gene Ontology (GO) which is one of the earliest and most frequently used vocabularies [17], there are a very few ontology on dental domain on the health sector. But there aren't any in dental extraction. Ontology-based systems provide reusable terminology resources and they can be used to improve the management of complex systems for different context information which can be captured and validated [15].

In order to integrate the knowledge, it has to be seamless and unaffected by the technological issues related to knowledge representation. In most of the knowledge ontologies, the experience of domain experts is key to design the ontologies [18]. Semantic representations help in these issues and enable interoperability. For a particular domain, unambiguous description of the objects and their relationship can be described by using domain ontology [19]. According to Gruber [11], *"ontology provides a structured view of domain knowledge and act as a repository of concepts in the domain"*. This structured view is essential to facilitate knowledge sharing, knowledge aggregation, information retrieval, and question answering. Therefore ontology can be used in the domain of dental to find the specific response to queries.

The use of ontologies in the health domain mainly focussed on the representation and re-organization of medical terminologies. The most significant benefit that ontologies in the health sector are its ability to support the integration of knowledge and data [20]. Even though ontologies are used in the information system (IS) design, the ontology development in the health sector is more challenging because of its complexity and the level of detail in it [16]. Even though there is some previous work which has evidenced knowledge sharing methods for various domains such as software testing [7, 10], economics [30] etc., a very little research into dental knowledge sharing using domain ontologies has been conducted.

Having discovered this research gap we have focused on our attention on developing a dental extraction forceps ontology to represent information needs according to tooth extraction context. That is, we intend to develop an ontology-based knowledge framework to manage extraction forceps-related knowledge. This would assist the doctors and their assistants in the dental hospitals to manage extraction forceps knowledge.

3   Methodology

Figure 1 depicts the overall methodological framework used by us for achieving our objective, i.e. development of the knowledge sharing portal for dental extraction forceps.

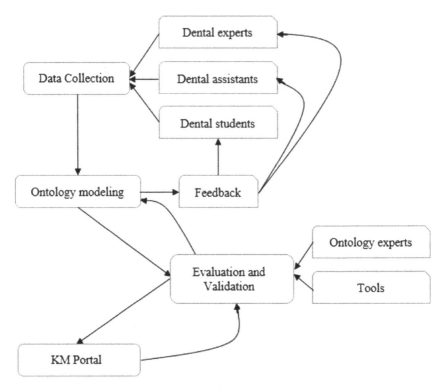

Fig. 1. Overall methodological framework for the development of the knowledge sharing portal for dental extraction forceps.

3.1   Data Collection

Our main focus is on simple extraction, more specifically on extraction forceps because these extraction forceps plays an important role on tooth extraction [4]. There are 32 teeth on an adult called as permanent dentition and 20 teeth on a child called as primary dentition. Further, each tooth has a crown and a root. Normally when extraction is done for the crown, the root also comes with the crown. But in some special cases like a broken tooth, while extracting crown, roots stay in jaw socket [4].

We used grounded theory for data collection. According to Strauss [21], grounded theory is a general methodology for developing theory in grounded data through systematically gathering and analysing. One of the key features of the grounded theory is that both data collection and analysis are interrelated and iterative. So, we can start the analysis as soon as the first data are collected [22].

Two dentists with extensive knowledge of dental (mainly on extraction) and an expert on ontology engineering took part. We also interviewed personnel from different hospitals regarding the idea of unifying forceps catalogues and the information that should be included in it. At the end of the interviews and questions to experts, we formalized some problems regarding dentists and their assistants in question form. Some of them are in Table 1.

From those problems, we gathered the needed data for our ontology modelling. We used various sources for this purpose; (i) various sources of literatures (books, journal articles, newspapers etc.), various sources of multimedia (radio, television, YouTube etc.) (iii) dental doctors and (iv) lecturers in dental field.

Table 1. Dental extraction problems

Dental Extraction Problems
Which is the most suitable extraction forceps to extract a particular tooth?
Which is the most suitable extraction forceps to extract a particular tooth if the crown is damaged, i.e. if the only root is there?
How to hold dental extraction forceps for a particular tooth?
What are the different types of dentitions in the human mouth?
What are the positions of the tooth located in the mouth?
What are the teeth of child and adult?
What are the different shapes of the dental extraction forceps used?
What are the movements of dental extraction forceps inside the jaw in order to remove a tooth?

3.2   Competency Questions (CQs)

CQs are a set of questions that can be answered only by ontology using its axioms [23]. CQs work as requirement's specification of the dental extraction forceps ontology. If CQs contains all the necessary and sufficient axioms that correctly answer the CQs, it is possible to know whether an ontology was created correctly [7]. Our ontology aims to answer competency questions. Some of them shown in Table 2.

We get the relevant data in order to answer these problems through an extensive literature survey and expert collaboration. We categorized the "Person" into two; "Adult" and "Child". The "Parts" of the tooth is divided into "Crown" and "Root". "Positions" also categorized as "Upper", "Lower", "Left" and "Right". Tooth have "Specific Names". They were classified into "Molar", "Premolar", "Canine" and "Incisor".

There are three international standard systems for naming teeth: the universal numbering system, the Palmer notation method and the two-digit FDI world dental federation notation. In this paper, we followed two-digit FDI world dental federation notation WHO and by other organizations such as the International Association for Dental Research. It provides a system for designating teeth or areas of the oral cavity using two digits [24]. We declared these notations into "ToothNotation" class.

Table 2. Competency questions

Competency questions
What is the position of central incisor of a child in the mouth?
Which tooth is in the upper left side of an adult?
Which extraction forceps are needed to extract the root of left second premolar of an adult?
Which extraction forceps are needed to extract the normal left central incisor of a child?
Which teeth are in the upper left side of an adult?
What is the tooth of lower left central incisor of a child in the mouth?
Which extraction forceps are S-shaped?
What type of movement is applied to the third molar of the upper left side of an adult
What type of dentition is for a child?

Since there are no standards for forceps classification, we formalized the forceps into two main categories; Crown Forces and Root Forceps. Here what we meant by the crown is the full tooth which includes both parts; crown and root. Further, we divided each forceps into many subclasses. The high-level class hierarchy is shown in Fig. 2.

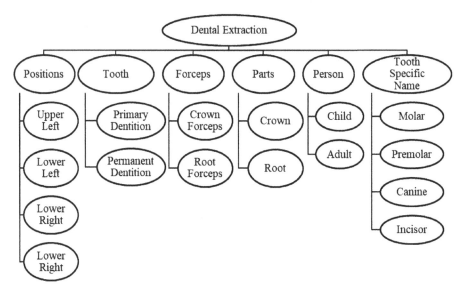

Fig. 2. High-level class hierarchy of dental extraction.

3.3 Ontology Modelling

Making the ontology manually is a tedious and time-consuming task [9]. According to Vasanthapriyan [7], the principles, methods, and tools for initiating, developing and maintaining ontologies are investigated in ontology engineering approach. There are many different methodologies proposed to model the ontologies in many works of literature [23, 25–27]. After reviewing all, we selected Grüninger and Fox's methodology [23] for our work. We made this decision because Grüninger and Fox's methodology publishes a formal approach for designing the ontology. Further, it also it provides a framework for evaluating the developed ontology [7]. The concepts and relationships are identified by the associative relationships. They help to define the relationships and their inverse relationships. Table 3 shows some associative relationships including their inverse.

Table 3. Associative relationships

Concept	Relationship	Concept
Dentition	hasSpecificName, isSpecificNameOf	SpecificName
Forceps	hasUsedToPluck, isPluckedBy	Dentition
Dentition	hasPosition, isPositionOf	Position
Child	hasPrimaryDentition, isPrimaryDentitionOf	PrimaryDentition
Dentition	hasCrown, isCrownOf	Crown

Datatype properties link an individual to an XML Schema Datatype value or an RDF literal. In other words, they describe relationships between an individual and data values. A datatype property can also be used in a restriction to relate individuals to members of a given datatype. Some of the data properties used are shown in Table 4.

Table 4. Data properties

Data property	Datatype
hasShape	String
hasHandleSize	String
hasJointBeaks	String
hasMovement	String

The ontology was implemented by using the Protégé-OWL Ontology Editor 5.1. Part of the dental extraction forceps ontology is shown in Fig. 3. Since we are designing with OWL 2 Web Ontology Language [28] for the semantic web, we use Description Logic (DL) which is a decidable fragment of FOL for our scenario. We have evaluated the competency questions to see whether the ontology meets the dentists' requirements during the internal design process. The DL expressions have been used to query the ontology. For this purpose, we used the DL query facility which is available in Protégé OWL Ontology Editor 5.1. Some of the DL query and their answers are shown in Table 5.

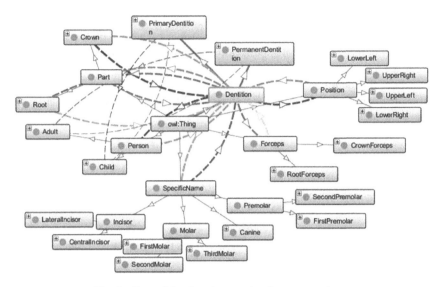

Fig. 3. Part of the dental extraction forceps ontology.

Table 5. DL query and their results

Competency questions	DL query	Answers
What forceps are used to pluck T55 dentition?	Forceps and hasUsedToPluck value T55	Instances (2) ● ChildUpperMolarCF ● ChildUpperRF
What are the dentitions which consist of specific name canine?	Dentition and hasSpecificName value Canine	Instances (8) ● T13 ● T53 ● T23 ● T63 ● T33 ● T73 ● T43 ● T83
What is the position of T34 dentition?	Position and isPositionOf value T34	Instances (1) ● LowerLeft
What is the specific name of T28 dentition?	SpecificName and isSpecificNameOf value T28	Instances (1) ● ThirdMolar

3.4   Development of Knowledge Sharing Portal

Powerful reasoning capabilities are provided by both the ontology and semantic web technologies. In this section, we describe the designing of knowledge framework to share dental extraction forceps knowledge. It was built upon the Java J2EE distributed component environment. The five layers of our knowledge framework are; Experience

Sharing, Ontology, Storage, Reasoning Engine, and Knowledge Retrieval Layer and they are shown in Fig. 4.

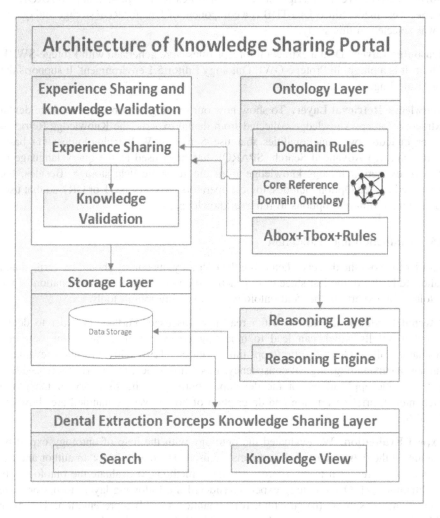

Fig. 4. The architecture of knowledge sharing portal.

Ontology Layer. Our developed dental extraction forceps ontology including its domain rules, axioms etc. is in the ontology layer. Using the Protégé-OWL Ontology Editor 5.1, these concepts and their relationships were partly described in the section "Ontology modelling".

Experience Sharing Layer. Through the Experience Sharing layer, the dental doctors can annotate their extraction knowledge with the support of the dental standard terms.

The shared knowledge is then transformed into the semantic data in a machine-understandable format of the triple structure by the semantic data generator.

Storage Layer. We used Triple-store, which stores RDF triples. Using SPARQL the queries were made. Since Jena TDB is a component of Jena for RDF storage and query, it was selected in this study.

Reasoning Layer. Dental extraction forceps rules were generated with Protégé-SWRL Editor. It is a plugin in Protégé-OWL Ontology Editor 5.1 environment. It supports the Jess Rule Engine.

Knowledge Retrieval Layer. To show how our ontology can be used to share dental extraction forceps knowledge collected from dental experts, the Knowledge Retrieval Layer includes two functionalities that use Semantic Web technologies: (1) basic search, and (2) Advanced Search. SPARQL has been used as the query language to retrieve extraction forceps knowledge from the semantic data storage. Besides, the Advanced Search Option includes, logical operators (AND or NOT or OR), so that user can combine different options to retrieve knowledge.

3.5   Evaluation and Validation

In order to avoid the defects when using the ontology, its quality should be verified and validated [29]. So, the last stage of our methodology consisted of an evaluation of the ontology by experts in the field ontology and by using inbuilt tools.

Internal Evaluation. FaCT++ 1.6.5 reasoner was used. Further, in order to detect potential pitfalls which can lead to modeling errors, we used an online ontology evaluator called OOPS! (http://oops.linkeddata.es/) [29]. This evaluator evaluates human understanding, logical consistency, modeling issues, real-world representation and semantic applications for the developed ontology. The summary of the pitfall encountered, brief description and description of how those are handled are shown in Table 6.

Expert Evaluation. We evaluated the ontology with the help of ontology expert by examining the deficiencies of the artifacts we used. The expert is not an author and not related to our research team. There were many methods to evaluate the ontologies in the literature [7]. Our ontology expert considered the following layers to perform the evaluation; (a) syntax, (b) structure, (c) semantics and (d) representation. The main objectives of the expert evaluation are; (a) whether the dental extraction forceps ontology meets its' requirements, standards, (b) coverage of the dental extraction forceps domain and (c) checking for internal consistencies. This methodology allows us a better focus because each level has a different evaluation objective. Table 7 summarizes the aspects of the evaluation method used.

Table 8 shows the suggestions and improvements highlighted by the ontology expert. Based on Ontology expert's responses, comments, and suggestions the ontology was redeveloped.

Table 6. Pitfall encountered, brief description and the solutions

Pitfall	Description	Solution
Creating unconnected ontology elements (2 cases | Minor)	Ontology elements are created, with no relation to the rest of the ontology	Relationships are created
Inverse relationships not explicitly declared (34 cases | Minor)	Except for the symmetric properties, others do not have an inverse relationship	Included missing inverse relationships
Missing annotations (176 cases | Minor)	Creating an ontology element without providing understandable annotations to it	Included the ontology annotations
Using different naming conventions in the ontology (8 cases | Minor)	Ontology elements are not named on the same convention	Corrected by using the uniform naming convention
Missing domain or range in properties (11 cases | Important)	Object and (or) datatype properties without domain or range	Added the missing domain and range
Defining multiple domains or ranges in properties (8 cases | Critical)	More than one domain or range is defined for a property	Modified the multiple domains and ranges

Table 7. Discussion topic of ontology experts

Layers	Description	Discussion topic
Syntax	The syntax of the formal language used	Standard syntax is used
Structure	The correctness of the concepts and the hierarchy	Whether is describes the is-a relationship between concepts
		Tools used in checking the structure
Semantics	Terms used to represent the knowledge	Understandable names of concepts and properties
Representation	Structural representation of the semantics	Proper taxonomy

Table 8. Review summary of ontology experts

Discussion topic	Ontology expert
Standard syntax is used	Manchester syntax was followed
Whether is describes the is-a relationship between concepts	All concepts follow is-a relationships
Tools used in checking the structure	Whole ontology was viewed using OntoGraph
Understandable names of concepts and properties	2 concepts and 8 object properties do not have understandable names
Proper taxonomy	Clearly viewed in OntoGraph

4 Discussions

Tooth extraction is one of the common surgical procedure in the field of dental, which mainly depends on the knowledge and experience of the dentists. Great importance on knowledge for dental extraction forceps is given in this research. An ontological approach to representing the necessary dental extraction forceps knowledge within the dentists' context was developed.

Designing this type of ontology is not a simple task, because we need to gain vast domain knowledge. In this paper, we have explained how we designed and developed the ontology to organize domain knowledge by meeting particular access requirements effectively. Using this approach, dental extraction forceps ontology to include information needs to be identified for dental extraction activities to be designed.

The validation and evaluation have been done separately. We validated the ontology in terms of accuracy and quality by using the FaCT++ reasoner which is and inbuilt tool in Protégé-OWL Ontology Editor 5.1 and by using web-based tool OOPS!. We evaluated the ontology with the help of ontology expert by examining the deficiencies of the artifacts we used. Based on Ontology experts' responses, comments, and suggestions the ontology was redeveloped.

5 Conclusions and Future Works

Tooth extraction is one of the common surgical procedure in the field of dental, which mainly depends on the knowledge and experience of the dentists. Therefore, in this research, great importance is given to knowledge for dental extraction forceps, and the potential benefits of managing dental extraction forceps knowledge. An ontological approach is needed to represent the necessary dental extraction forceps knowledge within the dentists' context [10]. Identification of the suitable dental extraction forceps for the given case is resolved by developing a domain ontology on dental extraction forceps. Our dental extraction forceps ontology not only solves the problem of selection of right dental extraction forceps but also, it provides a valuable knowledge sharing method for dental students and other researchers.

Designing the ontology in the dental domain is not a simple task. The complexities in the dental extraction domain and the need to gain vast domain knowledge made this task tedious. This research presents dental extraction forceps ontology which represents dental extraction forceps domain knowledge. It includes dental extraction forceps concepts, their properties, and their relationships. Since we have "Experience Sharing Layer" and "Knowledge Retrieval Layer", we strongly believe that our dental extraction forceps ontology can support the dental hospitals, dental students and other active researchers in this field to improve the sharing of knowledge and experiences.

Our future works have two main parts. Initially, we are planning to expand our research to the whole dental extraction process which includes all the devices used in the dental extraction process. Then as a next part, is to use more sophisticated query languages such as Query-enhanced Web Rule Language (SQWRL) for precise and effective knowledge sharing.

Acknowledgements. We acknowledge the experts and other personnel who directly and indirectly involved in order to complete the research work successfully.

References

1. Wikipedia: Dental Extraction. https://en.wikipedia.org/wiki/Dental_extraction. Accessed 01 and 30 Nov 2017
2. Kolosovas-Machuca, E.S., González, F.J., Pozos-Guillen, A.J., Campos-Lara, N.P., Pierdant-Perez, M.: Pain measurement through temperature changes in children undergoing dental extractions. Pain Res. Manag. **2016**, 5 (2016)
3. Anyanechi, C., Chukwuneke, F.: Survey of the reasons for dental extraction in eastern Nigeria. Ann. Med. Health Sci. Res. **2**, 129–133 (2012)
4. Cclyer, L.R.C.P.J.F.: Extraction of the Teeth. Claudius Ash & Sons, Limited, London (1986)
5. Walisadeera, A.I., Ginige, A., Wikramanayake, G.N.: User centered ontology for Sri Lankan farmers. Ecol. Inf. **26**, 140–150 (2015)
6. Choksi, A.T., Jinwala, D.C.: A novel way to relate ontology classes. Sci. World J. **2015**, 15 (2015)
7. Vasanthapriyan, S., Tian, J., Zhao, D., Xiong, S., Xiang, J.: An ontology-based knowledge management system for software testing. In: 29th International Conference on Software Engineering and Knowledge Engineering (SEKE), pp. 522–525 (2017)
8. Walisadeera, A.I., Wikramanayake, G.N., Ginige, A.: Designing a farmer centred ontology for social life network. In: DATA, pp. 238–247 (2013)
9. Walisadeera, A.I., Wikramanayake, G.N., Ginige, A.: An ontological approach to meet information needs of farmers in Sri Lanka. In: International Conference on Computational Science and its Applications, pp. 228–240 (2013)
10. Vasanthapriyan, S., Tian, J., Xiang, J.: An ontology-based knowledge framework for software testing. In: International Symposium on Knowledge and Systems Sciences, pp. 212–226 (2017)
11. Gruber, T.R.: Toward principles for the design of ontologies used for knowledge sharing? Int. J. Hum. Comput Stud. **43**, 907–928 (1995)
12. Balaji, S.: Burried broken extraction instrument fragment. Ann. Maxillofac. Surg. **3**, 93 (2013)
13. Heimann, W.: Extraction forceps for upper molars. In: Google Patents (Ed.) (1977)
14. Oğurel, T., Onaran, Z., Oğurel, R., Örnek, N., Büyüktortop GökçJnar, N., Örnek, K.: Branch retinal artery occlusion following dental extraction. Case Rep. Ophthalmol. Med. **2014**, 3 (2014)
15. Garcia-Valverde, T., Muñoz, A., Arcas, F., et al.: Heart health risk assessment system: a nonintrusive proposal using ontologies and expert rules. BioMed Res. Int. **2014**, 12 (2014)
16. Kuziemsky, C.E., Lau, F.: A four stage approach for ontology-based health information system design. Artif. Intell. Med. **50**, 133–148 (2010)
17. Hu, Y., Zhou, W., Ren, J., Dong, L., Wang, Y., Jin, S., et al.: Annotating the function of the human genome with gene ontology and disease ontology. Biomed. Res. Int. **2016**, 8 (2016)
18. Chen, R.-C., Jiang, H.Q., Huang, C.-Y., Bau, C.-T.: Clinical decision support system for diabetes based on ontology reasoning and TOPSIS analysis. J. Healthc. Eng. **2017**, 14 (2017)
19. Rao, R.R., Makkithaya, K., Gupta, N.: Ontology based semantic representation for public health data integration. In: 2014 International Conference on Contemporary Computing and Informatics (IC3I), 2014, pp. 357–362

20. Pisanelli, D.M.: Ontologies (2004). http://www.openclinical.org/ontologies.html. Accessed 22 Nov 2017
21. Strauss, A., Corbin, J.: Grounded theory methodology. Handb. Qual. Res. **17**, 273–285 (1994)
22. Rose, S., Spinks, N., Canhoto, A.I.: Management Research: Applying the Principles. Routledge, London (2014)
23. Grüninger, M., Fox, M.S.: Methodology for the Design and Evaluation of Ontologies (1995)
24. Park, S., Kim, H.-G.: Dental decision making on missing tooth represented in an ontology and rules. In: The Semantic Web—ASWC 2006, pp. 322–328 (2006)
25. Fernández-López, M.: Overview of Methodologies for Building Ontologies (1999)
26. Sure, Y., Staab, S., Studer, R.: On-to-knowledge methodology (OTKM). In: Springer (ed.) Handbook on Ontologies, pp. 117–132. Springer, Berlin (2004)
27. Noy, N.F., McGuinness, D.L.: Ontology development 101: a guide to creating your first ontology. In: Stanford Knowledge Systems Laboratory Technical Report KSL-01-05 and Stanford Medical Informatics Technical Report SMI-2001-0880, Stanford, CA (2001)
28. WWW Consortium: OWL 2 Web Ontology Language Document Overview (2012)
29. Poveda-Villalón, M., Suárez-Figueroa, M., Gómez-Pérez, A.: Validating ontologies with oops!. In: Knowledge Engineering and Knowledge Management, pp. 267–281 (2012)
30. Yoo, D., No, S.: Ontology-based economics knowledge sharing system. Expert Syst. Appl. **41**, 1331–1341 (2014)

Ontology Based Online Tourist Assistant

Pramodya Mendis[1(✉)], Sachini Siriwardene[1(✉)],
Ruwini Wijesiri[1(✉)], Upali Kohomban[2(✉)], and Subha Fernando[1(✉)]

[1] Faculty of Information Technology, University of Moratuwa,
Moratuwa, Sri Lanka
{134198V,134171H,subhaf}@uom.lk, ruwil025@gmail.com
[2] Codegen International Private Limited, Colombo, Sri Lanka
upali@codegem.net

Abstract. The services of travel agents have been widely replaced by online travel websites with the advent of Web 2.0. tripadvisor, a travel and restaurant website is one of the most popular websites used by tourists to obtain information about tourist attractions. However, majority of the information are presented as user reviews. This will result in tourists having to manually search through user reviews to find the needed information which is a time consuming and tedious task. This can be eliminated by the introduction of an online tourist assistant. We present an online tourist assistant agent, that allows tourists to obtain general information about a travel destination. The user can interact by asking questions in a textual format. The semantics of the question is analyzed and an answer is generated by querying the ontology. The ontology is populated using the data and reviews obtained from the tripadvisor website.

Keywords: Rule-based information extraction · POS tag classifier ·
Convolutional neural network · Recurrent neural network ·
Long short term memory

1 Introduction

Many online assistants can be found nowadays which assist people in day today tasks ranging from task management to disease prediction. The accuracy of these assistants has improved over time with the new technological advancements especially in the fields of natural language processing and machine learning. In order to replace a human with a virtual assistant, it should be capable of identifying the domain in discussion, search for the semantics of the query and present an answer that the customer can rely on. This research project suggests an online assistant for tourists which is able to understand the customer requirements and provide a response with basic information about a tourist attraction. The key research areas involved when developing information agents are information retrieval, semantic analysis and answer generation. Research conducted on the above mentioned areas are summarized in the following sections.

Chatbots can be classified into two categories as generative and retrieval based models. Generative models are capable of handling unseen queries and they generate the response based on the input sequence while retrieval based models use a predefined

© Springer Nature Singapore Pte Ltd. 2019
J. Hemanth et al. (Eds.): SLAAI-ICAI 2018, CCIS 890, pp. 161–174, 2019.
https://doi.org/10.1007/978-981-13-9129-3_12

repository of responses and answer the query by picking up a suitable response based on some heuristic. The common challenges involved in developing chat bots are in cooperating context, generating consistent replies to semantically identical queries, evaluating the system and generating relevant replies. The approach followed in this research is a hybrid one, where an answer is retrieved from the ontology and merged with a generated answer to formulate the final response.

2 Related Work

2.1 Information Extraction Techniques

Information extraction consists of 2 parts, the extraction of objective information(facts) and subjective information(opinions). In situations where data exhibits high variety, manual development of rules for information extraction can be a tedious and time-consuming task. Thus, most research focus using supervised, semi supervised or unsupervised machine learning methods which are more effective. However, the performance of these methods degrades in the face of small data sets.

Imsombut and Sirikayon [1] proposed an ontology population using machine learning using Conditional Random Fields (CRFs). It identifies uses lexico-syntactic patterns to identify instances and extract the relationships between the identified instance. However, although this approach produced acceptable results, it faces the limitation of the inability to account for long distance information dependencies.

Mooney et al. [2] proposed a supervised machine learning approach for information extraction based on word and word label sequence patterns. The sequence labeling is done by using either Hidden Markov Model, CRF or feature based inductive classifier. For objective information extraction, opinion mining can be performed at 3 levels; document level, sentence level or aspect level.

Muangon et al. [3] proposed a feature based opinion mining technique where features are identified using key words and polarity of the feature is computed using top 5 feature specific polar words. Although use of feature specific polar words increase accuracy, identifying the best polar words is challenging.

Afzaal and Usman [4] proposed an aspect based opinion classification system where overall opinion is calculated based on the identified aspect and their trends. The limitation of this approach is the difficulty involved with identifying trends and selecting the most significant trends.

Rahate and Emmanuel [5] proposed a support vector machine (SVM) approach for sentiment analysis of movie reviews. It identifies adjectives, adverbs and verbs as sentiment features. For each feature. a synset is obtained using WordNet and for each word in the synset positive, negative and objectivity scores are assigned. For words with multiple senses, an average score is calculated for positivity, negativity and objectivity. These scores are input into a SVM and the review is classified as negative or positive.

Hedge and Seema [6] proposed the use of incremental decision trees for sentiment analysis. In this approach, aspect based sentiment analysis is performed on the given data and then uses an iterative decision tree algorithm for opinion summarization. This method showed better results when compared with SVM and Naïve Bayes approaches.

Patil et al. [7] proposed an SVM approach for sentiment analysis. Each word (other than stop-words) is represented by its stem and its weight is calculated using TF-IDF. For classification, each word is considered as a feature and its weight is considered as the value. The use of TF-IDF rather than simply using TF, improves the performance of the classifier.

2.2   Semantic Analysis

Semantic parsing involves translating the natural language into a formal representation that can be understood by the underlying system such that an answer can be found for the question. Recent research of deep learning models in the field of NLP is discussed in [8].

2.2.1   Combinatory Categorical Grammar (CCG)

Recent approaches to building semantic parsers for question answering involve mapping the question to a logical form and then mapping the logical formats to the underlying ontological relationships. Logical form used widely for this purpose is known as combinatory categorical grammar (CCG). A CCG is defined by a lexicon and a set of combinators. The lexicon pairs words or phrase with CCG categories which include syntactic category such as noun, verb etc. and a meaning representation using a logical predicate or a combination of many. When parsing to CCG, first the lexical categories are assigned to each word or phrase and then they are combined to build a logical form that capture the meaning of the entire sentence.

A major challenge in semantic parsing is mapping of a large set of possible concepts into a single relationship or entity in the ontology which represents the meaning of the phrase. In [9], challenge of extending the semantic parsing to large scale open domain databases such as freebase is considered.

2.2.2   Generating Query Graphs

In another approach to semantic parsing, [10], constructs query graph which resemble subgraphs of the knowledge base and can be directly mapped to a logical form. This method leverages the use of the knowledge base to prune the search space in an early stage of the parsing process. The earlier two stage process which maps the phrases to generalized logical forms faces a problem when trying to reduce the intermediate logical form into a one which can be mapped to the ontology. Searching for the correct predicate in the large knowledge base is a tedious task. This method defines a query graph which can be directly mapped to a logical form in lambda calculus. The process consists of three main steps: identifying the topic entity, identifying the relationship between the answer and the topic entity and finally expanding the graph with additional constraints that describe properties that needs to be incorporated in the answer. A key advantage of this approach is the search for the matching predicate in the knowledge base is restricted to a limited space since the question is mapped to a topic entity in the knowledge base and the search is centered on the topic entity which is found.

2.2.3   Knowledge Graph Embeddings

Word embedding can also be used to extract the answer from the system [11]. This approach deals with encoding the words appearing in the question and the answer entity together with the surrounding relations in the knowledge base as vector embedding. The model learns a weight matrix of size N*K where K is the dimension of the embedding space and N is the dictionary of embedding to be learned. N include the total number of words, relationships and the entities in the knowledge base.

2.3   Answer Generation

The task of this component is to generate a suitable answer for the question asked, after considering about the context of the conversation as well. Recent approached focus on building chatbots based solely on generative approaches, where a large amount of question answer pairs are used to train the model.

2.3.1   Sequential Matching Network

This is based on a retrieval based chatbot system where the response is selected from an existing source. A response is selected to a question, based on the history of the conversation as well as the context. The two major challenges involved in this implementation are the selection of the important information in the context, crucial to selecting the correct response and modeling the relationships among the utterances in the context. This approach considers the task of maintaining a conversation which is not restricted to a single domain. Here, the order of the utterances is also important for accurate interpretation of the context.

The reason for loss of information in existing models is that they represent the whole context as a single vector and try to match with a response vector. The specific relationship between each query and response pair is not modeled and therefore an information loss takes place. The strategy taken in the above experiment to avoid information loss is matching the candidate response with each utterance in the context and forming two matrices for each utterance-response pair each encoding the word to word mapping and the sequence to sequence mapping. Having different levels of granularity helps to retain more information about the context and leads to a better response choice. The architecture consists of three layers where the first layer maps the response with each utterance, the second layer is a convolution and pooling and the final layer includes GRU (gated recurrent units) and finally outputs a score for the selected response being a suitable candidate answer [12].

2.3.2   Target Side Attention

A lot of the generation models are variants of the sequence to sequence neural network model used in machine translation. One drawback of the seq-to-seq model is the inability to generate longer responses since the decoder has to keep track of conversation history in its fixed length hidden state vector. As a solution, [13] suggests integrating target side attention separately to the network so that the hidden state can be freed to model more semantically complex responses.

A seq to seq model essentially maps an input sequence of words to a target output sequence based on the conditional probability of the output sequence given the input.

The existing seq to seq models with target side attention computes the conditional probability by considering the previous output generated, a hidden state vector and a fixed size encoding of the input sequence. This model is modified in the above mentioned experiment by adopting a new model called the glimpse model. In this model, the attention is augmented by considering the response which is generated so far. The response is split into glimpse size of k where the first part is generated normally and the second part is generated based on the input sequence as well as the output sequence which is generated so far or in other words taking a glimpse at the k output words generated so far.

3   Methodology

3.1   Information Extraction

The performance of machine learning approaches used for information extraction degrades in the absence of a large data set. However, manual development of rules is a tedious task. Furthermore, it's impossible to define rules to capture all possible ways an information can be presented. The solution to these problems is developing pattern rules based on co-location of cue-words. For information extraction, the basic details and user reviews about tourist attraction is obtained from tripadvisor, travel and restaurant website.

Firstly, an OWL ontology was developed using Protege 5.2.0 to model the domain knowledge. The ontology is then used to guide the information extraction process. Information extraction process attempts to identify values for higher level relationships first and once identified, the information is refined to identify values for sub-relationships of the higher level relationship.

As the first step in information extraction, the reviews will be preprocessed to remove inconsistencies such as duplicate reviews and non-English reviews. Then, during transformation phase sentence segmentation, tokenizing, part of speech tagging and lemmatization is performed. Once transformed, cue-word lists are used to identify features.

For fact extraction, additional cue-word lists will be used to perform word sense disambiguation (WSD). Pattern rules are used to filter features based on the proximity of the identified feature and WSD cue-word. Once features are filtered, cue-word lists that contain feature specific descriptors are used to identify potential information. Once features and feature descriptors are identified, their span is increased by concatenating it with information non-bearing words. Then pattern rules based on co-location and proximity of cue-words are used to extract facts from these features and feature descriptors.

Sentiment analysis is done using sentence level opinion mining. Sentences containing features are identified and for each sentence containing feature, the positive and negative polar words that describe the feature are identified using gazetteers. Next, cue-word lists are used to identify polarity shifting words (E.g.-negators) and the true polarity is identified by using the proximity of the polarity shifter and the polar word. The span of the feature and polar word is then increased by concatenating it with information non-bearing words. The overall polarity of the feature will be calculated by aggregating the negative and positive polar words. The extracted information is then processed to remove inconsistencies such as duplicate, redundant or contradicting information.

Once information about an attraction is extracted from text the ontology is populated with the attraction information. If the attraction already exists in the ontology, the attraction details will be updated according to the new information.

Example: Extraction of information regarding camera constraints from the sentence 'The exhibition of masterpieces was amazing. You can take pictures but without the flash.'

Step 1: Identify features using keywords.

```
//identify words refers/implies 'camera'
Document{->MARKFAST(Camera, CameraList2, true)};
Lemma{CONTAINS(Camera),INLIST(CameraList1,
      Lemma.value->MARK(Camera)};
//identify words refers/implies 'Photograph'
Lemma{INLIST(PhotographsList, Lemma.value)
      ->MARK(Photograph)};
```

Output: *'The exhibition of masterpieces was amazing. You can take <u>pictures</u> but without the flash.'*

The Ruta script segment above identifies words that relate to the feature camera/photography. The script uses lemma to identify single word or annotates a given character sequence to identify multiple words. This script would annotate the word 'pictures' with annotation 'Photograph'.

Step 2: Identify potential information bearing sentences

```
Sentence{CONTAINS(Camera)->MARK(CameraDetails)};
Sentence{CONTAINS(Photograph)
      ->MARK(PhotographDetails)};
```

Output: *'The exhibition of masterpieces was amazing. <u>You can take pictures but without the flash.</u>'*

The sentences containing either annotation 'Camera' or 'Photograph' are selected for further processing. This avoids computational waste of unnecessarily processing non-information bearing sentences.

Step 3: Filter features by performing word sense disambiguation using additional cue-words (if required).

Step 4: Identify feature specific descriptors to identify potential information.

```
// identify words implying allowed
Lemma{INLIST(AllowedList, Lemma.value)
       ->MARK(Allow)};
// identify words implying not allowed
Lemma{INLIST(NotAllowedList1, Lemma.value)
       ->MARK(NotAllowed)};
Document{->MARKFAST(NotAllowed, NotAllowedList2,
       true)};
// identify negators
Document{->MARKFAST(Negator, NegatorsList, true)};
("no" | "non"){->MARK(No)};
("flash" | "flasher" | "flashlight" | "flash light")
       {->MARK(Flash)};
```

Output: *'You can take pictures but without the flash.'*

The script annotates 'take' as 'Allow', 'without' as a 'Negator' and 'flash' as 'Flash'.

Step 5: Increase the span of the feature and feature descriptors by concatenating with information non-bearing words.

```
((pos.ART | pos.PP | pos.PR)+ Negator
       {->UNMARK(Negator)})
       {AND(-PARTOF(Photograph), -PARTOF(Nature),
       -CONTAINS(No))
       ->MARK(Negator)};
(Negator{->UNMARK(Negator)}
       (pos.ART | pos.PP | pos.PR)+)
       {AND(-PARTOF(Photograph), -PARTOF(Nature),
       -CONTAINS(No))->MARK(Negator)};
```

Output: *'You can take pictures but without the flash.'*

The span of the descriptor annotation 'Negator can be increased by concatenating with non-information bearing words such as articles, common nouns and prepositions.

Step 6: Identify negations of descriptors using proximity of descriptor and negators.

```
(Negator Flash{->UNMARK(Flash)})
       {->MARK(FlashNotAllowed)};
```

Output: *'You can take pictures but without the flash.'*

Whether flash is not allowed can be identified using the proximity of the annotation 'Negator' or 'NotAllowed' and 'Flash'. In the rule given, if a 'Flash' annotation is proceeded by a 'Negator' annotation, it's identified as flash not being allowed and is annotate 'FlashNotAllowed'.

Step 7: Identify information using pattern based rules based on co-location and proximity of feature and feature descriptors.

```
(Photograph{->UNMARK(Photograph)} # FlashNotAllowed)
      {-CONTAINS(FlashPhotographNotAllowed),
      -PARTOF(FlashPhotographNotAllowed)
      ->MARK(FlashPhotographNotAllowed)};
```

Output: *'You can take pictures but without the flash.'*

If an annotation 'Photograph' is followed by an annotation 'FlashNotAllowed', it is extracted as 'FlashPhotographNotAllowed'.

Step 8: Process to remove inconsistencies such as duplicate, redundant and contradicting information.

The information extracted using Ruta scripts are processed to remove inconsistencies. If there is information indicating camera is not allowed, it implicitly implies that flash camera is not allowed. Thus, firstly, if the extracted information contains camera not allowed information, it will not be further processed to find information about flash camera not allowed constraint. However, if the extracted nformation does not contain information on camera not allowed, then it is processed to find whether it contains information about flash camera not being allowed.

Step 9: Populate the ontology

If the ontology already contains information about the tourist attraction and it contains an entry for camera constraint, update the entry. Else if the attraction exists but doesn't have information about camera constraint, add an entry for camera constraint. Else if the attraction doesn't exist in the ontology, create an instance for the attraction and add the camera constraint information.

Figure 1 shows how information extracted about Ananta Samakhom Throne Hall is populated in the ontology.

3.2   Semantic Analysis

Most of the available researches focus on open domain question answering where the expected answer is not very complex and comprehensive most of the time. When addressing closed domain systems, a major obstacle is the lack of data. In addressing the tourism domain, this research focuses specifically on providing the basic details regarding an attraction. When analyzing the question provided by the user, first the question is classified and then the question is mapped to a specific ontology relationship using simple pattern matching.

The system is restricted to the domain of 11 categories which were identified as the basic groups a question can fall into. They are:

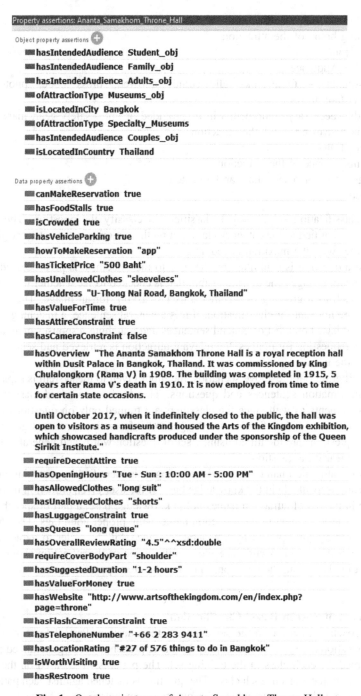

Fig. 1. Ontology instance of Ananta Samakhom Throne Hall

1. Duration to visit an attraction
2. Opening hours of the attraction
3. Busy Hours
4. Suitable Audience
5. Constraints – food/drinks allowed/not allowed, dress code, photography allowed/not allowed
6. Whether necessary equipment will be provided or not – safety gear, maps etc.
7. The best season to visit the attraction
8. Reservations
9. The importance of the attraction
10. Suggestions for places that can be visited
11. Tickets

The classification stage uses 3 classifiers to classify the question. The correct category is identified as the category classified by the majority or the category given by the classifier with the maximum accuracy.

When a question is submitted by the user to the system, it is preprocessed before the classification stage. The question submitted is checked to see whether it is a general sentence such as a greeting or whether a user is asking for an image. These kind of questions are not sent for classification. If it is a general sentence, a matching response is submitted based on a list of general sentences and matching responses maintained. If the user is requesting for images, the relevant attraction is retrieved and sent to display images to the user.

After filtering out the above scenarios, the input given to the system is separated as general information sentences and questions. This is done to avoid classifying the general statements as well since the classifiers are trained only on questions and will not give an accurate classification for the general informative sentences given by the user. The questions are identified using a set of question words and general key words that can appear on a question.

Then the attraction name the user is referring to is identified by matching against a list of locations available in the knowledge base. If the user given attraction name is not available in the list of attraction names in the knowledge base, a part of speech pattern matching is used to identify the attraction name using proper noun tags. The attraction names identified are replaced by a general reference, "it", in order to avoid the mis-classification that might occur since the specific name of the attraction should not be important in classifying the question. The classification approaches used are explained below.

3.2.1   Part of Speech Based Classification

This approach is focused on the semantics of the question. Part of Speech has been used in question classification tasks [14]. In this approach, a set of generalized patterns were formed for each class in the training set. The patterns were based on the part of speech tags of questions in each class. The question is matched against each pattern and a set of potential classes to which the question can belong are obtained. A set of trigrams are formed for the questions in in the training set for each class and the mutual trigram count between the question and the potential matched classes are obtained. The question is then classified to the class with the maximum amount of mutual trigrams.

3.2.2 Multi-layer Perceptron

The next classifier uses a neural network with 5 hidden layers. The model uses categorical cross entropy as the loss function and gradient descent to optimize the loss function. The inputs to the network are word vectors and vectors for the part of speech tags of the question. Both these input vectors are merged into one layer in the neural network.

The word and POS vectors are obtained by using the continuous bag of words algorithm. When obtaining word vectors, hierarchical softmax was used for model training.

3.2.3 Convolutional Network

The network has two convolutional layers of filter size 3 and 2 max pooling layers of pooling window size 3. The last two layers are fully connected layers with hidden neurons 256 and 12 respectively. The inputs to the network are the word vectors of the question.

Once the question is categorized into a major category, the question is further analyzed by searching for regular expressions. The regular expressions are based on the attributes that can be mapped to a question.

After classifying the question, it is mapped to a specific ontology relationship using predefined patterns based on regular expressions that contain key words identifying the attributes in the ontology. It is checked to see whether the previous utterance is a question or a general informative sentence. If it is a general sentence, it is processed to retrieve any information which will be useful to formulate the query.

For example, when analyzing the input "I will be traveling to London next week. What are the places I should visit?" The question is classified as a suggestion and the statement is processed to retrieve the location to query attractions located in London.

Also, any supplementary data needed to answer the question is retrieved from the question. For example, if a user is asking for historic attractions to visit in London, the data retrieved should include historic as the type and London as the location.

3.3   Answer Generation

Answer generation helps to maintain a natural conversation and chatbots on open domain are implemented using this technique [15]. The input given for this module include the question, the category being classified, the tag representing the ontology relationship to be used in the query and any supplementary data necessary to form the query. Once the data is received, a SPARQL query is formed based on the tag received to map the question to an ontology relationship. The answers retrieved are processed to obtain the correct answer. A sequence to sequence model is used to generate answers based on the words in the question.

3.3.1   Sequence to Sequence Model

The model uses one hidden layer each for the encoder and decoder and uses long short term memory (lstm). The hidden layer consists of 256 hidden lstm units. The training data set consists of question and answer pairs related to the questions asked about an attraction. Since the training data set is limited, a transfer learning approach is adopted. The hidden layer of the encoder is initialized with the encoder weights of a sequence to sequence model trained for a English to French translation task. The initial weights of the decoder are initialized to the output states given by the encoder. The model is then trained for the question and answer pairs in the training data set. Initial model is trained for 30000 English to French sentence pairs. When training the decoder, target sentences are appended with start and end tags at the beginning and end of the sentence to indicate the start and end of a sentence. The decoder is given the start tag and the word with the highest probability in output layer is taken as the next word in the answer. This answer is given as input to the decoder to predict the next word in the answer. The process continues until a end of sequence tag is reached or the sequence reaches the maximum length specified for the answer.

The Fig. 2 below show some sample questions and the responses generated by the chat bot.

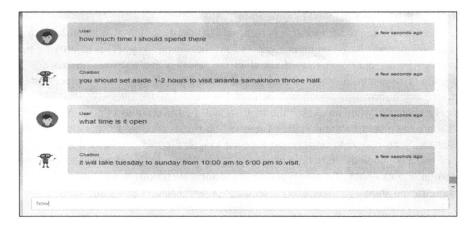

Fig. 2. Sample questions and answers generated by the chatbot

4   Evaluation

4.1   Information Extraction

The performance of the information extraction module is evaluated by analyzing the performance for each of the information category extracted in terms of accuracy, precision, recall and F1 score.

Test data set for evaluation was obtained from existing user reviews. The performance of categories with sub-categories was calculated by taking the simple average of the performance measures of the sub-categories. A list of information categories extracted and their performance measures are given below in Table 1 below.

(1) Accessibility

- Accessible to mobility impaired
- Accessible to visually impaired

(2) Access constraints

- Minimum and maximum age required for entrance
- Minimum and maximum height required for entrance

(3) Attire constraints

- Cloths that should be worn
- Cloths that shouldn't be worn
- Body parts that needs to be covered

(4) Audience (suitable audience; couples, family, friends, students, mobility impaired and vision impaired)
(5) Availability of banks and ATMs.
(6) Camera constraints

- Photography not being permitted
- Flash photography not being permitted

(7) Crowding information (whether attraction is heavily crowded or less crowded)
(8) Food and beverage constraint

- Food and beverages not being permitted
- Alcohol not being permitted
- Outside food and beverages allowed not being permitted
- Outside alcohol not being permitted

(9) Availability of food stalls and restaurants

- Food stalls and restaurants available
- Food stalls and restaurants available outside or nearby attraction

(10) Luggage constraint (Bags not being permitted)
(11) Pet details

- Pets not permitted
- Suitability of attraction for pets

(12) Queuing information (nature of queue and its movement)
(13) Making reservations

- Whether it's possible to make reservations
- Is it recommended to make a reservation?
- How to make reserve

(14) Availability of restrooms
(15) The peak season of the attraction
(16) Ticketing information

- Ticket price for a given audience
- Common ticket price
- Audience with free access
- Has free access

(17) Availability of vehicle parks
(18) Overall worth of the attraction

- Whether visiting attraction worth it
- Whether attraction has value for money
- Whether attraction has value for time

Natural Language Processing

Digital Assistant for Supporting Bank Customer Service

Dinithi Weerabahu, Agra Gamage, Chathurya Dulakshi,
Gamage Upeksha Ganegoda$^{(\boxtimes)}$, and Thanuja Sandanayake

Faculty of Information Technology, University of Moratuwa,
Katubedda, Moratuwa, Sri Lanka
weerabahu.wmd@gmail.com, agragamage93@gmail.com,
chathurya993@gmail.com, tcsandanayake@gmail.com,
upekshag@uom.lk

Abstract. Digital Assistants are trending in most industries. Despite the fact that it invaded the banking industry a few years ago, the concept is still new in the Sri Lankan banking context. A Chat-bot improves customer satisfaction providing solutions to customers, using the most preferred user interaction method called chat application as a solution to the usually inefficient, time-consuming processes which are followed in call centres. The proposed system is a question answering system which facilitates customers to solve their day-to-day banking related questions. The system provides answers to a set of most Frequently Asked Questions (FAQ) related to the banking domain. Customer inquiries are extracted and converted using natural language processing techniques understood by the system. It formulates and presents an appropriate answer using a set of preconfigured templates referring to the answer saved in a knowledge base. Knowledge is represented in the form of an Ontology.

Keywords: Banking chatbots · Natural language processing · Ontology · Template based systems · Machine learning

1 Introduction

For any business, customer satisfaction is one of the most crucial factors that drive the business towards success [1]. Because of that, customer service plays a vital role among all the business functionalities. During the past few decades, customer services have evolved a long way from physically travelling to the business locations to ask questions [2]. Then, the invention of the telephone has caused the eventual development of the call centre; but due to arisen frustrations, expectations of speed and automation have ascended with the time. Considering the widespread availability of technology and its advancements, successful businesses who are ahead of the curve are the ones who carry customer service to the forefront and adopt the technologies available to keep up with their changing expectations over time, which make lives of their customers easier [2].

Customer support services in many business environments; ranging from banking, educational etc. The customer service representatives handle activities which would include monitoring phone lines or live chats for customer inquiries and aiding when

J. Hemanth et al. (Eds.): SLAAI-ICAI 2018, CCIS 890, pp. 177–186, 2019.
https://doi.org/10.1007/978-981-13-9129-3_13

customers need assistance. This could be more easily and more effectively done using a digital assistant. But, Chat-bots need customization as per the requirement. As a result of this, there should be a defined scope. Non-banking chatbots cannot understand the scope of the banking domain and the banking vocabulary precisely. In this banking digital assistant, it manages questions and answers in ontology regarding banking domain. Moreover, managing banking vocabulary and uncommon question handling is done by the digital assistant. Due to those reasons, non- banking domain chatbots cannot be applied directly to derive answers for banking related questions and to handle uncommon questions.

When it comes to the banking domain, as sophisticated the customer lives have become with the technological advancements and having everything connected, customers expect banking services to integrate with their connected life. In this scenario not responding to customer expectations and having resistance towards evolving technologies could have negative results and will have adverse impacts in the near future. Time has passed where customers have to wait on hold for hours to talk to a customer service agent who cannot always provide the perfect solution. As a result, banks are moving forward to the era of digitizing all business functionalities and services where customers can get a seamless and a much simple customer experience [3].

This research study has focused on developing an automated chat bot for the banking domain. The concept of digital assistants has been derived from the much complex research areas of Artificial Intelligence (AI). At the same time, researchers in Natural Language Processing (NLP) and Semantic Web domains have proposed new approaches to model and implement more and more complex systems. Such systems are capable of interpreting natural languages, reasoning, and of assisting end-users such as Chatbot [4], Expert Systems [5], multi-agent systems [6], and Question and Answering systems [7]. They cover both open and closed domains such as social, commercial and scientific which aim to be independent, self-learning and can replace humans performing various tasks [8]. Integrating these concepts into the customer service digital agents in banking domain, they would not be able to replace human agents completely just yet. But with the growth of research areas in machine learning, the accuracy of these digital agents is increasing over time.

Research in Digital Assistant platform for supporting bank customer service is an emerging field in the world of financial services. In the local domain, there are no digital assistants in the banking field which can provide customized answers. Among the number of advantages of digital assistants, there are zero turnovers, no peak times or extra staffing projections for the holidays and cost reduction for the Bank. The limitation is not interpreting the question accurately which results in incorrect answers for the inquiries which the research tends to overcome. The system is capable of identifying the domain in the discussion, search for the semantics of the query and present a customized answer that the customer can rely on.

The research study is developed in three main modules i.e. Understanding and Extracting Natural Language, Generating and Maintaining Knowledge Base and Answer Generation using Natural Language Generation (NLG). An ontology has been used as the knowledge base which consists with Frequently Asked Questions (FAQs) of a bank by its customers.

2 Literature Review

There are few digitals assistant platforms which are available for banking domain, worldwide. These Chat-bots were developed based on decision tree techniques and machine learning techniques by providing an accurate, customized answer for bank clients [9].

2.1 Using Decision Trees

Santander SmartBank is capable of understanding the customer spending. Customer needs to ask questions such as "How much did I spend on March?", "where did I spend it?", "when did I spend?", etc. This digital assistant understands customer queries and responds accordingly [9].

PayPal has enabled features to make payments through voice assistant Apple Siri for iOS 10 users. Customers are allowed to ask Siri to send money or send a request for payment which is made through PayPal [9].

Being the first local financial institution to implement an online assistant, Seylan Bank has introduced a Chatbot that responds to customer queries using a third-party platform - Facebook Messenger. In addition to the bank's customer service channels, Seylan Messenger Bot helps to provide real-time responses to basic banking and financial queries. Basically, when a customer makes an inquiry, the bot automatically directs the user to the relevant web page of the main website.

These three bots are customized in their context and provide answers based on decisions chosen by the customer which can be taken as the limitation.

2.2 Using ML Techniques

IBM's Watson is a question answering computer system capable of answering questions posed in natural language. Watson can give financial institutes a 'deeper understanding' of their customers, and balance this with risk and compliance considerations. IBM Watson uses NLP techniques such as semantic parsing, POS tagging, Entity Recognition and Conference resolution and etc. [10].

Erica, the new Chatbot of Bank of America, takes inputs via text or voice. The more Erica collects data, customers will be able not only to make queries but also to make better financial decisions, as they have an advisor who will crunch more numbers than any given bank teller. Erica will provide the personal service of a top-tier customer, to the masses [9].

The proposed system has overcome the limitations of giving a common answer produced using decision trees, matching the words of the customer inquiry, instead it gives a customized answer using NLP, NLG and ML.

3 Research Objective

Objectives of the research are 1. Identification of the domain and extracting the required information from the user inquiry, 2. Understand the meaning of the input which customers express in various ways, 3. Generate and maintain the knowledge base, 4. Use classification to classify a new question and answer, in order to add it into the into the ontology, 5. Define an appropriate linguistic structure to formulate an answer using a template-based approach in order to provide a meaningful output to the end user.

4 Methodology

This section describes the main research approach with the three main modules; Understanding and Extracting Natural Language, Generating and Maintaining Knowledge Base and Answer Generation. Figure 1 shows the high-level architecture of the research.

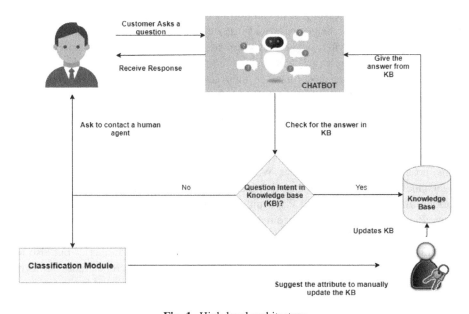

Fig. 1 High-level architecture

4.1 Understanding and Extracting Natural Language

The usage of the information extraction method is to automatically extract the structured information and other domain-specific (Banking domain) information. In this information extraction section, we used Natural Language Processing (NLP) techniques. The text preprocessing techniques will be used to Information retrieval of a question. There are words preprocessing techniques such as stop-words, stemming, lemmatization and part-of-speech tags (POS). It involves transferring raw data into an understandable format. The text preprocessing leads to sentence splitting, tokenization process and POS tagging process.

In the process of question extraction, text preprocessing techniques gives the keywords as the output. In that case, we used a separate database to maintain the banking domain vocabulary. Mainly, our data of banking domain information consists of cards, accounts, internet banking and mobile banking. With the use of text pre-processing techniques in NLP and domain related database, the digital assistant can identify the domain-specific questions and give the output as the extracted preprocessed text keywords. For an instance, if the user presents the inquiry as "How to apply for a credit card?", then the output is the extracted keywords of the question. Once the keywords are extracted, it will identify the domain of the digital assistant.

According to Fig. 1, the preprocessed keywords and domain identification lead the digital assistant into the meaning identification of the question. The similar question identification section was done by using the Bag-of-Words technique. The Bag-of-Words is a statistical representation which shows the vector quantization and object categorization. This technique assists to make a list of all words in given data set and create vectors. Then it checks the frequency of words from the given question and it creates a token which called a 'gram'. It helps to obtain the similarity between 2 questions by computing the number of same words in them by putting a weight to the words. It is a scoring method which satisfies the term frequency equation.

4.2 Generating and Maintaining Knowledge Base

As the project's knowledgebase, an ontology is used. The ontology is developed in a logical structure where a bank's products are saved as classes and subclasses. Answers to frequently asked questions are saved as the data property descriptions of instances. Data properties describe the attributes of the products. For an example, Dataset has frequently asked questions about the domains, Cards, Accounts, Electronic Banking, and services, which are taken the superclasses. If we take the superclass Cards as the example, it has subclasses such as Credit Cards, Debit Cards, Amex Cards, Supplementary Card, SET Plus etc. From that Credit Cards further classifies into subclasses which are the credit card types. Such as Visa Infinite Card, Visa Signature Card, Visa Platinum Card, Sampath Classic Card, Sampath Gold Card etc. Each of these subclasses has its instances, where each sub class's attributes are defined as data properties. Credit Card itself also has an instance where common attributes to all the credit card types are defined.

Answers will be retrieved from the ontology mapping keywords with Queries. A classification module is developed, which classifies keywords from the first module into its most suitable data property in the ontology, in order to add an uncommon answer for a given question. Classification module is developed using Naive Bayes and Support Vector Machine (SVM) classifiers in order to increase the accuracy.

Naive Bayes technique based on Bayes' Theorem with a hypothesis of independence among predictors. Naive Bayes classifier assumes that the presence of a particular feature in a class is unrelated to the presence of any other feature [11]. Among reasons to choose Naïve Bayes classification technique to the system, mainly it performs well in multiclass prediction which is needed as keywords are classified into many data properties. It performs easy and fast in predicting the class of the test data set. It only requires less training data as the data set of the bank consists with FAQs of mostly card related inquiries and very less no of inquiries of other domains, the data set given is very limited.

SVM is a supervised machine learning algorithm which can be used for both classification or regression. In the algorithm, each data item is plotted as a point in n-dimensional space with the value of each feature being the value of a particular coordinate. Then the classification is performed by finding the hyperplane that differentiates the two classes very well [12]. The reasons to choose SVM classifier are, it works well in clear margin separation and its ability to perform multiclass classification.

Like the first part, when a set of keywords (Different meanings, generalized into one.) given to this module, it will first go to the intermediate level of query mapping, where keywords and the query will be saved in a map. Once the keywords passed from the first module matches with the keywords of the map, the relevant query gets executed and the answer will be passed to the answer generation module. For an instance, "what is a corporate card?" and "I need to know about corporate card" has the same meaning. The question extraction and meaning identification module identifies the question and returns the keywords, 'what' and 'corporate' 'card' as the output. In such a scenario, once the keywords of the map, matched with 'what' 'corporate' and 'card', it will execute the relevant query and returns the answer saved in the ontology.

Once an uncommon question is being asked, when trying to match the keywords from the dictionary, the system identifies that such a question is not on the ontology. Then the system tries to get the question in other forms from the user and if it fails, the customer will be given the answer to contact a customer care agent. While this happens, the mapping module will direct the question (keywords) to a classification module and it will classify keywords from the first module into its most suitable data property in the ontology. The classified most suitable data property will be given to the Administration module where an authorized banking officer can add manually an uncommon answer into the ontology.

4.3   Answer Generation

This module mainly focuses on generating an appropriate answer whenever the user initiates his query. Answer generation is basically a template-based system. Whenever a user enters his query, text extraction module outputs certain keywords and it is matched with an answer saved in the knowledge base. This component formulates an answer using a pre-configured template adding the missing part of the template by filling the gap referring to ontology answer. This methodology works with questions that are clear to the system. This solution is an effort to combine two different methodologies to provide answers to its users. This module consists of two main components namely Template-Based Component and Deep Learning Component.

Extracted keywords from the text extracting module are the input values for generating an answer. Whenever a user input is received, it is necessary to identify whether it goes to either the Deep Learning Component or Template Based Component. If the user input falls under Deep Learning Category, pick a response which is almost matched to the user input and output it. If the user input does not match with the Deep Learning module, then it goes to the template based component match with the regular expression pattern which is already created and stored in the database. Keywords are continuously checked with the regular expression patterns and identify whether there is a match or not. If it does not match with any pattern in the database, it means digital assistant is unable to provide an exact answer for the given user query. Then he kindly requests to contact a human agent for further clarifications.

Answer Generation module receives the user query from the text understanding module. Then it is converted into a regular expression using NLP. Each and every question which has an answer in the knowledge base is converted into regular expression form. Considering the outcome of the regular expression form, a number of regular expression patterns can be generated. When some questions are converted into regular expressions (regex), it is possible to see common patterns can be obtained. Each question template has a corresponding answer template. A common answer format is used for common question template. An answer template has a gap to be filled. The gap is filled when the query is executed to get the value stored in the knowledge base. The answer is formulated if the gap is filled and then it is sent to the user.

Deep Learning Component is designed to handle user queries that produce output not based on the knowledge base. This component handles user greetings, thanking and some general details of the Bank. Furthermore, such information is more likely to fluctuate day by day. For instance, Local and Foreign interest rates, exchange rates and many more. That information needs to update frequently on the website. It's not quite efficient to keep the fluctuating values in the knowledge base as changing values in the knowledge base is troublesome if that occurs frequently. Possible user inputs are categorized under different tags and train them using a model. A threshold value is used to measure the accuracy of the output. When the threshold value decreases, the accuracy of the output becomes low. When the threshold value increases, the accuracy of the output becomes high.

5 Implementation

5.1 Preparing Data Set

This is a banking related dataset which consists of most Frequently Asked Questions (FAQ) of bank customers and corresponding answers given by the bank. Data has been gathered from the card centre of the bank and the website in order to narrow down the scope to the banking domain. The data set has been analyzed has and divided into several categories such as credit card, debit card, electronic banking and services for easy reference. Majority of the questions are related to credit card issues. According to the requirement, we have expanded the data set by doing certain modifications.

5.2 System Implementation

When a customer types a question, information should be extracted in order to provide an answer. Text preprocessing techniques are used to extract information. It involves transforming raw data into an understandable format. NLTK library is used for tokenizing, sentence segmentation and word removal. Most of the common words in the language such as 'is', 'are', 'can', and 'the' which do not need to be considered while preprocessing, are re-moved [12]. The statistical method is used as the preprocessing method. This preprocessed text leads to identify the banking domain questions. Similar question identification section is being developed using a bag of a sequence of words.

In here, python is used as core programming language. Moreover, the python web framework called Flask is used in the business logic layer. JavaScript, CSS and HTML5 will be used to develop the web application for the users to interact with the digital assistant.

Ontology is developed where all the classes, subclasses, data properties and object properties are developed manually according to the structure of the data set. Classes, subclasses, object properties and data properties are defined according to questions, and answers are saved when assigning data properties into instances. Queries to retrieve answers which are in the dataset are coded using SPARQL Queries. A mapping module is developed, in order to map passed keywords (from text extraction module) with the already developed queries. When an uncommon question is being asked, the question will be preprocessed by text extraction module and will be classified into a data property which is already defined in the ontology and it will be suggested to an authorized banking officer in order to add to the ontology.

User queries are matched against preconfigured patterns as to provide relevant answers to the questions being asked. Template Based Component uses a template based natural language generation approach to formulating answers to end users. This involves converting the user query into regular expression form and generates a pattern based on the regex form. Firstly, the user query is entered into the component and then it is tokenized into a list of tag words. When the sentence is tokenized, Lemmatization mechanism is used. Prior to converting the tokenized words into the regular expression, it is necessary to convert it into a POS tag. POS tagging is the basis for creating a list of Regex (Regular Expression) Patterns. The pattern should be matched with the user input to generate an answer. If the pattern is matched, then the answer is formulated for the relevant template by retrieving data from the knowledge base.

For the deep learning component, Deep Neural Network (DNN) is used to train the data with the tflearn library. Data is saved in Jason format. A threshold value is used to validate the output. In order to work both components accurately, this value is to being tested with the majority of the questions and responses.

6   Experimental Results

Our experiment is to compare the outcome of our digital assistant with respect to the existing banking chatbots in Sri Lankan context. By the time we started the research, there was only Seylan messenger chat bot. To measure the effectiveness of our system against the messenger bot, we have done a customer survey. Survey is used as it is the best way to mine user insights and get valuable feedback to better improve the system from their perspective while being usable.

This survey has been carried out using a random sample of banking customers and employees from both banks. They were expected to use both Seylan and Sampath chat bots providing sample dataset questions for both systems and evaluate the output. The digital assistant has been fed 150 questions and corresponding answers. For the evaluation purpose, we have created 50 sample dataset which contains exact same questions from the original dataset, differently asked questions, questions out of the dataset, greetings, banking related and not related questions etc. Once they evaluate system with sample dataset, they need to fill out the questionnaire. Test cases have created in such a way that it measures the chat bot response in terms of the user expected answer, usability, user friendliness, effectiveness and accuracy as illustrated in Fig. 2.

Summarized result of the questionnaire has shown that, in messenger bot, response for the customer inquiries is merely a URL of the website to find details. It acts as a search engine when providing answers to customers. Users have found that it is rather inconvenient as sometimes website does not provide latest updates. Our digital assistant works step ahead as it provides an exact answer to a user given query. Hence, customers are more satisfied when they are given answers in the chat window rather than searching a website.

This survey has further revealed that digital society is more comfortable getting solutions from a messenger platform rather than waiting hours on being hold in call centers. On the other hand, system is capable of providing answers to major issues that the customers frequently face when dealing with banks. Survey further shows that, this solution can improve the quality of customer service, level of customer satisfaction by minimizing rush in call centers and help desks.

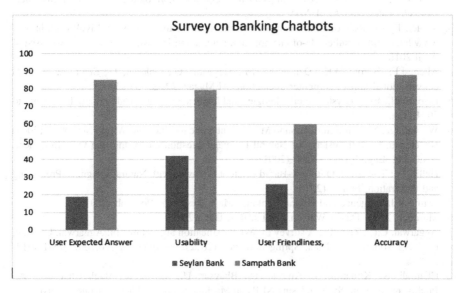

Fig. 2 Survey results

7 Conclusion

Since online assistants have gained a greater attraction on the banking domain which is an emerging field in the world of financial services, this paper proposes an online assistant for banking domain which is capable of processing customer queries and providing appropriate solutions while managing the knowledge base using Natural Language Processing (NLP) techniques. In Sri Lankan banking sector there are no any online assistants which can give customized answers. Moreover, there are some limitations like not getting the right answer and not interpreting the question correctly. This system is designed to overcome the issues in existing similar systems. Core Part of the project was achieved using three methodologies which are question extraction, knowledge base mapping and answer generation. Question extraction and meaning identification were done in using preprocessing techniques and Bag-of-Words method. Knowledgebase mapping was done by using a classification module and answer generation was done using pattern matching template-based system. The proposed online assistant consisting the question extraction and meaning identification, knowledge base mapping and answer generation is a helpful tool which assists to clarify customer queries and it drives the traditional banks into a change in the technology of chatbots.

References

1. Ozatac, N., Saner, T., Sen, Z.S.: Customer Satisfaction in the Banking Sector: The Case of North. In: Customer Satisfaction in the Banking Sector: The Case of North, Italy (2015)
2. Krainert, S.: The Evolution of Customer Service: 5 Progressions Spanning Past to Future, help shift, 19 January 2017. https://www.helpshift.com/blog/the-evolution-of-customer-service/. Accessed 3 April 2018
3. Kapler, J.: The Role of Chatbots and Automation in Customer Service. LiveWorld, https://www.liveworld.com/the-role-of-chatbots-and-automation-in-customer-service/. Accessed 4 April 2018
4. Allen, J.F., Byron, D.K., Dzikovska, M., Ferguson, G., Galescu, L., Stent, A.: Toward conversational human-computer interaction. AI Magaz. **22**, 27–37 (2001)
5. Liao, S.-H.: Expert system methodologies and applications—a decade review from 1995 to 2004. Taipei 251
6. Wooldridge, M.: An Introduction to MultiAgent Systems, 2nd edn. Wiley, New York (2009)
7. Hirschman, L., Gaizauskas, R.: Natural language question answering: the view from here. Nat. Lang. Eng. **7**(4), 275–300 (2001)
8. Hallili, A.: Toward an Ontology-Based Chatbot Endowed with Natural Language Processing and Generation, France (2014)
9. Artificial Intelligence and Digital Banking, Mapa Research, November 2016
10. Murdock, J.W.: This is Watson. IBM J. Res. Dev. (2012)
11. Aggarwal, C.C., Zhai, C.: A survey of text classification algorithms. In: Aggarwal, C., Zhai, C. (eds.) Mining Text Data. Springer, Boston (2012). https://doi.org/10.1007/978-1-4614-3223-4
12. Chaitrali, S., Kulkarni, S., Amruta, U., Bhavsar, U., Savita, R.: Bank Chat Bot—An Intelligent Assistant System, Using NLP and Machine Learning. https://irjet.net/archives/V4/i5/IRJET-V4I5611.pdf. Accessed 20 Feb 2018

A Novel Dialogue Manager Model for Spoken Dialogue Systems Based on User Input Learning

M. F. Ahmed Shariff and Ruwan D. Nawarathna[⊠]

Department of Statistics and Computer Science, Faculty of Science,
University of Peradeniya, Peradeniya 20400, Sri Lanka
shariff.mfa@outlook.com, ruwand@pdn.ac.lk

Abstract. The complexity of the dialogue manager is a major issue in spoken dialogue systems. In this work, a novel dialogue manager based on user input learning is proposed to overcome this issue. In the proposed model back-end functionality is considered as a set of functions a user can trigger through the dialogue manager. It uses these functions as classes for the classification of user inputs. To maintain the context of the dialogue interactions, a context tree is used. Consequently, the model performs its task as two classification tasks to identify the function a user input may trigger and use the context to maintain the discourse of the dialogue. The model shows promising results and proves that a dialogue manager can be integrated into a spoken dialogue system much more directly with less hassle.

Keywords: Dialogue manager · Spoken dialogue systems ·
Natural language processing · User input learning · Naïve Bayes

1 Introduction

Human Computer Interaction has evolved drastically since the inception of computers. Spoken dialogue systems provide an interface for the users to perform task directly by speaking to the system without being distracted by other elements of a user interface [1]. Also spoken dialogue applications provide companies a cost-effective way of communicating with the users. Yet developing a spoken dialogue system entails crafting the components required to deploy such a system, which is a tedious task that requires expertise and time, which prevents such systems being deployed by companies [2].

Spoken dialogue systems allow the user to access information or services that are available on a computer or over the internet using spoken language as the medium of interaction [3]. A spoken dialogue system contains five principle components, Automatic Speech Recognizer, Natural Language Understanding, Dialogue Manager, Natural Language Generation, and Text to Speech as shown in Fig. 1. The dialogue manager's primary role is to maintain the discourse of the dialogue and manage the tasks as dictated by the course of the dialogue. Hence having a functionally adequate dialogue manager is crucial in developing a successful spoken dialogue system.

© Springer Nature Singapore Pte Ltd. 2019
J. Hemanth et al. (Eds.): SLAAI-ICAI 2018, CCIS 890, pp. 187–199, 2019.
https://doi.org/10.1007/978-981-13-9129-3_14

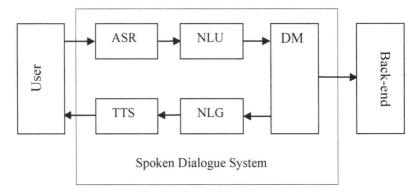

Fig. 1. Components of a spoken dialogue system: automatic speech recognizer (ASR), natural language understanding (NLU), dialogue manager (DM), natural language generation (NLG) and text to speech (TTS)

Interfacing a spoken dialogue system with a back-end system for which it acts as an interface for is a complex task. As it is the dialogue manager that manages the tasks the system performs it is the dialogue manager that will be interfaced to the back-end. Traditionally [4, 5], this integration requires the tasks the system can perform with respect to the back-end to be defined using a method specific to the scenario. Speech acts and dialogue moves are specified as domain independent components of the dialogue manager which utilizes the definitions specific to a domain to integrate with the back-end system. In this work, we propose a model for the dialogue manager which allows integrating a dialogue manager with the back-end system by including the back-end functionality in a more direct manner. Consequently, which can allow the dialogue manager to be integrated with a system with less hassle.

In order to do as such, we consider all functionalities of a system to be defined as functions. Every time a user interacts with the system, it is a function that is triggered and executed. This perspective is extended to define the primary tasks of the dialogue manager as a classification task. In order to maintain the discourse of the dialogue, a data structure is defined based on the relationship between the user's utterance and the functions.

2   Literature Review

Dialogue Acts are widely used to define the function of the utterances in a dialogue. In a speech processing system interpreting a user's utterance is primarily identifying the goal of the speaker. This can be said to be an extension of primary illocutionary acts Searle [6] identifies. Stolcke et al. [7] state that dialogue acts are approximately the same as the speech acts of Searle while also comparing it to other linguistic principles. It can be viewed as a tag set to classify utterances based on linguistic features that act as indicators to the speaker's intent. Though there is no consensus on the specification of dialogue acts.

There are attempts at standardizing dialogue acts [8, 9], yet dialogue act taxonomies have been developed to suit the task at hand [1, 10, 11]. The reason commonly cited by the authors who develop dialogue act schemes to suit their needs is that the standard dialogue act schemes such as DIT++ (Dynamic Interpretation Theory) [8] and DAMSL (Dialog Act Markup in Several Layers) [9] are too complex for the task at hand, and also too general for the tasks [1, 11].

In [1] the author defines a system-oriented Dialogue Act scheme to address the back-end functions he defines. He identifies three primary back-end functions, *getInfo*, *setInfo* and *do*. Subsequently, he defines three dialogue acts that directly represent the functions of the dialogue manager, *information-seeking act*, *information providing act* and *action requesting act*. These dialogue acts are used as the first phase of processing utterances. That is, they eliminate the ambiguity in the user's utterances, allowing to further simplify the process. These acts are used to identify if the user is requesting for information, providing some information or is requesting to perform an action. While the dialogue acts are identified from a classification task, the author further points out that a rule-based postprocessor will be needed when the result of the classification is an information providing act, as it would require an existing concern of the system that requires the user to provide more information.

For task-oriented dialogue systems, the representation of tasks is apparently of significance. Bohus and Rudnicky [12] define two layers, one is the dialog task specification which includes the domain-specific information of dialogue management, and the second layer is the dialogue engine which controls the dialogue by executing appropriate dialog task specifications. They use hierarchical task decomposition to represent the tasks. They also justify the use of tree structure to represent a hierarchy of tasks as it allows for the structure to be extended during run-time allowing the dialogue to grow dynamically. It captures the notion of the context through parent-child relationship of the tree and provides a chronological order for traversal. They conclude that the tree structure allows simplifying the operation of the dialogue engine. Each task is represented in the form of task agents. They define two different agents, fundamental dialog agents, and dialog agencies. Fundamental dialog agents being the atomic actions, which will be in the leaf nodes of the task tree. Dialog agencies, which will be the none-leaf nodes, will control the execution of their child nodes. The criteria for executing the task and the execution of the task itself are encapsulated in the agencies. The dialog engine executes the agents and builds a stack, which would capture the order in which the tasks are executed and their hierarchical relationship.

A similar approach is taken to represent tasks by Bangalore et al. [2]. In their work, they attempt to build a dialogue manager using a data-driven approach. In order to build such a model, they identify several components: (a) a model to identify the user's current action, for which they use a dialogue act scheme derived from DAMSL [9], (b) a model to identify the subtask being handled, and (c) a model to predict the next move of the dialogue manager. Here also tasks are represented in a tree structure. The root of the tree is the root task, and the sequence of subtasks are the child nodes, preferably in an order from left to right. As such tasks can be nested as subtasks. They test two methods of identifying subtasks, namely, chunk-based approach and parse-based approach. In the chunk-based approach, a subtask from a set of subtasks is predicted given an utterance in a dialogue. In the second approach, they take is a parse-based approach, reasoning that the chunk-based approach does not model the hierar-chical relationship between tasks. In this approach, they predict the plan tree given a sequence of utterances in a dialogue.

In another data-driven approach by Ha et al. [4], a task stream and a dialogue stream in a tutoring system are used to model a dialogue manager to spontaneously intervene while monitoring a user's tasks, in their case a tutoring session. When training their models, they test two approaches. First, a one-step dialogue management model, where not taking any action is also considered as a special dialogue act, predicts the next move based on the dialogue and task stream. In the second approach, a two-step dialogue management model is used. In the first step, it is decided that if an action should be taken or not, if the result of that step is that an action should be taken, the next step decides what step to take. The two-step model hence solves the shortcoming of the one-step model, which is that the probability distribution of dialogue acts can be skewed if the proportion of the special dialogue act is skewed. In their experiments, they show that the two-step dialogue management model has a better performance than the one-step dialogue management model.

In [1] a model is built in a bottom-up fashion. The dialogue model is created by identifying the back-ends functions and subsequently identifying how user's inputs can be used to perform more complex tasks through the back-end functions defined.

In an attempt to build a general spoken dialogue system development environment, all possible tasks a user can request a system to execute are divided into two broader tasks, which are communicating with a database or performing an action. Conse-quently, three primary functions a back-end can perform are defined. This helps to define a dialogue act scheme that could map to these back-end functions. As these acts are used only to identify the primary intent of an utterance, they are superficial to assist in performing further operations. That is, they are not sufficient to identify what the user's intents are. Hence, an Abstract Question Description (AQD) is defined, which models both system's questions and user's questions. Any answers would be matched to these AQD's to identify if it is indeed the answer. Subsequently, tasks are defined as a goal to be archived, such as getting information or performing an action. Each task may require more information, for which a set of AQDs is defined. The AQDs and the answers to them, together defined as an Information Transfer Object, are used to obtain the necessary information and perform the task.

It is worth noting that the work in [1], identifies a pattern in dialogues which is of particular interest in the proposed model in our work. Concerns (such as actions or questions) are elements in a dialogue that expect a response. Such a concern may require the other party to raise their own concerns. Clarifications are such instances. That is in order to define a concern completely, there can be other concerns that need to be resolved.

3 The Proposed Model

In any task-oriented dialogue, any utterance a user provides has an aim, which is to have the system perform an action. In this work, utterances of the user are mapped to the functions of the back-end system. That is, the user's utterances are considered as attempting to trigger a function in the back-end system. Hence the system will be working with the functions of the back-end directly. To simplify the identification of the function the user intends to trigger and to address situations where users provide information and the system communicating with the user, two broader dialogue acts are identified. They are concerns and replies, which are synonymous to the base elements of a dialogue identified in [1]. A concern is one party in the dialogue making a request to the other. A reply is when one party provides information to the other, which is always in response to a concern. Concerns and replies have different meanings for users and the system. When a user expresses a concern, it is requesting the system to execute a function. A system's concern is to request more information from the user. A user reply provides more information to the system. A system reply is the result of executing a function. All the concerns and replies together are defined as the context of a dialogue. The dialogue manager uses the context to perform actions, such as executing a function and determining the next step.

3.1   Representations of the User Input as Concerns and Replies in the Context

When a dialogue exchange is initiated between the user and the system, the context of the dialogue will have one concern of the system. The concern is the system's concern to know and perform what the user intends to have the system do. This is referred to as the *root-concern* of the system. As the dialogue progresses, any concern the user expresses is making a request to the system to execute a particular function in the back-end. This can be considered as a reply to the root concern. Following which the system attempts to execute the function the user attempts to trigger by the concern. The function the system attempts to execute may require parameters in order to execute successfully. The parameters are expressed by the system as concerns of the system. The user concern is resolved only if concerns which the system introduces are also successfully resolved. That is to say, the system can execute the function the user requested only if the user provides the values of the parameters of that function. Hence the user has to reply to the concerns the system introduces. The reply the user provides can be information that effectively resolves a concern of the system that represents a request for a value for a parameter. The reply the user provides can also be another concern that needs to be resolved in order to obtain the result that resolves the system's concern requesting a value for a parameter. As a concern the user introduces is a request to the system to execute a function, the system can introduce more child concerns of its own which are needed to be resolved. This relationship between concerns and replies can be expressed as follows: *A concern is resolved only if the concern has a direct reply or the child concerns introduced have been resolved.*

This hierarchical relationship between the concerns and replies, allows the context to be represented as a rooted tree where the root is the root-concern. This relationship can also be used to draw another conclusion, that all concerns, except the root-concern, are implicitly replies. Since all concerns and replies are closely related to the function, the distinction between a concern and a reply can be defined by how they are related to a function. The nodes in the context are referred to as *context-objects*. There are four types of context-objects, which are:

- *User-concern-context-object:* represents a user's utterance that intends to trigger one or more function in the back-end of the system.
- *System-concern-context-object:* represents a function that needs to be executed. There are two types of functions this can represent, a function in the system that performs an action, or a function that acts as a parameter extraction function.
- *User-reply-context-object:* represents a user's utterance that only provides information to a parameter extraction function.
- *System-reply-context-object:* represents the result of a function execution.

A user-context-object is used only to represent an utterance. Hence the function(s) the user intends to trigger by an utterance is added in the form of a system-concern-context-object as the child of the user-concern-context-object that represents the utterance. A system-concern-context-object represents a function which can be executed once the concern is successfully resolved. Hence a user-concern-context-object can be a parent or child only to a system-concern-context-object. That is, a user-concern-context-object is a user concern which is always a reply to a system concern. Since a user concern intends to trigger one or more functions, the child of a user-concern-context-object is one or more system-concern-context-objects that represent those functions which need to be executed to resolve the user's concern.

Each parameter values that are needed by a function are added as system-concern-context-objects that represent parameter extraction functions. The system-concern-context-objects that represent parameter extraction functions are added as child nodes of the system-concern-context-object that represents the function for which the parameters belong to. As such a concern-context-object is considered resolved only if the child nodes of it is resolved. Additionally, if it is a system-concern-context-object, it must successfully execute the function it represents. This entails that any reply-context-object is a leaf node in the context and they will be considered resolved by default. A dialogue exchange is considered completed when a root-concern of the context is resolved.

3.2   Proposed Dialogue Manager with User Input Learning

The dialogue manager's primary task is to interpret a user's utterance and determine the next step, which can include producing an utterance to the user or executing a function. The state change of the context can be used to determine the next step of the dialogue manager. State changes in the context will be triggered by a new user utterance. Hence the primary task of the dialogue manager is to process the user's utterances, following which other actions can be taken.

A user's utterance is represented by a user-context-object in the context. As all context-objects except the root-concern are implicitly replies, all user-context-objects are replies. Since a user-context-object can only be a child or parent to a system-concern-context-object and a system-concern-context-object always represents a function, to determine the parent system-concern-context-object of a user-context-object in the context, the functions can be directly used. That is to say the functions that can be represented in the context can be used as a set of classes to classify the user utterance.

This classification task will be referred to as *response-classifier*. The result of the response-classifier will be used to determine the parent system-concern-context-object of the user-context-object that represents the user utterance classified by the response-classifier. A user-context-object will be determined to be a user-concern-context-object only if it triggers a function. This also can be defined using a classifier whose classes are the functions that can be triggered by a user-concern-context-object. This classification task will be referred to as *trigger-classifier*.

The Fig. 2 shows the dialogue manager model proposed in this work. When the user provides a new utterance, first the response-classifier is used to determine for which system concern it is a reply for. Allowing to include the user-context-object to the context. Note that a user utterance can be a reply to multiple system concerns. In which case the user-context-object that represents the user's utterance has multiple parents. The trigger-classifier is used to determine if the user utterance is a user concern, if so, what is the function the user concern intends to trigger. If the user utterance is a user concern, a system-concern-context-object is included as a child of the user-context-object that represents the user's utterance. If the function that was included has parameters, the system-concern-context-objects representing each parameter will be included as child nodes of the system-concern-context-object that represents the function. Here a user utterance can trigger multiple functions simultaneously, in which case each function is represented by system-concern-context-objects and added as children to the user-concern-context-object.

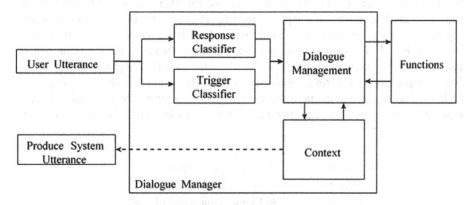

Fig. 2. Complete dialogue manager model. Solid arrows represent direct communication paths. The dashed arrow represents indirect communication. That is the information about the system utterance to produce is not conveyed directly from the context, rather that information is derived from the context by the dialogue manager.

Following each set of state changes of the context corresponding to a new user utterance, the context is scanned to determine if any of the concerns were resolved. If a system concern was resolved the function it represents is executed and its result is represented by a system-reply-context-object which is added as a child of the system-concern-context-object that represents the function. The system-concern-context-object will then be marked as resolved. Once all resolved concerns marked as resolved, the list of system-reply-concern-objects will be used to communicate the results to the user by sending appropriate signals to the component that can synthesize an utterance (which generally is a NLG component). When no new user utterance is provided, the unresolved system concerns are obtained from the context. From which the next systems concern to express can be determined and signaled to the NLG component. Note that system concern that represents functions that a user attempted to trigger cannot be expressed as such, only the system concerns that represent parameter extraction function can be expressed through the NLG. The parent of a system-concern-context-object can be used to determine the system concerns that can be expressed.

4   Results and Discussion

For the evaluation of the proposed dialogue manager, a text corpus containing simple dialogues was created. Each dialogue pertains the user requesting the system to perform a particular task. As all tasks are considered as an execution of a function. A set of functions that represents tasks that a back-end system can perform are defined. Every function designed for this experiment have one or more parameters. The parameter extraction functions are generated, where every parameter extraction function is unique to a single parameter in a function. In the experiments, it is assumed that a user's utterance can trigger only one function and will be a reply to one function. A 'nil' function is used as a placeholder function to represent when the user utterance does not trigger a function, making it a reply. This data set is used to train the two classifiers. Figure 3 shows a sample dialogue exchange which is represented in the data-set as shown in Fig. 4. The user in this dialogue exchange intends to book a train, that is, have the system execute a function *book-train*, whose function signature is *book-train* (*name, departure, destination, number-of-tickets*). Hence the data set contains a set of dialogues, where each dialogue is represented by a set of three element tuples. In each tuple, the first element is the utterance, the second element is the trigger function

System:	How may I help you?
User:	Can I book a train?
System:	Can I know your name please?
User:	It's Paul
System:	May I know when you are leaving?
User:	from Kandy
System:	Where are you traveling to?
User:	to Colombo
System:	How many tickets do you want?
User:	Five please

Fig. 3. Sample conversation in the text corpus. The user in this case intends to execute the function with signature: book-train (name, departure, destination, number-of-tickets)

("Can I book a train",   "book-train",   "root-concern")

("It's Paul",   "nil",   "book-train-name")

("from Kandy",   "nil",   "book-train-departure")

("to Colombo",   "nil",   "book-train-destination")

("five please",   "nil",   "book-train-number-of-tickets")

Fig. 4. Annotated data-set of sample dialogue shown in Fig. 3

(the function a user utterance intends to trigger) and the third element is the response-function (the function to which the user utterance is a reply to). Note that the parameter extraction functions are named as *'[function-name]-[parameter-name]'*, where the *function-name* is the name of the function to which the parameter extraction function is defined, and *parameter-name* is the name of the parameter itself as defined in the function signature. The system utterances are not included as the classifiers are for processing user utterances. The process in which the classifiers are to be trained is shown in Fig. 5.

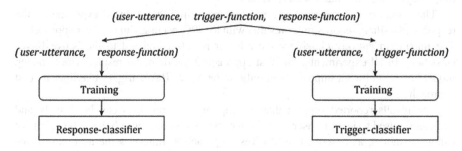

Fig. 5. The training of the two classifiers used in processing a user-utterance

The data set contains 103 user utterances from 29 individual dialogue exchanges. Each dialogue represents a scenario where the user expects to execute one of the 6 functions defined. The models trained were tested using two approaches. The first approach (*Test approach 1*) tests the classifiers in isolation for each utterance individually. The second approach (*Test approach 2*) tests the models trained with the whole dialogue manager model proposed, by providing the complete dialogue. The Test approach 1 assesses if a model is able to predict the name of the function related to the input user utterance. In the Test approach 2, each testing instance is a complete dialogue, which is represented by a set of user utterances. When testing one instance, the user utterance provided as the first input will be the utterance whose trigger function is not 'nil'. If the model is requesting any information, the name of the function[1] represented by the related system-concern-context-object will be the output of the

---

[1] These will be parameter extraction functions.

model. If the model is providing information, the output string that the relevant system-reply-context-object represents will be the output. The utterances provided to the model in the consequent turns will be the utterance whose response-function is the function name given as output. The user utterances can only be a reply to one of the system concerns already present in the context, hence the result of the response-classifier is filtered based on the list of system concerns which are expecting a user reply. When the test instance does not have an unused user utterance whose response-function is the output produced by the model, the turn is marked as a failure and the unused utterances will be discarded. The accuracy in Test approach 2 is the percentage of successful turns.

Following the *two-step dialogue management model* [4], the trigger-classifier was divided into two classifiers. The first classifier determines if the user utterance provided introduces a user concern, that is if the trigger-function of the user-utterance is 'nil'. If the first classifier determines that the user utterance introduces a user concern, the second classifier will determine the trigger-function.

For each trigger and response classifier, Naïve Bayes classifiers and maximum entropy classifiers were trained and compared[2]. Naïve Bayes classifiers use all words in input utterance as features due to the small data-set. Term frequency-inverse document frequency is used to obtain feature values.

The results of the experiments are summarized in Table 1. In all experiments, the response classifiers report similar results, with a 100% accuracy in the Test approach 2. The maximum entropy classifiers show better results compared to the Naïve Bayes classifiers. In all experiments, the Test approach 2 yields better results. The two-step model has a significant improvement only in the Naïve Bayes trigger-classifier in Test approach 2.

The results reported suggest that assumption that functions can be directly and sufficiently used to identify user's intent in providing an utterance holds. The results of using the model, as described by the Test approach 2, improves the accuracy of the response-classifier as the model functions as a filter that complements the response-classifier. The cause of the trigger-function classifier's lower accuracy is attributed to the data set not having a proportional number of trigger-functions. The two-step model was formulated to address this issue. Following which the accuracy of the trigger-classifier reports a 68% accuracy on the Naïve Bayes model, while it does not change the output of the maximum entropy model.

As the model does not provide any mechanism to filter the trigger functions the fluctuation of the accuracy of trigger functions between Test approach 1 and Test approach 2 should not be present. The fluctuations exist due to the testing approach taken in Test approach 2. When the trigger function classifier fails to produce a result with which the dialogue being tested cannot be completed, the dialogue is considered to be failed. Hence the remaining untested user utterances are not used. That is between the models, only 66% to 80% of the user utterances are used to test the models.

While the overall results suggest that our assumptions for the dialogue manager model hold since it is tested on a small data-set, practical results may differ from that

---

[2] All words in an input utterance are stemmed before being processed by the models.

Table 1. The accuracy of the proposed model with different classifiers

Model	Approach	Accuracy of the response classifier	Accuracy of the trigger classifier
Naive-Bayes without two-step dialogue management model	Test approach 1	71%	51%
	Test approach 2	100%	68%
Naive-Bayes with two-step dialogue management model	Test approach 1	71%	51%
	Test approach 2	100%	75%
Maximum entropy without two-step dialogue management model	Test approach 1	76%	54%
	Test approach 2	100%	88%
Maximum entropy with two-step dialogue management model	Test approach 1	76%	54%
	Test approach 2	100%	88%

are reported here. It also must be noted that dialogues in this data set are simple, in that, each utterance has only a simple function. Elements such as an utterance which can trigger multiple functions or responses to functions already available in the context are not tested.

The implication of the dialogue manager model designed here is that it allows to integrate a spoken dialogue system more directly. That is, the existing systems will already have a set of functions through which its services are provided. These functions can be employed in the process of understanding the user's requests in a more direct fashion. This also would imply that the complexity of developing a dialogue system can be reduced. Though an effort is required to provide a sufficient data set annotated with the function, and the work that needs to go in developing the linguistic aspects of the dialogue system can be significantly reduced. Also, the dialogue system can be employed as a separate module without making any significant alterations to the system which are factors that can influence spoken dialogue systems being adapted as interfaces to existing established systems.

5 Conclusions

A new dialogue management model is proposed where the back-end functionality of a system, to which the dialogue manager will act as an interface to, is used in a more direct fashion in mapping user input to the back-end functionality. To this effect, as base elements of a dialogue, concerns and replies are identified. Together all concerns and replies, of both user and system, are referred to as the context, which can be used to uniquely define a dialogue exchange. Further, the tasks user requests to perform and the tasks the system expects to perform are considered as functions in the system. A system reply is the result of executing a function. A user concern is when the utterance provided intends to trigger the system to execute a function. Since system concerns are defined as functions, system's request for information is also defined as a function. Hence a user's reply is a reply to a function. This allows to define the context in the form of a tree, where the root-node represents the system's concern to identify the user's concerns. Following that an important property of the user's concerns is identified. That is in the context, the user concern always precedes or follows system concerns. This is extended to argue that a user's utterance is always a reply to a function. A user utterance is a concern if and only if it intends to trigger a function. This is further refined to express the task of the dialogue manager as a simpler text classification problem. Two classifiers are defined, one to identify which function a user utterance is a reply to, second to identify if the utterance intends to trigger a function, and if so, what function it triggers.

To test the model, a simple dataset was created and tested using bigrams Naïve Bayes classifier and maximum entropy classifier. The results suggest the initial assumption that functions can be directly employed to extract the intent of a user from the utterances. The model proposed here provides a novel approach to implement and integrate a dialogue interface to an existing system. The approach alleviates the need to define and map the relationship between back-end functionality and speech acts or other intermediate states (which may require expert knowledge) allowing for a developer to integrate the dialogue manager with less work. In order for the model to be integrated to a system, it requires building a dataset corresponding to the system to which the dialogue manager is being integrated with.

The problems that are not handled by the proposed model include situations such as when there is a correction that needs to be made and when the task needs to be aborted. The ongoing work on this matter draws from the approach employed in RavenClaw [12]. That is, these functionalities are predefined built-in functions that can be triggered. The lacking functionality described in the proposed model can be defined as having to make alterations to the context of a dialogue. Corrections are replies that need to be assigned to concerns already considered to be resolved, which would imply the concern's state should be changed to not resolved. Aborting a task is forcefully marking a concern as resolved. Hence a set of in-built functions with access to the context can be used to address these limitations. Other shortcomings such as not being able to trigger multiple tasks, or processing over informative utterances, needs to be addressed by improving the process model of the dialogue manager.

Another limitation we intend to improve in the future is to incorporate unsupervised learning to perform the task of the dialogue manager. Such a model will address one of the primary drawbacks of the dialogue systems in general [2], which is having to build the data-set to train the system. This will allow us to ease the process of building a spoken dialogue system further.

The diversity in the way different dialogue managers are modeled makes objective comparisons of different models a difficult task. The recent body of work in end-to-end dialogue managers has given rise to several datasets to test the performance of dialogue systems in various domains and contexts [13–16]. These approaches don't address the limitation of integrating a dialogue manager with an existing system. The datasets proposed in this body of work tests the models from a general dialogue standpoint. Testing the proposed approach in this context requires addressing some of the previously mentioned limitations. While there is work done that proposes a framework to compare dialogue controls/strategies [5] it is insufficient to compare different models.

References

1. Berg, M.: Modelling of natural dialogues in the context of speech based information and control system. Ph.D. thesis, University of Kiel (2014)
2. Bangalore, S., Feng J., Rahim, M.G.: System and method of providing a spoken dialog interface to a website. United States Patent US 8,949,132 B2 (2015)
3. Jokinen, K., McTear, M.: Synthesis Lectures on Human Language Technologies, pp. 1–3. Morgan & Claypool, San Rafael (2010)
4. Ha, E.Y., Mitchell, C.M., Boyer, K.E., Letser, J.C.: Learning dialogue management models for task-oriented dialogue with parallel dialogue and task streams. In: SIGDIAL 2013 Conference, Metz, France (2013)
5. Larsson, S., Traum, D.R.: Information state and dialogue management in the TRINDI dialogue move engine toolkit. In: National Language Engineering Special Issue on Best Practice in Spoken Language Dialogue Systems Engineering, pp. 325–340 (2000)
6. Searle, J.R.: A classification of illocutionary acts. Lang. Soc. 1(1), 1–23 (1976)
7. Stolcke, A., et al.: Dialogue act modeling for automatic tagging and recognition of conversational speech. Comput. Linguist. 26, 339–373 (2000)
8. Bunt, H., et al.: Towards an iso standard for dialogue act annotation. In: 7th International Conference on Language Resources and Evaluation (2010)
9. Allen, M.C.J.: Draft of DAMSL: dialog act markup in several layers (1997). http://www.cs.rochester.edu/research/cisd/resources/damsl%20
10. Boyer, K.E., Ha, E.Y., Phillips, R., Wallis, M.D., Vouk, M.A., Lester, J.C.: Dialogue act modeling in a complex task-oriented domain. In: SIGDIAL 2010 Proceedings of the 11th Annual Meeting of the Special Interest Group on Discourse and Dialogue (Tokyo, Japan) (2010)
11. Bangalore, S., Fabbrizio, G.D., Stent, A.: Learning the structure of task-driven human-human dialogs. In: IEEE Transactions on Audio, Speech, and Language Processing, vol. 16, no. 7, pp. 1249–1259 (2008)
12. Bohus, D., Rudnicky, A.I.: RavenClaw: dialog management using hierarchical task decomposition and an expectation agenda. In: Research Showcase at CMU (2003)
13. Yang, X.: End-to-end joint learning of natural language understanding and dialogue manager. In: Proceedings of the IEEE International Conference on Acoustics, Speech, and Signal Processing, pp. 5690–5694 (2017)
14. Bordes, A., Weston, J.: Learning End-to-End Goal-Oriented Dialog. CoRR abs/1605.07683 (2016)
15. Weston, J., Bordes, A., Chopra S., Mikolov, T.: Towards AI-Complete Question Answering: A Set of Prerequisite Toy Tasks. CoRR abs/1502.05698 (2015)
16. Serban, I.V., Sordoni, A., Bengio, Y., Courville, A.C., Pineau, J.: Building end-to-end dialogue systems using generative hierarchical neural network models. AAAI 16, 3776–3784 (2016)

Text Mining-Based Human Computer Interaction Approach for On-line Purchasing

Nadeeka Malkanthi[✉] and Thashika D. Rupasinghe

Department of Industrial Management, Faculty of Science,
University of Kelaniya, Colombo, Sri Lanka
kanml@stu.kln.ac.lk, thashika@kln.ac.lk

Abstract. E-commerce websites have created a great opportunity not only for businesses but also for consumers to perform their transactions directly. These transactions can be classified into different types such as consumer-oriented factors, behavioral factors, and Human Computer Interaction (HCI)-based factors. This study uses a twofold approach. In the first phase, prominent HCI factors are identified through existing literature namely; accessibility, simplicity, and usefulness which enhances the interaction of people with E-commerce websites. In the second phase of the study, we conducted a detailed experiment by varying the identified HCI factors towards consumer interaction using text-mining approach. Various approaches have been utilized to identify the relationship between factors affecting the consumers' online purchasing behavior. Most of the cases, those studies focused on one website to identify the HCI factors pertaining to it. To overcome the research gap in current literature, the authors have built a novel and a unique approach to assess the factors related to HCI in enhancing online purchasing experience of diverse customer settings.

Keywords: Human Computer Interaction (HCI) · Online purchasing ·
Text mining · Sentiment analysis

1 Introduction

With the revolutionary development in the field of information technology for the past few years, it has impacted individuals as well as businesses in a massive way for communications and transactions related to businesses. Hence, this environment has made immense influences on businesses to create and continue e-commerce websites to improve their financial performance [1]. Furthermore, a significant number of consumers interact with e-commerce websites to complete their transactions, and day-by-day number of users and the reviews posted by them have increased drastically. Those reviews contained product-based reviews as well as website related reviews [2, 3].

In this environment, customer experience with the ecommerce websites are extended beyond the interaction to the website and include with starting from finding the web site to consumption of the product and service. Further this is different to each other with the social and cultural environment [4]. Hence high-quality user experience has become competitive factor for this environment and product development [5]. And

© Springer Nature Singapore Pte Ltd. 2019
J. Hemanth et al. (Eds.): SLAAI-ICAI 2018, CCIS 890, pp. 200–218, 2019.
https://doi.org/10.1007/978-981-13-9129-3_15

good quality information system is essential for achieving success in this rapidly growing e-commerce market [6].

The main goal of this paper is to develop a framework to evaluate the e-commerce website based on HCI factors and sentiment mining. That means to prioritize the factors which affect "good browsing "experience. To achieve this goal study has first identified the HCI factors and identifies the relationship between HCI and online purchasing.

2 Literature Review

Using a systematic review of the existing literature the authors identified the HCI related attributes which affect the consumers when they use e-commerce websites. Complex mixture of factors consisting social, cultural, educational, environmental factors influence the online consumer buying behaviour. Furthermore, the trust and the confidence placed on the website, attractiveness of the website, completeness of the information about goods and services encourage to make purchasing online [7]. Online purchasing is mainly based on three factors such as; personal, environmental, marketing, and web related factors. Furthermore, these factors can be further classified into consumer characteristics, consumer concerns in online shopping, and HCI related factors [8]. Trust is one of the main factors considered and it is a combination of Safety and privacy of information, security and delivery and return on time [9, 10] Furthermore, [11] conducted a study to investigate which graphic design elements were most likely to communicate trust in cyber-banking interfaces. Since their approach was exclusively empirical with little grounding in theory, it is argued that their results cannot be taken as high-level, generalizable HCI design principles. Similarly, a study by [12] discusses some heuristics susceptible to increase consumers' trust. However, the validity of these rules-of thumb is also seriously undermined, due to the lack of explicit knowledge from which the guidelines are derived. [13], on the other hand, propose a generic, analytical, model of trust for e-commerce. Although their model has not been tested empirically, it remains that it constitutes a good basis from which to derive a trust specific HCI design method. As a result of those studies has identified Consumers' lack of trust as a major barrier to the adoption of e- commerce web sites. So that [14] was developed a model of trust that describes what design factors affect consumers' assessment of online vendors' trustworthiness. Through that, it has identified six elements which can be categorized into three groups.

Consumer characteristics such as demographic factors, personality, tradition and cultural factors have played a major role and depends on other factors such as computer literacy, technology awareness, and past experiences. HCI in this study can be broadly defined and applied in the scope of website design, website interaction, and it's display for the user's easiness to learn. Furthermore, this is fulfilling through characteristic which are related to websites such as information available on website, visual effects and attractiveness, quality of content, ease of navigation, less time consuming and security assurance of the website [23].

According to the revolution of the web and internet, competition of e-commerce environment has ever grown. Hence, to increase the cited number of consumers to the website, it has to be designed with the fulfilment of user expectation [16].

In order to fulfil the user expectations, website designing needs pay to attention on 1. Web usability, 2. Interface design, 3. Trust [17]. When considering the e-commerce websites, it is a combination of three sub systems 1. Web store, 2. Customer, 3. Web technology. According to these subsystems, customer plays a stronger role and it starts with the consumer interaction to the e-commerce site. Therefore, HCI and web design guidelines are valuable to connect each subsystem [7, 18].

Usability is the ease of use and learnability of human made objects. Usefulness of an e-commerce website has increase through its designing factors and trustworthiness factors [19]. In addition, usability factors can be referred as 1. The ease of learning to use website, 2. The efficiency of the interface design, 3. The ease of memorizing how to use interfaces, 4. The ease of recovering from errors, 5. General satisfaction with the interface [20]. Within the web environment, human factors can be categorized into five types. 1. Entertainment, 2. Cognitive outcome, 3. User empowerment, 4. Visual appearance, 5. Organization of the information content. Since the number of web designing tools have increased, the purchasing intention and reuse intention of e-commerce sites have also increased [21]. In a recent study, HCI related attributes which affect e-commerce websites are highlighted as usefulness, accessibility, and simplicity [22]. Further, to success of e commerce environment website usability is imperative to aim for customer loyalty satisfaction along with the trust [22].

2.1   Text Mining

Text mining is the technology which is used to extract information and discover new knowledge from unstructured and semi-structured data sources like different written resources, and websites. According to the text mining process, it is a step by step process and it started with the collection of various types of documents [23]. Furthermore, text mining is a collection of different types of methods and techniques. Information extraction, summarization, categorization, clustering and information visualization, are the techniques used in the text mining process for filtering, analysis, generating the text. Moreover, it helps to manage a great amount of unstructured information for extracting patterns [24].

2.2   Sentiment Analysis and Opinion Mining

Sentiment analysis is a novel approach for text analysis which aims at determining the opinion and subjectivity of reviewers. Furthermore, it has helped to classify the huge number of texts through supervised learning [25]. Different techniques are used in analyzing the text to extract the sentiments. From a technical point of view, machine learning, lexicon-based, statistical and rule-based approaches have been used [26].

Machine Learning Methods: use this method for several algorithms such as a Naïve Bayes classifier to determine the sentiments after training it through known data set.

Lexicon-based Methods: use this method through calculating sentiment polarities for each and every semantic orientation of words in reviews.

Rule-based Method: use this method through identifying opinion words in a text and considering rules and classify those.

Statistical Method: use this method after representing each review as a mixture of latent aspects and rating.

Sentiment Analysis can be done in another aspect such as text view and rating view. The diagram shown below depicts all possible classifications carried out in sentiment analysis [26]. The Fig. 1 illustrates the techniques which are used in a most widely applicable sentiment analysis.

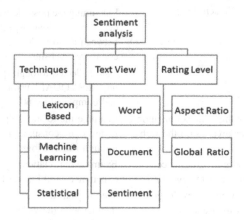

Fig. 1. Techniques in Sentiment Analysis [2]

2.3   Technology Acceptance Model (TAM)

When rapidly growing e-commerce environment, consumer behavior has investigated through Technology Acceptance Model (TAM). The TAM variables are perceived usefulness, perceived ease of use, and intentions which are correlated to the decision to adopt new technologies [27]. Furthermore, it has designed to explain new technology adoption and e-commerce behavior. But today mostly used That model to explore internet consumer behavior [28–32].

Under the section of literature review, the authors report a rigorous literature survey with the approaches, gaps, and applicability of those available studies related to this area. A summary of the systematic review is depicted on Table 1 with nine studies which are related to HCI and model formulations. With the findings of the below table, authors have summarized it into three stages and these stages are related to model formulation.

Most studies have used structured questionnaire and through observations consumer reviews have been used for analysing the data to identify the relationship between interaction to the website with the website usability factors.

The first two studies are formulated through questionnaire-based studies which identified the relationship between factors and consumer interaction to the e-commerce websites.

In the first study, Authors has collected data using a specified measuring instrument and it was a self-developed and standardized questionnaire. Furthermore, it consists two sections with The scale used for measurement was the Likert Scale; with answers

Table 1. Systematic review of existing literature

Name of the study	Objectives of the study
Effects of online shopping trends on consumer buying behaviour: an empirical study in Pakistan [41]	Examine the relationship between various factors and the consumer buying behaviour
Relationship between Website Attributes and Customer Satisfaction: A Study of E-Commerce Systems in Karachi [33]	Investigate the important attributes of online web stores in e-commerce
	Examining the possible website elements that determine different aspects of association between customer's satisfaction and e-commerce website
	Data collected through questionaries' based on "SERVQUAL" using 5-point Likert scale and completed by 60 respondents
Why are you telling me this? An examination into negative consumer reviews on the web [34]	Examine the relationship between product reviews and consumer buying behaviour through observations
Extracting usability and user experience information from online user reviews [35]	Examine the relationship between user experiences and buying behaviour
Web usage mining for web site evaluation-Making a site better fit its users [36]	Web log has analysis to identify how users interact with the website and identify the factors which interact to the website
How do users evaluate the credibility of web sites: A study with over 2,500 participants [37]	Survey based study to identify the credibility of the website
	Review data has evaluated and give scores to identify each websites credibility
Critical Design factors for successful e-commerce systems [38]	Survey based two studies to identify each website critical design factors
Review-based measurement of customer satisfaction in mobile service: Sentiment analysis and VIKOR approach [39]	Sentiment analysis used to analyse consumer reviews
	Proposed framework to measure the consumer satisfaction with mobile services by combining VIKOR and sentiment method. Lexicon based dictionaries are used
An approach towards feature specific opinion mining and sentimental analysis across e-commerce websites [40]	Sentiment analysis is used to analyse the product and service based reviews
	Proposed framework used to measure the consumer feature analysis of each product and services by combining score-based sentiment analysis method

ranging from 1 to 5, or strongly disagree to strongly agree respectively. Respondents were asked to rate their levels of agreement as pertaining to various criteria, mainly trust, convenience, time, product variety and privacy. The higher the score that was chosen, the greater the importance that the respondents assigned to the criterion when

Table 2. Pros and Cons of different techniques

Techniques	Advantages	Disadvantages
Questionnaire	The data gathered is standardized and therefore, easy to analyze	Responses might be inaccurate
	Can be gathered quickly from a large number of responds	Reasonable sample size is needed before the responses can be used to represent the population as a whole
	Online surveys are relatively	Response rates can be poor; people
	Inexpensive	may lack the motivation to complete or
	One person can administer the entire process if they have the necessary skills	return the Questionnaire
Observation	Ease of use	Lack of information about the quality
	Several observers can gather the same information and can check for reliability	More expensive rather than questionnaire
	Can focus on multiple human behaviors at the same time	Waste of time
Web log analyzing	Data is only as recent as last log file update	Time consuming

they were shopping online. Data sample has consisted 250 responds and analyzed through the SPSS software.

[33] as done their study based on 24 structured questions with the 1 to 5 Likert scale where "1" means Strongly Disagree and "5" means Strongly Agree. Furthermore, Sample data set has collected total 1082 registered IT firms in Pakistan which are doing web development activities as part of their businesses. As a result, total 60 responses were collected out of which male respondents accounted for 83% and 17% were female. Moreover, research has collected data for one dependent variable called as Satisfaction and five independent variables called as web structure, Web Adequacy, Web Security, Web Response and Web customization. Results has analyzed through a text of regression method.

Considering these studies, they have not more proper framework for mining the text to identify the relationship and consumer reviews have not used to identify the web usability. Further these studies have used software or simple methods to analyse the data which gathered through questionnaires.

[34] extracted consumer reviews from e-retailer websites and because of observation, data has analysed. [35] have used 9 usability experts for their study whom are active researchers in usability and as a result of observation from them 24 reviews are analysed, and results taken from it. As a result of these two studies, the authors have identified the above studies which use consumer review as primary data to derive the relationship of consumers' interaction with website and factors. Hence, studies of this stage used consumer reviews, but not text mining. Furthermore, e-commerce websites have become borderless marketplace and web users search products and services inspect and occasionally. Hence, to get competitive advantage from this race is

knowledge of those customers and establish personalized services for them. In this environment, [36] as evaluated the website to identify the relationship of web usage with web site design factors in order to this used group of users and define the activities that are expected to perform, such as surfing around, exploring the contents, and ordering products. Further, all operations are recorded. After that data has analyzed using web log with applying data mining techniques with formally or informally using recorded details.

[37] has done their study survey-based review collecting on credibility of website. 2500 participants have examined 10 content categories which include 100 websites and reviewed by them. Review comments are stored, and frequency of the comments are scored identify the credibility of each websites. [38] have e commerce system using survey-based techniques. Two studies have done for fulfill of research primary goal which identify the critical design factors that have a substantial impact on the performance of e-commerce systems.

In the final study, the authors have identified consumer reviews which are sentiment analysis VIKOR method-based study. Furthermore, VIKOR method is Multi Criteria Method which means it compares the number of criteria [39]. Furthermore, [40] as analysed using sentiment analysis for customer reviews which describe the online products and services. Furthermore, specific features have evaluated through those thousands of useful reviews. Moreover, this study has provided the summarized data for business for their improvements of business outcomes.

Through these studies, it has identified that the various approaches to identify the relationship between factors and consumers online purchasing behaviour used questionnaire based, observation etc. Furthermore, those studies basically focused on one website to identify the HCI factors which are related to it. Furthermore, Sentiment analysis also used for mining the reviews and little studies have touch this area. Hence, to overcome the research gap in current literature the authors have developed approach to identify the HCI related attributes which are embedded in websites to give better browsing experience to the consumers.

According to the literature, different methodologies have been identified to use to identify the relationships between consumer behavior and various.

3 Methodology

Study contains main two phases. First phase generates the HCI related words dictionary from online reviews and second phase is uses this HCI related word dictionary to identify the HCI attributes which affect the consumers for their satisfaction or dissatisfaction.

The objective of this model development is to extract the best and the worse attributes related to HCI pertaining to a particular e-commerce website when customers are browsing through.

As the initial step, the data source was Amazon product reviews which extracted from the Stanford data repository (https://snap.stanford.edu/data/web-Amazon.html). Further, this repository includes ∼35 million reviews from June 1995 to March 2013.

Reviews contain product reviews like ratings, text, votes, helpfulness and metadata like descriptions, features and links like also viewed from Amazon [42, 43] (Table 3).

Table 3. Data Statistics

Number of reviews	34,686,770
Number of users	6,643,669
Number of products	2,441,053
Users with > 50 reviews	56,772
Median no. of words per review	82
Timespan	Jun 1995–Mar 2013

Further, each and every review follows the below format.

{Product/product ID: B00006HAXW
Product/title: Heavenly Highway Hymns
Product/price: unknown
Review/user ID: A1RSDE90N6RSZF
Review/profile Name: Joseph M. Kotow
Review/helpfulness: 9/9
Review/score: 5.0
Review/time: 1042502400
Review/summary: Pittsburgh - Home of the OLDIES
Review/text: I": "I bought this for my husband who plays the piano. He is having a wonderful time playing these old hymns. The music is at times hard to read because we think the book was published for singing from more than playing from. Great purchase though!"}

And it consists with below information [42, 43].

- **Product/Product ID:** ID of the product
- **Product/Title:** title of the product
- **Product/Price:** price of the product
- **Review/User ID:** id of the user
- **Review/Profile Name:** name of the user
- **Review/Helpfulness:** fraction of users who found the review helpful
- **Review/Score:** rating of the product
- **Review/Time:** time of the review
- **Review/Summary:** review summary
- **Review/Text:** text of the review

Two small set of consumer reviews files have been extracted from this huge reading material related Amazon review file for the study. One file has used to the first phase of the study and Study has done through two phases. In the first phase,

Through an extensive review of literature, HCI related attribute dictionary has been created. This dictionary has hundreds of words which describe the features of a website through consumer reviews. According to that, a dictionary has been compiled with HCI related attributes connected to online purchasing website. Testing dataset has been used to compile this dictionary. For that, dataset has been loaded into R workspace as a corpus, and pre-processing steps have followed. As the results of pre-processing all punctuations, all numbers and all noisy words in the reviews have removed. Furthermore, removed stopping words which include in reviews don't make any information's. Moreover, all words convert into its stem format. Subsequently, that corpus was converted into Term Document Matrix and identifies the high frequency words [45].

3.1 Lexicon-Based Feature Extraction Model

A lexicon-based approach is a simple and practical approach to Sentiment Analysis and it is one of the main approaches to sentiment analysis and it involves calculating the sentiment from the semantic orientation of word or phrases that occurs in a text. For that, a dictionary which has positive and negative words is required. Through that model, represent the text as a bag of words. Following this representation of the message, sentiment values from the dictionary are assigned to all positive and negative words or phrases within the message. A combining function, such as sum or average, is applied in order to make the final prediction regarding the overall sentiment for the message. Using the final sentiment value, it's shown as overall value as negative or positive. Furthermore, lexicon-based approach can apply through dictionary based or corpus based [46].

This study has applied lexicon based approach and based on two dictionaries. Sentiment word dictionary and HCI related attributes dictionary. Using this method, it avoids creating the label and it is easier to understand and modify by a user. Further, this is not depending on a single language; it can be managing multi languages [46].

In here, Feature extraction from unstructured text is a major step in implementing the model which can identify the factors which give the better browsing experiences. This is one of the major challenges in the field of Natural Language Processing (NLP) and data mining. The step-by-step process which has been followed is depicted on the Fig. 2.

After compiling the HCI related attributes dictionary, it is imported to the working phase as dataset. Then the dataset has been initialized as a data frame and the reviews inside the data frame are split into sentences. Subsequently, the sentences are categorised into different categories based on lexical dictionaries which contained the attributes related to HCI. Then, all the sentences in each category have been split into bag of words. Afterwards, a bag of words has been further processed for extraction to classify as positive, negative or neutral opinions. Finally, the sentiment analysis has been carried out for each category by using visualization plots developed through open source R. The overall process of the sentiment analysis can be shown on the below Fig. 3.

3.2 Model Validation

Model validation is carried out by comparing SVM classifier with the proposed model [44]. It has been identified that the newly developed classifier compiles more attributes

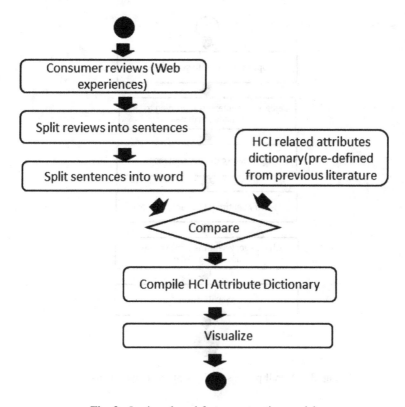

Fig. 2. Lexicon-based feature extraction model

from text than the SVM. Furthermore, through *Term document matrix* [11] and high frequency word cloud the newly developed classifier has been further validated.

4   Results

Results also have visualized into two stages. In the first stage, it has shown the results which identified after compiling the predefined dictionary and finally has shown the results of the model which apply for the consumer reviews files.

In the first stage, it has been identified that the words in consumer review data set and frequency of these words which used in the reviews are analysed. Among them highest frequency words could be compared with predefined dictionaries related to HCI and compile the HCI related words dictionary for model formulation.

In this study, results are taken through two sample test cases based on reviews, which are written by consumers related to their experiences about website are used to identify the high frequency words and compile with pre-defined dictionary and create HCI words dictionary for the next step of the study. Compilation of dictionary which is related to online purchasing website has been done through the lexicon-based feature extraction algorithm which has developed through this study.

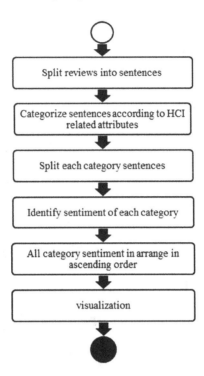

Fig. 3. Overall process of the sentiment analysis model

Figure 4 has depicted the high frequency words which are identified through the data set related to online purchasing website. Through that, it has identified the HCI related attributes which are mostly used in consumer reviews.

Further, after compilation of the dictionary it has built from HCI attributes which has highly frequency in the sample test cases. Hence, five attributes which has high frequency in the sample test cases which are embedded in online reading materials website are base for the compiled dictionary and these five attributes are used for model.

Table 2 is depicting the combination of HCI related attributes which are extracted from two test cases which has high frequency and it also depict HCI related attributes which are extracted from test cases individually (Table 4).

4.1   Analysing the Results of the Model

A developed model has been tested for data set related consumer reviews about online purchasing website. Through the model, polarity scores for each category has been calculated. Furthermore, the model has been calculated negative and positive polarities for each category. Those categories are the bag of sentences which connect with the attributes related to HCI that are embedded in online purchasing website.

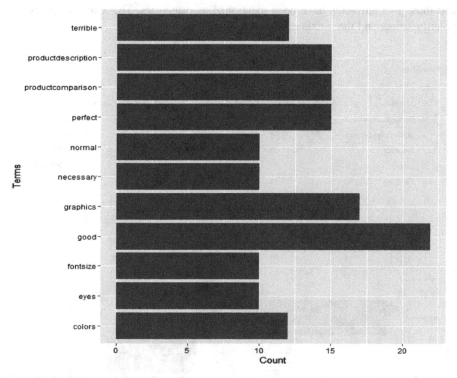

Fig. 4. High frequency words in dataset

Table 4. Human Computer Interaction related attributes which extracted from test cases

	Attributes from test case 1	Attributes from test case 2	Attributes from combination of test case 1 and 2
1	Graphics	Font Size	Graphics
2	Colours	Colours	Colours
3	Font size	Graphics	Font size
4	Product description	Product comparison	Product description
5	Product comparison		Product comparison

4.2 Test Results

The test result of testing data set is shown below. Figure 5 is the result gained from the R studio.

4.3 Polarity Scores for Each Attributes

Figure 6 shows the polarity scores for each category, and negative polarity categories are shown in red colour and positive score category is shown in green colour. Accordingly, the feature extraction step has been identified five HCI related attributes, and those five attributes have been mentioned as categories. The x axis displays the polarity scores and the y axis each category/attribute.

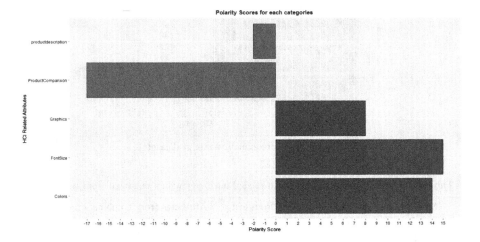

🔵 sortedvec   —

▽ Filter   🔍

	attributes	Positive_Count	Negative_Score	Neutral_Score	score	Average
4	ProductComparison	0	-17	0	-17	-1.0000000
3	productdescription	8	-10	0	-2	-0.1111111
1	Graphics	15	-7	0	8	0.3636364
2	Colors	14	0	0	14	1.0000000
5	FontSize	15	0	0	15	1.0000000

Fig. 5. Testing data set results in R studio

Fig. 6. Polarity scores for each attributes

According to the graph, colours, font size and graphics, there are positive polarity scores while product comparison and product description have negative polarity. Therefore, this shows the online reading material purchasing website's quality of graphics/photography, font sizes of text and colours of website are good whereas the product comparison and product description of the website are not sufficient to increase the interaction between consumers with the online purchasing website.

According to the results, it has been shown that the product description and product comparison details need to improve with the accuracy, and sufficiently to interact consumer with the website. Furthermore, graphics, colours and font size are not needed to be changed yet should be improved and continued. The consumer interaction with the website needs to continue those three attributes in a quality manner.

However, this diagram does not clearly show the consumer opinion as it shows the combination of polarity for a collection of different negative and positive opinion sentences. Finally, this diagram has helped to make prediction about the effect of website quality on interaction process of human with website.

4.4 Negative and Positive Opinion Score Comparison

The Fig. 7 shows the negative and positive opinion polarity scores for each attribute which are calculated from number of reviews. In the graph, the red colour bar refers to the positive opinions and blue ones are negative opinion Polarities.

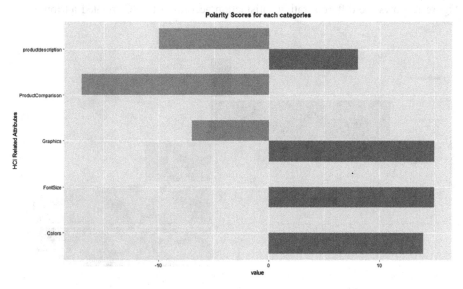

Fig. 7. Negative and positive opinion score comparison

According to the graph, it shows that colours and font size attributes have no any negative opinions. Hence, those two attributes have a good quality, and they help to increase and continue consumer interaction with online reading materials website. Furthermore, product description has no any positive opinions inside the bag of reviews. Therefore, it has an effect to decrease the consumer interaction with the website. Moreover, it must be improved, and given a better product comparison to get better knowledge and idea about products, and to help increase the consumer inter-action level with the website. According to the graphics attributes, it has the higher number of positive opinions more than the number of negative opinions. Therefore, it has been recommended that the graphics have good polarity, but it must be improved to continue the consumers' interaction with the website. Moreover, the product descrip-tion has positive and negative opinion reviews and scores of those opinions are closer. Nevertheless, there are more positive values rather than negative values. Therefore, there is a small negative value for this product description attribute. Therefore, according to this website product description, it is not much bad. Hence, increase the level of consumer interaction to website product description and product comparison need to be improved. Furthermore, level of improvement of product comparison is higher than compare to product description.

According to this diagram, it gives a clear idea about five factors which are embedded in online reading material purchasing website. The idea of what is to be improved and what factors are needed to continue its quality to make interaction with the consumers with the websites.

4.5   Satisfaction Scale According to Each HCI Factors

Figure 8 shows the different rating satisfaction according to HCI related attributes.

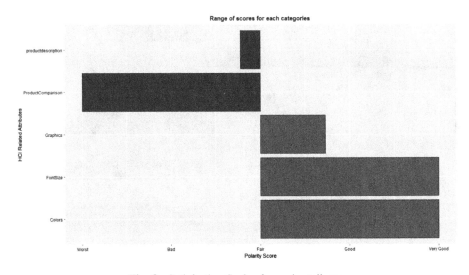

Fig. 8. Satisfaction Scales for each attributes

Satisfaction from website is core outcome measure for online reading material purchasing website. Hence, satisfaction of the consumer is depending on the quality of website HCI factors. Through the results from the model, a scale of consumer satisfaction about different factors has been recorded.

According to the graph, it has depicted the colours, font size and graphics of the website has positive satisfaction to the consumers compare to the satisfaction level of product description and product comparison. Hence, colours of the website, font size of the text and quality of the graphics are increase the consumer satisfaction level to the web site and it increase the level of interaction to the website. Furthermore, according to the results, product comparison has the lowest quality. As a result, while the consumers' buying process is in existence the product comparison gives a negative mindset for consumers, and it does not provide much help to consumers when buying the reading materials online.

Moreover, the graphics level of satisfaction is close to good scale type. These results come from the model and through the graph depicted from Fig. 8, the graphics do not help much to satisfy consumers about website when buying reading materials online. In addition to that, product description has satisfaction level closer to level of bad point in satisfaction scale. That means it does not help much to dissatisfy the website while in buying process.

According to the results of the model, it has been identified different factors help to change over the consumer buying behaviour from online purchasing reading material website. Among them, some factors help to increase the satisfaction level while increasing the revenue of the website. Further, some factors have decreased the satisfaction level of consumers about website and those factors have also influenced to decrease the revenue of the website.

5 Conclusions and Future Work

This study adds new knowledge to the HCI literature and sentiment analysis literature in several ways. Initially, feature extraction in sentiment analysis is a challenging area and it has many feature selection methods/techniques. They are NLP based methods, Machine learning or clustering based methods, statistical methods, hybrid methods. According to those methods, lexicon-based dictionary approach is a hybrid method which is used in this research to extract the attributes related to websites. This feature extraction has started after pre-processing the reviews and ended with compiling dictionary which has attributes related to HCI. Moreover, compiled dictionary has attributes related to HCI which reviews online purchasing websites.

According to the development process of model and developed model it has been used to classify the reviews. In this study, a lexicon-based approach is used to classify reviews and identify the HCI attributes which affect to different level of consumers to get good browsing experiences. The dataset has been used to split into sentences after the pre-process. Then after, through the HCI related words bag of sentences are categorized. Sense of each individual category is extracted after splitting each category into word of bag and compared with sentiment dictionary. Senses of all categories are arranged into one data frame. This sense is the polarity of those categories and positive, negative or neutral. This type of sentiment classification performs better than the document level semantic orientation.

Human Computer Interaction area has a growing literature and when it comes to web designing, designers and developers must concern those HCI factors while developing different attributes to make interact the users to the system/website. Therefore, online purchasing related e-commerce sites also follow those design styles since there are large number of organizations doing their businesses online. Therefore, the organizations have the need to watch and study about their websites regularly. Questionnaires based studies have been carried out to identify the product and mining the product related data. Furthermore, these types of questionnaires-based study have not shown rigorous quantitative analyses.

To the authors' knowledge, there is no past study about HCI based text mining approach carried out on the online purchasing. Therefore, this study identifies the factors which affect the consumer interaction with respect to the online purchasing experience and uses lexicon-based dictionary in text mining approach in improving the same.

This study can be easily extended develop models to identify other human factors related HCT such as; visual incompatibilities.

In the future, this study can be further generalized for enhancing predictive analytics dashboards to give better online purchasing experience for online shoppers in diverse set of applications.

References

1. Oh, A., Jo, Y.: Aspect and sentiment unification model for online review analysis. In: Proceedings of the Fourth ACM International Conference on Web Search and Data Mining (WSDM 2011) (2011)
2. Collomb, A., Costea, C., Joyeux, D., Hasan, O., Brunie, L.: A study and comparison of sentiment analysis methods for reputation evaluation (2014)
3. Hu, M., Liu, B.: Mining and summarizing customer reviews. In: Proceedings of the 2004 ACM SIGKDD international conference on Knowledge discovery and data mining (KDD 2004) (2004)
4. Kiringoda, N.M., Rupasinghe, T.D.: Predictive analytics for decision making: human computer interaction perspective from online purchasing. In: Proceedings of International Research Symposium for Pure and Applied Sciences (IRSPAS), Colombo (2016)
5. Kaasinen, E., et al.: Defining user experience goals to guide the design of industrial systems. Behav. Inf. Technol. **34**, 976–991 (2015)
6. Margherio, L., Henry, D., Cooke, S., Montes, S.: The Emerging Digital Economy. US Department, Washington, DC (1998)
7. Kotler, P., Keller, K.L.: Marketing Management. Pearson Education South Asia Pte Ltd, Singapore (2017)
8. Katawetawaraks, C., Wang, C.L.: Online shopper behavior: influences of online shopping decision. Asian J. Bus. Res. **1** (2011)
9. Prasad, C.J.S., Aryasri, A.: Determinants of shopper behavior in e-tailing: an empirical analysis. Paradigm **13**, 73–83 (2009)
10. Gefen, D., Karahanna, E., Straub, D.: Inexperience and experience with online stores: the importance of tam and trust. IEEE Trans. Eng. Manag. **50**, 307–321 (2003)
11. Kim, J., Moon, J.Y.: Designing towards emotional usability in customer interfaces—trustworthiness of cyber-banking system interfaces. Interact. Comput. **10**, 1–29 (1998)
12. Cheskin Research and Studio Archetype Deliver e-Commerce Trust Study. Free Online Library, https://www.thefreelibrary.com/Cheskin+Research+and+Studio+Archetype+Deliver+eCommerce+Trust+Study.-a053541794
13. Tan, Y., Thoen, W.: Towards a generic model of trust for electronic commerce. In: Proceedings of the 12th Bled E-Commerce Conference, Bled, SIovenia (1999)
14. Egger, F.N.: Trust me, Im an online vendor. In: CHI 00 Extended Abstracts on Human Factors in Computer Systems (CHI 2000) (2000)
15. Wan, H.A.: Opportunities to enhance a commercial website. Inf. Manag. **38**, 15–21 (2000)
16. Nah, F., Davis, S.: HCI research issues in E-commerce. J. Electron. Commer. Res. **3**(3), 98–113 (2002)
17. Nass, C., Brave, S.: Emotion in human computer interaction. In: The Human-Computer Interaction Handbook, pp. 81–96. L. Erlbaum Associates Inc., Hillsdale (2003)

18. Helander, M.G., Khalid, H.M.: Modeling the customer in electronic commerce. Appl. Ergon. **31**, 609–619 (2000)
19. Roy, M.C., Dewit, O., Aubert, B.A.: The impact of interface usability on trust in Web retailers. Internet Res. **11**, 388–398 (2001)
20. Usability 101: Introduction to Usability. https://www.nngroup.com/articles/usability-101-introduction-to-usability/
21. Hausman, A.V., Siekpe, J.S.: The effect of web interface features on consumer online purchase intentions. J. Bus. Res. **62**, 5–13 (2009)
22. Reichheld, F., Sasser, W.: Zero defections: quality comes to services. harvard business review. In: Harvard Business Review (1990)
23. Dijk, G.V., Minocha, S., Laing, A.: Consumers, channels and communication: online and offline communication in service consumption. Interact. Comput. **19**, 7–19 (2007)
24. Sukanya, M., Biruntha, S.: Techniques on text mining. In: 2012 IEEE International Conference on Advanced Communication Control and Computing Technologies (ICACCCT) (2012)
25. Vijaygaikwad, S., Chaugule, A., Patil, P.: Text mining methods and techniques. Int. J. Comput. Appl. **85**, 42–45 (2014)
26. Pang, B., Lee, L.: Opinion mining and sentiment analysis. Found. Trends® Inf. Retr. **2**(1–2), 1–135 (2008)
27. Davis, F.D., Bagozzi, R.P., Warshaw, P.R.: User acceptance of computer technology: a comparison of two theoretical models. Manag. Sci. **35**, 982–1003 (1989)
28. Bhattacherjee, A.: An empirical analysis of the antecedents of electronic commerce service continuance. Decis. Support Syst. **32**, 201–214 (2001)
29. Gefen, D., Karahanna, E., Straub, D.W.: Straub: trust and TAM in online shopping: an integrated model. MIS Q. **27**, 51–90 (2003)
30. Gefen, D., Straub, D.: The relative importance of perceived ease of use in IS adoption: a study of e-commerce adoption. J. Assoc. Inf. Syst. **1**, 1–30 (2000)
31. Koch, S., Toker, A., Brulez, P.: Extending the TAM with perceived community characteristics. Inf. Res. **16**(2) (2011)
32. Koufaris, M.: Applying the technology acceptance model and flow theory to online consumer behavior. Inf. Syst. Res. **13**, 205–223 (2002)
33. Hani, E., Qureshi, K.: Relationship between website attributes and customer satisfaction: a study of e-commerce systems in Karachi (2011)
34. Sen, S., Lerman, D.: Why are you telling me this? An examination into negative consumer reviews on the Web. J. Interact. Mark. **21**, 76–94 (2007)
35. Hedegaard, S., Simonsen, J.G.: Extracting usability and user experience information from online user reviews. In: Proceedings of the SIGCHI Conference on Human Factors in Computing Systems (CHI 2013) (2013)
36. Spiliopoulou, M.: Web usage mining for web site evaluation. Commun. ACM **43**, 127–134 (2000)
37. Fogg, B.J., Soohoo, C., Danielson, D.R., Marable, L.: How do users evaluate the credibility of web sites? A study with over 2500 participants. https://dl.acm.org/citation.cfm?id=997097
38. Kim, J., Lee, J.: Critical design factors for successful e-commerce systems. Behav. Inf. Technol. **21**, 185–199 (2002)
39. Kang, D., Park, Y.: Review-based measurement of customer satisfaction in mobile service: sentiment analysis and VIKOR approach. Expert Syst. Appl. **41**, 1041–1050 (2014)
40. Singh, P.K., Sachdeva, A., Mahajan, D., Pande, N., Sharma, A.: An approach towards feature specific opinion mining and sentimental analysis across e-commerce websites. In: 2014 5th International Conference-Confluence the Next Generation Information Technology Summit (Confluence) (2014)

41. Bashir, R., Mehboob, I., Bhatti, W.: Effects of online shopping trends on consumer-buying behavior: an empirical study of Pakistan. J. Manag. Res. **2** (2015)
42. SNAP: Web data: Amazon reviews. https://snap.stanford.edu/data/web-Amazon.html
43. Mcauley, J., Leskovec, J.: Hidden factors and hidden topics. In: Proceedings of the 7th ACM Conference on Recommender Systems (RecSys 2013) (2013)
44. Cortes, C., Vapnik, V.: Support-vector networks. Mach. Learn. **20**, 273–297 (1995)
45. Feinerer, I., Hornik, K., Meyer, D.: Text mining infrastructure in R. J. Stat. Softw. **25**, 1–54 (2008)
46. Taboada, M., Brooke, J., Tofiloski, M., Voll, K., Stede, M.: Lexicon-based methods for sentiment analysis. Comput. Linguist. J. **37**, 267–307 (2011)

Feature Based Opinion Mining
for Hotel Profiling

Dilum Gunathilaka[✉], Shamila Pathirana, Sasanka Senarathne,
Jithmi Weerasekara, and Thushari Silva

Faculty of Information Technology, University of Moratuwa, Katubedda,
Moratuwa, Sri Lanka
dilumgunathilaka@gmail.com,
shamilapathirana@gmail.com,
sasankatharaka93@gmail.com, jithmij@gmail.com,
thusharip@uom.lk

Abstract. Hotel profiling plays an important role in hotel recommendation. With the proliferation of huge amount of user-generated-reviews on web-sites, hotel profiling has become more challenging as these reviews and embedded opinions could indirectly drive hotels. Comprehensive hotel profiling based on review analysis could help people to get an overall opinion on hotels and hence to facilitate mindful tourism. To avoid deficiencies of many other recent researches, this research focuses more on the feature-based opining mining rather analysing only sentiments of the reviews. Thus, a semantic profiling approach which integrates a machine learning technique, part-of-speech (PoS) tagging and Ontology is proposed for feature-based hotel profiling. PoS tagging is used for recognising patterns of opinions and SentiWordNet is used to resolve semantic heterogeneity of the opinion phrases and to classify them. Feature-based analysis could generate the feature level opinion about a hotel in several aspects including food, hospitality and environment.

Keywords: Feature extraction · Opinion mining · Hotel profiling · Ontology · PoS tagging

1 Introduction

As a result of the emergence of technologies, tourism industry has been expanded opening a way to online reservation. Proliferation of information in websites and social media has greatly challenged the discovery of a hotel according to user's own interests. Thus, personalized hotel recommendation is crucial for successful hotel reservation and the core of personalized hotel recommendation is hotel profiling. In order to generate a comprehensive hotel profile, it is essential to automated extraction of several features and mine opinions from reviews. Thus, feature based opinion mining on multiple hotel reviews plays an essential role in hotel profiling.

TripAdvisor [1] and Hotels.com [2] web-sites provide a profile of a hotel based on user reviews. In TripAdvisor, polarity classification of the reviews has been achieved and a rating-based hotel profile for existing users indicating whether the hotel is

© Springer Nature Singapore Pte Ltd. 2019
J. Hemanth et al. (Eds.): SLAAI-ICAI 2018, CCIS 890, pp. 219–231, 2019.
https://doi.org/10.1007/978-981-13-9129-3_16

excellent, very good, average, poor or terrible has been generated. This rating-based hotel profiling is having cold start problem. Thus, a new user cannot get an idea of foods, the environment of the hotel, hospitality of the staff separately. Hotels.com, provides consider only a few aspects which are very general features e.g., locations, room details but failed to consider many features related to personalization including food categories and the opinion of those food items which are served in the hotel.

In the proposed method as the first step of hotel profiling, features of hotel reviews are identified and extracted. Then by using the Multinomial Naïve Bayes' classifier method, PoS tagging and ontology semantically classify features and aggregated summaries from reviews are generated. Patterns of PoS tagging are used to extract opinions and semantic ambiguity in generating a meaningful summary score for the opinion is resolved by using a SentiWordNet. As the polarity classification of opinion words is not enough to take useful conclusions regarding the hotels, opinions were extracted from reviews for each feature of the hotel.

The rest of the paper is organized as follows, Sect. 2 summarizes existing techniques in feature classification and opinion mining. In Sect. 3 the architecture of the proposed solution for feature extraction and opinion mining of hotel reviews is presented. Section 4 reports evaluation and summarized analysis of results of the experiments. Finally, Sect. 5 concludes the paper with future works which open a way for improving system accuracy.

2 Related Work

Sentiment analysis is a widely used technique for analysing features from textual content. The sentiment classification techniques can be divided into two major sections [3] Machine learning approach and Lexicon based approach. Machine learning techniques can be further divided as supervised and unsupervised approaches. The supervised machine learning approach deals with the training data set and testing data set to predict the sentiments. Most of the researchers focus on sentiment analysis and training the model by using supervised learning techniques. This method has the expected output for the inputs and supplied correct answers most of the times. And also, this method classifies the data, based on past experience. Most commonly used approaches of the supervised learning techniques are Naive Bayes classifier, maximum entropy, SVM [4, 5], Random Forest and Decision tree classifier. Naïve Bayes classification algorithm [4] comes under the supervised machine learning approach which belongs to probabilistic classifiers family and based on Bayes' theorem. Naive Bayes classifier is used to predict the class membership probabilities of given text for the most relevant class by performing probabilistic analysis. Maximum Entropy [6] is another probabilistic classifier method can be used for sentiment classification. Maximum entropy classification does not make independent assumptions for features. So, it is possible to add new features without overlapping. Neural Network and support vector machine (SVM) belong to linear classification approach which are part of the supervised machine learning techniques [6]. SVM partitions the data set with a line (boundary line) or a hyperplane. When the number of classes are low, SVM works very accurately. When the points are closer to the hyperplane, predictions are not much accurate [4].

In unsupervised learning techniques do not have an expected output for the particular input, the system is trained based on observations and adjust according to the error. Clustering techniques come under unsupervised learning can also be called as hierarchical or partitive clustering method. K-Means and Self Organizing Map (SOM) methods belong to the partitive clustering approach. Hidden Markov Model (HMM) [4] is another unsupervised learning approach which can be used for sentence classification.

In 2013, a set of researchers from Mumbai university, conducted a research about the sentiment detection on financial news. First, they collected financial related news from twitter and tokenize them into word vectors. Then they prepare a dictionary in a polarized set of words. In the above mentioned research, they collected 2360 positive words and 7383 Negative words. After creating the dictionary, they used Naive Bayes, Maximum entropy and random forest algorithms for the classification of the text and compared the results of each algorithm with evaluation methods like accuracy, precision and recall [7].

There are few limitations of using above machine learning algorithms in stock market sentiment classification. First one is algorithmic limitation. Though SVM, Naive Bayes are more suitable for text classification, sometimes they do not perform well because of the sentence structure. As an example, the position of the punctuations and emoticons in the sentence will vary the accuracy of the models [8]. The Naive Bayes technique does not properly work with some sentences which contain conjunction. The two or more phrases with different meanings can be combined by using conjunctions. So, it is difficult to understand the true meaning of the sentence by using Naive Bayes algorithm, when such sentences contain the conjunctions. When considering the SVM algorithm, it also having some limitations because of the sensitivity to the size of the data set [8]. When size of the data is not sufficient, the derived hyperplane may deviate from expected outcome. Both algorithms are highly depending on the selected features. Another limitation is data limitation. In stock market domain thousands of users express their own personal opinions about a company. But sometimes the irrelevant news may have a huge impact on the sentiment classification. That will affect for the final outcome as well.

Before the extraction of features and opinion words in customer reviews, the system should be able to identify and localize them. PoS tagging technique can be used for identification and localization. This mainly helps to identify opinion phrases in the sentences or customer reviews which contain nouns, verbs, adjectives and adverbs. And also, PoS tagging technique allows to generate language patterns. Htav and Lynn proposed Stanford–PoS tagger [9] to parse each sentence and yield the PoS tag of every word whether the word belongs to noun, verb, adjective or adverb. After that, they extract features and opinions based on pattern knowledge. To identify and extract opinion words, a pattern of adjectives or adverbs which are closer to noun phrase are used. But sometimes, the nearest adjective does not provide the real opinion word of the feature. Not only that, to identify opinion words, some verbs such as like, recommended, love, prefer...etc. and some adverbs such as not, never, overall, highly... etc. are used. So, to extract opinion words, two or three-word phrases are used [9].

After the extraction of opinion words, it is needed to classification in order to do the sentiment analysis. A vast number of techniques are available to classify the opinion. N-gram is one of the methodologies that is used to classify the opinion into negative, positive or neutral corpus [10].

Another feature extraction methodology is ontology. Ontology driven approaches can be categorized in two different ways. They are static and dynamic ontologies. Dynamic ontology is a modern approach to identify and extract features in an effective way. P. Baranikumar et al. (2016) proposed an ontology system which can be built and updated dynamically and is used for feature extraction. In there, features are separated from the opinions expressed by the user. The sentence which includes opinions contains the classes, individuals, datatype and object properties of the domain ontology and they are identified from the input. After that, the identified features are grouped based on their semantic distance and consider as a main concept of the ontology [11].

After the feature and opinion classification process, profiles can be created on the related domain. This is helpful to access all information of domain at once. This task can be done using an ontology driven approach. Ontologies can be developed in different languages such as RDF, RDF Schema, XML, XML Schema and OWL [12]. OWL is the latest and widely used language. Using the ontology, parametric search can be done. And also, it allows intelligent access to an online services and information. Ananthapadmanaban et al., (2011) proposed a new platform on tourism ontology for Tamilnadu and it focuses on the integration of tourism information from various websites and efficient retrieval of the accurate information that user needs by using the semantic web services [12]. In there, the tourism ontology for Tamilnadu is built to conceptualize tourism spots, accommodation and activities during travel. The ontology contains eight important classes and each class has subclasses. Then agents interact to perform tasks such as, crawling internet for tourism websites for new data, then if any found, annotation manager stored them in a database, then that information is added to predefined ontology, GUI is accessed remotely by end users for information same as in a search engine, User requests are passed to web agent, then when ontology schema is performed, instance data by the activation of a reasoner and finally SPARQL queries are formulated and processed by the agents in conjunction with Jena and results displayed to the end user via GUI [13].

3   Methodology

The proposed feature-based opinion mining and hotel profiling approach can be divided into three sub components:

(1) Sentiment Classification and Feature Extraction module
(2) Opinion Mining module
(3) Hotel profiling module

Figure 1 shows the architecture of the proposed solution. The complete process inclusive of feature extraction, opinion mining and hotel profiling is planned to be executed according to the proposed design in Fig. 1. The first module identifies the features and classifies them into pre-defined feature categories. The second module

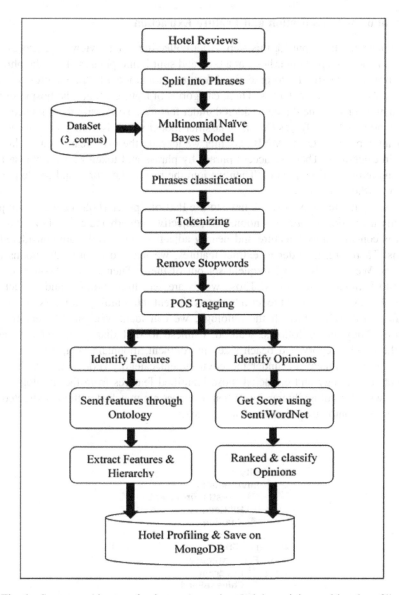

Fig. 1. System architecture for feature extraction, opinion mining and hotel profiling

identifies the opinion and classifies them. The third module creates the hotel profile. That profile is helpful to get feature-wise overall image of the hotel.

In this proposed architecture we take hotel reviews as input to the system. Hotel reviews are taken from Hotels.com by crawling. Hotel profile is done based on the customer reviews.

3.1 Sentiment Classification and Feature Extraction

Hotel reviews are the input for this step. After collecting hotel reviews, we access one review sentence of a particular hotel at a time and split it into phrases. Then the phrases of sentences are classified into predefined feature set and identify the features of hotel using the above review sentences. Three categories of features; food, the hospitality of staff and hotel environment are considered under features. To classify the sentences, we use Multinomial Naive Bayes (MNB) Classifier model which is trained on prior to the classification process. Using MNB classifier we identify the main features and classify into main categories. Then we access phrase by phrase and tokenize each phrase into words and remove the stop word. Then we join the rest of the words and create phrase to use in further process.

To extract the features, first, we have to use Part-of-Speech (PoS) tagger techniques to classify the words of phrase as noun, verb, adjective, adverb and etc.... For example, a noun is considered as a feature and nearby adjectives or adverbs are considered as opinions. Therefore, in order to extract features, we need to identify the nouns and adjectives. We filter the most frequent set out of them. Then we use WordNetLemmatizer to lemmatize the words. Those words are sent into ontology and extract the features. For example, when the term "prawns" is sent into ontology it infers the output as seafood. Likewise, through the ontology, we can identify eight different feature categories. They are as follows, seafood, Chinese food, Indian food and beverages under the Food category and beach side environment, mountain area, rural area and urban side environment are under the environment category. For that, first, have to construct an ontology and extracted those identified features from the ontology. Figure 2 shows the ontology hierarchy. When instances are matched with the extracted set of words, then ontology infers the related class.

Fig. 2. Ontology hierarchy design for feature extraction

3.2   Opinion Mining

In this phase, we used the above mentioned PoS tagging techniques and related algorithm for pattern identification. To identify opinion phrase we use sequences of patterns of adjectives, nouns, adverbs and verbs. We used eight different patterns for extract opinion phrases with related to our domain of hotel reviews. They are as follows,

(1) Adjective(JJ) + Noun(NN)
(2) Adjective(JJ) + Noun(NN) + Noun(NN)
(3) Adverb(RB) + Adjective(JJ)
(4) Adverb(RB) + Adjective(JJ) + Noun(NN)
(5) Adverb(RB) + Verb(VBN)
(6) Adverb(RB) + Adverb(RB) + Adjective(JJ)
(7) Verb(VBN) + Noun(NN)
(8) Verb(VBN) + Adverb(RB)

To extract those related sequences, regular expressions are used. Table 1 shows some of the extracted opinion phrases extracted from hotel reviews by using above PoS tag sequences.

Table 1. Identified opinion phrases

Opinion identification	
Pattern	Identified opinion phrase
(Adjective, noun)	Quality foods
(Adjective, noun, noun)	Good staff service
(Adverb, adjective)	Very helpful
(Adverb, adjective, noun)	Very good service
(Adverb, verb)	Personally recommend
(Adverb, adverb, adjective)	Not so bad
(Verb, noun)	Appreciate service
(Verb, adverb)	Served well

The identified opinion phrases are categorized using SentiWordNet library. Their scores are calculated for the positive and negative opinions of the particular sentences which belong to particular feature category set respectively. Based on these scores opinions are ranked and classified. Algorithm 1 shows the calculation of the score for the opinion phrases.

```
Algorithm 1
Input: Opinion phrase list of particular category L
Output: Score for the opinion list
Begin
L' ← findOpinionScore(L)
P ← opinion_phrase
For each P ∈ L
   W ← Opinion Word in a P
   Score_list = []
   For each W ∈ P
      Tag ← Pos_tag(W)
      Lem ← Lemmatize ( Tag[0] )
      if Tag[1] startswith( 'NN' )
         Newtag = 'n'
      else if Tag[1] startswith( 'JJ' )
         Newtag = 'a'
      else if Tag[1] startswith( 'V )
         Newtag = 'v'
      else if Tag[1] startswith( 'R )
         Newtag = 'r'
      else
         Newtag = ''
      if ( Newtag != '' )
         Synsets←findSynonymsUsingSentiWordNet(Lem,Newtag)
         Score = 0
         if (length (Synsets) > 0)
            S ← synonym for opinion word
            For each S ∈ Synsets
               Score += S.pos_score() - S.neg_score()
               W_Score = Score / length ( Synsets )
               PSLoL ← append Score_list ( W_Score )

   phrase_scorelist = []
   PS ← One Phare Score list
   For each PS ∈ PSLoL
      if length (PS) != 0
         For each W_Score ∈ PS
            PScore = Sum(W_Score) / length (PS)
            PL ← append phrase_scorelist (PScore)

   opinion_list_score=sum(phrase_scorelist)
   classifyOpinion (opinion_list_score)
```

We rated the food category up to five classes. They are worst, bad, average, good and excellent. And also staff categories were rated into three classes and they are bad, normal and good. In same way opinions related to the environment category are classified into two classes, good and bad. These ratings were converted into numerical values for each category according to the classified class as above mentioned way.

3.3   Hotel Profiling

To build the hotel profile, above mention features under several categories and opinion classification values are used. These values are stored in a MongoDB along with the hotel name, the image of the hotel and hotel class. Then automatically build the hotel profile for each and every hotel. The stored profiles of the hotels can also be used for recommendation systems. Figure 3 shows the one of the hotel profile which is stored in MongoDB.

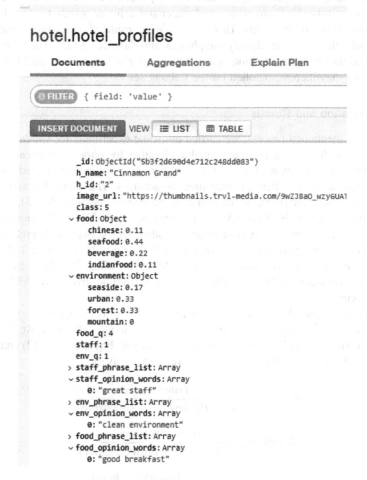

Fig. 3. Hotel profile on MongoDB

4 Experiments

4.1 Dataset

We have collected data i.e., reviews under three different categories: food, environment and hospitality of the staff from TripAdvisor and Hotels.com. Those reviews are manually classified into three corpora named as food, staff and environment to create training samples. Food corpus consists of a total of 427 review phrases, staff corpus contains 193 review phrases and environment corpus consists of a total of 178 review phrases. During the pre-processing phase, the reviews were converted into lower case letters, removed stop words, punctuation marks and all the other non-related characters.

After creating the dataset, the reviews which are belonging to three categories were tagged according to related category and then appended them into a list. These three data sets were tokenized into words and generated a list of words to find the most frequent words out of all words. Those words are considered as features which were used to make the dataset to classify the phrases into three categories. Then the dataset was divided into two parts: training data set and testing data set. Then the Multinomial Naive Bayes classifier was applied on the training set.

4.2 Evaluation and Results

In the above mentioned process, we carried out some experiment for validation of our approach. In order to find the most suitable classifier for phrase classification, some experiments were conducted on existing classifiers by using earlier created three corpora and trained the classifiers and measured the accuracy. The selected classifiers were Naïve Bayes classifier (NB), Multinomial Naïve Bayes classifier (MNB), Bernoulli Naïve Bayes classifier (BNB) and Support Vector classifier (SVC). Multinomial Naïve Bayes classifier's accuracy was higher than the other three classifiers. Therefore, MNB was selected for the phrase classification module of the project. Figure 4 shows the results of the accuracy of these classifiers; MNB provides 78.08% accuracy, NB provides the accuracy of 74.38%, BNB provides 52.78% accuracy and SVC provides 52.62% accuracy.

After the phrase classification, we evaluate the results in order to measure the performance and accuracy of our phrase classification module. For that, we used most popular metrics such as Precision, Recall and F-measure. Equations (1), (2) and (3) are represent the Precision, Recall and F-measure in respectively.

$$Precision = \frac{True\,Positives}{True\,Positives + False\,Positives} \tag{1}$$

$$Recall = \frac{True\,Positives}{True\,Positives + False\,Negatives} \tag{2}$$

$$F - measure = 2 * \frac{Precision * Recall}{Precision + Recall} \tag{3}$$

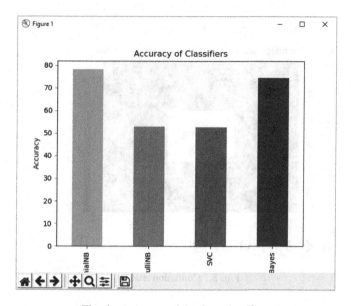

Fig. 4. Accuracy of the four classifiers

Table 2 shows the results obtained through the evaluation along with the supported phrases in each category.

Table 2. The results of the evaluation metrics

	Precision	Recall	f1-score	Support
Environment	0.86	0.51	0.64	143
Food	0.77	0.96	0.85	345
Staff	0.76	0.64	0.70	160
Avg/total	0.79	0.78	0.77	648

Figure 5 shows the confusion matrix of the classified categories. Actual values are shown in the y-axis and predicted values are shown in the x-axis. Using this confusion matrix, we can conclude that staff and food phrases are classified with high accuracy while environment phrases are classified in average accuracy. In the confusion matrix, middle values is 330 and right bottom corner value is 103.

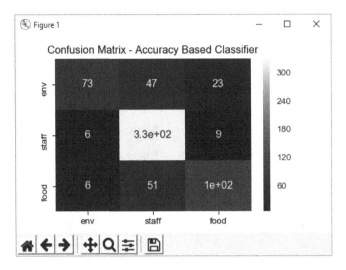

Fig. 5. Confusion matrix

5 Conclusions

The paper presented a feature-based opinion mining and a hotel profiling system with the use of hotel reviews from the tourist or other users. The main challenge in creating the automated hotel profile by user reviews is to extract features and related opinion words in an accurate manner. TripAdvisor and Hotels.com use their own approaches to make the hotel profiles. But, those approaches consist of some limitations. TripAdvisor mostly does not provide feature-based hotel profiling. It provides an overall rating based hotel profiling indicating whether it is good or bad. Even though hotels.com provides a feature-based hotel profiling, under the foods, it has overlooked the hierarchical categories e.g., several types of food such as Chinese, Indian and seafood through reviews.

Through our approach, we have overcome the above limitations and identified patterns using a hybrid approach to extract features and opinions. Moreover, an ontology which is used to resolve semantic heterogeneity in feature extraction and semantic similarity of identified opinion phrases is calculated with the help of SentiWordNet.

Initial experimental results have been presented for validation of the proposed approach. The average results for the precision, recall and F-score are 79%, 78% and 77%, respectively. These values are represented in all categories (food, environment and staff). The above experiment results were obtained through the supported of 648 review phrases.

References

1. TripAdvisor. https://www.tripadvisor.com
2. Hotels.com. https://www.hotels.com
3. Wojcik, K., Tuchowski, J.: Feature based sentiment analysis. In: 3rd International Scientific Conference on Contemporary Issues in Economics, Business and Management (2014)
4. Medhat, W., Hassan, A., Korashy, H.: Sentiment analysis algorithms and applications: a survey. Ain Shams Eng. J. **5**(4), 1093–1113 (2014)
5. Devi, D.V.N., Kumar, C.K., Prasad, S.: A feature based approach for sentiment analysis by using support vector machine. In: IEEE 6th International Conference on Advanced Computing (2016)
6. Bhardwaj, A., Narayan, Y., Pawan, V., Dutta, M.: Sentiment analysis for indian stock market prediction using sensex and nifty. Procedia Comput. Sci. **70**, 85–91 (2015)
7. Kalyani, J., Bharathi, P., Jyothi, P.: Stock trend prediction using news sentiment analysis. CoRR. ArXiv Prepr. ArXiv:1607.01958 (2016)
8. Bapat, P.: A comprehensive review of sentiment analysis of stocks. Int. J Comput. Appl. **106**(18), 1–3 (2014)
9. Htay, S.S., Lynn, K.T.: Extracting product features and opinion words using pattern knowledge in customer reviews. Sci. World J. **2013**, 1–5 (2013)
10. Mars, A., Gouider, M.S.: Big data analysis to features opinions extraction of customer. Procedia Comput. Sci. **112**, 906–916 (2017)
11. Baranikumar, P., Gobi, N.: Feature extraction of opinion mining using ontology. Int J. Adv. Comput. Electron. Eng. **1**(1), 18–22 (2016)
12. Ananthapadmanaban, K.R., Srivatsa, S.K.: Personalization of user profile: creating user profile ontology for Tamilnadu Tourism. Int. J. Comput. Appl. **23**, 42–47 (2011). (0975–8887)
13. Corcho, O., Hauswirth, M., Koubarakis, M.: In: 1st International Workshop on the Semantic Sensor Web (2009)

Agent Based System

A Hybrid Agent System to Detect Stress Using Emotions and Social Media Data to Provide Coping Methodologies

Ridmal Liyanagamage[1]([⊠]), Shakina Kitchilan[1],
Roshan Maddumage[1], Shazeeka Kitchilan[1],
Nishantha Kumarasinghe[2], and Subha Fernando[1]

[1] Faculty of Information Technology, University of Moratuwa,
Moratuwa, Sri Lanka
ridmal19@gmail.com, shakikit2@gmail.com,
uomroshan@gmail.com, shazeekit@gmail.com,
subhaf@uom.lk
[2] Kotelawala Defence University, Rathmalana, Sri Lanka
drkumarasinghe2015@gmail.com, nishantha@kdu.lk

Abstract. Final year undergraduates in Sri Lanka are more likely to experience high levels of stress due to the high competition in the education system. Living with high levels of stress has the possibility of putting a person's entire well-being at a great risk. Today more and more students are suffering from various levels of stress. Too much stress will bring a variety of physical and psychological problems including anxiety, depression and even suicide to growing youths. Traditional face-to-face stress detection and relief methods do not work, confronted with undergraduates who are reluctant to express their negative emotions to the people in real life. In this paper, the authors present undergraduates-oriented intelligent chatting system which aims to act as a virtual friend to listen, understand, comfort, encourage, and guide stressful undergraduates to pour out their bad feelings and thus release the stress by suggesting stress coping mechanisms to follow and to be guided. Our user study demonstrates *that this system* is effective on sensing and coping with undergraduates stress.

Keywords: Stress coping mechanisms · Chat bot ·
Agent based knowledge system · Neural networks ·
Video processing and machine learning

1 Introduction

Stress is a necessary factor to challenge and motivate undergraduates to learn and perform well in their academic work load. But some approaches are required to reduce the negative aspect of stress which might result in serious damage over health or which would reduce good academic performance [1]. In medical terms, stress is a state or a condition of mind that has the ability to affect both physically and psychologically. Stress is understood as a psychological reaction which people experience daily in their

© Springer Nature Singapore Pte Ltd. 2019
J. Hemanth et al. (Eds.): SLAAI-ICAI 2018, CCIS 890, pp. 235–255, 2019.
https://doi.org/10.1007/978-981-13-9129-3_17

lives. In some cases, Stress in less quantities can be identified as a motivating factor while high levels of stress can result in very harmful problems in health [1]. High levels of stress have many negative effects such as strokes, poor performance, hypertension, heart failures, dysfunction of body systems and in some cases even sudden deaths. Because of the high competition in the education of Sri Lanka, students are more likely to experience these stressful conditions which might lead to hamper and escalate their academic performance and social well-being as well as their personal health [2].

Being a student in a competitive environment can be the most interesting and challenging time period of a person's life. Adapting to a new environment, balancing the academic work load, making new friends, financial issues, exam pressures and coping with the society while learning can be very challenging which can lead to different levels of stress. So it is very important to manage these varying degrees of stress of students to make sure their well-being and good performance [3]. The paper proposes an online stress coping assistant for final year students of Universities which helps to manage stress that can be observed during their university lives.

In serious situations such as depression, anxiety or very high level of stress the authors recommend the help of counseling, meeting a psychologist or an experienced physician. But minor stress detection that can affect long term health and its diagnosis and decision making can highly depend on the experience of the physician when interpreting the measurements [4]. Therefore, an online stress management assistant which analyze psychological stress level from social media and detect stress from facial expressions through the web camera will provide the stress level for an expert knowledge system which will propose multiple solutions and these solutions will be communicated via the chat bot using stress releasing communication methods. Therefore, the proposed system suggests stress coping mechanisms with the intention of handling a stressed student [1, 4] in a more positive and effective way.

The remainder of the paper is organized as following. The authors have review related work in Sect. 2 and outlined the overall *system* in Sect. 3. The four core components which includes social media psychological stress detection module, emotion detection module, agent based expert system and chat manager modules are detailed in Sects. 3.1, 3.2, 3.3 and 3.4 respectively. Evaluations results of each model and user study are analyzed in Sect. 4. Section 5 concludes the paper and discusses future work.

2 Related Work

There are many researches on social media such as twitter use to predict mental health care and personal event detection and binary stress detection but very few on Twitter used to measure the psychological stress using texts, emoticons, punctuation marks, gender, age and time of comment. According to Huijie Lin et al. [5] less attention has been paid to determine stress using social media data due to challenges such as stressor subject identification, stressor event detection, data collection and representation etc. Therefore, few have overcome these challenges and have used different methodologies to estimate stress via social media.

To overcome the above challenges Huijie Lin et al. [5] have used a comprehensive scheme to estimate the users stress level from the users twitter messages. Therefore, a benchmark data set is built to extract the features which are in the context of stress. Then they developed a hybrid multi-task model to identify the stressor events and subjects. The scheme proposed by Huijie Lin et al. [5] comprises following three major modules. The description component, the detection component and the measurement component. Another significant approach is using a deep sparse neural network to detect psychological stress from cross media micro-blog data [6]. It extracts three aspects from the tweet messages namely, linguistic attributes such as words phrases from the messages, visual attributes such as images brightness, color and social attributes such as how much attention has attracted for a treat from friends etc. were considered. Contrast to previous models this approach outputs five different categories of psychological stress namely affection, social, psychological, work and others. The final category expresses stress caused by others or external factors. Likewise, many other researchers have used Convolutional Neural Networks, Linera SV classifier to detect stress from social media which are mainly classified into binary categories and have used polarity data sets.

Over the last few years, a lot of researchers have done human-computer interaction related works based on computer vision. Researchers have significantly advanced human facial emotions (Happiness, Anger, Fear, Disgust, Sad, Surprise and Neutral) recognition with computer vision. There are more traditional approaches but now have more novel approaches for this problem.

The last few years "Convolution Neural Networks" (CNNs) have become the most popular approach in research fields for face emotion recognition. Recent submissions [7, 8] all used Convolution Neural Network approaches to achieve high accuracy. But few research papers [9–12] published recently on video-based human facial emotions using CNNs. Emotion detection from human facial expression and its use to define the stress level of a human and identify the relationships between stress level using individual emotions and emotions mixture was done more accurately by Dr. Suvashis Das [13].

Psychologists or counselors use several methods to identify the user stress level and they implement methods to help people to avoid stress related problems occurred in day to day life with their expertise and experiences. Several researches have tried to develop knowledge based systems to determine the user stress level and to provide virtual consultancies to the users in a stressed situation. Awanis Romli and Arnidcha Peri Cha conducted a research to build an expert system to substitute the role of a psychologist or counselor with a computer system (ESSM system) [14]. Basically it conducts two tests called Career test and stress test to extract the input information form the user. Combination of those two tests will help to determine and provide best solution for stress related problems based on user's interest area.

V.J. Madhuri, Madhumitha R. Mohan, Kaavya R developed a fuzzy based system for stress management. In this system, Stress detection was done by using psychological signals such as heart rate, galvanic skin response, body temperature, blood pressure and muscle tension. But reaction of the stress depends on the body condition, age, gender, experience of the user [15]. So they believe that while defining the user's stress occurrence of the complexity and uncertainty can be overcome with the fuzzy logic. Input of the psychological signals were collected using wearable sensors.

Anusha Ghosh, Jeffery W. Tweedale and Andrew Nafalski developed multi agent system for analyzing work stress data and providing feedback in real time [16]. This system will classify and grade work-stress level using hybridized approach called Intelligent Multi-Agent Decision Analyzer (IMADA). A Neural network model is used for classification and a fuzzy logic approach is used to transform the outputs generate form the neural network to the linguistic grades. This hybrid approach was able to achieve efficient classification and measures user's stress level in human readable format.

Eliza was developed to act like a psychotherapist which was developed in 1960s. It provides the feeling of being listened and understood by making certain dialogue driven conversations with the user [17]. Based on a predefined set of key words a set of decomposition rules are triggered to analyze the sentences inputted by the user. The reassembly rules associated with the triggered decomposition rules will generate the responses to the user by trying to make a meaningful conversation.

ALICE chat bot the Lobner Prize winner in 200, 2001 and 2004 for the most human-like computer is another famous chat bot [18]. The architecture of it is clearly separated as in to 'chat bot engine' and 'language knowledge model' to plug and play alternative language knowledge models if necessary. This architecture mainly uses pattern matching algorithms to generate responses by trying to match word by word and obtain the longest pattern match [19]. The knowledge of ALICE about English conversation patterns are stored in AIML (Artificial Intelligence Markup) files which is a derivative of XML [5].

TeenChat is a chatterbot system that is developed to sense and release stress of adolescents. The system framework is comprised of three main components which are as following. The Chatting Manager, The Stress Detector and the Response Generation component. By mapping and linking the inputted words and the lexicons using a dependence tree the system will detect whether the user is at stress or not and will provide a response based on the category from the local knowledge base to comfort and guide users to have positive feelings [18] (Fig. 1).

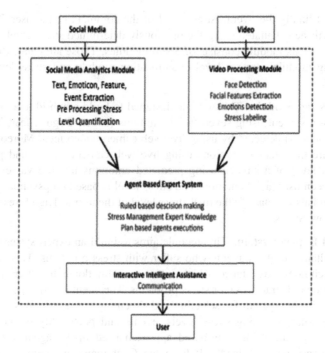

Fig. 1. High level architecture of the proposed system

3 Methodology

3.1 System Architecture

In this study the aim is to build an online chatting system targeted for final year students in universities which can detect stress and then help to reduce the stress to make the affected student feel better. The detection of stress is done by monitoring and analyzing the facial emotions of the student. In addition, since there is a growing trend among students to express their feelings in social media rather than turning to share their feelings with people the authors use their Facebook activities to detect whether the student is experiencing any stress. By using these inputs when the system identifies the student is stressed then the Chat Bot module is used to communicate and interact with the stressed student to assist and reduce his/her stress level by suggesting stress coping mechanisms.

The above diagram provides the high-level architecture of the system. It shows how each module of the system is connected with each other and illustrates the functionalities of each module.

Social Media Psychological Stress Detection Module. Social media psychological stress detection module is responsible for detecting and measuring stress level of a person using word phrases, emoji's, punctuation marks, gender, age and time of comment in social media such as twitter and Facebook. Therefore, the outputs of the module would be the average stress level of the text, the average stress level of the emoticons and finally the overall stress level of the comment of the user. The overall stress level will be calculated using the previously determined stress levels of the text and emoticons. This module consists of 3 sub modules. Those are data extraction and pre-processing module, stressor level quantification module and stress level identification module.

Video Processing Module. This module designed to build a hybrid model to classify stress level of a student using seven facial emotions (anger, disgust, fear, happy, sad, surprise and neutral) detected by using live web camera video feed. Moreover, allows user to capture their facial emotions using live web camera frames and provide the current stress level of a student using predicted emotions mixture values. The relationship between user facial emotions and stress level is based on psychological expert knowledge and also to classify the final stress level of the user as High Stress, Moderate Stress and Low Stress.

Agent Based Expert System. This module aims to build an expert system to provide virtual consultancy to the students who suffer with stress problems. This will act as a personal psychologist assistance which intent to calm down the user and provide suitable solutions (distractions) for stress problems. The agent based expert system will be introduced in this system for selecting and executing stress solutions. This derives stress coping solutions using stress levels, events and personality of the user. And solutions will execute using plan-based approach used in the agent system. Every execution process will get feedback from the Chat manager module and maintain continuous evaluation with the help of user feedback.

Chat Manager Module. This module is used to manage and maintain conversations with a stressed student to relief stress by suggesting the stressed student to share their personal feelings through chatting which would not be confident enough to say out loud with someone else. This online chatting system is aimed to provide their users the sense of being listened, comforted and understood which allows the user to gradually pour out their uncomfortable feelings while actively interacting with the user by suggesting positive thoughts. The conversation between the user and the system will be driven based on psychological aspects to ensure that the user will gradually develop positive and motivated feelings at the end of the conversation. This module is aimed to conduct an interactive and meaningful conversation with user and try to calm down the user (distract the user from a stress problem) by using solutions gain from the expert system.

3.2 Social Media Psychological Stress Detection Module

The authors have worked towards quantifying and identifying stress via social media specially twitter and Facebook data which can be considered as non-trivial due to the following challenges which can be identified as certain research areas that the authors have worked through. Those are namely difficulties on finding large-scale-benchmark data set that is publicly-available. Many researches focus on categorizing into two stress levels and there is no categorized data set for multi class stress levels that is suitable for the study of research area. User's behaviors on social media have ambiguity. Analyzing and quantifying the level of stress using the words of a particular user in social media are some of the challenges authors had to face.

Stress Measurement. To address the mentioned challenges, the authors have derived a comprehensive scheme that is able to automatically detect stress level of a user and further estimate and quantify the overall stress levels. As illustrated, the scheme consists of three components. In particular, first the extraction and pre-processing module will extract a set of discriminant features including text and emoticons. Then theses will be pre-processed to capture the most important features for sentiment analysis. Second the stress level quantification module will be conducted in two schemes. First text will be classified to identify the level of stress using a logistic regression model. The model is improved to increase the accuracy of classification using different methods. Then the emoticons will be analyzed separately to measure the level of stress. This uses three approaches to make the quantification and via weighted average methods and linear regression models. Finally, the stress level identification module will calculate the overall stress of a particular user considering both text and emoticons used. It is worth mentioning that the relatedness among stressed text as well as emoticons is well captured and modeled in the system. To verify the scheme, authors have construct a representative data set from twitter and a data set which has already labeled the emotion as joy, sad, fear and anger. Extensive experiments well validates the proposed scheme (Fig. 2).

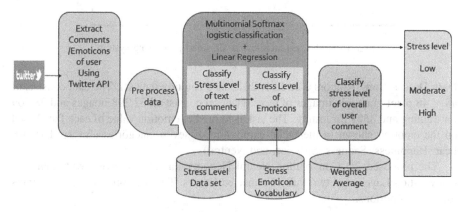

Fig. 2. High level architecture of social media stress detection module.

3.3   Video Processing Module

Authors collect data from university student-based survey as video clips for each individual student. The collected video clips are divided into frames for pre-processing. Captured video data from laptop web camera are with the size of 1280 × 800 and videos are saved in mp4 file format. After collecting all videos, created 2 min video clips from those captured videos to reduce the time to identify the stress level and reduce the error rate. All video clips labeled as High, Moderate or Low stress by analyzing the data by the psychological doctors.

Normal web camera has 30fps capture rate and to create the data set it is split as video clip into frames and calculated the emotion level values for each frame. Finally calculated the average emotion level values for each video clips. Using Chen et al. [20] (haar cascade classifier) face detection approach used for face detection and then cropped frame to get face of the frame. Haar cascade classifier helps to identify all faces on a frame and then the collected video frames have only one face and therefore this will get only one face as a cropped image. Then convert RGB image to GRAY scale image and resize (48 × 48) the images to reduce processing power and match to input size of the Convolution Neural Network (CNN). Then converted the image into NumPy array and expand the dimension of the array to match the input size of the CNN.

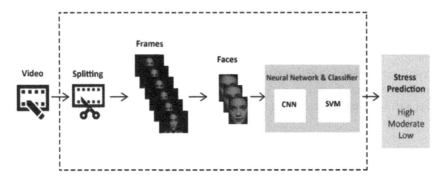

Fig. 3. High level architecture of video processing system.

Data Description. Authors used FER-2013 face emotion data set. The data consists of 48 × 48 pixel grayscale images of faces. Data set consist all 32,298 images and 28,709 for training and 3589 for testing. The task is to predict emotion value of each face based on the emotion shown in the facial expression of seven categories (Angry, Disgust, Fear, Happiness, Sadness, Surprise, and Neutral).

The proposed 2D Convolution Neural Network has all six layers with four 2D-Convolution Layers and two Fully Connected Layers. This will produce seven outputs for seven emotions.

Stress Measurement. In the recent few years' researches [21] have achieved best performance from Convolution Neural Network approaches for emotion detection methods. Therefore, the authors uses a Convolution Neural Networks to achieve high performance as shown in Fig. 3.

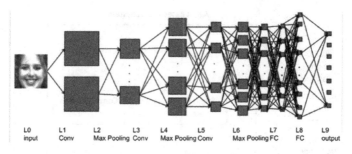

Fig. 4. CNN model used for video processing system.

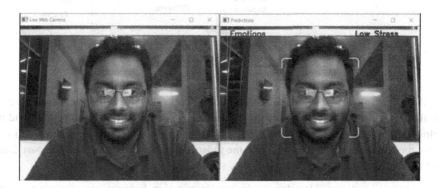

Fig. 5. Implementation of video processing system.

3.4 Agent Based Expert System

The agent based expert system consist of several components which helps to determine and provide the stress coping solutions based on the stress level, stress event and the personality. The components of this module are described as following (Figs. 4 and 5).

Agents. The software agent is an application that can perceive its environment with the help of sensors and acts through the effectors for changing the environment. JASON is used to develop the agent system and in the proposed system mainly two types of agents exists (Fig. 6).

Stress Coping Agent. Handles all the processes which needs to provide stress coping solutions for the user. This agent focus on fetching the most suitable stress coping solutions from the knowledge base considering the given inputs and executing the solution by selecting relevant plans in the plan library.

Ex: Solution – Listen to a relax music

- Step 1: Ask about the preferences for listening to a relax music
- Step 2: Execute the action (listen to a relax music) based on the user preferences.
- Step 3: get the feedback about the solution
- Step 4: go to the next solution or end the solution execution based on the user feedback.

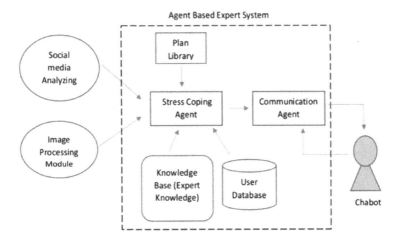

Fig. 6. High level architecture of agent based expert system

After fetching the relevant solutions from the knowledge base the agent uses cosine similarity to re-arrange the solution array based on the similarity of the solutions. And it helps to avoid providing the same type of solution again when user rejects a solution. Also, the stress coping agent will fetch the most preferable solutions from the past data and present the solution to the users as a start.

Communication Agent. Handles all the communication between stress coping agent and the environment (Chatbot). Main characteristics of the proposed agent based expert system is as following.

Main characteristic of the Agent system is mentioned below.

- Two Agents (Communication and stress Coping Agent) will allocate for each user
- Agents works independently
- Synchronized communication (message passing) between agents
- Provide solutions for the Chabot (different users) asynchronously
- Used centralized architecture.
- Solutions will change each time when user stress level is changed
- Used cosine similarity for sort the solution array based on the similarity between solutions. (Similar solutions will not provide one after the other. This will help to prevent providing same type of solutions to user when user ignoring that type of solutions.)
- Used Spring boot web application to implement the web portal between agent and the chat application which will help to communicate with the agent system using set of API calls.

Knowledge base and inference Engine. Knowledge base of the system is developed using expert knowledge of the domain experts. (Psychologist, Psychiatry, Counselors) Ruled based techniques are used to input the expert knowledge to the system with the help of PROLOG language which have pre-build inference engine.

Sample rule-based representation of data.

- IF Stress is HIGH AND personality type is INTROVERT AND stress event EXAM

  THEN SOLUTION breathing exercises, listen to relax music

- IF Stress is MEDUIM AND personality type is EXTROVERT AND stress event FINANCIAL

  THEN SOLUTION mindfulness, call a close friend (Fig. 7)

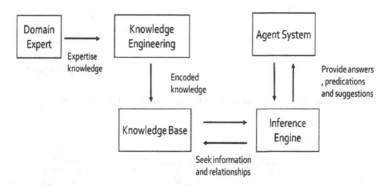

Fig. 7. Flow diagram of the knowledge-based development process in agent based expert system.

User and Solution Database User database stores all the information relevant to the user which can be used to retrieve the stress coping solutions such as personality type, name etc. And solution database stores information related to the solution executions. It holds sequence of the solution used to relive the user's stress based on the stress event, personality and stress level which will used by the agent to determine the best solution sequence for given inputs (Fig. 8).

3.5   Chat Manager Module

The chat manager module compromises three main components. The text classification using NLP and machine learning algorithms, the decision engine that decides the response type whether it should be a general conversation response or an agent-based response type and will trigger the relevant response. The data layer holds all the data that require to analyze user inputted sentences and the relevant responses. Below diagram shows the flow diagram of the approach.

Analyzation of User Inputted Sentences Using NLP and Machine Learning. The input text entered by a user will be processed using NLP technologies to extract the semantic meaning of the sentence. The sentence will be classified in to predefined intent object which will be in one of the fixed categories. Before classifying preprocessing, the data is required.

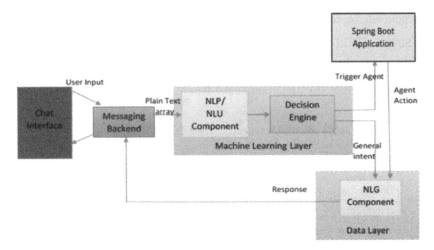

Fig. 8. High level architecture of chant manager system

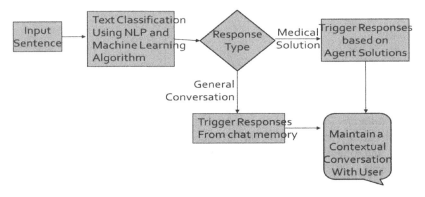

Fig. 9. Flow diagram of the chat managing module

Processing Text using NLP. The NLP/NLU component is responsible for tokenizing, stopper filtering, stemming and synonym handling of the inputted sentence so the expert system can decide which rules in the knowledge base should be triggered by searching and matching the keywords. In tokenization a set of splitters will be used to split the user text input and the stored words into tokens. In stopper filtering phase it removes the set of words that can occur frequently but has less contribution in creating meaning such as determiners, prepositions, conjunctions, coordination etc. Word stemming is important for indexing and searching the keywords in the system. In this process the authors will be searching for a match between roots of words from both the stored word and inputted word.

Text Classification Using Artificial Neural Networks. To classify sentence a neural network is used. The model is created using tflearn to classify the new text inputs entered by the user in to the defined categories. This classification will be done based on what the model learned from the training data set. The neural network model will learn features from the training data set and will used them for the prediction against new input text. It will be classified in to one of the predefined intents either a general conversation intent or an agent-based solution required intent.

Furthermore, if the user provides a response for a suggested agent-based solution, this solution will be classified based on its polarity either positive, negative or neutral and will maintain a contextual conversation with the user by providing a meaningful response with the respective sentiment analysis.

Data Layer. The chat modules data layer is where the Chatbot holds general conversations that can have with the user. The conversations that can be driven by a user is classified in to two main types as the general conversation intents and the agent solution required conversation intents. All the data are stored in json format because it is easy and is a fast data structure compared to AIML.

Below given the main intents and their categories that would be classified.

- General intents – greetings, good bye, thanks, stressed, leaving, happy, need help, already told you, nobody to talk, cannot study, who are you, boost me up, anger, agreeable, not agreeable, not sure, feeling down
- Agent based intents – exam, project, job, internship, relationships, financial
- Polarity intents – positive, negative, neutral

Response Provider. The response providing component will provide meaningful sentences to respond to the user based on the decision engine's triggers which will be based on the solutions that are received from the agent expert system. This component will result in maintaining a meaningful and comfortable conversation that will gradually drive the user to have positive feelings. The user has the freedom to accept the suggested solutions or deny it where at denials the component will send it back to the agent system and will suggest other feasible solutions.

The json file will hold all the responses for the format of agent solutions where the responses stored in each 'action' tag will be triggered when the agent sends a solution tag to the decision engine based on the level of stress. If a certain user sentence is not classified in to a predefined category, then it will be redirected to provide default responses which uses regex mechanisms and pattern matching to generate a meaningful response.

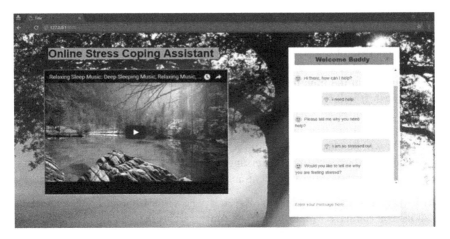

Fig. 10. Implementation of the chat managing module

4 User Study

4.1 Experimental Setup

The authors invited 30 students (aged between 24 and 25) from university of Moratuwa faculty of Information Technology to participate in the study. The authors chose these students because the majority of those who suffers from high levels of stress were identified through a survey and the selected students were suffering from high or medium stress, as evidenced by their Cohen's Perceived Stress Scale (CPSS-14) results [8], which is commonly used to measure human stress level worldwide in psychology. To begin with, the users were told that this was a chatting system which could help them release stress and they could chat with the system whenever necessary. During the experiment, the authors asked the users to do the following things: (1) Whenever they feel stressed out due to their academics, chat with the system. (2) Evaluate the releasing effect of each conversation. (3) Give the ground truth to the stress status of each sentence

4.2 Experimental Results

The authors evaluated the effectiveness of the stress relief mechanisms that are suggested by the agent based expert system by providing a pop-up message for the user to rate the perceived stress from a 1 to 5 scale after providing each solution for a stress related problem (1–5: represent feeling worse, not changed, a bit better, better and much better respectively).

Furthermore, after evaluating the user's perceived stress and its reduction the authors were able to get the ratings of the importance and the usefulness of the system from those who have used the system and the results were as following.

The evaluation of the classification models used to classify the intents in the chat manager module are as following. The Tensorflow tflearn model has given the highest accuracy and for polarity classification the ANN model that had been developed using numpy had given the highest accuracy (Fig. 10). Also, the confusion matrix for intent classification and polarity classification are shown in Figs. 9 and 11 respectively (Figs. 12, 13, 14, 15 and 16).

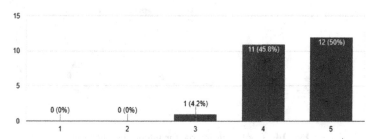

Fig. 11. Provides the results for the question whether the user stressed had been reduced or not. And it shows 40% of the users have been able to reduce their stress and feels much better after using the system, 44% users feel better and 4.2% users feel bit better.

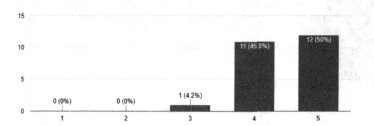

Fig. 12. Shows that 52% of the users has rated that the system is highly useful and 44% of the users had rated the system as moderately useful and only 4.2% of the users had rated as the system is somewhat useful.

	Naïve Based	Linear SVC	Logistic Regression	Multinomial NB	Random Forest Classifier	Ridge Classifier	Feed forward ANN	Tensorflow tflearn
Correctly classified intents	60.32%	71.71%	68.86%	60.95%	50.82%	70.65%	79.6%	88.39%
Incorrectly classified intents	39.68%	28.29%	20.19%	39.05%	49.18%	29.35%	20.4%	11.61%

Fig. 13. Intent classification model accuracy

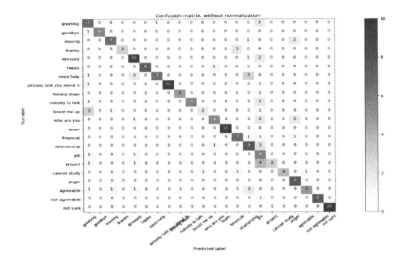

Fig. 14. Confusion matrix for intent classification

	Naïve Based	Linear SVC	Logistic Regression	Multinomial NB	Random Forest Classifier	Ridge Classifier	Feed forward ANN
Correctly classified intents	59.26%	58.64%	58.50%	53.67%	41.62%	57.81%	79.8%
Incorrectly classified intents	38.74%	41.36%	41.5%	39.05%	49.18%	29.35%	20.2%

Fig. 15. Polarity classification model accuracy

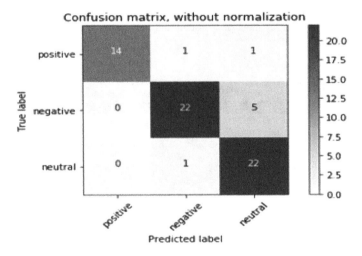

Fig. 16. Confusion matrix for polarity classification

For the emotions detection model authors had tried out with Support Vector Machine (SVM) and 2D-CNN. SVM model gives 54.63% accuracy for Cohn Canade face data set and from 2D-CNN achieved 65.70% accuracy. When comparing both models best accuracy was given from 2D-CNN. Therefore 2D-CNN approach was chosen for emotions detection part (Fig. 17).

Method	Dataset	Accuracy
SVM	CK+	54.63%
2D-CNN	Fer2013	65.70%

Fig. 17. Emotions detection models

The stress level classification part had been tried out with different approaches and received following results for our own data set. When evaluating the stress detection models the best approach was SVC Gaussian Classifier with rbf kernel. It gives the best accuracy for random sampled data set. Other model was also good but did not reach above 60% of testing data accuracy (Figs. 18 and 19).

Dataset	SVC - rbf	FFNN	SVC - linear
Before Class Balance	36.36%	42.50%	45.45%
After Class Balance	53.33%	48.54%	46.67%
After Random Sampling	_71.43%_	54.30%	57.14%

Fig. 18. Stress level classification models

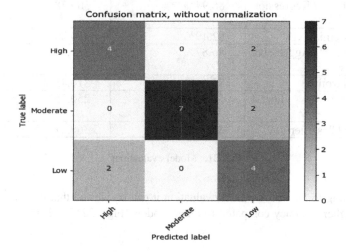

Fig. 19. Confusion matrix for emotion detection model.

The classification report gives a comprehensive detail about precision, recall and F1 score. Precision – Accuracy of positive predictions. Precision = TP/(TP + FP). Recall - Fraction of positives that were correctly identified.

Recall = TP/(TP + FN) F1 Score - compare two classifiers. F1 Score takes into account precision and the recall. It is created by finding the harmonic mean of precision and recall. F1 = 2 × (precision × recall)/(precision + recall).

Accuracy = TP + TN/TP + FP + FN + TN

A ratio of correctly predicted observation to the total observations (Fig. 20).

Precision	Recall	F1-Score
0.67	0.67	0.67
1.00	0.78	0.88
0.5	0.67	0.57

Fig. 20. Classification report for emotion detection module.

This section consists the evaluation of Social Media Stress Detection Module. Therefore, based on the accuracy of each model authors have used Logistic Regression to implement the module (Fig. 21).

Model	Validation Set Accuracy	Test Time (s)
Ada Boost Classifier	71.78%	320.26
Bernoulli NB	84.45%	340.98
Linear SVC	85.96%	330.56
Logistic Regression CV	86.94%	309.78
Multinomial NB	82.49%	310.89
Passive Aggressive Classifier	86.87%	311.49
Perceptron	82.65%	310.45
Random Forest Classifier	58.96%	250.75
Ridge Classifier	85.28%	360.41

Fig. 21. Model evaluations

According to the above model evaluation it can be viewed that logistic regression CV has higher accuracy compared to other models (Figs. 22, 23, 24).

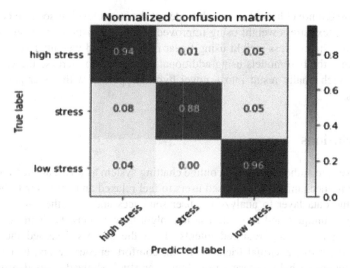

Fig. 22. Confusion matrix for social media stress detection module

	Precision	Recall	F1-score	Support
Class 0	0.90	0.94	0.92	126
Class 1	0.99	0.88	0.93	106
Class 2	0.91	0.96	0.94	122
Avg/Total	0.93	0.93	0.93	354

Fig. 23. Classification report for social media stress detection module

Final Output Per Comment	Accuracy
Average Approach 01	90.6%
Weighted Average Approach 02	91.68%
Neural Network Approach 03	88.7%

Fig. 24. Overall system accuracy for social media stress detection module

Therefore, the proposed hybrid social media analysis model achieves an accuracy of 91.68% which adds another novelty for the module. Also, it can be observed that individual sub components of the overall system also have achieved higher accuracy levels (more than 91%) which increases the novelty of the overall system. The authors have proposed a novel hybrid approach to detect the stress level of social media model by analyzing text stress weight using improved softmax logistic regression model and analyzing emoticon stress weight using linear regression and weighted average values and combines the two models using additional parameters to increase the validity and accuracy which finally result into a novel hybrid approach with better performances and results.

5   Conclusions

In this paper, the authors present an online chatting system as a virtual friend to suggest stress coping mechanisms for stressed users to feel relaxed and calm. First, the authors had built the data layer to analyze the user sentences and used the natural language processing techniques and machine learning algorithms to classify them in to general intents or agent solution required intents. Then the authors designed the response strategies to act like a virtual friend to listen, comfort, encourage and understand the stressful student to help release stress. Our user study showed a good result of the system in stress detection and stress release. In future work, the authors will make use of abundant resources in social network to improve the response effect, including collecting more answers with higher pertinence and efficiency.

References

1. Oguntimilehin, A., Abiola, O.B., Adeyemo, O.A.: A Clinical Decision Support System for Managing Stress, vol. 6, no. 8 (2015)
2. Devi, R.S., Mohan, S.: A study on stress and its effects on college students. Int. J. Sci. Eng. Appl. Sci. 1(7), (2015)
3. Jayakumar, A.: An empirical study on stress management for higher secondary students in a Salem-District-Tamil Nadu. Int. J. Recent Adv. Org. Behav. Decision Sci. 1(1), (2014)
4. Madhuri, V., Mohan, M.R., Kaavya, R.: Stress management using artificial intelligence 54–57 (2013)
5. AbuShawar, B., Atwell, E.: ALICE Chatbot: trials and outputs. Comput. Sist. 19(4), (2015)
6. Marksberry, K.: What is stress? The American Institute of Stress. https://www.stress.org/what-is-stress
7. Dan, D., Gautam, S., Chris, E.: Facial emotion recognition in real time. Report (2016)
8. Molchanov, P., Gupta, S., Kim, K., Kautz, J.: Hand gesture recognition with 3D convolutional neural networks. In: IEEE Conference on Computer Vision and Pattern Recognition Workshops (CVPRW) (2015)
9. Byeon, Y., Kwak*, K.: Facial expression recognition using 3D convolutional neural network. Int. J. Adv. Comput. Sci. Appl. 5(12), (2014)
10. Hasani, B., Mahoor, M.H.: Facial expression recognition using enhanced deep 3D convolutional neural networks. In: IEEE Conference on Computer Vision and Pattern Recognition Workshops (CVPRW) (2017)
11. Fan, Y., Lu, X., Li, D., Liu, Y.: Video-based emotion recognition using CNN-RNN and C3D hybrid networks. In: Proceedings of the 18th ACM International Conference on Multimodal Interaction - ICMI 2016, pp. 445–450 (2016)

12. Bargal, S., Barsoum, E., Canton, C.F., Zhang, C.: Emotion recognition in the wild from videos using images. In: Proceedings of the 18th ACM International Conference on Multimodal Interaction - ICMI (2016)
13. Suvashis, D., Koichi, Y.: Emotion detection from facial expression and its use in the evaluation of stress (2013)
14. Karanta, I., Rautila, M.: An expert system for mitigation actions. In: 20th Conference of Open Innovations Association (FRUCT) (2017)
15. Cha, A.P., Romli, A.: Human-computer interaction of design rules and usability elements in expert system for personality-based stress management. Int. J. Intell. Comput. Res. 1(1), 20–29 (2010)
16. Ghosh, A., Tweedale, J.W., Nafalski, A.: Modified hybridized multi-agent oriented approach to analyze work-stress data providing feedback in real time. Procedia Comput. Sci. 22, 1092–1101 (2013)
17. Lin, H.: Psychological stress detection from cross-media microblog data using deep sparse neural network. In: IEEE International Conference on Multimedia and Expo (ICME), pp. 1–6 (2014)
18. Yin, X., Ho, K., Zeng, D., Aickelin, U., Zhou, R., Wang, H.: Health Information Science, vol. 9085. Springer, Cham (2015)
19. Al-Zubaide, H., Issa, A.A.: OntBot: ontology based chatbot. In: Fourth International Symposium on Innovation in Information & Communication Technology (ISIICT), pp. 7–12 (2011)
20. Hinton, G.E.: Learning multiple layers of representation. Trends Cogn. Sci. 11(10), 428–434
21. Vidhyapathi, C.M., Joseph, A.N.: Advances in the analysis of human gesture recognition using kinect sensor: a review. ARPN J. Eng. Appl. Sci. 11(11) (2016)
22. Schager, B., AB M.P.S.: Stress and Human Functioning 1 (2009)
23. O'Brien, N.: Academic stress, coping mechanisms, and outcome measures among college students of today (2014)

Thinking Like Humans: A New Approach to Machine Translation

Budditha Hettige$^{(\boxtimes)}$, Asoka Karunananda, and Gorge Rzevski

Department of Computational Mathematics, Faculty of Information Technology,
University of Moratuwa, Moratuwa, Sri Lanka
bhettige@gmail.com, asokakaru@uom.lk,
rzevski@gmail.com

Abstract. Existing machine translation approaches do not adequately mimic how humans do translation from one natural language to another. This paper presents a novel approach to machine translation that is inspired by how humans translate natural languages. We have exploited the theory of psycholinguistic sentence-parsing to develop a human-like machine translation system. This approach has been modeled as a multi-agent system, named EnSiMaS, which translates an English sentence into Sinhala sentence. The multi-agent system has been implemented through the MaSMT framework with two manager agents and over 100 agents which deliberate on different aspects of machine translation. These agents are clustered into eight-agent swarms to consider morphological, syntactic, and semantic concerns of the source and the target languages. The EnSiMaS system has been tested with the different types of sentences and successful results were obtained.

Keywords: Machine translation · Multi-agent system · Psycholinguistic

1 Introduction

In 1956, the field of Artificial Intelligence (AI) was born with the primary objective to build intelligent machines. First time in the history, in 1950, Alan Turing's classic article, "Computing Machinery and Intelligence" has postulated the concept of intelligence machines [1]. From the inception of AI, computer-based natural language processing, commonly known as NLP, has been recognized as a major area of AI. NLP is concerned with computer-based natural language understanding and machine translation among natural languages. As compared with tremendous developments in AI, machine translation remains a research challenge. A typical machine translation systems automatically translate texts in a source natural language to corresponding texts in a target language by preserving the meaning [2]. In general, machine translation systems first analyze the given source language sentence and identify morphological, syntactical, and semantical relationships. In the second step, corresponding morphological, syntactical and semantical details of the source language text are identified within the target language. Finally, the corresponding text in the target language generates by the machine translation system.

© Springer Nature Singapore Pte Ltd. 2019
J. Hemanth et al. (Eds.): SLAAI-ICAI 2018, CCIS 890, pp. 256–268, 2019.
https://doi.org/10.1007/978-981-13-9129-3_18

Most of the existing machine translation systems follow this general pipeline for natural language translation [3]. For that, these systems also handle morphology, syntax, and semantics of both source and target language on different levels. According to the level of language processing and generation of morphology, syntax, and semantics, machine translation systems are broadly categorized into three groups: namely, direct transfer system, syntax transfer system, and interlingua transfer system [4]. A direct transfer system gives much attention to morphological concerns, but less attention to syntax and semantics aspects of translation. In syntax transfer systems, sound attention has been given to morphology and syntax while sematic concerns are almost disregarded. In contrast, the interlingua transfer systems give full attention to all three concerns. Further, based on the translation approach, machine translation systems are also classified as rule-based, statistical, neuro-linguistic, example-based, hybrid and so on. All these machine translation approaches have their own strengths and weaknesses. However, none of these approaches have been able to achieve up to the expectation of the NLP community. There is still a considerable translation quality gap between automated machine translation and translation by humans. As such it is worth investigating why human translations have been better than a translation by machines.

Human translation is based on psycholinguistic parsing techniques [5] that can provide the most suitable translation between two natural languages. Psycholinguistic parsing is driven by four main factors: phrase-structure, semantic features, thematic rules, and associated probability [6]. However, the exact weight of each of these factors' contribution is unknown. In addition, a number of theories are also available for English language parsing, including the garden path model [7] and the constraint satisfaction model [8]. These theories demonstrate how people parse an English sentence together with meaning. Based on these theories and psycholinguistic parsing techniques, we propose a hybrid approach to machine translation, inspired by phrase-based and multi-agent approaches. The proposed approach has been simulated through the multi-agent system [9], named EnSiMaS, which can be used to translate English text into Sinhala. EnSiMaS consists of four different types of translation tools: a word translator, phrase translator [10], sentence editor, and a classical text translator. The word translator translates Sinhala words considering only the morphology of both languages' words. The phrase translator is capable of translating an English phrase into multiple Sinhala phrases. The sentence editor is capable of translating English sentences into Sinhala with multiple solutions. The editor can also be used as an intermediate editing tool for professional translators to make a better solution. The classical text translator can translate English text (paragraphs) into Sinhala considering the morphology, syntax, semantics, and pragmatics on both languages.

This paper presents a psycholinguistic approach to machine translation together with a brief description of how the EnSiMaS sentence editor translates a given English sentence into Sinhala.

The rest of the paper is organized as follows. Section 2 reports the Existing approach for machine translation including strengths and weaknesses. Then Sect. 3 explains the proposed approach to machine translation. Section 4 gives a brief description of EnSiMaS including design, implementation and results of the translations Finally, Sect. 5 provides a note on the conclusion and further direction of the research.

2 Existing Approach to Machine Translation

Machine translation is an automated language translation process, which depends on the approach used for the translation. There are numbers of approaches available for machine translation. These approaches can be classified into several categories, including human-assisted, rule-based, statistical, example-based, knowledge-based, hybrid, agent-based, neuro translation etc. These machine translation approaches have their own strengths and weakness.

The human-assisted approach uses human interaction for the pre-editing, post editing, and/or intermediate editing stages [11]. Thus, human-assisted machine translation systems can be categorized as semi-automated systems.

The rule-based approach gives grammatically correct translations by considering a set of rules. In general, rule-based systems consist of source and target language processing modules including a source language morphological analyzer, a source language parser, translator, target language morphological analyzer, target language parser, and several lexicon dictionaries. Most of the rule-based systems provide accurate translations only for a limited domain. Anusaarka [12] is a popular rule-based system that is capable of translating English to Indian languages.

Statistical machine translation [13] is a successful approach to machine translation so far. Generally, in statistical machine translation, phrases are translated from source to target using a bilingual corpus with the support of the statistically generated decision.

Neural machine translation [14] is an approach to machine translation that uses a large artificial neural network to predict the translation. Now, Google uses Google Neural Machine Translation to improve the quality of the translation compared to previous statistical methods.

Considering the English to Sinhala machine translation, only a few numbers of systems are available. Among others, Google translation [15] is the most commonly used machine translation system so far. This system also uses a statistical method for machine translation and it was improved through neural machine translation methods. However, the statistical machine translation system required more resources from both languages for sufficient training. Thus, the English to Sinhala Google machine translation system gives less accuracy for uncommon sentences.

BEES is an English to Sinhala rule-based machine translation system [16] that uses the concept of Varanegeema (conjugation) [17] in the Sinhala language as the philosophical basis. This system is capable of providing grammatically correct translation for simple English sentences.

In addition to the above, there are few other prototype systems also available for English to Sinhala including, SEES [18] (a translator from Sinhala to English and English to Sinhala) and ESANA [19].

Further, according to the complexity of natural languages, machine translation is still achieving less accuracy than human translation in some complex situations. Therefore, reducing the translation quality gap in between human translation and machine translation is still research challenging task.

3   A Novel Approach to Machine Translation

This section briefly describes a novel approach to machine translation, which has been implemented as a multi-agent system that exploits the theory of psycholinguistic parsing for phrase-based machine translation.

3.1   Theoretical Basis for the Approach

Psycholinguistic theory offers two models, namely, garden path model and the constraint satisfaction model for parsing natural languages. These psycholinguistic models demonstrate how people parse an English sentence together with meaning. According to the garden path model, the reader takes a solution (translation) for a first noun phrase available in the input sentence and proceeds in the right direction with the syntactic structure and making the correct assumptions as they are reading. New information presented later in the sentence, causes the reader to fall down the rabbit hole. Then reader should able to find another solution for existing context that suitable for the new information. Thus, garden path model restricts to a single context, which was selected by the reader in the bingeing of the reading. The constraint satisfaction model also states that the reader uses all the available information at once when engaging in the parsing of a sentence.

In addition, psycholinguistic parsing is also based on four main factors: namely, phrase structure, probability, thematic roles, and semantic features. Figure 1 shows the four factors contributing to translation.

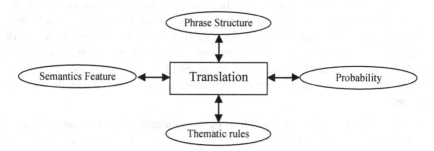

Fig. 1. Four factors contribute to parsing a phrase or sentence

Phrase structure consists of syntactical and grammatical rules for each phrase. English phrases are translated into Sinhala by considering these grammar rules. For Instance, some English verb phrases represent only a single Sinhala verb (The English phrase 'will read' translates into *kiyawanneya* ((කියවන්නේය))). According to the phrase structure, head word (that contain a main meaning) and other supporting words are also recognized.

Probability is a measure that is used to identify the most suitable phrase from existing multiple phrases. For instance, each English word consists of one or more Sinhala meanings. Probability is calculated considering the availability of these words (in here, it is calculated through Google search results). For instance, consider the simple English phrase "the good boy." The words 'good' and 'boy' have multiple Sinhala meanings. Therefore, the system can generate more Sinhala phrases considering all these options. After generating multiple Sinhala phrases, usage of each phrase is calculated. The probability of a Sinhala phrase P(x) is calculated through Eq. 1:

$$Probability\ P(x) = \frac{Usage\ of\ the\ P(x)}{\sum Usage\ of\ P} \tag{1}$$

The thematic roles focus on the lexical information being presented [20]. The syntax analysis system should take required thematic relation of each English phase. With this information, it should also be capable of calculating probability values for multiple Sinhala translations. The probability was calculated for subject-verb and verb-object relations.

The semantic feature gives a clear idea about words. This should be used to take the best solution than acceptable more solutions. However, the present system does not recode the semantic features of a word. Thus, the system can provide multiple results.

Note that, multi-agent systems are opportunistic rather than algorithmic activities [21]. Therefore, the multi-agent approach is used to simulate the translation. Considering the translation process, each translated phrase acts as an agent and provides better solutions by communicating with each other through the messages.

3.2 English to Sinhala Machine Translation

This section briefly explains how the above theoretical based approach is used to translate English sentences into Sinhala. It should be noted that different people phrase and translate one language sentence into another through different methods (the approach is the same but follows a different order). Considering the ability to simulate through the computer application, a suitable human language translation process was identified. Then human's language translation process was pipelined with the following seven steps.

Step 1: Read the input sentence left to right and identify the grammatical category (part of speech) of each word in the input sentence. This was done through the English morphological processing system. Note that, some English words have only one grammatical category, and some have one or more. For instance, the English word 'books' consist of two categories: noun and verb. After this analysis, all the grammatical information for each word is recorded. If out-of-vocabulary words are available, then mark them as unknown or if an unknown word begins with an uppercase letter then mark it as a proper noun.

Step 2: Identify the available Sinhala meaning (Sinhala base word) from an English-Sinhala bilingual dictionary for each English word in the sentence by considering the identified grammatical category. Note that, some words do not have direct Sinhala meanings and some have one or more. For instance, the English word 'the' is only the noun modifier and the English word 'boy' has more Sinhala meanings, including පිරිමි ළමයා, කොල්ලා, ගැටයා etc.

Step 3: After arranging the morphological information on each word, the English syntactical processing system (swarm) can identify available English phrases in the input sentence with considering the grammatical category and available Sinhala meaning of each English word. Considering all the available phrases, the syntactical processing system can detect suitable English phrases from the available phrase list.

Step 4: Use existing English phrases, thematic relationship (syntax) for the input sentence is identified. In this step, the subject, object, action verb and modifiers, and their relationship of the input sentence are also recorded.

Step 5: Considering phrase structure and the thematic relationship of each phrase, multiple Sinhala translations (Sinhala phrases) are generated for each English phrase. In this point, a Sinhala phrase agent is assigned to each English phrase. These phrase agents communicate with relevant other Sinhala phrase agents for further translations.

Step 6: Through the relevant communication between Sinhala phrase agents, subject phrase agents can identify suitable verb phrases according to its calculated probability. Same as the above, the Sinhala verb phrase agent(s) capable of identifying relevant object phrases. Note that, a Sinhala phrase agent does not agree to the existing context, then other agents' cable to re-arrange there Sinhala phrase context according to the new situation.

Step 7: According to the syntax of the existing English sentence, Sinhala syntax processing system capable to re-arrange the Sinhala phrases to generate a grammatically correct Sinhala sentence.

Further, the thematic relationship in the previous translated Sinhala sentence is recorded for the pragmatic analysis. The next section briefly explains the design and implementation of the EnSiMaS with how EnSiMaS sentence editor translates the given input English sentence.

4 EnSiMaS: Multi-agent System for Machine Translation

The English to Sinhala Machine Translation system, namely EnSiMaS, has been designed and developed as a multi-agent system. EnSiMaS has been also implemented through the MaSMT framework [23] with seven agent swarms for different processes, including the English morphological analyzing swarm, the English syntax analyzing swarm, the phrase-based translation swarm, the Sinhala morphological generation swarm, the Sinhala syntax generation swarm, the Sinhala semantics processing swarm, and the ontology managing swarm. In addition to the above seven swarms, the EnSiMaS Manager and GUI agent are used to completing the translation process. Figure 2 shows the design diagram of the EnSiMaS. A brief description of each swarm is given below.

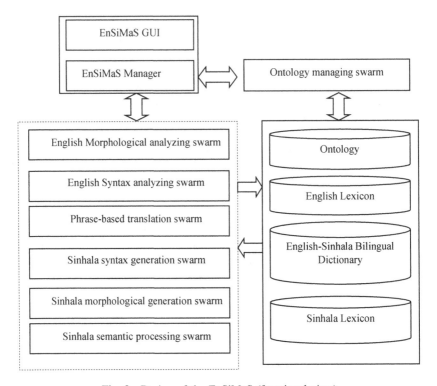

Fig. 2. Design of the EnSiMaS (functional view)

4.1   The English Morphological Analyzing Swarm

The English morphological analyzing swarm can analyze English morphology for the given English words. This swarm comprises nine morphological processing agents to handle English language morphology. Theoretically, the morphological analysis has been done by the English morphological agents and each agent follows a rule-based root-fixing method [22] to identify the existing morphology of given English words. The result of the morphological analysis is stored in the ontology for further usage.

4.2   The Sinhala Semantics Processing Swarm

The Sinhala semantics processing swarm communicates with the ontology and loads relevant Sinhala meanings for each English word. Semantics agents are also capable of calculating and updating probability values for each phrase from the internet or existing storage.

4.3   The Ontology Managing Swarm

The ontology managing swarm is capable of handling ontologies in the multi-agent system as required. Agents in the swarm create, load, update, and store ontological information as required for the translation.

4.4   The Sinhala Semantics Processing Swarm

The Sinhala semantics processing swarm communicates with the ontology and loads relevant Sinhala meanings for each English word. Semantics agents are also capable of finding the usage for the existing phrase from the internet or existing storage. The ontology managing swarm is capable of handling ontologies in the multi-agent system as required. Agents in the swarm create, load, update, and store ontological information as required for the translation.

4.5   English Syntax Analyzing Swarm

Syntax analysis is the process of analyzing the syntax of the given English sentence or part of the sentence. The English syntax analyzing swarm uses bottom-up, phrase-based parsing methods to analyze the English sentence structure. According to the proposed human-based approach, phrase agents are capable of identifying existing phrases, with left-to-right parts of speech tag reading. Then, agents read all the available phrases and identify valid phrases and structures for the input sentence. After the syntactic structure identification, thematic agents are capable of identifying existing thematic rules and relations by communicating with relevant agents.

4.6   Sinhala Morphological Generation Swarm

Morphological generation is the opposite task of the English morphological analysis. In this Sinhala morphological generation swarm capable to generate Sinhala words according to the given grammar. The Sinhala morphological generation is through the hybrid approach (multi-agent and rule-based). Each morphological rule is stored as an add-remove rule for the Sinhala based word. The system reads the Sinhala-based word and the required morphology, then Sinhala morphological generation agents are capable of generating the correct Sinhala word form according to the given grammar.

4.7   The Sinhala Syntax Generation Swarm

The Sinhala syntax generation swarm provides a grammatically correct translation. This system uses a multi-agent-based syntax transfer method to generate the final Sinhala translation. This approach is powered through the set of syntax transfer rules that are used to generate Sinhala sentence structure from the English sentence. System translation is done through the phrase based and each phrase in the sentence is put into the correct order that how human rearrange the Sinhala phrase in a sentence from its original English sentence.

4.8   The Phrase-Based Translation Swarm

The phrase-based translation swarm generates appropriate Sinhala phrase agents to represent existing Sinhala phrases. These Sinhala phrase agents can handle the rest of the translation process through communication among relevant agents. The Sinhala phrase agent consists of the Sinhala context, phrase structure, headword information, and thematic relationship according to the existing English phrase and the Sinhala phrase grammar. The Sinhala phrase agent takes different activities for their thematic relation and the structure of the phrase. According to the thematic rules and phrase structure, a Sinhala phrase agent is categorized as a subject agent, verb agent, object agent, subject modifier etc. The subject agent sends a message to the verb phrase (final verb) agent and asks for a suitable verb phrase. Note that, the subject agent also sends headword information for a verb phrase agent. Then the verb phrase re-calculates the probability of considering the subject-verb relationship. After calculating the subject-verb probability, the verb phrase agent sends a reply message for the subject phrase. Then the subject phrase takes all results and identifies a suitable verb phrase according to the calculated probability. Following the same procedure, the verb phrase agent communicates with the object phrase agent and takes the best object phrase.

Assume that, the input sentence "The good boy is reading a new book" has three English phrases. According to the input sentence structure, "the good boy" is the subject phrase and has multiple Sinhala translations ""හොඳ පිරිමි ළමයා, දක්ෂ කොල්ලා,, දක්ෂ ළමයා, හොඳ කුමාරයෝ etc." The Sinhala subject phrase agent with context ""හොඳ පිරිමි ළමයා"" sends a message for the Sinhala verb phrase with the headword ""පිරිමි ළමයා"". Then the Sinhala verb phrase agent reads the message and calculates the probabilities of the available verb phrases. After probability calculation, verb phrase agent takes maximum probability for ""පිරිමි ළමයා කියවයි"" (subject-verb relation) and sends the reply for the subject phrase agent. Further, according to this probability calculation process, the verb ""කඳාරනවා"" takes the maximum probability for the headword ""කුමාරයා"". After relevant communication among agents, the subject agent takes ""කියවනවා"" as the best verb phrase and අලුත් පොතක් is taken as the best object for the verb phrase ""කියවනවා"". The Fig. 3 shows the phrase relation of the given sentence.

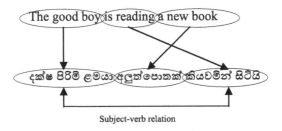

Subject-verb relation

Fig. 3. Phrase relation for the input sentence "The good boy is reading a good book"

This phrase selection method follows three factors, such as phrase structure, thematic feature, and probability as same as the psycholinguistic parsing techniques. However, the present system does not consider the semantic features and for that multiple translations are provided (each head word of the subject agent takes a solution). Figure 4 shows the user interface of the EnSiMaS sentence editor, which shows the translation results for the input sentence "The good boy is reading a new book." The EnSiMaS editor shows multiple Sinhala translation for the input sentence and a number of Sinhala phrases for the selected English phrase.

Performance of the EnSiMaS system has been tested with considering the 200 sample sentences. To calculate the performance of the EnSiMaS, translation results are compared with a human translation results with the Google translation. Among those sample sentences, Table 1 shows selected five sample English sentences and results on both EnSiMaS and Google translations. With considering the 200 sample sentences, the word error rate has been calculated through the equation given in Eq. 2. According to the calculation, the system shows 4.65 word error rate.

$$Word\ Error\ Rate = \frac{\sum Incorrect\ words\ in\ the\ sentence}{\sum Total\ numbers\ of\ words\ in\ the\ sentence} \tag{2}$$

In addition, system performance has been calculated for 200 sample sentences through human evaluation. Table 2 shows the human evaluation results for 200 samples. According to the evaluation, EnSiMaS system capable to translate English sentence into Sinhala with approximately 93% accuracy.

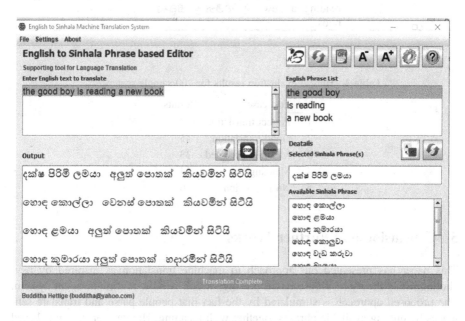

Fig. 4. EnSiMaS sentence editor

Table 1. Translation results for 5 sample sentences

No	Sample Sentence	EnSiMaS	Google Translator
1	The good boy reads a new book	දක්ෂ පිරිමි ළමයා අලුත් පොතක් කියවයි	හොඳ පිරිමි ළමයා නව පොත කියවන්න
2	the good girl will read books at the school	දක්ෂ ගැහැනු ළමයා විද්‍යාස්ථාය දී පොත් කියවන්නේය	හොඳ කෙල්ල පාසලේ පොත් කියවන්න
3	I write a letter at home	මම නිවස දී ලිපියක් ලියමි	මම ගෙදර ලිපියක් ලියන්න
4	The boy shall have been reading a book	පිරිමි ළමයා පොතක් මතු කියවමින් උන්නෙමු වන්නේය	පිරිමි ළමයා පොත කියවීම කර තිබීම
5	the good boy had been reading a new book	දක්ෂ පිරිමි ළමයා අලුත් පොතක් කියවමින් ඉඳ තිබුණි	හොඳ පිරිමි ළමයා නව පොත කියවීම කර ඇති

Table 2. Human evaluation results for 200 sample sentences.

No	Test case	Results
1	Perfect translation	108
2	Good translation	45
3	Meaning accepted	33
4	Meaningless	14
5	No translation	0

5   Conclusion and Further Works

This paper has presented our approach to machine translation as inspired by psycholinguistics theory of phrase-based parsing, which is built as a multi-agent system. The proposed approach is stimulated by the fact that people parse and translate sentences by putting available phrases together with meaning. Human translation is based on psycholinguistic parsing techniques to investigate correct meanings and it differs from existing systematic machine translation approaches. The system, EnSiMaS, was implemented for simulating the proposed approach, with seven swarms of agents, namely the English morphological swarm, the English syntactical swarm, the English-Sinhala semantic swarm, the Sinhala morphological swarm, the Sinhala syntactical swarm, the ontology management swarm, and the translation swarm. The translation swarm is the key subsystem of the EnSiMaS, which can create a number of Sinhala phrase agents for generating accurate Sinhala translation. These Sinhala phrase agents communicate with other relevant Sinhala phrase agents to take better solutions. For instance, Sinhala subject phrase agents communicate with verb phrase agents and take the most suitable verb phrase for the exiting subject phrase. Same as the above, Sinhala verb phrase agent communicates with the Sinhala object phrase agent and takes a suitable Sinhala object phrase from the existing object phrases. EnSiMaS is also capable of providing multiple solutions for the given English sentence. The system was tested with different types of sentences and results were compared with human translation and Google translation. According to the experimental results, the system gives 4.65 word error rate and approximately more than 93% human accepted translation. Thus, this multi-agent through phrase-based translation approach can overcome the gap between human translation and machine translation. Further, this system can be improved as a bilingual translator by including more capabilities for each language processing system. In addition, generated English and Sinhala phrases can be used to train other statistical or neural machine translation systems.

References

1. Turing, A.M.: Computing machinery and intelligence. Mind **49**, 433–460 (1950)
2. Jurafsky, D., Martin, J.H.: Speech and Language Processing. Pearson Education, London (2005)
3. Hutchins, W.J., Somers, H.L.: An Introduction to Machine Translation. Academic Press, London (1992)
4. Hettige, B., Karunananda, A.S.: Existing systems and approaches for machine translation: a review. In: Proceedings of the 8th Annual Sessions, Sri Lanka Association for Artificial Intelligence (2011)
5. Marinis, T.: Psycholinguistic techniques in second language acquisition research. Second Lang. Res. **19**(2), 144–161 (2003)
6. Psycholinguistics/Parsing-Wikiversity.   https://en.wikiversity.org/wiki/Psycholinguistics/Parsing
7. Ferreira, F., Christianson, K., Hollingworth, A.: Misinterpretations of garden-path sentences: implications for models of sentence processing and reanalysis. J. Psycholinguist. Res. **30**(1), 3–20 (2001)
8. Frazier, L.: Constraint satisfaction as a theory of sentence processing. J. Psycholinguist. Res. **24**(6), 437–468 (1995)
9. Hettige, B., Karunananda, A.S., Rzevski, G.: A multi-agent solution for managing complexity in English to Sinhala machine translation. Int. J. Des. Nat. Ecodyn. **11**(2), 88–96 (2016)
10. Hettige, B., Karunananda, A.S., Rzevski, G.: Phrase-level English to Sinhala machine translation with multi-agent approach. In: 2017 IEEE International Conference on Industrial and Information Systems (ICIIS) (2017)
11. Craciunescu, O., Gerding-Salas, C., Stringer-O'Keeffe, S.: Machine translation and computer assisted translation. Transl. J. **8**(3), 11 (2004)
12. Anusaarka Machine Translation System. http://sampark.iiit.ac.in/anusaaraka
13. Statistical Machine Translation (ebook) by Philipp Koehn. eBooks.com. http://www.ebooks.com/502350/statistical-machine-translation/koehn-philipp/
14. Wu, Y., et al.: Google's neural machine translation system: bridging the gap between human and machine translation. Google AI (2016). https://ai.google/research/pubs/pub45610
15. Google Translate. https://translate.google.com/

16. Hettige, B.: A computational grammar of Sinhala for English–Sinhala machine translation. M.Phil. thesis, University of Moratuwa, Sri Lanka, Moratuwa (2011)
17. Hettige, B., Karunananda, A.S.: A novel approach for English to Sinhala machine translation. In: ITRU Research Symposium, Moratuwa (2010)
18. A translator from Sinhala to English and English to Sinhala (SEES). In: International Conference on Advances in ICT for Emerging Regions. http://www.icter.org/conference/icter2016/?q=icter2012/paper/43
19. Ekanayake, A.E., Maduranga, G.L.D., Maddewithana, D.A., Fernando, M.P.H., Wijesiriwardana, C.P., Mufitha, M.B.: Int. J. Emerg. Technol. Comput. Appl. Sci. (IJETCAS), 6 (2014). www.iasir.net
20. Christianson, K., Hollingworth, A., Halliwell, J.F., Ferreira, F.: Thematic roles assigned along the garden path linger. Cognit. Psychol. **42**(4), 368–407 (2001)
21. Rzevski, G., Skobelev, P.: Managing Complexity. WIT Press, Boston (2014)
22. Hettige, B., Karunananda, A.S., Rzevski, G.: Multi-agent system technology for morphological analysis. In: Proceedings 9th Annual Sessions Sri Lanka Association for Artificial Intelligence SLAAI Colombo (2012)
23. Hettige, B., Karunananda, A.S., Rzevski, G.: MaSMT: a multi-agent system development framework for English-Sinhala machine translation. Int. J. Comput. Linguist. Nat. Lang. Process. **2**(7), 411–416 (2013)

Rice Express: A Communication Platform for Rice Production Industry

M. A. S. T. Goonatilleke$^{(\boxtimes)}$, M. W. G. Jayampath$^{(\boxtimes)}$, and B. Hettige$^{(\boxtimes)}$

Department of Computer Science, Faculty of Computing,
General Sir John Kotelawala Defence University, Ratmalana, Sri Lanka
sandali07@hotmail.com, 33-cosc-004@kdu.ac.lk,
budditha@yahoo.com

Abstract. Rice production can consider as the main production area in the agriculture industry. Because of the poor communication among farmers, buyers and transporters Sri Lanka is a high-cost rice producer. Rice production cost can significantly reduce through the communication between relevant persons in right time. Thus Multi-Agent technology can be used to handle the communication productively. This paper presents a multi-agent solution for the agriculture industry, namely, Rice Express, which is capable of communicating between the persons in the rice production industry. Rice Express has been developed through the MaSMT framework. The system comprises three types of agents, namely, farmers, buyers and transporters. With the relevant agent communication among farmers, buyers, and transporters, the system should be capable of reducing transport cost significantly. The Rice Express has been successfully tested in the practical environment, and successful results were obtained.

Keywords: Agriculture · Rice production · Multi-Agent Systems · MaSMT framework

1 Introduction

The agriculture industry is the largest and oldest occupation in the world. Millions of people in the world are involved in this industry and contribute a lot in food production. When compared to other economic sectors, the agricultural industry is the leading actor for economic in most of the countries including Sri Lanka. Further, 31.8% are engaged in agricultural activities out of the total population [1]. The agricultural industry can be classified as rice cultivation, tea plantation, oilseed crops, fruits, and vegetables. The primary form of the agricultural industry in Sri Lanka is rice production industry. Rice is cultivated during two seasons which can be named as Maha and Yala. Rice crop occupies 34% of the total cultivated area in Sri Lanka, According to the web resources, 1.8 million farmer families are engaged in paddy cultivation island-wide. Sri Lanka currently produces more than 2.7 million tonnes of rough rice annually and satisfies around 95% of the domestic requirement [2].

© Springer Nature Singapore Pte Ltd. 2019
J. Hemanth et al. (Eds.): SLAAI-ICAI 2018, CCIS 890, pp. 269–277, 2019.
https://doi.org/10.1007/978-981-13-9129-3_19

The rice production industry in Sri Lanka still could not be obtained the success due to several reasons. They are; weak delivery services in rural areas, low farm gate price and poor communication between the community and so on [3]. However, most of the issues can solve using proper communication mechanisms between the people who are involved in the industry. Further, many governments and private sectors are involved in reducing these problems and leading the sector to succeed.

Efficient and effective communication can help to achieve many goals of any industry because it acts as a source of information and helps to make decisions. Similarly, rice production industry also suffers from lack of communication. Innovations do not go to the lowest level of this sector, and according to this situation, farmers face many problems such as the problems involved in cultivating and selling products. Not only that, but also there are no proper tools and suitable technology that can hold among the people who involved in this industry. As a result, the industry is lagging.

Farmers, buyers, sellers, and transporters are the principal persons of the rice production industry. When considering them separately, they are very busy with their occupations. Not only that, but also most of them have minimal computer knowledge and skills. As a result, there is no inclination of using computerized systems as they cannot handle complex systems and no time to interact with computers. Because of this situation, they are seeking for simple systems to fulfil their requirements. Therefore, most of the existing computerized systems have become useless.

With the above, research has been conducted to provide relevant fast and effective communication among people in the rice production industry to reduce the cost of rice production. Thus, a multi-agent system has been developed named Rice Express. Rice Express is a Multi-Agent system has been designed to communicate with the people who are involved in the rice production industry. The system was developed using MaSMT [4]. MaSMT is freely available Java-based Multi agent development framework which was initially designed to develop machine translation systems [5] with a large number of agents runs on a single machine. The Rice Express provides three types of agents consists of farmers, buyers, and transporters which deputize community in the industry. In this system farmers are the sellers who sell rice, the buyers are the people, or a company who buy rice from farmers and transporters are the people who collect and transport rice from place to place. The system consists of two modes. They are manual mode and the automated mode. In the manual mode farmers and buyers can perform tasks through a graphical user interface and then the system will start to work as an automated mode. In the automated mode, an agent has been working as a person in the field. These rice express agents can communicate with each other through the message parsing.

This paper presents the design and development of the Rice Expert system which handles the communications between related persons in the rice production industry. The rest of the paper is structured as follows. Section 2 gives a brief description of existing systems in the rice production industry. Section 3 gives a brief introduction about Multi-Agent system technology and some existing Multi-agent systems in the rice production industry and related agricultural industries. Section 3 presents descriptions about models in Rice Expert System. Section 4 reports how the system works in the practical environment and Sect. 5 presents the experimental results of the system. Finally, Sect. 6 gives a conclusion and further works for the project.

2 Related Works

This section briefly describes existing supporting systems for rice production. The Department of Agriculture, Government of Sri Lanka [6], provides some useful information on rice production industry; including several and particular technologies for crop and post-harvest details about fertilizers including organic fertilizers and chemical fertilizers, pests management systems for general pest management, integrated pest management, biological pest management and weed management.

Further, a number of web resources are available to provide information on rice production. Wiki Goviya [7] website is an interactive web tool for agriculture development in Sri Lanka which acts as a meeting place for farmers, experts, academics, students and private sector organizations. It provides a platform to share and discuss agricultural information, agriculture policies and their implementations.

There are many systems which have been developed for the rice production industry. Among them, many of these systems have used Multi-agent system Technology. The subsection below gives a brief description of multi-agent system technology and existing multi-agent systems in the rice production industry.

The multi-agent system technology is a modern computerized system technology that is designed to interact with intelligent agents [8]. This technology consists of a large number of small programs which can be known as agents. Agents can run in parallel and communicate with others to make a solution. Multi-Agent Systems consist of a set of agents and their environment where agents perceive inputs and perform actions. Multi-Agent Systems are referred to software agents could be either robots or humans. Typically, agents can be divided into passive agents, active agents and cognitive agents. The environment that agent lives can be classified as virtual, discrete and continuous. Basically, any Multi-Agent System contains four major components namely Multi-Agent Engine, Virtual World, Ontology and Interfaces. Design and develop a multi-agent system for a specific problem is a bit challenging task and it required to select the most suitable agent development framework. There are several toolkits and frameworks are available for the development of Multi-Agent Systems. JADE (Java Agent Development Framework) is a free software framework which designed to develop intelligent agents [9]. This is implemented in Java. JADE provides support to maintain the coordination between several agents FIPA and use FIPA-ACL as the communication language. Not only that but also JADE is a middleware that provides facilities for the development of Multi-Agent Systems by creating multiple containers for the agents, and each of them can run on one or more systems. Accordingly, JADE provides an environment for the execution of agents, class libraries to create agents using heritage and redefinition of behaviours and graphical toolkit to monitor and manage the platform of the intelligent agents. Jason is an open source, java based platform which distributed under GNU for the development of Multi-Agent Systems [10]. It is an extension of the AgentSpeak agent-oriented programming language. It comes as a plugin of jEdit and Eclipse.

MaDKit [11] (Multiagent Development Kit) is a Multi-Agent-based development platform implemented in Java. It provides facilities to build distributed applications and simulations that can easily use the Multi-Agent paradigm. MaDKit is built upon the

AGR (Agent/Group/Role) organizational model and does not rely on a predefined agent model.

MaSMT [4] (Multi-Agent System for Machine Translation) is a modern software palindrome to handle the complexity of a software system and can provide intelligent solutions using the power of the agents. It is a free and lightweight Multi-Agent System development framework which is designed through the Java environment. This framework provides three types of agents. They are an ordinary agent, manager agent and root agent. The manager agent can have a set of ordinary agents, and the root agent consists of a set of manager agents.

There are several numbers of systems which have been designed using Multi-Agent System Technology. Among them, there are some systems that have been designed for the rice production industry and the agricultural industry. But most of the systems have been designed to the entire agricultural industry by giving the priority for the rice production industry.

Ponweera and Premaratne have developed an Information and Decision Support System to Enrich Paddy Cultivation in Sri Lanka [12]. This system has been developed to enable decision making authorities and farmers to make effective decision making. In addition, they have developed a classification model based on a decision tree to predict the harvest. Above system was evaluated based on the information which is collected from different Govi Jana Kendra.

Jayarathna and Hettige have developed AgriCom: A Communication Platform for Agriculture Sector [13] which is an innovation practical Multi-Agent System for Agricultural Communication. They state that Multi-Agent technology can be used to handle the required communication successfully among related persons in the agricultural sector. Accordingly, the system has provided four types of agents; farmer buyer, seller, and instructor. The system was developed through the MaSMT architecture.

Adikari and Karunananda have developed a Multi-Agent System for Agriculture stakeholders [14]. The system is contained with five agents. They are Message Agent, Interface Agent, User Profile Agent, Crop Management Agent, and Selling Agent. The Message Agent plays a crucial role in guiding and passing messages to other agents and Interface Agent displays and distributes the information in a suitable form for the user whereas User Profiler Agent creates individual user profiles according to individual preferences. Crop Management agent and Selling Agent are the two primary agents who make decisions using external and internal information. This system has been developed on JADE environment and can be connected via web access.

Tharaka and Kulawansa have developed an Information System for Cultivation [15]. They have developed a framework based on modern IT infrastructure such as web services, and mobile services to address the critical need of disseminating domain knowledge to the farmer with the aim of enhancing the cultivation process. The proposed framework is based on fuzzy predictive models to impart, expert domain knowledge and recommendations to solve many of the problems faced by the farmer.

3 Design

Rice Express system has been developed by using MaSMT architecture. MaSMT consists of three types of agents namely ordinary agent, manager agent and root agent. These agents can be considered as simple java programs which support specific tasks. The ordinary agents work under the control of manager agent. The agents can make communication with other agents using the message space. It can be peer-peer or object-object communication methods. Rice Expert has been developed with the MaSMT manager and a number of MaSMT agents. Figure 1 shows the design architecture of the Rice Express System. The system consists of three modules namely user interface, task manager and MaSMT agents. All the communication messages and agent-based information has been stored in an XML based ontology. A brief description of each module has given below.

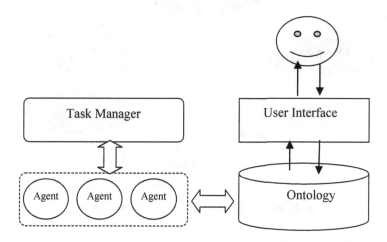

Fig. 1. Design of the Rice Express

A. User Interface
The user interface of the system is used to communicate between the agent and the user. Through the user interface seller, farmer and transporter can submit their information. For instance, farmers have kept the details of what they cultivate, produce and sell, registered buyers have kept the details of what they buy and order products.

B. Task Manager
Task manager is the controlling module of the Rice Express. This module makes the communication between user and agents. Through the task manager, the user can create a new task, update task and delete when they need. In addition, users can manually send messages, getting a reply from others, sending auto-replies and making the communication etc. If the system has been switched to automated mode, then task manager create new agents for each user registered into the system. Then task manager allows agents to communicate with each other and find the most suitable solutions.

C. MaSMT Agent

MasMT agent works as an agent of the Rice Express. Through the MaSMT communication module, Rice express agents communicate with each other. For that agents use existing methods for message parsing. Note that, MaSMT allows, peer-to-peer, broadcast and notice board method to message parsing [16]. Rice Express system provides three types of agents namely farmer, buyer and transporter which represents the farmer's buyers and transporters in Sri Lanka, Each agent in this system works in the different places and uses common XML database as ontology and the universal message space of the agents. Figure 2 shows the Agents' structure of the Rice Express system.

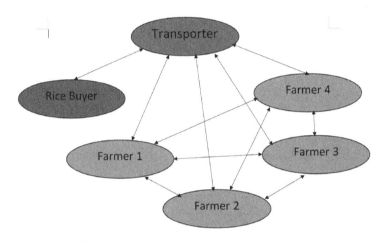

Fig. 2. Agents' structure of the Rice Express System

4   Rice Express in Action

This section describes how Rice Express system works in the test environment. Assume that, there are many agents appear as farmers, buyers and transporters.

The buyer agent consists of location, required rice quantity and type, maximum price per 1-kilogram and the date rice required. The farmer agent consists of location, available rice quantity and type, minimum price per 1-kilogram and the date rice were ready. The transporter consists with location travel charge for a kilometre and cargo capacity.

The buyer agent can make a request when a buyer wants to buy rice from the farmer. This request will be sent to the farmers. Then if the farmer can supply the required rice quantity with the buyer conditions farmer agent directly communicate with the buyer. Assume that farmer has less amount of rice then farmer work as a buyer and ask remaining amount from other farmers. (Farmer asks to join to sell rice as a join selling) with other farmers communication farmer send that join request for the buyer. The buyer can select a suitable option. The same communication method is also applied for transporters. Then transporter communicates with farmers and collects rice according to the farmer's request. Further, in the Rice Express, the users can register as a buyer or as a farmer. If a user registered as a buyer, he can add, update and delete the details of buying products. If the user registered as a farmer, he can add, update and delete the details of their cultivated crops and selling products. In this system farmers and buyers are the persons that add tasks through the GUI. After adding the required task, the user can leave from the system. At that time system comes to the automated mode and agents communicate with each other by sending and receiving messages automatically.

Figure 3 shows the communication diagram of the Rice Express System. This diagram shows the way of how agents communicate with others. In this diagram, there are four types of agents as rice buyer, transporter, farmer clubs and individual farmers. Farmer clubs is also a farmer, and he is the manager agent of all the individual farmers. First, the rice buyer makes the request, and it will send to the transporter, and then this will be forwarded to the farmer clubs: farmer clubs requests each and every individual farmer. Then finally he will receive all the response of these farmers and send the final solution to the transporter. Finally, it will send to the rice buyer.

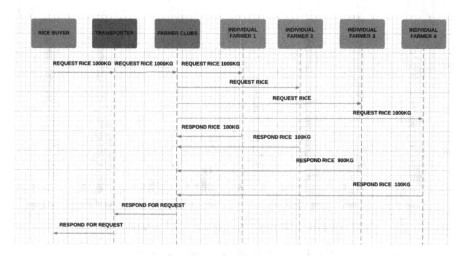

Fig. 3. Communication diagram for buying rice from multiple farmers

5 Evaluation

Rice Express has been successfully evaluated through a test environment using 30 persons who are involved in the rice production industry. Accordingly, farmers, buyers and transporters were involved as they are key persons in this system. Therefore, the system was freely distributed among these 30 persons. Then allow them to register and provide facilities to use this system within 6 day period. During these 6 days, questioners are provided to them and obtained results which are shown in Table 1 (Fig. 4).

Table 1. Results obtained by the questioner.

Parameter	Very easy	Easy	Difficult	Very difficult
Installability	16	14	0	0
Usability	8	21	1	0
Understandability	10	20	0	0
Ability to sell a product	5	12	3	0
Ability to buy a product	2	3	0	0
Ability to order a product	3	2	0	0
Parameter	Very good	Good	Poor	Very poor
Attractiveness	7	20	3	0
Usefulness	11	18	1	0

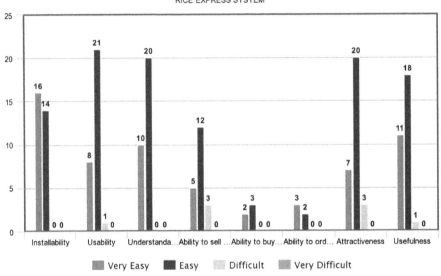

Fig. 4. Summary of the evaluation results

6 Conclusion and Further Works

Rice Express is an innovation practical Multi-Agent System that is designed to fulfil communication aspects of the rice production industry in Sri Lanka. The system provides three types of agents as farmers, sellers, and transporters who represent the rice production community. These agents have been designed and developed through the MaSMT framework—the system consists of two modes which are manual mode and automated mode. If the user is working with the application, the agent works in the manual mode and provides several facilities for users to communicate with each other through a GUI. In this system farmers and buyers are the persons who add tasks through the GUI. After adding the required task, the user can leave from the system. At that time system comes to the automated mode as the next step agents will start to communicate with each other by sending and receiving messages automatically. In addition, the system provides automated responses for the received messages. Finally, Rice Express has been tested using 30 persons who were selected from rice production industry and were obtained successful results.

According to evaluation results, Rice Express System is a very user-friendly and a simple system for the rice production industry. Accordingly, this system has been specialized only for rice production Industry this system can be improved for any buying and selling system.

References

1. LFS_Q1_Bulletin_WEB_2017_final.pdf. http://www.statistics.gov.lk/samplesurvey/LFS_Q1_Bulletin_WEB_2017_final.pdf. Accessed 08 Dec 2018
2. Paddy Statistics. http://www.statistics.gov.lk/agriculture/Paddy%20Statistics/PaddyStats.htm. Accessed 08 Dec 2018
3. Dairy Farming Sector in Sri Lanka | Livestock | Dairy Farming: Scribd. https://www.scribd.com/document/90172870/Dairy-Farming-Sector-in-Sri-Lanka. Accessed 08 Dec 2018
Hettige, B., Karunananda, A.S., Rzevski, G.: MaSMT: a multi-agent system development framework for English-Sinhala machine translation. Int. J. Comput. Linguist. Nat. Lang. Process. IJCLNLP 2(7), 411–416 (2013)
5. Hettige, B., Karunananda, A.S., Rzevski, G.: A multi-agent solution for managing complexity in English to Sinhala machine translation. Complex Syst. Fundam. Appl. 90, 251 (2016)
6. Department of Agriculture. https://www.doa.gov.lk/index.php/en/. Accessed 08 Dec 2018
7. "ඉර් 8ඉව.". https://www.goviya.lk/index.php/si/. Accessed 08 Dec 2018
8. George, R.: A new direction of research into artificial intelligence. In: Presented at the Proceeding of the Fifth Annual Sessions, Sri Lanka Association for Artificial Intelligence (SLAAI) (2008)
9. Jade Site | Java Agent DEvelopment Framework. http://jade.tilab.com/. Accessed 13 Sept 2017
10. Jason (multi-agent systems development platform). Wikipedia, 20 September 2016. https://en.wikipedia.org/w/index.php?title=Jason_(multi-agent_systems_development_platform)&oldid=740305186. Accessed 13 Sept 2017
11. Gutknecht, Olivier, Ferber, Jacques: The MADKIT Agent Platform Architecture. In: Wagner, Tom, Rana, Omer F. (eds.) AGENTS 2000. LNCS (LNAI), vol. 1887, pp. 48–55. Springer, Heidelberg (2001). https://doi.org/10.1007/3-540-47772-1_5
12. Ponweera, P., Premaratne, S.C.: Information and decision support system to enrich paddy cultivation in Sri Lanka (2013)
13. Jayarathna, H., Hettige, B.: AgriCom: a communication platform for the agriculture sector. In: 2013 8th IEEE International Conference on Industrial and Information Systems (ICIIS), pp. 439–444 (2013)
14. Adikari, A., Karunananda, A.S.: Multi-agent systems for agricultural stakeholders, October 2013. http://dl.lib.mrt.ac.lk/handle/123/8414. Accessed 08 Dec 2018
15. Tharaka, K.J., Kulawansa, K.: Information system for cultivation, October 2013. http://dl.lib.mrt.ac.lk/handle/123/8437. Accessed 08 Dec 2018
16. (PDF) MaSMT 3.0 Development Guide. ResearchGate. https://www.researchgate.net/publication/319101813_MaSMT_30_Development_Guide. Accessed 08 Dec 2018

Signal and Image Processing

Diagnosis of Coronary Artery Diseases and Carotid Atherosclerosis Using Intravascular Ultrasound Images

K. V. Archana[✉] and R. Vanithamani

Avinashilingam Institute for Home Science and Higher Education for Women,
Coimbatore, India
warchanaavjkmr@gmail.com, vanithamani_bmie@avinuty.ac.in

Abstract. Cardiovascular diseases are of paramount importance as large number of deaths is caused, if not diagnosed and treated at the right time. Ultrasound examination complements other imaging modalities such as radiography, and allows more definite diagnostic tests to be conducted. This modality is non-invasive in nature, widely used in diagnosis of cardiovascular diseases. Recently, two leading ultrasound based techniques are used for the assessment of atherosclerosis: B-mode ultrasound used in measurement of carotid artery intima thickness and intravascular ultrasound. These techniques provide images in real time, portable, substantially lower in cost and no harmful ionizing radiations are used in imaging. The processing of ultrasound image takes a major role in the accurate diagnosis of the disease level. The diagnostic accuracy depends on the time to read the image and the experience of the practitioner to interpret the correct information. Computer aided methods for the analysis of the intravascular ultrasound images can assist in better measurement of plaque deposition in the coronary artery. In this paper, the level of plaque deposition is identified using Otsu's segmentation method and classification of plaque deposition level is performed using Back Propagation Network (BPN) and Support Vector Machine (SVM). The result shows SVM classifies more significantly in comparison with the BPN network.

Keywords: Intra vascular ultrasound · Atherosclerosis ·
Carotid artery intima thickness · Plaque deposition · Support Vector Machine

1 Introduction

Cardiovascular Diseases (CVDs) are the major cause of death globally [3]. The World Health Organisation (WHO) report states approximately 17.7 million people died from CVDs in 2015, representing 31% of all global death factors. Out of which, 7.4 million are due to coronary heart diseases and 6.7 million are due to stroke. The major risk factors for the CVDs are altered blood cholesterol levels, high blood pressure, diabetes, smoking, being obese, excessive alcohol consumption and excessive stress [2]. Most CVD's can be prevented by following healthy diet, physical activity and avoiding usage of alcohol and tobacco.

© Springer Nature Singapore Pte Ltd. 2019
J. Hemanth et al. (Eds.): SLAAI-ICAI 2018, CCIS 890, pp. 281–288, 2019.
https://doi.org/10.1007/978-981-13-9129-3_20

Coronary artery diseases are caused due to atherosclerosis of the arteries that resists the flow of blood to the heart. Patients may experience stable angina, discomfort during exertion or emotional stress or remain asymptomatic until the plaque ruptures [4]. The diagnosis and treatment of coronary artery diseases depends on the degree of stenosis and plaque characterization. The traditional methods for the diagnosis of CVD's are:

- **Electrocardiogram (ECG):** records the electrical signals that travel through the heart.
- **Echocardiogram:** where sound waves used to produce images of heart. Doctors can analyze, whether all the parts of the heart wall contribute normally to the heart pumping function.
- **Cardiac Catheterization and Angiogram:** views the blood flow through the heart vessels by injecting special dye into coronary artery.

Though these techniques are used traditionally in diagnosis of CVD's, they fail in determining the plaque level and their characterization. The accumulation and oxidation of Low Density Lipoproteins (LDL) particles are the primary steps in the formation of atherosclerotic lesions. Oxidized LDL causes cell death and leucocyte deposition in the inner layer of the artery. This leads to the generation of complex atherosclerotic plaques. Cardiac angiogram does not provide the cross sectional view of the vessel wall, there by progress of the plaque formation cannot be determined. Whereas the carotid ultrasound images determine the flow of blood through the arteries and measures the inner layer of the artery.

In IVUS (Intravascular Ultrasound) imaging, the reflected ultrasound signals are converted into electrical signals and these signals are processed for the formation of grey scale IVUS image. The IVUS system consists of a transducer incorporated into a catheter and a console structure to capture the back scattered signal for reconstructing and displaying the image. Currently, two types of IVUS system are available based on their operation. First type is the mechanical IVUS probe, which rotates at a rate of 1800 rpm based on single piezoelectric transducer and the operating frequency is between 30 and 45 MHz. Second type is electronic phased array system with a centre frequency of 20 MHz [8]. Electronic system consists up to 64 transducers placed annularly to generate the cross sectional view of the artery. They have the ability to display the blood flow in color that facilitates the distinction between lumen and the blood walls.

The IVUS image provides vital information for the diagnosis of coronary artery disease and carotid atherosclerosis. However these images are highly prone to acquisition distortions. The main types of artifacts that exist in the IVUS images are: presence of guided wire, reverberation effect, non-uniform rotational distortion, discontinuity of tissue appearance. The major challenge in diagnosis of the coronary heart disease using IVUS image involve the novel techniques for image enhancement and segmentation of region of interest to identify the plaques accurately. The early detection can help in better treatment of the disease.

In this work Otsu's segmentation technique is used in segmenting the plaque deposited region and GLCM (Grey Level Co-occurrence Matrix) technique is used to extract the features like Correlation, Cluster Shade, Dissimilarity and Entropy. Then the classification is performed using SVM (Support Vector Machine) and BPN (Back Propagation Network). A data set consisting of 51 images are used for the plaque identification. The plaque deposition level is classified as either mild or moderate.

2 Methodology

The proposed method in this paper aims at identifying the plaque by masking the Region of Interest (ROI), segmenting the ROI, feature extraction and classifying the level of plaque deposition. The overall work is depicted in Fig. 1.

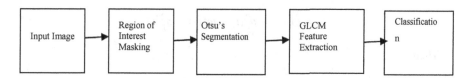

Fig. 1. Stages of plaque identification

The ROI masking divides the original IVUS image into luminal area and the plaque deposited region. A circular mask is applied over the plaque deposited area to segment it from the lumen of the coronary arterial wall. The GLCM features are extracted from the segmented region.

2.1   Otsu's Segmentation

Segmentation is the process which involves the partitioning of image into distinct regions. For the meaningful image analysis and interpretation, the region has to be strongly related to the feature of interest. The edge of the image consists of local discontinuous pixels that are the most significant part in image segmentation. In this paper Otsu's technique is used for segmenting IVUS images.

Otsu's method uses a linear discriminant criterion that assumes the image consists only of the object and background. The diversity and heterogeneity of the background image is eliminated for the processing. The Otsu's method involves segmenting the image into two regions T_0 and T_1 (light and dark). The intensity level of T_0 is set from 0 to t and T_1 is set from t + 1 to L, where t is the threshold value and l is the maximum grey scale value of 256. T_0 and T_1 can be set to object and background or vice versa. The method scans all the possible value and calculates the minimum value for each pixel based on the thresholding level. The threshold is set with the minimum entropy for the sum of object and background. The threshold value is determined using the statistical information of the image. For the chosen threshold value the variance of the set T_0 and T_1 can be determined. The threshold value is calculated by minimizing the sum of the weighted group variances.

The weights are the probabilities of the respective group. The histogram probabilities of the given grey value i = 1, 2, ..., L is given as

$$P(i) = \{number(r,c) \mid image(r,c) = i\} \div (R,C))$$

(1)

Where r, c are the index for the row and column of the image and R, C are the number of rows and columns in the image.

Let the weight, mean and variance of the set T_0 in the range 0 to t is represented as $w_b(t)$, $\mu_b(t)$ and σ_b^2 (t). The weight, mean and variance of T_1 set is denoted as $w_f(t)$, $\mu_f(t)$ and σ_f^2 (t). The optimal threshold value t is minimum sum of the group variances and given as

$$\sigma_\omega^2 = \omega_b(t) \times \sigma_b^2(t) + \omega_f^2(t) \times \sigma_f^2(t)$$

(2)

Where

$$\omega_b(t) = \sum_{i=1}^{t} P(i)$$

(3)

$$\omega_f(t) = \sum_{i=t+1}^{l} P(i)$$

(4)

$$\mu_b(t) = \sum_{i=1}^{t} i * P(i) \div \omega_b(t)$$

(5)

$$\mu_f(t) = \sum_{i=t+1}^{l} i * P(i) \div \omega_f(t)$$

(6)

$$\sigma_b^2(t) = \left\{ \sum_{i=1}^{t} (i - \mu_b(t))^2 * P(i) \right\} \div \omega_b(t)$$

(7)

$$\sigma_f^2(t) = \left\{ \sum_{i=t+1}^{t} (i - \mu_f(t))^2 * P(i) \right\} \div \omega_f(t)$$

(8)

2.2 Feature Extraction

Feature extraction involves determining the relevant information contained in the image pattern so as to make the process of classification more easy and accurate. It is a method of dimensionality reduction technique where the more relevant data from the image are extracted and represented in lower dimensional space [9]. In this work Gray-Level Co-occurrence Matrix (GLCM) feature extraction method is used to obtain the correlation, cluster shade, dissimilarity and entropy. The textural feature utilizes the contents of the GLCM to provide the measure of variation in intensity at the pixel of interest. The features are extracted by pair wise spatial co-occurrences of pixels separated by some angle and distance which are tabulated using the GLCM. The GLCM consist of an N × N matrix, where N is the number of gray levels in the image.

Correlation is the grey level linear dependence between the pixels at a specified position to each other and given as

$$\text{Correlation} = \frac{\sum_i \sum_j (i,j) p(i,j) - \mu_x \mu_y}{\sigma_x \sigma_y} \tag{9}$$

Cluster shade is a measure of the skewness of the matrix or lack of symmetry. When the value of cluster shade is higher, the image is not symmetric with respect to the texture value. The cluster shade is estimated as

$$\text{Cluster shade} = \sum_{i,j}^{i,j} \left((i - \mu_i) + (j + \mu_j) \right)^3 c(i,j) \tag{10}$$

C(i, j) – is the (i, j) the entry in co-occurrence matrix C

$\sum_i$ means $\sum_{i=1}^{i=M}$ where M is the number of rows

$\sum_j$ means $\sum_{j=1}^{j=N}$ where N is the number of columns

$\sum_{i,j}$ means $\sum_i, \sum_j$

μ_i is defined as $\mu_i = \sum_i i \sum_j c(i,j)$

μ_j is defined as $\mu_j = \sum_i j \sum_j c(i,j)$

Dissimilarity is a measure that defines the variation of grey level pairs in an image. It is computed as

$$\text{Dissimilarity} = \sum_{i,j} |i - j| p(i,j) \tag{11}$$

It is expected that these two measures behave in the same way for the same texture because they calculate the same parameter with different weights. Contrast will always be slightly higher than the dissimilarity value. Dissimilarity ranges from [0, 1] and obtain maximum when the grey level of the reference and neighbor pixel is at the extremes of the possible grey levels in the texture sample.

Entropy shows the amount of information of the image that is needed for the image compression. Entropy measures the loss of information in a transmitted image as in Eq. (6).

$$\text{Entropy} = -\sum_{i,j} p(i,j) * \log(p(i,j)) \tag{12}$$

A completely random distribution would have very high entropy because it represents disorder. Solid tone image would have an entropy value of 0.

2.3 Classification

Classification helps to identify the classes with similar features. GLCM features such as correlation, cluster shade, dissimilarity, and entropy are extracted. In this work, two machine learning classifiers used for classification of plaque are Back Propagation Network (BPN) and Support Vector Machine (SVM). The results are compared to identity the significant classifier.

2.3.1 Support Vector Machine

SVMs are efficient learning approaches for training classifiers based on several functions like polynomial functions, radial basis functions, neural networks etc. SVM is a linear classifier that maps the points into the space with separate categories such that they have wider space with a clear gap in between. A hyper-plane is chosen to classify the data.

The separating hyper-plane must satisfy the constraints.

$$y_i[(w.x_i) + b] \geq 1 - \xi_i, \quad \xi_i \geq 0 \tag{13}$$

Where
w = the weight vector
b = the bias
ξ_i = The slack variable
The SVM requires the parameters such as the kernel function and the regularization parameter C.

2.3.2 Back Propagation Network

BPN is the predominantly used supervised artificial neural network. The structure consists of three-layers and selection of the architecture is crucial before beginning a process. An input vector is required and the corresponding desired output is necessary. The input is propagated forward through the network to compute the output vector. The output vector is compared with the desired output and errors are determined. The process is repeated until the errors are minimized. The weight values are updated based on the difference value. During the training phase, the weights of the network performance are iteratively adjusted to minimize the network performance function.

$$E = \sum (T - Y)^2 \tag{14}$$

Where T is the target vector, Y is the output vector.

3 Results and Discussion

The training set consists of 20 images of both mild and moderate level of plaque deposition. Testing the result is done for image set of 31. Figure 2(a) shows the Test image - 1. The results of various stages of plaques detection are shown in Fig. 2(b) and (c). Initially the Region of plaque is determined and extracted from the input image.

GLCM features are extracted for classification using SVM and BPN network. The GLCM features extracted for a set of 10 images are shown in the Table 1.

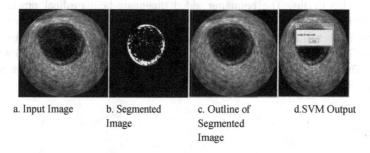

a. Input Image   b. Segmented   c. Outline of   d.SVM Output
                     Image   Segmented
                                     Image

Fig. 2. Plaque identification of Test Image – 1

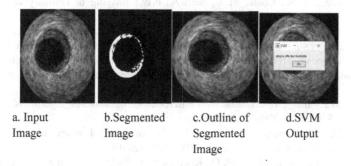

a. Input   b.Segmented   c.Outline of   d.SVM
Image   Image   Segmented   Output
                             Image

Fig. 3. Plaque identification of Test Image – 2

Table 1. GLCM features

S. no.	Correlation	Cluster shade	Dissimilarity	Entropy
1	0.86	0.31	0.01	0.26
2	0.87	0.26	0.01	0.22
3	0.83	0.42	0.02	0.37
4	0.86	0.45	0.02	0.37
5	0.85	0.13	0.01	0.12
6	0.85	0.38	0.02	0.32
7	0.85	0.45	0.02	0.38
8	0.85	0.44	0.02	0.37
9	0.86	0.46	0.02	0.38
10	0.86	0.45	0.02	0.37

The extracted features are trained and classification is performed using SVM and BPN network. The SVM network provides a significant result of 96% accuracy (Fig. 3).

4   Conclusion

The early diagnosis of the cardiovascular diseases can aid in better treatment and prevent sudden deaths. The computer aided diagnosis help medical practitioner in making better determination of plaque deposition in arterial walls. In this work the deposition is segmented using Otsu's method and features are extracted by GLCM technique. These features are classified as mild or moderate using the SVM and BPN network. The classification results show that the SVM classifier gives more significant result compared to BPN network.

References

1. Bland, T., Tong, J., Ward, B., Parker, N.G.: Geometric distortion of area in medical ultrasound images. J. Phys: Conf. Ser. **797**, 012002 (2018)
2. Garcia-Garcia, H.M., Costa, M.A., Serruys, P.W.: Imaging of coronary atherosclerosis intravascular ultrasound. Eur. Heart J. **31**, 2456–2469 (2010)
3. Benjamin, E.J., Blaha, M.J., Chiuve, S.E., Cushman, M., Das, S.R., Deo, R.: American heart association statistics committee and stroke statistics subcommittee. In: Heart Disease and Stroke Statistics—2017 Update: A Report from the American Heart Association (2017)
4. Chauhan, S., Aeri, B.T.: Prevalence of cardiovascular disease in India and its economic impact—a review. Int. J. Sci. Res. Publ. 3(10) (2013)
5. Robust, M.F.: Image binarization with ensembles of thresholding algorithms. J. Electron. Imaging **15**, 023010 (2006)
6. Basu, J.K., Bhattacharyya, D., Kim, T.: Use of artificial neural network in pattern recognition. Int. J. Softw. Eng. Appl. **4**(2), 23–34 (2010)
7. Caballero, K.L., Barajas, J., Pujol, O., Rodriguez, O., Radeva, P.: Using reconstructed IVUS images for coronary plaque classification. In: Proceedings of the 29th Annual International Conference of the IEEE EMBS (2007)
8. Katouzian, A., Angelini, E.D., Carlier, S.G., Suri, J.S., Navab, N., Laine, A.F.: A state-of-the-art review on segmentation algorithms in intravascular ultrasound (IVUS) images. IEEE Trans. Inf. Technol. Biomed. **16**(5), 823–834 (2012)
9. Papadogiorgaki, M., Mezaris, V., Chatzizisis, S., Giannoglou, D., Kompatsiaris, I.: Automated IVUS contour detection using intensity features and Radial Basis Function approximation. In: Twentieth IEEE International Symposium on Computer-Based Medical Systems (CBMS'07) (2007)
10. Wong-od, A., Rodtook, A., Rasmequan, S., Chinnasarn, K.: Intravascular ultrasound image recovery and segmentation based on circular analysis. In: 9th International Conference on Information Technology and Electrical Engineering (ICITEE) (2017)
11. Papadogiorgaki, M., Mezaris, V., Chatzizisis, Y.S., Giannoglou, G.D., Kompatsiaris, I.: Texture analysis and radial basis function approximation for IVUS image segmentation. Open Biomed. Eng. J. **1**, 53–59 (2007)

Performance Analysis: Preprocessing of Respiratory Lung Sounds

G. Shanthakumari$^{(\boxtimes)}$ and E. Priya

Department of Electronics and Communication Engineering,
Sri Sai Ram Engineering College,
Sai Leo Nagar, West Tambaram, Chennai 600044, India
{shanthakumari.ece, priya.ece}@sairam.edu.in

Abstract. Computerized lung sound analysis for automatic detection and classification of adventitious lung sounds is an emerging technique for the diagnosis of pulmonary diseases. Automated analysis of lung sound signals involves acquisition of clean lung sounds and identification of key factors present in the signal to aid the physician in recognizing the category of adventitious lung sounds. There is a possibility that the acquired lung sounds may be corrupted with interferences such as heart sound, artifacts due to improper mounting of sensor and power line interference. It also depends upon the environment in which the signals are recorded. Therefore preprocessing of the signal plays the key role in diagnosis and interpretation of lung sound. In this work the lung sounds are preprocessed using Recursive Least Mean Square (RLS), Least Mean Square (LMS), Square root Recursive Least Mean Square (SRLS), Discrete Wavelet Transform (DWT) and Total Variation De-noising (TVD) methods. The performance metrics Mean Square Error (MSE), Mean Absolute Error (MAE), Signal to Noise Ratio (SNR), Peak Signal to Noise Ratio (PSNR) and Cross Correlation (CC) are computed for the evaluation of RLS, LMS, SRLS, DWT and TVD. It is observed from the results that the DWT performs better compared to RLS, LMS, SRLS and TVD in removing the artifacts from the lung sounds.

Keywords: Lung sounds · Adaptive filters · Wavelet transform ·
Total variation de-noising · De-noising metrics

1 Introduction

The statistics of World Health Organization reveals that more than 3 million people die each year due to chronic obstructive pulmonary diseases. Lung sounds convey useful information regarding pulmonary pathology. Most often used clinical practice in pulmonary disease diagnosis is auscultation. The accuracy of diagnosis using auscultation depends on the experience of the physician ability to differentiate the adventitious lung sounds and also the hearing capacity. The major hitch is that continuous monitoring is not possible using auscultation and hence it is a subjective process [1]. These limitations can be overcome by computerized lung sound analysis that automatically detects and classifies the adventitious lung sound.

© Springer Nature Singapore Pte Ltd. 2019
J. Hemanth et al. (Eds.): SLAAI-ICAI 2018, CCIS 890, pp. 289–300, 2019.
https://doi.org/10.1007/978-981-13-9129-3_21

Respiratory sounds include lung sounds heard over the chest region, trachea and near mouth. These sounds are demarcated as normal breath and adventitious sounds. Normal respiratory sounds are categorized as vesicular, tracheal, bronchial and bronchio-vesicular depending upon the region over which the sound is heard [2]. Adventitious lung sounds are categorized into Continuous Adventitious Sound (CAS) and Discontinuous Adventitious Sounds (DAS). Wheezes, stridors, rhonci and squawks are categorized as CAS whereas crackles (fine and coarse) are DAS. In general the frequency range of lung sound is from 50 to 6 kHz [3].

The spectral analyses of lung sounds convey useful diagnostic information. Recent advancements in digital signal processing techniques and computerized analysis of waveforms paved the way for researchers to attempt computerized lung sound analysis [4]. Computerized analysis of lung sound involves digital recording, preprocessing, extraction of useful features and classification. The recorded lung sound comprises of lung sounds embedded in heart sounds and other noises. Thus preprocessing need to be performed to remove the unwanted signals from the recorded lung sounds.

The conventional methods perform either time or frequency domain analysis of the lung sounds. A granular to fine multi-resolution perception of the signal is enabled in the time frequency analysis when compared to the conventional time and frequency domain analysis [5].

Literature reveals that wide range of filters is implemented to de-noise the recorded or acquired signals in the field of biomedical engineering. Adaptive filters involve a technique of building a relationship between the input and the output in an iterative manner. An adaptive filter is used to cancel the heart sound present along with the lung sound. Recursive Least Mean Square (RLMS) and Normalized Least Mean Square (NLMS) adaptive filters are used to cancel the heart signal. NLMS has less computing complexity but convergence time is more compared to RLMS algorithm [6]. Digital Butterworth low pass Finite Impulse Response (FIR) filter and high pass filter with 20 Hz cutoff frequency is designed to preprocess the signal followed by feature extraction using spectrogram analysis [7]. Besides Butterworth band pass filter designed with a pass band from 50 to 2400 Hz did not improve the results and execution time [8].

The diagnosis of lung sounds using only temporal and spectral characteristics is difficult as those signals are non-linear and non-stationary. Wavelet transform analysis enables multiple window durations. The compression and stretching of the wavelet is obtained by setting the scale as low and high respectively. So non-stationary signals can be analyzed using wavelet transforms [9].

Literature identifies Total Variation De-noising (TVD) method as a procedure that involves total variation mathematical function. This identifies the marginally different parameters related to the co-domain measure or the local variation. It depends on the standard that noisy signal is prone to high total variations [10]. In real life applications it is not possible to determine the local characteristics and TVD does not require any knowledge about this. Since conventional filters are based on the Gaussian distribution, they do alter the characteristics of the signal. Apart from that TVD has Bayesian interpretation and hence it preserves the basic characteristics of the signal [11].

In this work, lung sounds are preprocessed by time, frequency and time frequency domain. The performance metrics such as Mean Square Error (MSE), Mean Absolute Error (MAE), Signal to Noise Ratio (SNR), Peak Signal to Noise Ratio (PSNR) and Cross Correlation (CC) are computed to find out suitable method for de-noising of lung sounds.

This paper is organized as follows. Methodology is discussed in Sect. 2. Section 3 describes experimental results of the preprocessing algorithms attempted for the lung sounds. The conclusion of the work is summarized in Sect. 4.

2 Methodology

The lung sounds utilized in this work are obtained from the RALE database. The R.A. L.E repository presents digital recordings of respiratory sounds in health and disease conditions. It provides a collection of respiratory sounds that includes normal breath sounds (vesicular, tracheal, bronchial and bronchiovesicular) and adventitious sounds such as wheezes, fine and coarse crackles, stridors, rhochi and squawks. The respiratory sounds presented in this database are recorded with EMT25C Siemens contact accelerometer and ECM 140 Sony electret microphone [12]. These recorded signals need to be preprocessed before it is further analyzed.

Twenty two lung sound signals that include sixteen abnormal and six normal signals are considered for this analysis. These signals are de-noised using RLMS, SRLMS, LMS, DWT and TVD techniques. The preprocessing methods attempted are detailed as follows.

2.1 Adaptive Filters

Adaptive filters involve a technique of building a relationship between the input and the output in an iterative manner. The adaptive filter is advantageous over the conventional filter in the aspect that it automatically tunes its filter coefficients to the new inputs [10].

The LMS algorithm is an approximate steepest descent algorithm which uses an instantaneous estimate of gradient vector [11]. The LMS algorithm involves two fundamental processes, one to predict the residue error by comparing the output from the linear filtering and input response. The second one is the estimated error in updating the filter vector. The weight updating relation is given as

$$W(n+1) = W(n) + 2\mu E(n)X(n) \tag{1}$$

where μ is the learning rate which controls the stability and rate of convergence [13].

The standard RLS filter is comprised of FIR transversal filter. In RLS algorithm two inputs are applied one is primary input vector and the other is the reference input vector. The primary signal is the signal that obtains information as well as noise. The reference signal is highly correlated with noise signal. The output of the RLS filter is a close value to the noise signal. The output error signal needs to be minimized in further iteration. The output of the filter is subtracted from the primary input signal and the noise is removed from the input signal [10]. The output equation of the RLS filter is mathematically expressed as

$$y(n) = \sum_{k=0}^{M-1} w_k^* r(n-k) = \underline{w}^H(n)\underline{u}(n) \tag{2}$$

where M is the order of the filter, $\underline{w}^H$ is called the Hermitian transposition of the w_k tap-weight vector of the FIR filter calculated for the current iteration n, and $\underline{u}(n)$ is the nth column of the covariance matrix of the reference input $r(n)$. The output of the filter is $e(n)$ and it is mathematically expressed as

$$e(n) = x(n) - y(n) = [b(n) + m(n)] - y(n) \tag{3}$$

Substituting the value of $y(n)$ in the equation $e(n)$ and by developing a matrix inversion lemma RLS algorithm is obtained. The continuous iteration performed in the equation $e(n)$ removes the noise from the lung sound. The LMS algorithm calculates the mean square of the error and subtracts from the input signal. So that it updates the weights automatically until the noise is removed from the input signal.

The SRLS calculates the square root of the least mean square and subtracts it from the input signal and updates the weights accordingly until the noise in the input signal is reduced or completely removed. However convergence time of adaptive filter is more and it depends on an input reference vector.

2.2   Total Variance De-noising

TVD is a slope preserving technique proposed by Rudin et al. (1992) [14]. The objective of this technique is to minimize the function

$$E = ||Y - f(x)||^2 + \alpha |Df(x)| \tag{4}$$

where Y is the measured noisy signal, $f(x)$ represents the filtered signal, D signifies the first derivative of the filtered signal and α denotes the regularization parameter respectively. This regularization factor α plays a critical role in de-noising process. Smoothing is not performed when $\alpha = 0$ and it cannot be very close to zero and also not very far away and hence an optimal value of α need to be chosen. The first term in Eq. (4) signifies the Euclidean squares norm whereas the second term in Eq. (4) utilizes the Manhattan norm of first derivative from the filtered output. The second term in Eq. (4) is the function that calculates the total variation and it can be defined as

$$S_{TV}(f(x)) = \int_0^1 |f'(x)| dx \tag{5}$$

The slope preserving ability of the TVD is achieved using the Eq. (5). The disadvantage of TVD is that there is no closed loop solution for minimization [15]. It is not an iterative procedure and is a feed forward technique but determining the regularization factor α is a difficult process. The main drawback of classical models and algorithms for de-noising is that they are based on least squares, Fourier series and other L_2 approximation. The results of these techniques are contaminated by oscillations put forth by Gibbs phenomena and smearing near the prominent features of the signals. Yet TVD avoids spurious oscillations and Gibbs phenomenon [16].

2.3   Discrete Wavelet Transform

Wavelet analysis is a powerful mathematical tool for bio-signal analysis. The conventional Fourier Transform does not present enough information when non- stationary signals are presented. The Short Time Fourier Transforms maps the signal in time and frequency domain but uses a fixed single window. These disadvantages are overcome in wavelet transform as the signal is mapped in time as well as frequency domain and uses multiple windows [17]. The DWT is a suitable technique for multi-resolution time frequency analysis of non-stationary signals. The high frequency components are decomposed with fine time resolution and coarse frequency resolution in DWT, whereas the low frequency components are decomposed with coarse time domain resolution and fine frequency resolution [18]. In DWT a signal is reconstructed based on the original approximations coefficients from level 1 to N [19]. The discrete wavelet can be defined as

$$T_{m,n} = \int_{-\infty}^{\infty} x(t)\psi_{m,n}(t)dt \qquad (6)$$

$x(t)$ is the noisy input signal, $\psi_{m,n}(t)$ is the mother wavelet and $T_{m,n}$ is the de-noised signal. m and n are the integers that control the wavelet dilation and translation. The inverse discrete wavelet transform is defined as

$$\sum_{m=-\infty}^{\infty} \sum_{n=-\infty}^{\infty} T_{m,n}\psi_{m,n}(t) \qquad (7)$$

The term wavelet means a small wave. Mother wavelet is the one that derives the functions used for transformation from one main function. The accuracy of classification depends on type of the selected wavelet. The wavelet can be expressed as

$$\psi_{s,\tau}(t) = |s|1/2\psi[(t-\tau)/s] \qquad (8)$$

τ is the shift parameter. It determines the part of the input signal to be analyzed and s is the scaling variable [17]. In this work, symlet is taken as the mother wavelet as the basis function resembles the lung sounds that are being processed.

2.4   Performance Metrics

The preprocessing algorithms are evaluated using the metrics such as MSE, MAE SNR, PSNR and CC [20, 21]. These metrics are used to validate the preprocessing algorithms. These de-nosing metrics can be defined as

Mean squared error

$$MSE = \frac{\sum_{n=1}^{N}(x(n) - x'(n))^2}{N} \qquad (9)$$

where $x(n)$ is the noisy lung sound signal and $x'(n)$ is the de-noised signal. N represents length of the sequence and n represents the sample number. The accuracy of the de-noising algorithm is measured using the mean square error. MSE is calculates the average value of the square of the error.

Mean absolute error

$$MAE = \frac{\sum_{n=1}^{N} (x(n) - x'(n))}{N} \tag{10}$$

Mean absolute error is obtained by calculating the average value of the difference between the original and the de-noised signal.

Signal to noise ratio

$$SNR = 10 \log_{10} \frac{\sum_{n=1}^{N} x(n)^2}{\sum_{n=1}^{N} (x(n) - x'(n))^2} \tag{11}$$

Signal to noise ratio is the ratio of the signal power to noise power. It is obtained by taking the ratio of the square of the noisy input to the square of the difference between the input and de-noised signal. It is usually calculated in decibels. As the ratio is taken between square of the input and noisy signal the logarithm value is multiplied by 10.

Peak signal to noise ratio

$$PSNR = 20 \log_{10} \frac{\max(x(n))}{RMSE} \tag{12}$$

Peak signal to noise ratio is the ratio between maximum possible signal power to the root mean square of the noise power. PSNR gives different values when the inputs with different dynamic ranges are corrupted with the same noise. PSNR is much more content specific than SNR.

Cross Correlation

$$xcorr = \frac{E(x'(n) - \mu_{x'})(x(n) - \mu_n)}{\sigma_{x'}\sigma_x} \tag{13}$$

where $\mu_{x'}$ and μ_n represents the average values of the signal $x'(n)$ and $x(n)$ respectively and the corresponding standard deviation is presented as $\sigma_{x'}$ and σ_x. The operator $E()$ is the statistical expectation or mean. Cross correlation is a measure of similarity between the two input signals.

3   Results and Discussion

A representation of a wheeze lung sound is presented in Fig. 1a. The strong bursts represent the wheeze during the exhale cycle and the weak bursts represent the wheeze during the inhale cycle. The wheeze lung sounds are preprocessed by RLMS, LMS, SRLMS, TVD and DWT. Not much difference could be noticed from the original and de-noised wheeze signal. Much variation is not perceived by visual inspection but the signals are found to contain valuable clinical information. Hence to find the suitable method for de-noising performance metrics are computed.

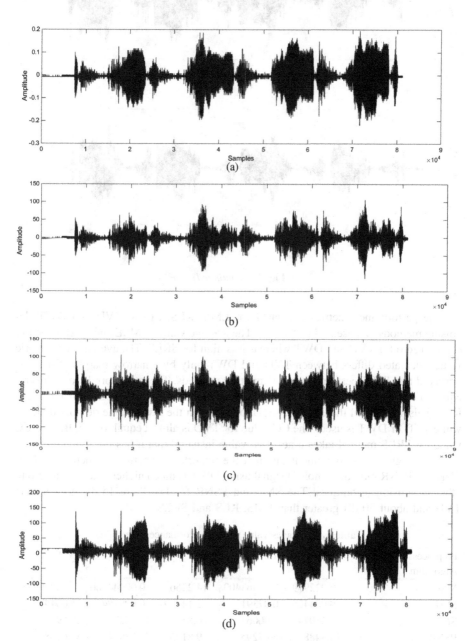

Fig. 1. Lung sound signal (**a**) raw wheeze signal, de-noised by (**b**) LMS (**c**) RLS (**d**) SRLS (**e**) TVD (**f**) DWT

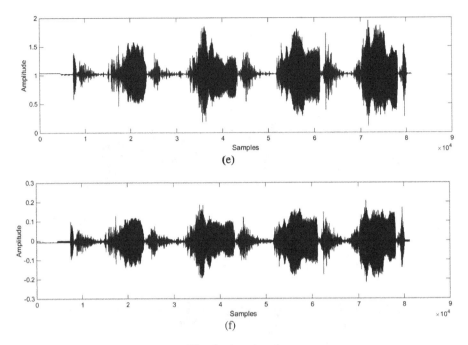

Fig. 1. (*continued*)

The performance metrics evaluated for LMS, RLS, SRLS, TVD and DWT denoising methods is presented in Table 1. The average value of MSE and MAE is nearly equal to zero for TVD and DWT whereas it is high for SRLS. The average error metric value calculated differs between TVD and DWT only by a narrow margin. Thus it is observed that DWT performs better than other methods. The cross correlation is nearly equal to one for both TVD and DWT whereas it is nearly equal to zero for LMS and RLS. This shows that there is no correlation between the raw and the de-noised signal while TVD or DWT is used. The CC value for TVD is almost equal to one. But the CC value for SRLS method takes a negative value insisting that it has not much removed the noise signal. Results demonstrate that the important performance metrics such as SNR and PSNR ratio of de-noised signal using DWT is much higher when compared to other de-noising techniques. The SNR and PSNR for DWT are 15 dB greater than TVD and about 30 dB greater than LMS, RLS and SRLS.

Table 1. Averages value of the performance metrics

Preprocessing Algorithm	LMS	RLS	SRLS	TVD	DWT
MSE	0.022979	0.01363409	14.2266	0.00044106	0.00040973
MAE	0.084425	0.073912	2.149091	0.009784	0.00497
SNR	2.11074	0.00066	−26.8338	14.8527	28.5968
PSNR	14.84889	14.67295	9.8145	31.03964	45.6578
CC	0.02654	0.015571	−0.56979	0.928041	0.974873

Further analysis is done by computing the Power Spectral Density (PSD) of the signals. PSD for raw wheeze and de-noised signal using LMS, RLS, SRLS, TVD and DWT are plotted and compared. The PSD plot shows the strength of the signal distributed in frequency domain in relative to the other components present in the signal.

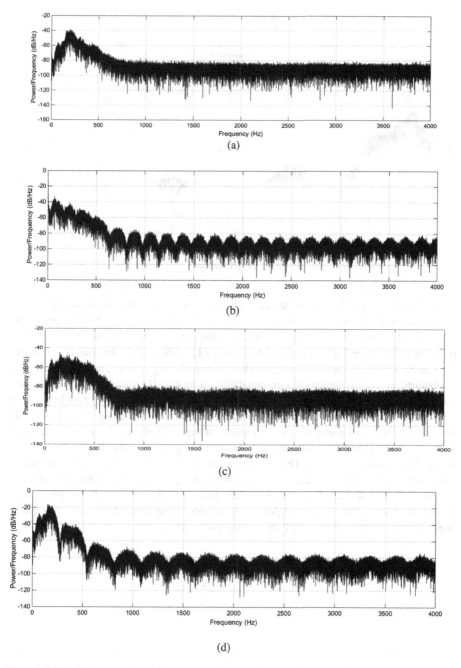

Fig. 2. PSD of (a) raw wheeze lung sound, de-noised by (b) LMS (c) RLS (d) SRLS (e) TVD (f) DWT

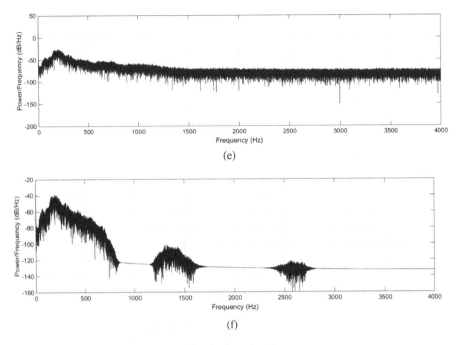

(e)

(f)

Fig. 2. (*continued*)

Figure 2a shows the PSD of the raw wheeze sound. The PSD of the wheeze sound de-noised by LMS, RLS, SRLS, TVD and DWT are shown Fig. 2b–f respectively. The PSD of the raw wheeze lung sound shows the presence of spurious noise. The PSD of de-noised wheeze lung sound by LMS and SRLS shows more sub-bands and hence the noise components are still present in the de-noised lung sound. The maximum peak is obtained at the frequency approximately equal to 200 Hz which lies in the normal lung sound range. It is observed that PSD for the RLS method not performs better than other methods as almost all the frequency components of the signal and noise is present. There is not much difference present in the PSD obtained for de-noised lung sound using TVD and the raw wheeze lung sound. Figure 2f shows the PSD of the de-noised lung sound by DWT. The maximum peak power is obtained at the dominant frequency of the wheeze signal. The observed bandwidth is form 60 to 800 Hz which is the frequency band for wheeze signal with two sub-bands present in the plot. Analyzing the PSD plots of the preprocessed wheeze lung sounds, most of the noise components are filtered by DWT de-noising process.

4 Conclusion

In today's scenario computer assisted methods for analysis and evaluation of lung sound is inevitable as this would help the clinicians in decision making. Also automated analysis for lung sounds is indispensable for mass screening of the diseases rather than manual analysis by human experts. There are few processing stages involved in the lung sound analysis. The initial stage involved in the lung sound analysis includes preprocessing which could remove the unwanted signals present.

In this work, the preprocessing of lung sound signals is carried out. The lung sounds are preprocessed using LMS, RLS, SRLS, TVD and DWT methods. Further the performance of these methods is evaluated by the error metrics such as MSE, MAE, SNR, PSNR and CC.

Results demonstrate that DWT de-noising algorithm performs better in removing the noise from the lung sounds compared to other methods such as LMS, RLS, SRLS, TVD and DWT. It is inferred from PSD plot that the DWT out performs other preprocessing methods that are attempted for the lung sound signals. The CC obtained using DWT is 0.97 which is approximately equal to 1. Thus DWT is found to perform better in preprocessing the noisy lung sounds and make it suitable for further analysis.

References

1. Bahoura, M.: Pattern recognition methods applied to respiratory sounds classification into normal and wheeze classes. Comput. Biol. Med. **39**(9), 824–843 (2009)
2. Sovijarvi, A.R.A., Vanderschoot, J., Earis, J.E.: Standardization of computerized respiratory sound analysis. Eur. Respir. Rev. **10**(77), 585 (2000)
3. Gurung, A., Scrafford, C.G., Tielsch, J.M., Levine, O.S., Checkley, W.: Computerized lung sound analysis as diagnostic aid for the detection of abnormal lung sounds: a systematic review and meta-analysis. Respir. Med. **105**(9), 1396–1403 (2011)
4. Alsmadi, S., Kahya, Y.P.: Design of a DSP-based instrument for real-time classification of pulmonary sounds. Comput. Biol. Med. **38**(1), 53–61 (2008)
5. Kandaswamy, A., Kumar, C.S., Ramanathan, R.P., Jayaraman, S., Malmurugan, N.: Neural classification of lung sounds using wavelet coefficients. Comput. Biol. Med. **34**(6), 523–537 (2004)
6. Saatci, E., Akan, A.: Heart sound reduction in lung sounds by spectrogram. In: IFMBE Proceedings, vol. 11, no. 1, pp. 1727–1983 (2005)
7. Riella, R.J., Nohama, P., Maia, J.M.: Method for automatic detection of wheezing in lung sounds. Braz. J. Med. Biol. Res. **42**(7), 674–684 (2009)
8. National Center for Biotechnology Information. http://www.ncbi.nlm.nih.gov
9. Jayachandran, E.S.: Analysis of myocardial infarction using discrete wavelet transform. J. Med. Syst. **34**(6), 985–992 (2010)
10. Sundar, A., Pahwa, V., Das, C., Deshmukh, M., Robinson, N.: A comprehensive assessment of the performance of modern algorithms for enhancement of digital volume pulse signals. Int. J. Pharma Med. Biol. Sci. **5**(1), 91 (2016)
11. Carini, A., Mumolo, E.: Fast square-root RLS adaptive filtering algorithms. Sig. Process. **57**(3), 233–250 (1997)
12. http://www.rale.ca/Recordings.html

13. Carini, A., Mumolo, E.: A numerically stable fast RLS algorithm for adaptive filtering and prediction based on the UD factorization. IEEE Trans. Signal Process. **47**(8), 2309–2313 (1999)
14. Gribok, A.V., Buller, M.J., Rumpler, W., Hoyt, R.W.: Total variation electrocardiogram filtering. In: AAAI Spring Symposium: Computational Physiology (2011)
15. Condat, L.: A direct algorithm for 1-D total variation denoising. IEEE Signal Process. Lett. **20**(11), 1054–1057 (2013)
16. Torres, A., Marquina, A., Font, J.A., Ibáñez, J.M.: Total-variation-based methods for gravitational wave denoising. Phys. Rev. D **90**(8), 084029 (2014)
17. Hadjileontiadis, L.J.: Lung sounds: an advanced signal processing perspective. Synth. Lect. Biomed. Eng. **3**(1), 1–100 (2008)
18. Göğüş, F.Z., Karlik, B., Harman, G.: Classification of asthmatic breath sounds by using wavelet transforms and neural networks. Int. J. Signal Process. Syst. **3**(2), 106–111 (2015)
19. Sharma, A., Sharma, R., Toshniwal, S.: Efficient use of bi-orthogonal wavelet transform for cardiac signals. Int. J. Appl. Biomed. Eng. **7**(9), 429–435 (2014)
20. Vidya, K.V., Priya, E.: Frailty analysis of SEMG signals for different hand movements based on temporal and spectral approach. Biomed. Sci. Instrum. **51**, 91–98 (2015)
21. Priya, E.: Digital image enhancement techniques for dental radiographs: a support to clinicians. In: Computational Techniques for Dental Image Analysis, pp. 1–39. IGI Global (2019)

A Classification Based Approach to Predict the Gender Using Craniofacial Measurements

Maneesha M. M. Arachchi[1], Lakshika S. Nawarathna[1(⊠)],
Roshan Peiris[2], and Deepthi Nanayakkara[2]

[1] Department of Statistics and Computer Science, Faculty of Science,
University of Peradeniya, Peradeniya, Sri Lanka
maneesha.mudugamuwa@gmail.com, lakshikas@pdn.ac.lk
[2] Division of Anatomy, Department of Basic Sciences,
Faculty of Dental Sciences, University of Peradeniya, Peradeniya, Sri Lanka
rdpeiris@gmail.com, deepthinanayakkara@yahoo.com

Abstract. In archaeological, forensic, clinical and surgical fields, it is important to decide the gender of an individual and to know the facial asymmetry. The objective of this study is to ascertain the asymmetry of the skull and to predict the gender based on the shape and dimensions of the infraorbital foramina (IOF) and its position in relation to maxillary teeth, supraorbital foramen (SOF) and clinically relevant anatomical landmarks. Linear discriminant analysis (LDA), binary logistic regression (BLR), support vector machine (SVM) and bagging CART algorithms were used to predict the gender and results were validated using 10-fold cross-validation technique. A significant variation on the position of IOF in relation to anatomical landmarks was observed and the relative position of the IOF varies between the genders. Moreover, the left side measurements were larger than the right-side measurements and hence human skull is asymmetric. The outcome of the study proposes the classification-based approach to predict the gender of the individuals. The Bagging CART model performed well in terms of both accuracy and precision when compared with other methods.

Keywords: Bagging CART algorithm · Binary logistic regression ·
Craniofacial measurements · Linear discriminant analysis ·
Support vector machine

1 Introduction

The human skull is one of the most intricate structures in the human skeleton. Analyses carried on the human skull have revealed that male skulls are thicker, heavier, and notably larger than female skulls in generally [1–3].

Infraorbital foramina (IOF) are a pair of holes into the floor of the eye socket which transmits infraorbital nerve, a branch of the maxillary nerve, infraorbital artery, and vein. Typically, IOF identified about 1 cm below the infraorbital margin on the maxillary bone of the skull [4]. Infraorbital nerve is solely a sensory nerve which is a branch of the maxillary division of the trigeminal nerve. Damaging this nerve is a

© Springer Nature Singapore Pte Ltd. 2019
J. Hemanth et al. (Eds.): SLAAI-ICAI 2018, CCIS 890, pp. 301–314, 2019.
https://doi.org/10.1007/978-981-13-9129-3_22

critical situation because it supplies the skin and mucous membrane of the middle face. Infraorbital nerve is considered as the prime candidate for a regional nerve block as it provides a larger area of sensory innervation. When the infraorbital nerve is successfully blocked, it provides anaesthesia for the area between the upper lip and the lower eyelid, fulfilling anesthesia in midface area surgeries and paranasal sinuses [5, 6]. Bleeding and hypoesthesia or paresthesia or anesthesia can be resulted due to traumatic or iatrogenic injury to the infraorbital neurovascular bundle. Therefore, it is crucial to identify the exact anatomical location of IOF and possible variations to provide safe and successful anaesthetic and surgical interventions for the midface region.

It has been proven in various studies that the relative position of the IOF varies between the genders [7–10]. It also varies from population groups in various regions [11, 12]. Several soft tissues, anatomical and bony landmarks have been used to ascertain the precise location of the IOF. It has been reported in the existing studies that, there is a significant variation of the position of IOF in relation to the infraorbital margin [8, 9, 11, 13, 14]. Moreover, the relative position of the maxillary teeth varies among the population groups [11, 15, 16].

The identification of a deceased person's gender has been a serious challenge in archeological and forensic fields. It is important to have a method to predict the gender using only the craniofacial skeleton when a long-decomposed and unidentified individual is found with no other possessions on the person. In the forensics field this prediction may help to resolve a mystery and in the archaeological field, it may help to assure facts that are important to the society.

There were not enough studies to identify the dimensions and the relative position of the IOF in the Sri Lankan population. Hence, the present study was undertaken to ascertain the asymmetry of the skull and to predict the gender based on the shape and dimensions of the IOF and its position in relation to maxillary teeth, supraorbital foramen (SOF), and clinically relevant anatomical landmarks.

2 Data and Methods

2.1 Data

In this study, 55 Sri Lankan adult dry human skulls (43 male skulls and 12 female skulls) have been used. These skulls have been collected from the Division of Anatomy, Department of Basic Sciences, Faculty of Dental Sciences, University of Peradeniya, Sri Lanka.

Table 1 shows the twelve measurements which are related to the IOF. Six of them are continuous and the other six are categorical. In order to fit a model and predict the gender, all of these variables are analyzed together and separately. Figure 1 shows relative position of the IOF in relation to maxillary teeth while Fig. 2 shows the measurements taken to determine the position of the IOF.

Table 1. Description of the variables.

Variable	Description
RIOF-ANS	The distance between the right IOF and the anterior nasal spine (ANS)
LIOF-ANS	The distance between the left IOF and the ANS
RIOF-IOM	The vertical distance between the right IOF and the inferior orbital margin (IOM)
LIOF-IOM	The vertical distance between the left IOF and the IOM
RIOF-FNZ	The distance between the right IOF and the nasion (NA)
LIOF-FNZ	The distance between the left IOF and the NA
Shape – R	Shape of the hole for right side (Triangular-1, Oval-2, Semilunar-3, Round-4)
Shape – L	Shape of the hole for left side (Triangular-1, Oval-2, Semilunar-3, Round-4)
SOF – R	Relationship to the supraorbital foramen (SOF) for the right side (Medially-1, in between-2, Laterally-3)
SOF – L	Relationship to the SOF for the left side (Medially-1, in between-2, Laterally-3)
Teeth – R	Relationship to upper teeth for right side (1, 2, 3, 4, 5) (see Fig. 1)
Teeth – L	Relationship to upper teeth for left side (1, 2, 3, 4, 5) (see Fig. 1)

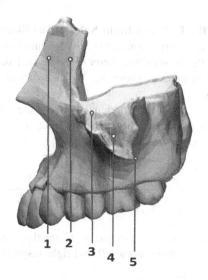

Fig. 1. Relative position of the IOF in relation to maxillary teeth. 1: line passing through the cusp tip/middle of the buccal socket margin of the maxillary canine. 2: passing through the buccal cusp tip/middle of the buccal socket margin of the maxillary first premolar. 3: passing through the buccal cusp tip/middle of the buccal socket margin of the maxillary second premolar. 4: passing through the cusp tip/middle of the buccal socket margin of the mesiobuccally cusp of the maxillary first molar. 5: passing through the cusp tip/middle of the buccal socket margin of the distobuccal cusp of the maxillary first molar.

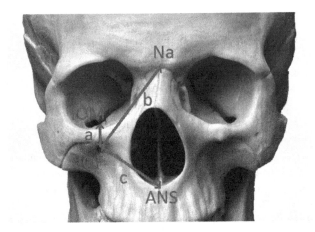

Fig. 2. Measurements taken to determine the position of the IOF. a: vertical distance from IOF to IOM. b: distance from IOF to NA. c: distance from IOF to ANS.

2.2   Methods

2.2.1   Asymmetry of the Left and Right Sides of the Skull

The left and right sides of the organism can be divided into near mirror images of each along the midline called the bilateral symmetry of the body. Due to various factors, it is hard to find the bilateral symmetry. Therefore, Welch t-statistic is used to compare the two sides; left and right.

The hypothesis is H_0: There is no difference between the means of two groups; left and right vs. H_1: There is a difference between two group means. The t-statistic and the degrees of freedom for the test are defined in Eq. (1).

$$t = \frac{\mu_l - \mu_r}{\sqrt{\frac{s_{ll}^2}{n_l} + \frac{s_r^2}{n_r}}} \quad df = \frac{\frac{s_l^2}{n_l} + \frac{s_r^2}{n_r}}{\frac{s_l^4}{n_l^2(n_l-1)} + \frac{s_r^4}{n_r^2(n_r-1)}} \tag{1}$$

where μ_l, μ_r are means of the two groups, s_l, s_r are the standard deviation of two groups, n_l, n_r are the size of two groups left and right respectively.

2.2.2   Classification of the Gender

Classification is the problem of identifying to which of a set of categories (subpopulations) a new observation belongs, based on a training set of data containing observations whose category membership is known. In this study, classification-based methods namely linear discriminant analysis (LDA), binary logistic regression (BLR), bagging cart algorithm and support vector machine (SVM) are used to predict the gender.

A. Linear Discriminant Analysis (LDA)

LDA is applied to predict the gender using the distance related to IOF by taking Male and Female as the two sets. We assume multivariate normality, homogeneity of variance/covariance (homoscedasticity) and the independence of randomly selected participants. Let π_1 be the female(F) group and π_2 be the male(M) group. Also let μ_1 and μ_2 be the population means of the males and females respectively, and X is the observation matrix. Then the Fisher's linear discrimination function can be written as

$$y = (\mu_1 - \mu_2)' \Sigma^{-1} X \tag{2}$$

where Σ be the dispersion matrix of X. The mid-point between the two univariate population means is $m = \frac{1}{2}(\mu_1 - \mu_2)' \Sigma^{-1} (\mu_1 + \mu_2)$. Let y_o be the value of the discriminant function for a new observation x_o. Then, the classification rule can be defined as in Eq. (3).

$$\begin{aligned}
&\text{Allocate } x_0 \text{ to } \pi_1 \text{ if } y_o = (\mu_1 - \mu_2)' \Sigma^{-1} x_o \geq m \text{ or } y_o - m \geq 0 \\
&\text{Allocate } x_0 \text{ to } \pi_2 \text{ if } y_o = (\mu_1 - \mu_2)' \Sigma^{-1} x_o \geq m \text{ or } y_o - m < 0
\end{aligned} \tag{3}$$

B. Binary Logistic Regression (BLR)

BLR is a classification model that doesn't involve decision trees. It applied when the target variable is categorical and with two categories. In order to predict the gender, we have used gender as the target variable where the two categories were male and female. Six continuous variables described in Table 1 were used as the explanatory variables. The assumptions of the binary logistic regression are the independence of the observations and no high intercorrelations among the predictors [17]. The BLR model can be written as

$$Prob(event) = \frac{1}{1 + e^{-z}} \tag{4}$$

where $Z = b_0 + b_1(RIOF\text{-}ANS) + b_2(LIOF\text{-}ANS) + b_3(RIOF\text{-}IOM) + b_4(LIOF\text{-}IOM) + b_5(RIOF\text{-}NA) + b_6(LIOF\text{-}NA)$ and $b_0, b_1, b_2, b_3, b_4, b_5, b_6$ are coefficients.

C. Support Vector Machine (SVM)

SVM is a supervised learning algorithm which is based on the decision plane concept [18] and used for classification, regression and outlier detection. Algorithm SVM performs classification by finding the hyperplane which separates two classes after plotting each data in an n-dimensional space [19]. It can be linear or nonlinear. SVM has a technique known as kernel trick to convert none separable problems to separable which mostly used in non-linear cases. Linear, polynomial, radial basis function (RBF) and sigmoid are mostly used kernels. Gamma and c are important parameters having the higher impact on model performance where higher gamma values cause overfitting and c is the penalty parameter of the error term which controls the tradeoff. In the present study the SVM method with polynomial kernel was used as it gave the highest model accuracy.

D. Bagging CART Algorithm

(Breiman, 1996) proposed the technique of bagging to reduce the variance associated with the prediction which helps to improve the prediction process [20]. It is an application of the Bootstrap procedure to a high-variance machine learning algorithm, typically decision trees [21]. In the bagging process, the model is trained on each bootstrap sample. The predicted outcome is an average of all the models as we get the aggregated models of all samples. In this study, Bagging CART algorithm is applied to all 12 numerical and categorical variables.

2.3   Model Validation

Accuracy, misclassification error, sensitivity, specificity and the F1 score of each model is considered to select the best model. Accuracy and the misclassification error are calculated comparing the actual and predicted values using the 10-fold cross-validation technique. We used the confusion matrix to display the results as given below (Table 2).

Table 2. Confusion matrix.

	Predicted No	Predicted Yes
Actual No	True Negative (TN)	False Positive (FP)
Actual Yes	False Negative (FN)	True Positive (TP)

Accuracy shows how often classifier is correct.

$$\text{Accuracy} = \frac{TP + TN}{Total} \tag{5}$$

Misclassification rate gives how often classifier is wrong.

$$\text{Misclassification Error} = \frac{FP + FN}{Total} \tag{6}$$

Sensitivity (Recall) is the proportion of positives that are correctly identified.

$$\text{Sensitivity} = \frac{TP}{TP + FN} \tag{7}$$

The proportion of negatives that are correctly identified is called Specificity.

$$\text{Specificity} = \frac{TN}{TN + FP} \tag{8}$$

Precision is if it predicts yes, how often is it correct.

$$\text{Precision} = \frac{TP}{Predicted\ Yes} = \frac{TP}{FP + TP} \tag{9}$$

Using the average confusion matrix, sensitivity (true positive rate) and specificity (true negative rate) values for each model can be found. In our study, sensitivity gives the proportion of males that are correctly classified, and specificity gives the proportion of females that are correctly classified. For a better model, both sensitivity and specificity should be maximum.

F1 is also a measurement of a test's accuracy which reaches its best value at 1 and poorest value at 0.

$$\text{F1 Score} = 2\frac{(Precision * Recall)}{(Precision + Recall)} \tag{10}$$

3 Results

We used several statistical methods, algorithm and classifiers to check the asymmetry of the skull and construct a model to predict the gender using IOF related variables.

3.1 Checking of Asymmetry of the Left and Right Sides of the Skull

Table 3 shows a comparison of IOF on left and right sides of the crania. All the averages are greater on the left side than the average measurements for the right side. According to the Welch t-statistic, the measurements were not statistically different except for the distance from IOF to IOM.

Table 3. Comparison of IOF on the right and left sides of the crania.

Measurement	Left			Right			p-value
	Min	Max	Mean ± SD	Min	Max	Mean ± SD	
Maximum vertical diameter	2.42	4.16	3.31 ± 0.55	1.46	3.78	3.11 ± 0.61	0.319
Maximum transverse diameter	2.55	4.47	3.33 ± 0.59	2.10	4.17	3.27 ± 0.58	0.736
Distance from IOF to ANS	23.99	39.76	34.23 ± 2.56	25.35	40.47	33.81 ± 2.68	0.463
Distance from IOF to IOM	3.38	11.53	7.30 ± 1.57	3.28	15.47	6.53 ± 2.03	0.038
Distance from IOF to NA	34.22	49.37	42.52 ± 3.28	33.27	53.37	42.37 ± 3.52	0.829

Table 4 shows the similarity between the left and right side of the IOF. It is observed that 69.23% of the individual has the same hole shape in both sides of the crania while 30.77% of individuals have the different type of hole shapes. Further, 87.5% of individuals have a similar relationship with SOF for both sides whereas 12.50% individuals have different relationships. Moreover, 47.83% of individuals have the same type of relationship with teeth for both sides and 52.17% have the different type of relationships when considering the sides of the crania. This concludes the asymmetric shape of the skull of the human.

Table 4. Similarity and differences between left and right side of IOF.

Measurement	Similarity % (Count)	Difference % (Count)
Shape of the hole	69.23(27)	30.77(12)
Relationship with SOF	87.50(35)	12.50(5)
Relationship with teeth	47.83(11)	52.17(12)

Tables 5 and 6 display the vertical and transverse diameters and distance from IOF to ANS, IOM and NA. It is found that the average distance of these measurements was lager in males than in females. Also, the observed measurements were greater on the left side than the right side. According to Table 5, the distance from IOF-ANS, IOF-IOM and IOF-FNZ(NA) were greater for males than females for both sides of the crania. Only the left distance of IOF-IOM was statistically significant ($p < 0.05$). Moreover, Table 6 shows that all the measurements are greater for males than females and differences were not statistically significant except for the instance with the distance from IOF to IOM ($p < 0.05$). Figure 3 displays box plot for the distance from (a) IOF-ANS (b) IOF-IOM (c) IOF-FNZ with respective to the gender. From the Fig. 3 the measurements taken for males were larger than those taken for females.

Table 5. Measurements of the IOF on left and right sides in males and females.

Side	Measurements	Male			Female			p-value
		Min	Max	Mean ± SD	Min	Max	Mean ± SD	
Right	Maximum vertical diameter	1.46	3.69	3.06 ± 0.72	2.34	3.78	3.17 ± 0.51	0.719
	Maximum transverse diameter	2.10	3.83	3.21 ± 0.68	2.67	4.17	3.32 ± 0.50	0.587
	Distance from IOF to ANS	28.54	40.47	34.25 ± 2.24	25.35	36.77	32.41 ± 3.56	0.057
	Distance from IOF to IOM	4.13	15.47	6.83 ± 1.97	3.28	9.25	5.52 ± 1.96	0.137
	Distance from IOF to IOM	4.13	15.47	6.83 ± 1.97	3.28	9.25	5.52 ± 1.96	0.137
	Distance from IOF to NA	33.27	53.37	42.70 ± 3.63	37.67	46.92	41.2 ± 3.00	0.238
Left	Maximum vertical diameter	2.42	4.06	3.36 ± 0.52	2.47	4.16	3.22 ± 0.61	0.709
	Maximum transverse diameter	2.55	4.47	3.33 ± 0.62	2.55	4.06	3.34 ± 0.59	0.525
	Distance from IOF to ANS	28.60	39.76	34.4 ± 1.99	23.99	38.24	33.3 ± 4.05	0.223
	Distance from IOF to IOM	5.12	11.53	7.55 ± 1.45	3.38	8.67	6.40 ± 1.71	0.029
	Distance from IOF to NA	34.22	49.37	42.79 ± 3.36	37.72	47.85	41.5 ± 2.92	0.284

Table 7 displays the shape of the IOF on the right and left sides of the crania. The predominant shape of the IOF of males was oval followed by semilunar, triangular and round. However, the order is different in females and the order is semilunar followed by oval, triangular and round.

Table 6. Measurements of IOF on the right and left sides with respect to gender of the crania.

Measurements	Male			Female			p-value
	Min	Max	Mean ± SD	Min	Max	Mean ± SD	
Maximum vertical diameter	1.46	3.69	3.06 ± 0.72	2.34	3.78	3.17 ± 0.51	0.474
Maximum transverse diameter	2.72	4.08	3.43 ± 0.55	2.61	3.75	3.40 ± 0.41	0.433
Distance from IOF to ANS	28.57	40.11	34.44 ± 2.01	24.67	37.51	33.10 ± 3.81	0.169
Distance from IOF to IOM	4.63	13.50	7.32 ± 1.61	3.38	8.35	5.85 ± 1.76	0.032
Distance from IOF to NA	33.74	50.92	42.77 ± 3.31	37.94	47.38	41.49 ± 3.05	0.302

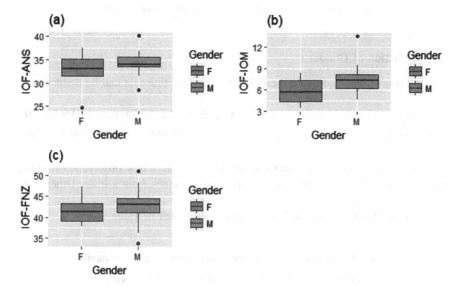

Fig. 3. Box plot for the distance from (a) IOF-ANS (b) IOF-IOM (c) IOF-FNZ with respective to the gender.

Table 7. Shape of the IOF on the right and left sides of the crania.

Shape	Right % (Count)			Left % (Count)		
	Male	Female	Total	Male	Female	Total
Triangular	21.21(7)	10.00(1)	18.60(8)	17.14(6)	18.18(2)	17.39(8)
Oval	45.45(15)	20.00(2)	39.53(17)	42.86(15)	18.18(2)	36.96(17)
Semilunar	24.24(8)	50.00(5)	30.23(13)	18.18(7)	54.54(6)	28.26(13)
Round	9.09(3)	20.00(2)	11.63(5)	20.00(7)	9.09(1)	17.39(8)

Table 8 shows the majority of IOF were located medially to the SOF (93.02% of right side and 91.11% of left side) followed by both IOF and SOF located in same vertical plane (4.65% of right side and 8.89% of left side) and located lateral to the SOF (2.33% of right side and 0.00% of left side) of the skull.

Table 8. The relative position of the IOF in relation to the SOF/N.

Position	Male %			Female %		
	Right	Left	Total	Right	Left	Total
Medially	91.18	88.57	93.02	100.00	100.00	91.11
In between	5.88	11.43	4.65	0.00	0.00	8.89
Laterally	2.94	0.00	2.33	0.00	0.00	0.00

3.2 Prediction of Gender

From the results obtained using the LDA, the classification rule can be defined as,

Allocate x_0 to π_1 if $y_o = (\mu_1 - \mu_2)' \, \Sigma^{-1} x_o \geq \hat{m} = 12.55633 \text{ or } y_o - 12.55633 \geq 0$

Allocate x_0 to π_2 if $y_o = (\mu_1 - \mu_2)' \, \Sigma^{-1} x_o \geq \hat{m} = 12.55633 \text{ or } y_o - 12.55633 < 0.$

If the Fisher's linear discrimination function value for a new observation is greater than or equal to the 12.09348 then the observation comes from a male. Otherwise it comes from a female.

Summary results of the fitted BLR model were listed in Table 9.

Table 9. Summary results of the binary logistic regression model.

Variable	Coefficient	Std. error	z-value	p-value
Intercept	− 8.3872015	10.632847	− 0.789	0.430
RIOF-ANS	0.1780243	0.2160750	0.824	0.410
LIOF-ANS	− 0.0516093	0.2864494	− 0.180	0.857
RIOF-IOM	0.2225711	0.3759534	0.592	0.554
LIOF-IOM	0.3343810	0.3682933	0.908	0.364
RIOF-NA	0.0412076	0.1941070	0.212	0.832
LIOF-NA	0.0003674	0.2108989	0.002	0.999

Since high p-values (>0.05) are observed, all the coefficients are significant in the binary logistic model. Therefore, the final BLR model can be written using all the coefficients in Table 9 as follows.

$$Prob(event) = \frac{1}{1 + e^{-z}}$$

where $Z = -8.3872015 + 0.1780243$ *(RIOF-ANS)* $+ -0.0516093$ *(LIOF-ANS)* $+ 0.2225711$ *(RIOF-IOM)* $+ 0.3343810(LIOF-IOM) + 0.0412076$ *(RIOF-NA)* $+ 0.000 3674$ *(LIOF-NA)*.

Figure 4 depicts the accuracy graph of SVM polynomial model. A more accurate model is observed when using a second order polynomial model with 0.1 scale and 0.5 cost.

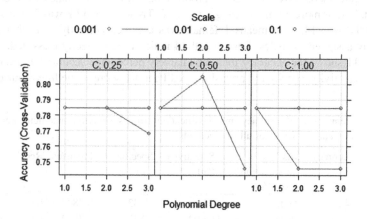

Fig. 4. Accuracy graph of SVM polynomial models.

Several methods and classification models are applied to construct a model to predict the gender using several skull anatomies. The actual values and predicted values of all the proposed models are checked, using 10-fold cross-validation technique. The results of the confusion matrix are shown in Table 10.

Table 10. Confusion matrix with average percentages and counts for LDA, BLR, SVM and Bagging CART methods.

Method	Actual group	Predicted group membership% (Count)					
		Original group			Cross-validated group		
		F	M	T	F	M	Total
LDA	F	5.4(3)	16.4(9)	21.8(12)	1.8(1)	20(11)	21.8(12)
	M	5.5(3)	72.7(40)	78.2(43)	5.5(3)	72.7(40)	78.2(43)
	Total	10.9(6)	89.1(49)	100(55)	7.3(4)	92.7(51)	100(55)
BLR	F	10.9(6)	10.9(6)	21.8(12)	1.8(1)	20.0(11)	21.8(12)
	M	5.5(3)	72.7(40)	78.2(43)	5.5(3)	72.7(40)	78.2(43)
	Total	16.4 (9)	83.6(46)	100(55)	7.3(4)	92.7(51)	100(55)
SVM	F	5.4(3)	16.4(9)	21.8(12)	1.8(1)	20.0(11)	21.8(12)
	M	0(0)	78.3(43)	78.2(43)	0(0)	78.2(43)	78.2(43)
	Total	5.4(3)	94.6(52)	100(55)	1.8(1)	98.2(54)	100(55)
Bagging CART	F	17.6(3)	0(0)	17.6(3)	5.9(1)	11.7(2)	17.6(3)
	M	0(0)	82.4(14)	82.4(14)	0(0)	82.4(14)	82.4(14)
	Total	17.6(3)	82.4(14)	100(17)	5.9(1)	94.1(16)	100(17)

According to Table 10 for both LDA and BLR models; TN, FP, FN and TP were 1, 11, 3 and 40 respectively. Therefore, only one female was assigned correctly, whereas other 11 were incorrectly assigned to group male. Further, 3 of group male observations were incorrectly assigned to group female and the other 40 males were correctly classified in both LDA and BLR models. Moreover, for the model SVM, TN, FP, FN and TP were 1, 11, 0 and 43 respectively. That means 1 female was assigned correctly, other 11 were incorrectly assigned to group male while all 43 males were correctly classified. Furthermore, in model bagging CART; TN was 1 and FP was 2. The FN was zero and TP was 14. That means 1 female was assigned correctly and other 2 were incorrectly assigned as males. Besides, all 14 males were correctly classified.

Table 11 shows the accuracy measures namely percentage accuracy, misclassification rate, sensitivity, specificity, precision, recall and F1-score of the fitted four models.

Table 11. Comparison of accuracy, misclassification error, sensitivity, specificity percentage, precision, recall and F1 score for all the methods.

Method	Accuracy (%)	Mis-classification error (%)	Sensitivity (%)	Specificity (%)	Precision	Recall	F1 score
LDA	74.55	25.45	93.02	8.33	0.7843	0.9302	0.8510
BLR	74.55	25.45	93.02	8.33	0.7843	0.9302	0.8510
SVM	80.00	20.00	100	33.33	0.7962	1.0000	0.8865
Bagging CART	88.24	11.76	100	33.33	0.8750	1.0000	0.9333

Bagging CART model recorded the highest accuracy (88.24%) and the highest F1 score (0.9333). Next the SVM model provided the second-best values. i.e., 80% accuracy and 0.8865 F1 score. LDA and Binary logistic regression models presented the equal lower accuracy (74.55%) and F1 score (0.8510) when compared to the other models.

4   Discussion

Prior work has shown that the male skulls are typically notably larger than female ones [2, 3]. The same result was obtained in the present study. Moreover, it was found that the observed measurements were greater in left side than the right side. Further, there were about 31% of individuals who have different hole shapes in left and right sides. The relationship with the SOF was different in the left and right sides for 12% of the individuals. The relationship with teeth for the left and right sides were different for the majority which was about 52% of individuals.

The predominant shape was oval, followed by semilunar, triangle and round for the sample. Though this case was the same for the male for the female the predominant shape was semilunar followed by oval, triangle and round. For the studied sample the majority of IOF were located medially to the SOF followed by both IOF and SOF located in the same vertical plane and located lateral to the SOF of the skull.

Among the four classification methods used to predict the gender of the individual, bagging CART model has the highest accuracy. Therefore, bagging CART algorithm is the best method to predict the gender among these methods.

5 Conclusion

Predicting the gender using the skull is an important task in archeology and forensics fields. With a case of a long-decomposed and unidentified individual with no other effects on their person than the skull, it is important to have a method to predict gender using the skull anatomy. In this paper, a computational model using machine learning techniques known as bagging CART has been proposed to predict the gender of an individual using craniofacial measurements.

The results of the predictive model show that it performs with an accuracy of 88.24% and 0.9333 F1 score, proving that this model can be used to predict the gender of an individual using craniofacial measurements.

References

1. Spradley, M.K., Jantz, R.L.: Sex estimation in forensic anthropology: skull versus postcranial elements. J. Forensic Sci. **56**(2), 289–296 (2011)
2. Junior, E.A., Reis, F.P., Galvão, L.C.C., Alves, M.C., Vasconcelos, D.: Investigação do sexo e idade por meio de mensurações interforames em crânios secos de adultos. RevCiênc Méd. Biol. **12**(1), 55–59 (2013)
3. Junior, E.A., Araújo, T.M., Galvão, L.C.C., Campos, P.S.F.: Investigação do sexoatravés de umaárea triangular facial formada pela interseção dos pontos: forame infra-orbital direito, esquerdo e o próstio, emcrâniossecos de adultos. Rev. CiêncMéd. Biol. **9**(1), 8–12 (2010)
4. Standring, S.: Gray's Anatomy: Anatomical Basis of Clinical Practice, 40th edn. Churchill Livingstone Elsevier, London (2008)
5. Zide, B.M., Swift, R.: How to block and tackle the face. Plast. Reconstr. Surg. **101**(3), 840–851 (1998)
6. Aziz, S.R., Marchena, J.M., Puran, A.: Anatomic characteristics of the infraorbital foramen: a cadaver study. J. Oral Maxillofac. Surg. **58**(9), 992–996 (2000)
7. Elsheikh, E., Nazr, W.F., Ibrahim, A.: Anatomical variations of infraorbital foramen in dry human adult Egyptian skulls, anthropometric measurements and surgical relevance. Otorhinolaryngol. Clin. **5**(3), 125–129 (2013)
8. Apinhasmit, W., Chompoopong, S., Methathrathip, D., Sansuk, R., Phetphunphiphat, W.: Supraorbital notch/foramen, infraorbital foramen and mental foramen in Thais: anthropometric measurements and surgical relevance. J. Med. Assoc. Thai. **89**(5), 675–682 (2006)
9. Agthong, S., Huanmanop, T., Chentanez, V.: Anatomical variations of the supraorbital, infraorbital, and mental foramina related to gender and side. J. Oral Maxillofac. Surg. **63**(6), 800–804 (2005)
10. Karakas, P., Bozkir, M.G., Oguz, O.: Morphometric measurements from various reference points in the orbit of male Caucasians. Surg. Radiol. Anat. **24**(6), 358–362 (2002)

11. Azir, S.R., Marchena, J.M., Puran, A.: Anatomic characteristics of the infraorbital foramen; a cadaver study. J. Oral Maxilliofac. Surg. **58**, 992–996 (2000)
12. Kazkayasi, M., Ergin, A., Ersoy, M., Tekdemir, I., Elhan, A.: Microscopic anatomy of the infraorbital canal, nerve and foramen. Otolaryngol. Head Neck Surg. **129**, 692–701 (2003)
13. Kazkayasi, M., Ergin, A., Ersoy, M., Bengi, O., Tekdemir, I., Elhan, A.: Certain anatomical relations and the precise morphometry of the infraorbital foramen-canal and groove: an anatomical and cephalometric study. Laryngoscope **111**(4), 609–614 (2001)
14. Boopathi, S., Chakravarthy, M.S., Dhalapathy, S., Anupa, S.: Anthropometric analysis of the infraorbital foramen in a south indian population. Singap. Med. J. **51**(9), 730–735 (2010)
15. Ilayperuma, I., Nanayakkara, G., Palahepitiya, N.: Morphometric analysis of the infraorbital foramen in adult Sri Lankan skulls. Int. J. Morphol. **28**(3), 777–782 (2010)
16. Singh, R.: Morphometric analysis of infraorbital foramen in Indian dry skulls. Anat. Cell Biol. **44**(1), 79–83 (2011)
17. Logistic Regression. http://faculty.chass.ncsu.edu/garson/PA765/logistic.htm
18. TIBCO Statistica, support vector machines (SVM). http://www.statsoft.com/Textbook/Support-Vector-Machines
19. Analytics Vidhya : Understanding Support Vector Machine algorithm from examples (along with code) (2017). https://www.analyticsvidhya.com/blog/2017/09/understaing-support-vector-machine-example-code
20. Breiman, L.: Bagging predictors. Mach. Learn. **24**(2), 123–140 (1996)
21. Bagging and random forest ensemble algorithms for machine learning. machine learning mastery. https://machinelearningmastery.com/bagging-and-random-forest-ensemble-algorithms-for-machine-learning/

An Optimized Predictive Coding Algorithm for Medical Image Compression

J. Anitha[1]($\boxtimes$), P. Eben Sophia[2], and D. Jude Hemanth[1]

[1] Department of ECE, Karunya Institute of Technology and Sciences,
Coimbatore, India
anithaj@karunya.edu
[2] Department of ECE, Karpagam College of Engineering, Coimbatore, India

Abstract. This article proposes a novel algorithm which helps in efficient transmission and storage of medical images. The conventional prediction algorithm is modified in such a way that they provide high compression without any further degradation in the image quality. A binary mask is generated based on the optimized threshold value for the image data. Then prediction is done for the masked coefficients to eliminate high error values caused by lower range of coefficients. An appropriate prediction function which gives less entropy for the input image is selected and encoded. The experimental results showed a maximum of 45% improvement in compression ratio compared to the normal prediction process. The proposed modified prediction algorithm can efficiently replace the prediction step in any lossy or lossless compression algorithms. They can also be utilized as a part of compression in any contextual compression techniques. Any kind of transformation approach can be used in hybridization with this proposed optimized prediction model to perform better.

Keywords: Predictive coding algorithm · Thresholding ·
Particle Swarm Optimization (PSO) · Medical image compression ·
Magnetic Resonance Imaging (MRI) · Computed Tomography (CT)

1 Introduction

Medical imaging technology is one of the major technologies which represent the interior analysis of the human body. This helps physicians to analyze the injuries or disease even without tending to intrude, especially upon privacy. Magnetic Resonance Imaging (MRI) and Computed Tomography (CT) images are used in analyzing the anatomy of human body. Large numbers of these images are generated in hospitals every day and an efficient way of storing and transmitting these images will be of great advantage. The complexity of these images also makes them impractical for telemedicine. So it is absolutely essential to study on a lossless compression approach for these medical images [1]. Compression helps in reducing the size of the image data, there-by enabling easy storage and transmission. Lossy compression helps in large reduction in size and also produces good visual quality by capturing the redundancies in the image pixels and rounding off. There are many lossy compression techniques for dimensionality reduction [2]. But, in case of medical images they are less important.

© Springer Nature Singapore Pte Ltd. 2019
J. Hemanth et al. (Eds.): SLAAI-ICAI 2018, CCIS 890, pp. 315–324, 2019.
https://doi.org/10.1007/978-981-13-9129-3_23

This is because any loss of diagnostic information might result in wrong diagnosis. But, lossless compression provides efficient way of reducing the size without loss of diagnostic information [3–5]. The amount of compression achieved here is less. Hence, universally accepted lossy compression limit has been provided by the European Society of Radiology [6] for all types of medical imaging modalities. Some loss is allowed even for medical images provided the compression achieved is within the acceptable range.

Predictive compression is a method of capturing the correlation between image or video pixels. This method is widely utilized in image processing and video processing applications [7–10]. In case of compression, the unpredictable part which is the prediction error is encoded and transmitted to the decoder. The decoder, with the knowledge of the prediction model, performs the same procedure as the encoder, adds the transmitted prediction error for reconstructing the image. Prediction schemes are fully reversible and are used by several lossless encoding schemes [11]. Medical images are complex and require a near lossless compression to avoid loss of diagnostic data and also to compress efficiently. For example, in [12] they used prediction in hybridization with wavelet transforms along with arithmetic encoding for implementing a compression technique. In [13] the authors have used prediction for hyperspectral image compression along with fractals to lower the complexity of the encoding algorithm. In [14] prediction has been used for reconstructing a multi-dimensional signal in hybridization with transformation. Thus Predictive coding is one of the lossless coding techniques and can assist any transform based coding or other hybrid techniques to improve compression. There are several non-adaptive transform domain methods such as Wavelet transform [15, 16], Contourlet transform [17], Ripplet transform [18] etc., which are widely used for many image processing applications. Other transforms like curvelet [19], ridgelet [20] etc., are other non-adaptive methods. But brushlet [21], bandelet [22], and directionlet [23] require prior knowledge of the image. All these transforms decompose image data into coefficients of orthogonal functions. Compression is obtained by eliminating the insignificant coefficients are quantizing the data in the transformed domain. These transform based approaches are generally lossy but produces superior compression performance [24]. Transform based compression are also investigated in lossless image compression [25]. Prediction assists in reducing the source entropy to further provide compression. Several techniques uses predictive coding in hybridization with transform based compression techniques to provide high compression [11–14]. In this paper, a modified prediction algorithm based on thresholding and optimization has been proposed which helps in reducing the size of the image data more efficiently than the normal prediction approach. Section 2 discusses the proposed methodology and Sect. 3 shows the results obtained to prove the efficiency of the proposed algorithm.

2 Proposed Methodology

Conventional prediction methods predict a pixel value using the previous pixel values based on prediction function. They try to exploit the correlation between the image pixels. In case of compression the prediction error which has less entropy will be coded instead of the original image. The decoder, with the knowledge of the prediction function, performs the same procedure to get the predicted image. This predicted image will then be added to the prediction error to reconstruct the original image. This normal prediction approach provides less compression. This conventional method is slightly modified to produce a better compression ratio for the same quality. This is done by means of random thresholding and masking. The proposed block diagram using random thresholding is shown below in Fig. 1. Initially, the image data f(x, y) is read and the mean value is calculated. To start with initial threshold value is set as half of the mean value and the data are masked above that threshold. Normal prediction is performed for the masked coefficients alone, using the prediction function which gives less entropy and prediction error is encoded using arithmetic encoding. The lower data values are masked to reduce the prediction error that occurs for smaller values, which may be greater than the actual one. After calculating the compression ratio process is repeated by increasing the threshold value and masking again. The threshold which gives the highest compression is selected. The process stops when the compression ratio decreases than the previous one.

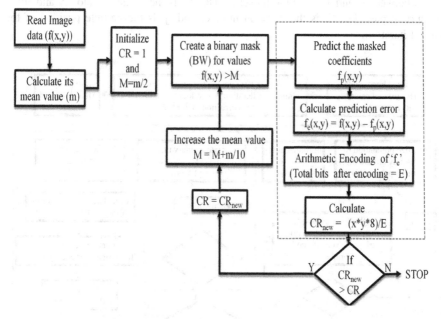

Fig. 1. Proposed threshold based prediction algorithm

The dotted line representing the selected part in Fig. 1 is the normal prediction which is subjected to modifications in the proposed algorithm. The threshold here is selected randomly and there may be better threshold which gives better results. So the process can be improvised by finding the optimized threshold value which gives highest compression ratio. Any optimization technique can be used. Here, we used Particle Swarm Optimization (PSO) technique which is the simplest and efficient method for fast calculation. The improved block diagram using PSO is shown below in Fig. 2. The optimized method is used for finding the exact threshold value for masking. Initially the PSO parameters are set and the compression ratio is the fitness function. The threshold value has to be optimized so that they provide high compression ratio. The swarm particles are randomly generated around the mean value for first iteration. Then the prediction process is done for all the swarm particles and the compression ratio is obtained. The swarm particle which gave high compression ratio is selected and used for updating the velocity and for generating new swarm particles. The process gets repeated and moves towards obtaining optimum threshold value until we get improved compression performance or until the specified number of iterations. The equations for updating the velocity and swarm particle are given in Eqs. 1 and 2 respectively.

$$V_{ij} = \left(I * V_{ij}\right) + \left(c_{f1} * r_{v1}\left(pbest - P_{ij}\right)\right) + \left(c_{f2} * r_{v2}\left(gbest - P_{ij}\right)\right) \qquad (1)$$

$$P_{ij} = P_{ij} + V_{ij} \qquad (2)$$

where 'c_f1' and 'c_f2' are the correction factors set to 2, r_v1 and r_v2 are random values between 0 and 1, 'I' is inertia set to 0.8, 'V' is the particles velocity and 'P' is the current particles. 'i' is the iteration number and 'j' is the particle position of the current iteration.

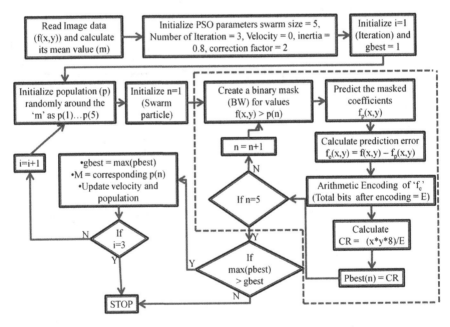

Fig. 2. Optimized threshold based prediction approach

The 'gbest' (global best) is the maximum of 'pbest' (particle best) and gets updated after each iteration when, the new maximum is greater than the previous one. Maximum of three iterations is considered as an example in the Fig. 2 shown. The iteration number is kept less in order to reduce the extra time consumed in case of large data set. The dotted line represents the mask based prediction approach which is then merged with optimization process. When this prediction approach is carried out after transformation and quantization the iteration number can be increased further since the size of dataset will be reduced and the loop operation does not consume more time. The results and discussion section shows the improved performance of the proposed prediction algorithm over the conventional one.

3 Results and Discussion

The set of test images were obtained from Aarthi scan centre, Chennai, India, and are viewed using a DICOM viewer application called Singo – fastview from Siemens medical solutions. The experiment was carried out using 2D MRI brain images and 2D CT images. Sample test image are shown in Fig. 3. The conventional method of prediction and the proposed algorithm are compared in terms of Bits Per Pixel (BPP) and Compression Ratio (CR). The compression ratio is given by

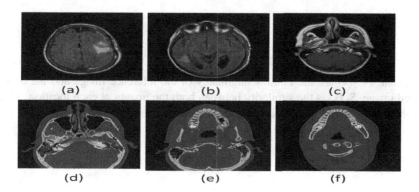

Fig. 3. Test images used for experimental analysis (a), (b), (c) 2D MRI brain images and (d), (e), (f) 2D CT brain images

$$CR = \text{Size of original image/size of compressed image} \qquad (3)$$

The reconstructed images are compared with original images to calculate PSNR, SSIM, FSM and Q. The PSNR is given by

$$PSNR = 10 \log_{10}\left((255)^2/MSE\right) \tag{4}$$

Where the Mean Square Error (MSE) is given by

$$MSE = \frac{1}{mn}\sum_{i=1}^{m}\sum_{j=1}^{n}\left|x_{ij} - y_{ij}\right| \tag{5}$$

The equation for Structural SIMilarity (SSIM) index is given by

$$SSIM = \frac{\left(2\mu_f\mu_{\bar{f}} + c_1\right)\left(2\delta_{f\bar{f}} + c_2\right)}{\left(\mu_f^2 + \mu_{\bar{f}}^2 + c_1\right)\left(\delta_f^2 + \delta_{\bar{f}}^2 + c_2\right)} \tag{6}$$

where f is the original image and $\bar{f}$ is reconstructed image, μ represents the average gray value, δ represents the variance and c_1 and c_2 are constants to prevent unstable results. The equation for FSIM (Feature SIMilarity index) is given in Eq. 7.

$$FSIM = \frac{\sum_{x\in\Omega} S_L(X)PC_m(X)}{\sum_{x\in\Omega} PC_m(X)} \tag{7}$$

where,

$$PC_m(X) = \max(PC_1(x), PC_2(x)) \tag{8}$$

$PC_1(x)$ and $PC_2(x)$ are the Phase Congruency of the reference image and the decompressed image, $S_L(x)$ is the similarity between both the images at each location 'x' and Ω is the whole image spatial domain. The universal quality index is given by

$$Q = \frac{1}{M}\sum_{j=1}^{M} Q_j \tag{9}$$

where 'M' is the number of local regions covered by the sliding window and 'Q_j' is the local quality index at the local region 'j' which is given by

$$Q_j = \frac{4\sigma_{xy}\bar{x}\bar{y}}{\left(\sigma_x^2 + \sigma_y^2\right)\left((\bar{x})^2 + (\bar{y})^2\right)} \tag{10}$$

where x and y are the original and the decompressed images, x and y are the estimate of the contrast of x and y. The experiment was carried out using Intel Core 2 with 1.50 GHz CPU, and 32-bit Operating System and MATLAB software. The results are obtained for the test images shown in Fig. 3. The reconstructed images are compared with original images to calculate PSNR, SSIM, FSM and Q. Figures 4 and 5 show the

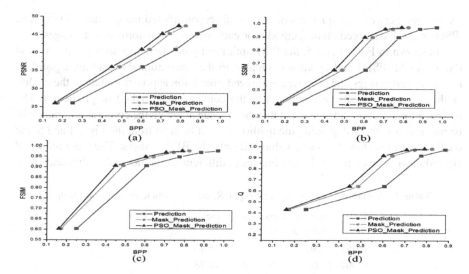

Fig. 4. Comparison between Prediction, Mask based Prediction and PSO-Mask based Prediction in terms of quality measures using Fig. 3(e). (a) PSNR vs BPP (b) SSIM vs BPP (c) FSIM vs BPP (d) Q vs BPP

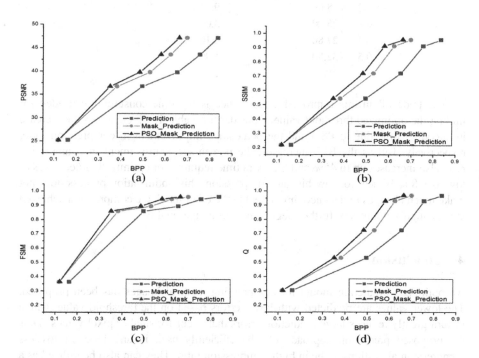

Fig. 5. Comparison between Prediction, Mask based Prediction and PSO-Mask based Prediction in terms of quality measures using Fig. 3(f). (a) PSNR vs BPP (b) SSIM vs BPP (c) FSIM vs BPP (d) Q vs BPP

comparison between the qualities of the sample reconstructed images using Optimized (PSO) mask based prediction methods for each wavelet transformed test images.

As shown in Figs. 4 and 5, the PSO optimized prediction approach produces good PSNR, SSIM, FSIM and Q when compared to the conventional prediction algorithm. For all the test images, the proposed optimized-prediction approach enhances the quality of the reconstructed image compared to the conventional method of prediction. The optimization process finds the exact threshold value at which the compression ratio will be maximum without degrading the quality. As can be seen from the Figs. 4 and 5, the quality measures show the same value and only the BPP changes. Thus, the proposed algorithm works well for all the test images of different modalities and of different sizes.

Table 1. Variation in encoding time and CR, due to particle swarm optimization

BPP	Increase in encoding timing due to PSO (s)	Increase in CR (%)
0.055	9.80	45.40
0.064	11.60	41.78
0.076	12.72	32.68
0.087	13.21	29.99
0.1	15.48	24.36
0.2	18.09	9.79
0.3	25.00	3.06
0.4	27.80	2.10
0.5	32.80	1.90

The trade off in this improved performance is the time consumption needed for finding the optimized threshold value. Consider the Table 1, which shows the increase in encoding time due to PSO and the percentage improvement in compression ratio, respectively. But as the BPP increases, the percentage improvement in compression ratio also increases up to 45% and the extra time required for optimization decreases as low as 9.8 s. Hence, for low bit rate compression, this optimization process does not make much changes in the encoding time. On the other hand, the compression achieved is very high without any further degradation in image quality.

4   Conclusion

An optimized prediction model for compressing medical images has been proposed. The lower values are predicted with lower errors based on the threshold value, which in-turn greatly reduces large prediction errors that occur for smaller pixel values. Thus the proposed prediction approach can be efficiently used in any lossy or lossless compression algorithm to obtain high compression ratio. They can also be utilized as a part of compression in any contextual compression techniques also. Any kind of transformation approach can be used in hybridization with this proposed optimization based prediction approach to perform better at lower bit rates with high compression performance. Experimental results show that the algorithm achieves 45% improvement in compression ratio compared to the conventional prediction model at 0.055 bit rate. The proposed algorithm performs better for both MRI and CT images of different sizes. This algorithm can efficiently replace conventional prediction approach in any digital image processing applications for improved performance.

References

1. Zuo, Z., Lan, X., Deng, L., Yao, S., Wang, X.: An improved medical image compression technique with lossless region of interest. Optik Int. J. Light Electron. **126**, 2825–2831 (2015)
2. Ballester-Ripoll, R., Pajarola, R.: Lossy volume compression using Tucker truncation and thresholding. Vis. Comput. **32**, 1433–1446 (2016)
3. Martchenko, A., Deng, G.: Bayesian predictor combination for lossless image compression. IEEE Trans. Image Process. **22**(12), 5263–5270 (2013)
4. Li, J.: An improved wavelet image lossless compression algorithm. Optik **124**(11), 1041–1044 (2013)
5. Miaou, S.-G., Ke, F.-S., Chen, S.-C.: A lossless compression method for medical image sequences using JPEG-LS and interframe coding. IEEE Trans. Inf Technol. Biomed. **13**(5), 818–821 (2009)
6. European Society of Radiology: Usability of irreversible image compression in radiological imaging. Insights Imaging **2**(2), 103–115 (2011)
7. Kamisli, F.: A low-complexity image compression approach with single spatial prediction mode and transform. Signal Image Video Process. **10**, 1409–1416 (2016)
8. Zhao, D., Zhu, S., Wang, F.: Lossy hyperspectral image compression based on intra-band prediction and inter-band fractal encoding. Comput. Electr. Eng. **54**, 494–505 (2016)
9. Venugopal, D., Mohan, S., Raja, S.: An efficient block based lossless compression of medical images. Optik **127**, 754–758 (2016)
10. Herrero, R., Ingle, V.K.: Ultraspectral image compression using two-stage prediction: prediction gain and rate-distortion analysis. Signal Image Video Process. **10**, 729–736 (2016)
11. Shirsat, T.G., Bairagi, V.K.: Lossless medical image compression by integer wavelet and predictive coding. ISRN Biomed. Eng. **2013**, 1–6 (2013). Article ID 832527
12. Hussain, A.J., Al-Jumeilya, D., Radib, N., Lisboa, P.J.G.: Hybrid neural network predictive-wavelet image compression system. Neurocomputing **151**(3), 975–984 (2014)
13. Zhu, S., Zhao, D., Wang, F.: Hybrid prediction and fractal hyperspectral image compression. Math. Probl. Eng. **2015**, 1–10 (2015)
14. Coluccia, G., Kuiteing, S.K., Abrardo, A., Barni, M., Magli, E.: Progressive compressed sensing and reconstruction of multidimensional signals using hybrid transform/prediction sparsity model. IEEE J. Emerg. Sel. Top. Circuits Syst. **2**(3), 340–352 (2012)
15. Zadeh, P.B., Akbari, A.S., Buggy, T.: Wavelet-based image compression techniques. In: Advances in wavelet theory and their applications in engineering, physics and technology (Chapter 18), pp. 423–448. Intech Open Access Publisher, London (2012). ISBN 979-953-307-385-8
16. Deshmukh Miete, P.R., Ghatol Fiete, A.A.: Multiwavelet and image compression. IETE J. Res. **48**(3–4), 217–220 (2012)
17. Do, M.N., Vetterli, M.: The contourlet transform: an efficient directional multiresolution image representation. IEEE Trans. Image Process. **14**(12), 2091–2106 (2005)

18. Sujitha, J., Rajsingh, E.B., Ezra, K.: A novel medical image compression using ripplet transform. J. Real-Time Image Process. **11**(2), 401–412 (2016)
19. Candès, E.J., Donoho, D.L.: Curvelets – a surprisingly effective nonadaptive representation for objects with edges. In: Rabut, C., Cohen, A., Schumaker, L.L. (eds.) Curves and surfaces. Vanderbilt University Press, Nashville, TN (2000)
20. Do, M.N., Vetterli, M.: The finite Ridgelet transform for image representation. IEEE Trans. Image Process. **12**(1), 16–28 (2003)
21. Meyer, F.G., Coifman, R.R.: Brushlets: a tool for directional image analysis and image compression. Appl. Comput. Harmon. Anal. **4**, 147–187 (1997)
22. Le Pennec, E., Mallat, S.: Sparse geometric image representations with bandelets. IEEE Trans. Image Process. **14**(4), 423–438 (2005)
23. Velisavljević, V., Beferull-Lozano, B., Vetterli, M., Dragotti, P.L.: Directionlets: anisotropic multi-directional representation with separable filtering. IEEE Trans. Image Process. **15**(7), 1916–1933 (2006)
24. Andries, B., Lemeire, J., Munteanu, A.: Scalable texture compression using the wavelet transform. Vis. Comput. **33**, 1–19 (2016)
25. Xiao, B., Gang, L., Zhang, Y., Li, W., Wang, G.: Lossless image compression based on integer discrete tchebichef transform. Neurocomputing **214**, 587–593 (2014)

Palm Vein Recognition Based on Competitive Code, LBP and DCA Fusion Strategy

Xiyu Wang and Hengjian Li[✉]

School of Information Science and Engineering,
University of JiNan, Jinan 250022, China
ise_lihj@ujn.edu.cn

Abstract. Information fusion mainly includes feature level fusion, matching-score level fusion and decision level fusion. However, the feature level fusion is considered to be a more effective fusion method because of the more biometric data than the matching fraction fusion and the decision level fusion. Feature level fusion is the extraction of feature information from the source image and the multiple features are analyzed, processed and integrated to get a single fusion image feature. In this paper, the palm vein features are extracted with Competition code and local binary pattern (LBP), respectively, to obtain two different palm vein features. Then two features are fused using discriminant correlation analysis (DCA). DCA is a feature level fusion technology, which associates class associations to the correlation analysis of feature sets. DCA implements effective feature fusion by maximizing the pairwise correlation between the two feature sets, and eliminating inter class correlation and restricting the correlation within the class. The Competition code uses the directional characteristics of the image to extract the palm vein features, while the LBP is an operator used to describe the local texture features of the image. The two features are complementary. Using DCA to combine the two characteristics of the palm vein can achieve a good classification effect. This paper uses the multispectral near-infrared palm vein image database of Hong Kong Polytech University for testing. Compared with the single palm vein Competition code feature or LBP feature, the DCA combines the two characteristics of the palm vein, which not only shortens the classification time in some degree, but also improves the recognition rate to 99.8% in the case of training samples of 9 and test samples of 3.

Keywords: Feature level fusion · Competition coding · Local binary pattern ·
Discriminant correlation analysis · Palm vein recognition

1 Introduction

With the development of technology, palm vein recognition has become an important part of biometric identification in 2006 [1]. The palm vein recognition technology is gradually being applied to the technical defense system, such as the palm vein recognition instrument. The palm vein recognition system has not only become the basic equipment of the ATM systems of various banks in Japan, but also has been increasingly diversified in Taiwan [2, 3]. Intelligent monitoring combined with basic

© Springer Nature Singapore Pte Ltd. 2019
J. Hemanth et al. (Eds.): SLAAI-ICAI 2018, CCIS 890, pp. 325–334, 2019.
https://doi.org/10.1007/978-981-13-9129-3_24

access control systems and RFID (radio frequency identification) has become practical [4].

The research results of multi-biometric fusion and recognition technology have a great effect on improving the performance of biometric recognition systems [5]. At present, the image feature extraction, fusion, and recognition methods studied have a certain scope of application. Since each method has advantages, how to effectively combine multiple methods will be a trend in future research. In addition, how to maximize and organically combine the acquired information is also a topic of universal significance [6].

The Competition coding is a direction-based expression method for finding each pixel of the palm vein image. It maps images from grayscale space to direction information space, then matching. LBP is an operator used to describe the local features of images. LBP features have significant advantages such as gray invariance and rotation invariance. The Competitive code features of the palm vein and the LBP features can complement each other. Using DCA to fuse the two features, you can get a better classification effect. DCA implements effective feature fusion by maximizing the pairwise correlation between the two feature sets, and eliminating inter class correlation and restricting the correlation within the class.

This paper is organized as follows: Sect. 2 mainly introduces the principle of Competitive code and LBP extracting palm vein features. Section 3 introduces the main algorithm DCA principle. The experiments are conducted and analyzed in Sect. 4. Finally, Sect. 5 concludes the paper.

2 Palm Vein Feature Extraction Using Competitive Code and LBP

2.1 Competitive Code

During the feature extraction of the palm vein with Competitive code stage, six different directions of Gabor filter are used to surround the palm vein image, and the filter in the dominant direction is encoded into a bitwise representation [7]. The competitive coding is a direction-based expression method for finding each pixel of the palm vein image. It maps images from grayscale space to direction information space, then matching [8].

The direction information of the palm print can be obtained by using a Gabor filter. The Gabor filter is defined as follows.

$$\Psi(x, y, \omega, \theta) = \frac{\omega}{\sqrt{2\pi}\kappa} e^{-\frac{\omega^2}{8\kappa^2}\left(4x'^2 + y'^2\right)} \left(e^{i\omega x'} - e^{-\frac{\kappa^2}{2}}\right) \tag{1}$$

where $x' = (x - x_0)\cos\theta + (y - y_0)\sin\theta$, $y' = -(x - x_0)\sin\theta + (y - y_0)\cos\theta$; (x_0, y_0) represents the filter center point; ω represents radial frequency; θ indicates the filter angle; $\kappa = \sqrt{2\ln 2}\left(\frac{2^\delta + 1}{2^\delta - 1}\right)$, δ represents the half bandwidth of the frequency response.

According to Euler's formula, the Gabor filter can be expressed in the following form:

$$\psi(x, y, x_0, y_0, \omega, \theta, \kappa) = \frac{\omega}{\sqrt{2\pi\kappa}} e^{-\frac{\omega^2}{8\kappa^2}(4x'^2 + y'^2)} \left(\cos(\omega x') - e^{-\frac{\kappa^2}{2}} \right) \tag{2}$$

First, create a line segment model, which is a top-down Gaussian shape, defined as follows:

$$L(x, y) = M \left[1 - \exp \left(-\frac{((x - x_p)\cos\theta_L + (y - y_p)\sin\theta_L)^2}{2\sigma_L^2} \right) \right] + N \tag{3}$$

where σ_L, the standard deviation of the profile, can be considered as the width of the line. (x_p, y_p) is the center of the line. M is a positive real number used to control the size of the line, depending on the contrast of the capture device. N is the brightness of the line, which is the direction of the line in response to capturing the brightness of the device and capturing ambient light. θ_L represents the angle of a straight line.

For a straight line $x\cos\theta_L + y\sin\theta_L = 0$, using a Gabor filter at its mid-point, the response is as follows.

$$R(x, y, \phi, \omega, k, \sigma_L) = -\frac{M\sqrt{8\pi}k\sigma_L}{\sqrt{\omega^2\sigma_L^2 + k^2(1 + 3\sin^2\phi)}} \left\{ e^{-\frac{k^2}{2}g} - e^{\frac{k^2}{2}} \right\} \tag{4}$$

where $\phi = \theta^2\theta_L$ and $g = \left(1 - \frac{k^2\cos^2\phi}{\omega^2\sigma_L^2 + k^2(1 + 3\sin^2\phi)} \right)$.

The aim of the algorithm is to encode the straight line. At this point of view, all kinds of lines are undifferent and need not to be related to the environment and the acquisition equipment. Therefore, there is no direct use of the corresponding R here, but it uses a competition rule to get the straight line angle. The rules of competition can be defined as: $\arg\min_j (H(x, y) * \Psi R(x, y, \omega\theta_j))$.

H is the preprocessed image, which is the real part of the Gabor filter. Is the filter angle, where j = {0, 1, 2, 3, 4, 5}. Represents the six angles of [0, π/6, ... π] selected by the filter.

2.2 Local Binary Pattern

LBP is an operator used to describe the local features of images. LBP features have significant advantages such as gray invariance and rotation invariance. It was proposed by Ojala, Pietikäinen, and Harwood [9, 10] in 1994. LBP is widely used in many fields of computer vision because of its simpleness to calculate and great effect [11].

The original LBP operator is defined in the neighborhood of the pixel 3 × 3, with the neighborhood center pixel as the threshold. The gray values of the adjacent 8 pixels are compared with the pixel values of the neighborhood center, if the surrounding pixels are larger than the central pixel value, the position of the pixel is marked as 1, otherwise 0. Thus, 8 points in the 3 × 3 neighborhood are compared to generate an 8-

bit binary number, and the 8-bit binary numbers are sequentially arranged to form a binary number. This binary number is the LBP value of the center pixel. Therefore, there are 256 LBP values. The LBP value of the center pixel reflects the texture information of the area around the pixel [12].

The above process is shown in Figs. 1 and 2.

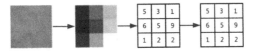

Fig. 1. Original LBP process

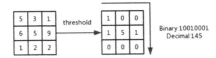

Fig. 2. Threshold processing

Since the original LBP feature uses the gray value in the fixed neighborhood, when the scale of the image changes, the encoding of the LBP feature would be wrong. The biggest drawback of the basic LBP operator is that it covers only a small area within a fixed radius, which obviously does not meet the needs of different size and frequency textures. In order to adapt to the texture features of different scales and achieve the requirements of gray scale and rotation invariance, researchers improved the LBP operator. They extended the 3×3 neighborhood to any neighborhood and replaced the square neighbor with a circular neighborhood [13]. The improved LBP operator allows for any number of pixels within a circular neighborhood of radius R. Thus, an LBP operator with P sampling points in a circular region such as radius R is obtained (Fig. 3).

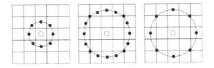

Fig. 3. Circular LBP

For a given center point (x_c, y_c), its neighborhood pixel position is (x_p, y_p), $p \in P$, its sampling point (x_p, y_p) calculated by the following formula:

$$x_p = x_c + R \cos\left(\frac{2\pi p}{P}\right)$$

$$y_p = y_c - R\sin\left(\frac{2\pi p}{P}\right)$$

R is the sampling radius, p is the sampling point, and P is the number of samples.

The Competition code encodes the direction angle of the collected palm vein image, and proposes a similarity measurement method. The LBP processes the texture information of the collected palm vein image to extract the palm vein features. Both have their own advantages and disadvantages. By merging them in the right way, you can get better classification results.

3 Feature-Level Fusion Using Discriminant Correlation Analysis

3.1 DCA Introduction

DCA is a feature-level fusion technique that incorporates class associations into the correlation analysis of feature sets. DCA performs efficient feature fusion by maximizing the pairwise correlation between two feature sets while eliminating inter-class correlation and limiting dependencies within the class [14]. This method can be used in pattern recognition applications to fuse features extracted from multiple modalities or to combine different feature vectors extracted from a single modality [15]. It is worth that DCA is the first technique to consider the class structure in feature fusion. In addition, it has very low computational complexity and can be used for real-time applications [16, 17]. DCA is described below.

Suppose that the samples in the data matrix are collected from c separate classes. Therefore, the n column of the data matrix is divided into c separate groups, where the n_i column belongs to the ith class ($n = \sum_{i=1}^{c} n_i$). Let $x_{ij} \in X$ represent the eigenvector corresponding to the jth sample in class i^{th}. $\bar{x}_i$ and $\bar{x}$ respectively denote the mean values of x_{ij} vectors in class i^{th} and the whole feature set. That is, $\bar{x}_i = \frac{1}{n_i}\sum_{j=1}^{n_i} x_{ij}$ and $\bar{x} = \frac{1}{n}\sum_{i=1}^{c}\sum_{j=1}^{n_i} x_{ij} = \frac{1}{n}\sum_{i=1}^{c} n_i\bar{x}_i$. Interclass scatter matrix is defined as

$$S_{bx_{(p\times p)}} = \sum_{i=1}^{c} n_i(\bar{x}_i - \bar{x})(\bar{x}_i - \bar{x})^T = \Phi_{bx}\Phi_{bx}^T$$

where $\Phi_{bx_{(p\times c)}} = \left[\sqrt{n_1}(\bar{x}_1 - \bar{x}), \sqrt{n_2}(\bar{x}_2 - \bar{x}), \ldots, \sqrt{nc}(\bar{x}c - \bar{x})\right]$.

If the number of features is higher than the number ($p \gg c$), it is more computationally easier to calculate the covariance matrix as $\left(\Phi_{bx}^T\Phi_{bx}\right)_{c\times c}$ rather than $\left(\Phi_{bx}\Phi_{bx}^T\right)_{c\times c}$. Presentation of the, and the most important eigenvector of $\Phi_{bx}\Phi_{bx}^T$ can be effectively obtained by mapping the eigenvectors of the $\Phi_{bx}^T\Phi_{bx}$. So, we just need to find the eigenvectors of the $c \times c$ covariance matrix $\Phi_{bx}^T\Phi_{bx}$.

If classes are well separated, $\Phi_{bx}^T\Phi_{bx}$ will be diagonal matrices. Since $\Phi_{bx}^T\Phi_{bx}$ is symmetric positive semidefinite, we can find the transformation of diagonalization:

$$P^T\left(\Phi_{bx}^T\Phi_{bx}\right)P = \hat{\Lambda}$$

where P is the matrix of orthogonal eigenvectors, $\hat{\Lambda}$ is the diagonal matrix of real eigenvalues and non negative eigenvalues sorted in descending order.

Let $Q_{(c\times r)}$ be composed of the first r eigenvector, where correspond comes from r largest nonzero eigenvalue of matrix P. We have:

$$Q^T\left(\Phi_{bx}^T\Phi_{bx}\right)Q = \Lambda_{(r\times r)}$$

The r most significant eigenvectors of S_{bx} can be obtained with the mapping: $Q \to \Phi_{bx}Q$:

$$(\Phi_{bx}Q)^T S_{bx}(\Phi_{bx}Q) = \Lambda_{(r\times r)}$$

$W_{bx} = \Phi_{bx}Q\Lambda^{-\frac{1}{2}}$ is the transformation that unitizes S_{bx} and reduces the dimensionality of the data matrix, X, from p to r. That is:

$$W_{bx}^T S_{bx} W_{bx} = I$$

$$X'_{(r\times n)} = W_{bx_{(r\times p)}}^T X_{(p\times n)}$$

X' is the projection of X in space, where the scatter matrix between classes is I, and classes are separated. Note that there are at most $c-1$ nonzero generalized eigenvalues; therefore, the upper limit of r is $c-1$. The other upper limit of r is the level of the data matrix, i.e., $r \leq \min(c-1, rank(X), rank(Y))$.

Similar to the above method, we solve second feature sets Y and find a transformation matrix W_{by}, which unifies the S_{by} inter class scattering matrix of second modes and reduces the dimension of Y from q to r:

$$W_{by}^T S_{by} W_{by} = I$$

$$Y'_{(r\times n)} = W_{by_{(r\times q)}}^T Y_{(q\times n)}$$

The updated Φ'_{bx} and Φ'_{by} are non-square $r \times c$ orthogonal matrices. Although $S'_{bx} = S'_{by} = I$, the matrix $\Phi'^T_{bx}\Phi'_{bx}$ and $\Phi'^T_{by}\Phi'_{by}$, 0 by are strictly diagonally dominant matrices $\left(\forall i : |a_{ii}| > \sum_{j\neq i}|a_{ij}|\right)$, where diagonal elements are close to one and non-diagonal elements close to zero. This makes the centroids of the classes have minimal correlation with each other, so classes are separated.

Now we have converted X and Y to X' and Y', where the interclass scatter matrix is cellular, and we need to make the features in a set only nonzero correlation with the corresponding features in the other sets. To achieve this, we need to diagonalization the set covariance matrix of the transformed feature set, $S'_{xy} = X'Y'^T$.

3.2 Algorithm Step

The DCA palm vein feature fusion steps are as follows:

Step 1: The Competition code features and LBP features of the palm vein are extracted separately to obtain corresponding data sets.
Step 2: We calculate the eigenvector of the data covariance matrix.
Step 3: The dimension of palm vein feature data is reduced.
Step 4: The two feature data are uniformly mapped to the same spatial domain by convolution.
Step 5: In the same spatial domain, the two feature data are correspondingly added or multiplied to perform feature fusion. We get the fusion characteristics of the palm vein, and finally classify.

4 Experimental Results

This paper uses the multispectral near-infrared palm vein image database of Hong Kong Polytech University. The multispectral palm vein database was a multispectral palm vein image collected from 500 volunteers. The palm vein image is captured using near-infrared light. It is divided into two sessions, each of which collects six palm vein images from each palm. Each person collected a total of 12 palm vein images, and the entire palm vein dataset totaled 6000 palm vein images.

The experimental results are measured using matlab2010 on a host with the frequency of Intel(R) Xeon(R) CPU E5620 @ 2.40 GHz and the memory of 8.00 GB.

We input the original palm vein image, and use the Competition code and LBP algorithm to obtain the characteristics of the palm vein. As shown in Fig. 4, (a) is 3 original palm vein images extracted from 6000 palm vein data sets; (b) is Competitive code feature images of (a); (c) is the LBP feature images of (a).

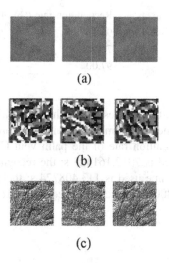

(a)

(b)

(c)

Fig. 4. (a) Original palm vein image, (b) Competitive code feature image, (c) LBP feature image

The extracted palm vein Competitive code features and LBP features were fused using DCA and then classified. The results are as follows.

First, we divided each of the 12 palm vein images into training samples and test samples in a 9:3 ratio. The experimental results obtained are shown in Table 1 below:

Table 1. The recognition rate of the training samples and test samples for 9:3

	Recognition rate (%)	Time (s)
Competitive_Code	97.33	7912.16
LBP	84.08	113.41
dcaFuse	99.80	271.19

We divided each of the 12 palm vein images into two groups according to a ratio of 6:6. The experimental results obtained are shown in Table 2 below:

Table 2. The recognition rate of the training samples and test samples for 6:6

	Recognition rate (%)	Time (s)
Competitive_Code	95.99	8123.18
LBP	81.27	131.18
dcaFuse	98.15	266.21

The 12 palm vein images from each person were divided into training samples and test samples according to a ratio of 3:9. The experimental results obtained are shown in Table 3 below:

Table 3. The recognition rate of the training samples and test samples for 3:9

	Recognition rate (%)	Time (s)
Competitive_Code	94.16	7856.16
LBP	72.96	88.26
dcaFuse	97.00	249.81

As can be seen from the three tables above, the recognition rate after feature fusion is improved. In Table 1, when the number of training samples is 9 and the number of test samples is 3, the recognition rate of the palm vein Competition code feature is 97.3280% and the time used is 7912.161423 s; the recognition rate of the palm vein LBP is 84.0756% and the time used is 113.408724 s; the recognition rate of the two features after fusion is 99.8000 and the time used is 271.189720 s. It can be seen that the use of DCA to fuse the two palm vein features not only greatly reduces the classification time than the Competition code feature, but also improves the recognition rate. The ratios of the training samples and test samples in Tables 2 and 3 are 6:6 and 3:9. Although the recognition rates of the three features are reduced under these two ratios, the feature recognition rate of DCA fusion is higher than the other two. The decrease in the recognition rate of Tables 2 and 3 is due to the decrease in the number of training samples and the increase in the number of test samples. The more the number of training samples, the less the number of test samples, the higher the recognition rate. However, the recognition rate of the DCA fusion feature is the highest regardless of the ratio, which proves the effectiveness of the feature fusion algorithm in the palm vein.

5 Conclusions

In this paper, we use a feature fusion based on feature set correlation analysis called a discriminant correlation analysis to fuse the Competition code features of the palm vein with the LBP features. This feature fusion approach uses the class association of the samples in the analysis. It is designed to find the transformation that maximizes the pairwise correlations in the two feature sets, while separating the classes in each set. These characteristics allow DCA to be used in the fusion of palm vein features to achieve a higher recognition rate. In addition, DCA has computational efficiency and can be used for real-time applications. We tested the multispectral near-infrared palm vein data set of the Hong Kong Polytechnic University with a size of 6000, demonstrating the effectiveness of the method, regardless of the ratio of the test set and the training set. However, there are still some shortcomings in this method, and we still need to continue to work hard to improve.

References

1. Srinivasan, R., Roy-Chowdhury, A.: Robust face recognition based on saliency maps of sigma sets. In: 10th IEEE International Conference on Biometrics Theory, pp. 1–6 (2015)
2. Haghighat, M., Zonouz, S., Abdel-Mottaleb, M.: Identification using encrypted biometrics. In: Wilson, R., Hancock, E., Bors, A., Smith, W. (eds.) CAIP 2013. LNCS, vol. 8048, pp. 440–448. Springer, Heidelberg (2013). https://doi.org/10.1007/978-3-642-40246-3_55
3. Felzenszwalb, P.F., Girshick, R.B., McAllester, D., Ramanan, D.: Object detection with discriminatively trained part-based models. IEEE Trans. Pattern Anal. Mach. Intel. 32(9), 1627–1645 (2010)
4. Park, U., Jillela, R., Ross, A., Jain, A.K.: Periocular biometrics in the visible spectrum. IEEE Trans. Inf. Forensics Secur. 6(1), 96–106 (2011)
5. Bahrampour, S., Nasrabadi, N.M., Ray, A., Jenkins, W.K.: Multimodal task-driven dictionary learning for image classification. IEEE Trans. Image Process. 25(1), 24–38 (2016)
6. Li, H.K., Toh, A., Li, L.: Advanced Topics in Biometrics. World Scientific, Singapore (2012)

7. Han, H., Klare, B.F., Bonnen, K., Jain, A.K.: Matching composite sketches to face photos: a component-based approach. IEEE Trans. Inf. Forensics Secur. **8**(1), 191–204 (2013)

8. Adams, W.K., David, Z.: Competitive coding scheme for palmprint verification. In: International Conference on Pattern Recognition, vol 1, pp. 520–523 (2004)

9. Ojala, T., Pietikäinen, M., Harwood, D.: Performance evaluation of texture measures with classification based on Kullback discrimination of distributions. In: Proceedings of the 12th IAPR International Conference on Pattern Recognition, vol 1, pp. 582–585 (1994)

10. Ojala, T., Pietikäinen, M., Harwood, D.: A comparative study of texture measures with classification based on feature distributions. Pattern Recogn. **29**, 51–59 (1996)

11. Liao, S., Zhu, X., Lei, Z., Zhang, L., Li, S.Z.: Learning multi-scale block local binary patterns for face recognition. In: Lee, S.-W., Li, S.Z. (eds.) ICB 2007. LNCS, vol. 4642, pp. 828–837. Springer, Heidelberg (2007). https://doi.org/10.1007/978-3-540-74549-5_87

12. Ahonen, T., Hadid, A., Pietikäinen, M.: Face description with local binary patterns: application to face recognition. IEEE Trans. Pattern Anal. Mach. Intell. **28**(12), 2037–2041 (2006)

13. Ahonen, T., Hadid, A., Pietikäinen, M.: Face recognition with local binary patterns. In: Pajdla, T., Matas, J. (eds.) Computer Vision - ECCV 2004. LNCS, vol. 3021, pp. 469–481. Springer, Heidelberg (2004). https://doi.org/10.1007/978-3-540-24670-1_36

14. Haghighat, M., Abdel-Mottaleb, M., Alhalabi, W.: Discriminant correlation analysis for feature level fusion with application to multimodal biometrics. In: IEEE International Conference on Acoustics, Speech and Signal Processing, pp. 1866–1870 (2016)

15. Mohammad, H., Mohamed, A.M., Wadee, A.: Discriminant correlation analysis: real-time feature level fusion for multimodal biometric recognition. IEEE Trans. Inf. Forensics Secur. **11**(9), 114–120 (2016)

16. Correa, N.M., Adali, T., Li, Y.O., Calhoun, V.D.: Canonical correlation analysis for data fusion and group inferences. IEEE Signal Process. Mag. **27**(4), 39–50 (2010)

17. Li, W.P., Yang, J., Zhang, J.P.: Uncertain canonical correlation analysis for multi-view feature extraction from uncertain data streams. Neurocomputing **149**, 1337–1347 (2015)

Author Index

Ahmed Shariff, M. F. 187
Anitha, J. 315
Arachchi, Maneesha M. M. 301
Archana, K. V. 281

Dias, Naomal 32
Dulakshi, Chathurya 177

Eben Sophia, P. 315

Fernando, Subha 161, 235

Gamage, Agra 177
Gamage, Dhananjali 92
Ganegoda, Gamage Upeksha 129, 177
Goonatilleke, M. A. S. T. 269
Gunathilaka, Dilum 219

Hepsiba, D. 103
Hettige, B. 269
Hettige, Budditha 256

Ilmini, Kalani 92

Jayampath, M. W. G. 269
Jude Hemanth, D. 315
Justin, Judith 103

Kapila Tharanga Rathnayaka, R. M. 79
Karunananda, Asoka 32, 67, 256
Kevin, R. 3
Kitchilan, Shakina 235
Kitchilan, Shazeeka 235
Kohomban, Upali 161
Kumarasinghe, Nishantha 235

Li, Hengjian 325
Liyanagamage, Ridmal 235

Maddumage, Roshan 235
Malkanthi, Nadeeka 200
Meedin, G. S. N. 49
Mendis, Pramodya 161

Nanayakkara, Deepthi 301
Nawarathna, Lakshika S. 301
Nawarathna, Ruwan D. 187

Pathirana, Shamila 219
Peiris, Roshan 301
Praboda, Erandi 15
Premaratne, I. A. 113
Priya, E. 3, 289

Ratnayake, H. U. W. 49, 113
Rupasinghe, Thashika D. 200
Rzevski, Gorge 256

Sandanayake, Thanuja 177
Savithri, C. N. 3
Senarathne, Sasanka 219
Seneviratna, D. M. K. N. 79
Shafeeque, Shazir 49
Shanthakumari, G. 289
Silva, Thushari 15, 219
Siriwardene, Sachini 161
Sohan Janaka, M. W. 113

Vanithamani, R. 281
Vasanthapriyan, Shanmuganathan 147

Wagarachchi, Mihirini 67
Wang, Xiyu 325
Weerabahu, Dinithi 177
Weerakoon, Chinthanie 32
Weerasekara, Jithmi 219
Wickramarathna, Nishan Chathuranga 129
Wijesiri, Ruwini 161

Printed in the United States
By Bookmasters